'An outstanding contribution to the literature, which deepens our understanding of the jurisprudence of the European Court of Human Rights on political rights. However, the book does much more than that by setting the legal analysis within a clear theoretical framework, which explores a range of democratic theories to enable a clear and rigorous interrogation of the Court's conceptions of democracy. From being a background ideal complacently left in the backwaters of legal analysis, democracy is now at the forefront of the battle over European values, and the Court finds itself at the fulcrum of debates concerning the very future of European democracy. This book will be an invaluable reference point for those involved, and to anyone interested in human rights, democracy, and the role of the Court in the democratic enterprise.'

Nigel White, Professor of Public International Law, University of Nottingham

'Never was a book timelier as 47 Council of Europe States and the Court that binds them grapple with maintaining open, just and accountable societies. This meticulously researched book traverses the kaleidoscope of rights essential to democratic societies. Essential reading in the era of human rights retreat and democratic push-back.'

Fionnuala Ní Aoláin, Regents Professor, Robina Chair in Law, Public Policy, and Society, University of Minnesota Law School and Professor of Law, Queen's University of Belfast.

'A deeply researched but lightly written account of how the European Court of Human Rights engages with democracy, a fundamental question related to the Court's very rationale and one that is brilliantly answered here. Authoritative and very well-organised. Worth developing a course on this exact issue in order to have such a good core text so readily to hand!'

Conor Gearty, Professor, London School of Economics and Political Science

LAW, DEMOCRACY AND THE EUROPEAN COURT OF HUMAN RIGHTS

Law, Democracy and the European Court of Human Rights examines the political rights jurisprudence of the European Court of Human Rights. It discusses how the Court supports a liberal representative and substantive model of democracy, and outlines the potential for the Court to interpret the Convention so as to support more deliberative, participatory and inclusive democratic practices. The book commences with an overview of different theories of democracy and then discusses the origins of the Council of Europe and the Convention and presents the basic principles on the interpretation and application of the Convention. Subsequent chapters explore issues around free expression, free assembly and association, the scope of the electoral rights, the right to vote, the right to run for election and issues about electoral systems. Issues discussed include rights relating to referendums, voting rights for prisoners and non-nationals, trade union rights and freedom of information.

RORY O'CONNELL is Professor of Human Rights and Constitutional Law at the School of Law & Transitional Justice Institute, Ulster University; from 2014–2020 he was the Director of the Transitional Justice Institute. He is a member of the Executive of the Committee on the Administration of Justice, a member of the Global Challenges Research Hub on Gender, Justice and Security and a former member of the BrexitLawNI ESRC project on the constitutional, legal, human rights and equality aspects of Brexit for Northern Ireland.

Law, Democracy and the European Court of Human Rights

RORY O'CONNELL

Ulster University

CAMBRIDGE
UNIVERSITY PRESS

University Printing House, Cambridge CB2 8BS, United Kingdom

One Liberty Plaza, 20th Floor, New York, NY 10006, USA

477 Williamstown Road, Port Melbourne, VIC 3207, Australia

314–321, 3rd Floor, Plot 3, Splendor Forum, Jasola District Centre, New Delhi – 110025, India

79 Anson Road, #06–04/06, Singapore 079906

Cambridge University Press is part of the University of Cambridge.

It furthers the University's mission by disseminating knowledge in the pursuit of education, learning, and research at the highest international levels of excellence.

www.cambridge.org
Information on this title: www.cambridge.org/9781107035072
DOI: 10.1017/9781139547246

© Cambridge University Press 2020

This publication is in copyright. Subject to statutory exception and to the provisions of relevant collective licensing agreements, no reproduction of any part may take place without the written permission of Cambridge University Press.

First published 2020

A catalogue record for this publication is available from the British Library.

Library of Congress Cataloging-in-Publication Data
NAMES: O'Connell, Rory, author.
TITLE: Law, democracy and the European Court of Human Rights / Rory O'Connell, Ulster University.
DESCRIPTION: Cambridge, United Kingdom ; New York, NY : Cambridge University Press, 2020. | Includes bibliographical references and index.
IDENTIFIERS: LCCN 2020014091 (print) | LCCN 2020014092 (ebook) | ISBN 9781107035072 (hardback) | ISBN 9781139547246 (epub)
SUBJECTS: LCSH: Political rights–Europe–Cases. | European Court of Human Rights.
CLASSIFICATION: LCC KJC5132 .O26 2020 (print) | LCC KJC5132 (ebook) | DDC 341.4/8094–dc23
LC record available at https://lccn.loc.gov/2020014091
LC ebook record available at https://lccn.loc.gov/2020014092

ISBN 978-1-107-03507-2 Hardback

Cambridge University Press has no responsibility for the persistence or accuracy of URLs for external or third-party internet websites referred to in this publication and does not guarantee that any content on such websites is, or will remain, accurate or appropriate.

For Eva and Joshua

Contents

Acknowledgements	*page* xiii
Table of Cases	xv
Table of Treaty Provisions	xxv
List of Abbreviations	xxix
Introduction	1

1 Theories of Democracy — 5

Liberal Democracy	6
Representative Democracy	9
Substantive Democracy	14
The Convention, the Court and Liberal Representative Substantive Democracy	15
Beyond Liberal Representative Substantive Democracy	18
Participation	18
Deliberative Democracy	23
Equality, Difference and Inclusion: Parity Democracy, Group Representation, Consociationalism	26
The Challenges of Governance	27
Conclusion: Towards Deliberative, Inclusive and Participatory Democracy	31

2 Council, Convention and Court: Origins and Evolution — 33

The United Nations and the Universal Declaration of Human Rights	33
European Regional Developments: Integration Movements	36
A Question of Democracy?	38
The Council of Europe	41

ix

	Drafting the European Convention on Human Rights	43
	Convention Rights: Inclusion and Definition	46
	The Convention Institutions	50
	Evolution of the Council of Europe and the Convention Institutions	51
	Competences of the Modern Court	54
	Other Council of Europe Institutions	57
	The International Law Context	59
	Conclusion	63
3	**European Principles of Interpretation and Application**	65
	The Interpretation of the Convention	65
	The Principles on Limitations of Rights	70
	Positive Obligations	75
	The Margin of Appreciation	78
	Convention Principles and Democracy	80
	Conclusion	83
4	**Freedom of Expression**	84
	General Approach	84
	The Importance of Free Expression	87
	Liberal Democracy	89
	The Liberal Democratic State and National Security	92
	Substantive Conception I	95
	Substantive Conception II	99
	Deliberative and Participatory Democracy	108
	Free Expression during Campaigns and Political Advertising	109
	Animal Defenders International and Deliberative Democracy	113
	Participation and Freedom of Information	115
	Conclusion	116
5	**Association, Assembly and Political Parties**	120
	Liberal Democracy	120
	Political Parties	123
	Substantive Democracy	128
	Deliberative and Participatory Democracy	133
	Conclusion	141
6	**Scope of the Electoral Rights**	143
	Legislature	144
	Other National Political Institutions	147

	Federal, Devolved and Local Institutions	152
	Globalisations	155
	The Convention and International Institutions	158
	Conclusion	163
7	**The Right to Vote**	166
	Identifying the Rights in P1–3	167
	The Right to Vote	170
	Substantive Democracy	197
	Participation and Effective Inclusion	198
	Deliberative Democracy	200
	Conclusion	201
8	**The Right to Run for Election**	204
	Legitimate Aim	204
	Legality or Lawfulness	207
	Proportionality	210
	Substantive Democracy	217
	Inclusion	218
	Deliberative Democracy	224
	Conclusion	225
9	**Regulation of Elections**	228
	Types of Electoral System	229
	Proportional Representation Systems: Thresholds	233
	Proportional Representation Systems: List Membership, Closed Party Lists and Bonus Seats	241
	Electoral Systems and Constituencies	244
	Clarity of Electoral Legislation	247
	The Timing of Amendments to Electoral Laws	247
	Electoral Commissions	250
	Integrity of the Electoral Process	252
	Campaign and Party Finance	258
	Electoral Systems and Minorities	261
	Conclusion	264
	Conclusion: Deliberation, Inclusion and Participation	268
	Bibliography	281
	Index	287

Acknowledgements

I am grateful to everyone who has contributed to this book. Academic and administrative colleagues at both Ulster University and Queen's University of Belfast have provided encouragement, suggestions and critical commentary along the way. I especially thank Fionnuala Ní Aoláin, Brice Dickson, Tom Hadden, Sylvie Langlaude, Colin Harvey, Ruth Rubio Marin and Aoife Nolan who at different points have provided support and advice. Others, too numerous to mention, have helped shape the content of the book with comments at conferences and workshops along the path. I have had the opportunity to discuss much of the contents of the book with different cohorts of students on postgraduate degrees at Ulster and Queen's University Belfast; preparing for these classes and discussing issues with my students helped me enormously, so thank you to them. All flaws and inadequacies in the text naturally remain my responsibility.

Ulster University provided me with an invaluable period of sabbatical leave to enable me to finish this book. Prof Siobhán Wills stepped in to cover my administrative responsibilities at that time, and I am in her debt for that. Acting Head of School Amanda Zacharopoulou and Head of School Eugene McNamee were supportive of my request to prioritise this project over the last few months before submission. My administrative colleagues Sadie Magee, Maria Prince, Lisa Thompson and Rhonda Black helped both by their consummate professionalism as well as keeping me on track with their kind inquiries about my progress.

Anonymous reviewers at Cambridge University Press provided much needed critical feedback early on in the project, and the editors at the Press have been helpful and generous throughout the process.

Finally, I am deeply indebted to my wife Fiona for her unwavering support, and to Chris, Deirdre and Padraic for keeping me grounded.

Table of Cases

A v United Kingdom App no 3455/05 (2009) 49 EHRR 29
(Grand Chamber) 79
Abil v Azerbaijan (No 2) App no 8513/11 (5 December 2019) 211
Açık and Others v Turkey App no 31451/03 (13 January 2009) 85
Ādamsons v Latvia App no 3669/03 (24 June 2008) 74
ADQ v Belgium App no 1028/61 (1961) 4 Yearbook 324
(European Commission of Human Rights) 167
Advisory Opinion on certain legal questions concerning the lists
of candidates submitted with a view to the election of judges to
the European Court of Human Rights (12 February 2008) 55
Airey v Ireland App no 6289/73 (1979) 2 EHRR 305 66
Aksu v Turkey App no 4149/04 and 41029/04 (2012) 56 EHRR 4
(Grand Chamber) 106
Al Skeini v United Kingdom App no 55721/07, (2011) 53 EHRR 18
(Grand Chamber) 56
Alajos Kiss v Hungary App no 38832/06 (20 May 2010) 186
Alliance des Belges de la Communauté Européenne v Belgium
App no 8612/79 (1979) DR 259 (European Commission of
Human Rights) 158
Anchugov and Gladkov v Russia App no 11157/04 (4 July 2013) 148
Andrejeva v Latvia App no 55707/00 (2010) 51 EHRR 28 68
Animal Defenders International v United Kingdom
App no 48876/08 (2013) 57 EHRR 21 (Grand Chamber) 77, 112
Antonopoulos v Greece App no 58333/00 (29 March 2001) 260
Asensio Serqueda v Spain App no 23151/94 77B DR 122
(European Commission of Human Rights) 206
August v Electoral Commission CCT 8/99, [2000] 1 Law Reports of the
Commonwealth 608 190
Axel Springer AG v Germany App no 39954/08 (2012) 55 EHRR 6 90
Aziz v Cyprus App no 69949/01 (2005) 41 EHRR 11 (22 June 2004) 188

B v France App no 13343/87 (1992) 16 EHRR 1 67
Babenko v Ukraine App no 43476/98 (4 May 1999) 252

xv

Table of Cases

Bader v Austria App no 26633/95 (European Commission of
Human Rights, 15 May 1996) 150
Bankovic v Belgium and 16 other states App no 52207/99, (2001) 44
EHRR SE5 56
Baškauskaitė v Lithuania App no 41090/98 (1999) 27 EHRR CD 341
(European Commission of Human Rights) 147
Beian v Romania App no 30658/05 (6 December 2007) 72
Ben el Mahi and others v Denmark App no 5853/06
(11 December 2006) 96
Bladet Tromso and Stensaas v Norway App no 21980/93 (2000)
29 EHRR 125 90
Bompard v France App no 44081/02 (4 June 2006) 245
Booth-Clibborn v United Kingdom App no 11391/85 (1986)
8 EHRR CD 99 (European Commission of Human Rights) 154
Boskoski v FYRM App no 11676/04 (2 September 2004) 147
Bowman v United Kingdom App no 141/1996/760/961 (1998)
26 EHRR 1 111
Brânduse v Romania App no 39951/08 (27 October 2015) 194
Brind v United Kingdom (1994) 77 D&R 262 (European
Commission of Human Rights) 92
Brita da Silva Magno v Portugal App no 26720/06 (17 June 2008) 206

Calmanovici v Romania App no 42250/02 (1 July 2008) 193
Campagnano v Italy App no 77955/01 (2006) 48 EHRR 43 188
Centro Europa 7 srl v Italy App no 38433/09
(Grand Chamber, 7 May 2012) 109
Cernea v Romania App no 43609/10 (27 February 2018) 205
Cherepkov v Russia App no 51501/99 (25 January 2000) 154
Christian Democratic People's Party v Moldova App no 28793/02
(2006) 45 EHRR 13 126
Cisse v France App no 51346/99 (18 January 2001) 122
Clerfayt and Legros v Belgium App no 10650/83
(European Commission of Human Rights, 17 May 1985) 153
Clerfayt v Belgium App no 27120/95, (European
Commission of Human Rights, 8 September 1997) 187
Communist Party of Russia and Others v Russia App no 29400/05
(19 June 2012) 110
Cumhuriyet Halk Partisi v Turkey App no 19920/13 (26 April 2016) 259
Cumhuriyet Halk Partisi v Turkey App no 48818/17 (21 November 2017) ..151

Danilenkov v Russia App no 67336/01 (2014) 58 EHRR 19 138
Davydov and Others v Russia App no 75947/11 (2018) 67 EHRR 25 ..152, 228
*Decision on the competence of the Court to give an advisory
opinion on whether the CIS Commission could be regarded as 'another
procedure of international investigation or settlement'* (2 June 2004) 55
Demir and Baykara v Turkey App no 34503/97 (2008) 48 EHRR 54
(Grand Chamber) 139

Table of Cases

Denmark and others v Greece (The Greek case) App no 3321/67
(European Commission of Human Rights, 5 November 1969) 55
DH v Czech Republic App no 57325/00 (2008) 47 EHRR 3
(Grand Chamber) 198
Djavit An v Turkey App no 20652/92 (2005) 40 EHRR 45 121
Doyle v United Kingdom App no 30158/06 (2007) 45 EHRR SE 3 176

EB v France App no 43546/02 (2008) 47 EHRR 21 79
Ekoglasnost v Bulgaria App no 30386/05 (6 November 2012) 248
Eman and Sevinger v Netherlands Case 300/04 (Court of Justice of the
European Union, 12 September 2006) 176

Federación Nacionalista Canaria v Spain App no 56618/00
(7 June 2001) 152, 235
Féret v Belgium App no 15615/07 (16 July 2009) 101
Filini v Greece App no 30244/11 (6 May 2014) 239
Firth and others v United Kingdom App nos 47784/09, 47806/09,
47812/09, 47818/09, 47829/09, 49001/09, 49007/09, 49018/09,
49033/09 and 49036/09 (2016) 63 EHRR 25 162
Fretté v France App no 36515/97 (2004) 38 EHRR 21 79
Frodl v Austria App no 20201/04 (2011) 52 EHRR 5 193
Fuentes Bobo v Spain App no 39293/98 (2001)
31 EHRR 50 77

Gahramanli and Others v Azerbaijan App no 36503/11
(8 October 2015) 256
Gajcsi v Hungary App no 62924/10 (23 September 2014) 187
Georgian Labour Party v Georgia App no 9103/04 (2008)
48 EHRR 14 170
Gitonas v Greece App nos 68/1996/687/877-879 17/1997/801/1004
and 23/1997/807/1010 (1998) 26 EHRR 691 205
GK v Belgium App no 58302/10 (21 May 2019) 207
Glasenapp v Germany App no 9228/80 (1986) 9 EHRR 25 86
Glimmerveen v Netherlands App nos 8348/78 and 8406/78 (1979)
4 EHRR 260, (European Commission of Human Rights) 217
Golder v United Kingdom App no 4451/70 (1975) 1 EHRR 524 66
Goodwin v United Kingdom App no 28957/95 (2002)
35 EHRR 18 67
Gorizdra v Moldova App no 53180/99 (2 July 2002) 153
Gorzelik v Poland App no 44158/98 (2005) 40 EHRR 4
(Grand Chamber) 122
Gözel and Özer v Turkey App no 43453/04 (6 July 2010) 94
Greens and MT v United Kingdom App nos 60041/08 and 60054/08
(23 November 2010) 193
Grosaru v Romania App no 78039/01 (2015) 61 EHRR 1 210
Guerra v Italy App no 14967/89 (1998) 26 EHRR 357 76
Gül and Others v Turkey App no 4870/02 (8 June 2010) 94

xviii — Table of Cases

H v Netherlands App no 9914/82 (European Commission of
  Human Rights, 4 July 1983) 190
Hajili v Azerbaijan App no 6984/06 (10 January 2012) 254
Handyside v United Kingdom (Little Red Schoolbook case) (1979)
  1 EHRR 737 18
Harmati v Hungary App no 63012/10 (21 October 2014) 187
Herri Batasuna v Spain App nos 25803/04 and 25817/04 (30 June 2009) ..121
Hilbe v Liechtenstein App no 31981/96 (7 September 1999) 150, 174
Hirst v United Kingdom (2004) 38 EHRR 825 (Chamber) 191
Hirst v United Kingdom (No. 2) App no 74025/01 (2006)
  42 EHRR 41 (Grand Chamber) 2
Holland v Ireland App no 24827/94 (European Commission of
  Human Rights, 14 April 1998) 190
Huggett v United Kingdom App no 24744/94
  (European Commission of Human Rights, 28 June 1995) 109

IA v Turkey App no 42571/98 (2007) 45 EHRR 30 96
Isakov v Russia App no 54446/07 (4 July 2017) 195
IZ v Greece App no 18997/91 (European Commission of
  Human Rights, 28 February 1994) 252

Janowiec v Russia App no 55508/07 and 29520/09, 58 EHRR
  30 (Grand Chamber) 56
Jersild v Denmark App no 15890/89 (1994) 19 EHRR 1 100

Karimov v Azerbaijan App no 12535/06 (25 September 2014) 255
Kasymakhunov and Saybatalov v Russia App nos 26261/05
  and 26377/06 (14 March 2013) 130
Kavakci v Turkey App no 71907/01 (5 April 2007) 207, 212
Kerimova v Azerbaijan App no 20799/06 (30 September 2010) 253
Klein v Slovakia App no 72208/01 (2010) 50 EHRR 15 96
Kosiek v Germany App no 9704/82 (1986) 9 EHRR 328 86
Kovach v Ukraine App no 39424/02 (7 February 2008) 207
Krasnov and Skuratov v Russia App nos 17864/c4 and 21396/04 (2007)
  47 EHRR 46 154
Krivobokov v Ukraine App no 38707/04 (19 February 2013) 148
Kulinski and Sabev v Bulgaria App no 63849/09 (21 July 2017) 161
Kurić v Slovenia App no 26828/06 (Chamber, 26 June 2012) 184
Kurić v Slovenia App no 26828/06 (Grand Chamber, 12 March 2014) 184

Labita v Italy App no 26772/95 (2008) 46 EHRR 50 190
Le Lievre v United Kingdom App no 36522/15 (2016) 62 EHRR SE 20 233
Le Pen v France App no 18788/09 (7 May 2010) 104
Leander v Sweden App no 9248/81 (1987) 9 EHRR 433 115
Leyla Sahin v Turkey App no 44774/98 (2005) 41 EHRR 8 18
Liberal Party v United Kingdom App no 8765/79, (1980) 21 DR 211
  (European Commission of Human Rights) 232

Table of Cases

Lindsay v United Kingdom App no 8364/78 (1979) 15 DR 247
(European Commission of Human Rights) 158, 231
Lingens v Austria App no 9815/82 (1986) 8 EHRR 407 89
Luksch v Germany App no 35385/97 (European Commission
of Human Rights, 21 May 1997) 173
Luksch v Italy App no 27614/95 (European Commission
of Human Rights, 21 May 1997) 183
Lustig-Prean v United Kingdom App nos 31417/96 and 32377/96 (1999)
29 EHRR 548 72
Lykourezos v Greece App no 33554/03 (2008) 46 EHRR 7 213

M v United Kingdom App no 10316/83 (European Commission
of Human Rights, 7 March 1984) 146
Magnago and Sudtiroler Volkspartei v Italy App no 25035/94
(European Commission of Human Rights, 15 April 1996) 234
Magyar Helsinki Bizottság v Hungary App no 18030/11
(Grand Chamber, 8 November 2016) 115
Makuc v Slovenia App no 26828/06 (31 May 2007) 152
Manole v Moldova App no 13936/02 (17 September 2009) 109
Marckx v Belgium App no 6833/74 (1979) 2 EHRR 330 67
Marinov v Bulgaria (communicated) App no 26081/17 187
Mathieu-Mohin and Clerfayt v Belgium App no 9267/81 (1987)
10 EHRR 1 ....146, 152
Matthews v United Kingdom App no 24833/94 (1999) 28 EHRR 361
(Grand Chamber) 63
McGuinness v United Kingdom Admissibility Decision
App no 39511/98 (8 June 1999) 221
McLean v United Kingdom App nos 12626/13 and 2522/12 (2013)
57 EHRR SE 8 153
MDU v Italy App no 58540/00 (European Commission
of Human Rights, 28 January 2003) 190
Melnychenko v Ukraine App no 17707/02 (2004) 42 EHRR 39 206
Merabishvili v Georgia App no 72508/13 (Grand Chamber,
28 November 2017) 72
Mihaela Mihai Neagu v Romania App no 66345/09 (6 March 2014) 206
Molka v Poland App no 56550/00 (11 April 2006) 153
Moohan and Gillon v United Kingdom App nos 22962/15
and 23345/15 (13 June 2017) 150
Mouvement raëlien suisse v Switzerland App no 16354/06 (2013)
56 EHRR 14 97
Müller v Switzerland App no 10737/84 (1991) 13 EHRR 212 85
Murat Vural v Turkey App no 9540/07 (21 October 2014) 91
Murphy v Ireland App no 44179/98 (2004) 38 EHRR 13 112

Namat Aliyev v Azerbaijan App no 18705/06 (8 April 2010) 254
National Union of Belgian Police v Belgium App no 4464/70 (1979-80)
1 EHRR 578 137

Table of Cases

National Union of Rail Maritime and Transport Workers v United Kingdom
App no 31045/10 (2015) 60 EHRR 10 139
Navalnyy v Russia App no 29580/12 and four others (Grand Chamber,
15 November 2018) 72
Nedim Şener v Turkey App no 38270/11 (8 July 2014) 94
Nemtsov v Russia App no 1774/11 (31 July 2014) 88
Niedzwiedz v Poland App no 1345/06 (2008) 47 EHRR SE 2 150
Norris v Ireland App no 10581/83 (1991) 13 EHRR 186 81
Norwood v United Kingdom App no 23131/03 (2005) 40 EHRR SE 11 99

Occhetto v Italy App no 14507/07 (12 November 2013) 204
Okçuoğlu v Turkey App no 24246/94 (8 July 1999) 91–3
Ollinger v Austria App no 76900/01 (2008) 46 EHRR 38 122
Opuz v Turkey App no 33401/02 (2010) 50 EHRR 28 .... 69, 77
Oran v Turkey App nos 28881/07 and 37920/07 (15 April 2014) 180
Osman v United Kingdom App no 23452/94 (1999) 29 EHRR 245
(Grand Chamber) 76
Otto v Germany App no 27574/02 (24 November 2005) 86
Otto-Preminger-Institut v Austria App no 13470/87 (1994)
19 EHRR 34 .... 18, 87, 97
Ouranio Toxo v Greece App no 74989/01 (2007)
45 EHRR 8 122
Özgürlük Ve Dayanişma Partisi (ÖDP) v Turkey App no 7819/03
(10 May 2012) 261

Palomo Sanchez v Spain App nos 28955/06, 28957/06, 28959/06
and 28964/06 (2012) 54 EHRR 24 (Grand Chamber) 86
Partei Die Friesen v Germany App no 65480/10 (28 January 2016) 263
Parti nationaliste basque v France App no 71251/01 (2007) 47 EHRR 47 .. 264
Partija 'Jaunie Demokrati' and Partija 'Musu Zeme' v Latvia
App nos 10547/07 and 34049/07 (29 November 2007) 228
Paschalidis Koutmeridis and Zaharakis v Greece
App nos 27863/05 28422/05 and 28028/05 (10 April 2008) 213
Paunović and Milivojević v Serbia App no 41683/06
(24 May 2016) 244, 265
Pedersen and Baadsgaard v Denmark App no 49017/99 (2004)
42 EHRR 24 .... 90, 108
Petkov and others v Bulgaria App nos 178/02, 505/02 and
77568/01 (11 June 2009) 207
Pilav v Bosnia and Herzegovina App no 41939/07
(9 June 2016) 149, 224
Podkolzina v Latvia App no 46726/99 (9 April 2002) 204
Polacco and Garofalo v Italy App no 23450/94
(European Commission of Human Rights, 15 September 1997) 174
Purcell v Ireland App no 15404/89, (European Commission
of Human Rights, 16 April 1991) 92
Py v France App no 66289/01 (2005) 42 EHRR 26 153

Table of Cases

Rai and Evans v United Kingdom App nos 26258/07 and 26255/07
(17 November 2009) 122
Rantsev v Cyprus and Russia App no 25965/04 (2010) 51 EHRR 1 76
Rees v United Kingdom App no 9532/81 (1987) 9 EHRR 56 67
Refah Paritisi (Welfare Party) v Turkey App nos 41340/98
41342/98 41343/98 and 41344/98 (2003) 37 EHRR1 2
Republican Party of Russia v Russia App no 12976/07 (2015)
61 EHRR 20 .... 126, 129, 240
Riza and DPS v Bulgaria App no 48555/10 (13 October 2015) 170, 177
Russian Conservative Party of Entrepreneurs v Russia
App nos 55066/00 and 55638/00 (2007) 46 EHRR 39 170

Saccomanno v Italy App no 11583/08 (13 March 2012) 242
Sadak and others v Turkey App nos 25144/94; 26149/95
to 26154/95; 27100/95 and 27101/95 (2002) 36 EHRR 23 212
Santoro v Italy App no 36681/97 (2004) 42 EHRR 38 154
Sarukhanyan v Armenia App no 38978/03 (27 May 2008) 216
Schalk and Kopf v Austria App no 30141/04 (2011) 53 EHRR 20 69
Scoppola v Italy (No 3) App no 126/05 (Chamber, 18 January 2011) 193
Scoppola v Italy (No 3) App no 126/05 (Grand Chamber, 22 May 2012) ... 74
Sejdic and Finci v Bosnia and Herzegovina App nos 27996/06
and 34836/06 (2009) 22 BHRC 201 (Grand Chamber) 2
Sevinger and Eman v Netherlands App nos 17173/07 and 17180/07 (2008)
46 EHRR SE 14 175
Shindler v United Kingdom App no 19840/09 (2014) 58 EHRR 5 172
Shukurova v Azerbaijan App no 37614/11 (27 October 2016) 256
Sidabras v Lithuania App nos 55480/00 and 59330/00 (2006)
42 EHRR 6 68
Sik v Turkey App no 53413/11 (8 July 2014) 94
Sitaropoulos and Others v Greece App no 42202/07
(Chamber, 8 July 2010) 177
Sitaropoulos and Others v Greece App no 42202/07 (Grand Chamber,
15 March 2012) 178
Šlaku v Bosnia and Herzegovina App no 56666/12 (25 May 2016) 223
Sobaci v Turkey App no 26733/02 (29 November 2007) 207
Soberanía de la Razón v Spain App no 30537/12 (26 May 2015) 206
Söyler v Turkey App no 29411/07 (17 September 2013) 194
Staatkundig Gereformeerde Partij v Netherlands App no 58369/10
(10 July 2012) 219
Steel and Morris v United Kingdom App no 68416/01 (2005)
41 EHRR 22 76
Steel v United Kingdom App no 24838/94 (1999) 28 EHRR 603 85
Strack and Richter v Germany App nos 28811/12 and 50303/12
(5 July 2017) 240
Sukhovetskyy v Ukraine App no 13716/02 (2007) 44 EHRR 57 206
Şükran Aydin and Others v Turkey App nos 23196/07, 49197/06,
50242/08, 60912/08 and 14871/09 (22 January 2013) 220

xxii *Table of Cases*

Sunday Times v United Kingdom App no 6538/74 (1979)
2 EHRR 245 .... 77, 86
Sunday Times v United Kingdom No 2 App no 13166/87 (1991)
14 EHRR 229 88

Tănase and Chirtoaca v Moldova App no 7/08 (18 November 2008) 208
Tănase v Moldova App no 7/08 (2011) 53 EHRR 22 (Grand Chamber) ... 207
Taranenko v Russia App no 19554/05 (15 May 2014) 85, 88
Társaság a Szabadságjogokért v Hungary App no 37374/05
(14 April 2009) 115
Tatár and Fáber v Hungary App nos 26005/08 and 26160/08 (2014)
59 EHRR 8 85
Tete v France App no 11123/84 (1987) 54 DR 52 (European Commission of
Human Rights) 158
Timke v Germany App no 52731/95 (1995) 20 EHRR CD 133
(European Commission of Human Rights) 152
Timurhan v Turkey App no 28882/07 (16 December 2014) 181
Tsonev v Bulgaria App no 45963/99 (2008) 46 EHRR 8 127
Tuskia v Georgia App no 14237/07 (11 October 2018) 122
TV Vest AS & Rogaland Pensjonistparti v Norway
App no 21132/05 (2009) 48 EHRR 51 112
Tyrer v United Kingdom App no 5856/72 (1978) 2 EHRR 1 67

Uçar v Turkey App no 4692/09 (24 June 2014) 153
UNITE the Union v United Kingdom App no 65397/13 (3 May 2016) 135
United Communist Party of Turkey v Turkey App no 19392/92
(1998) 26 EHRR 121 (Grand Chamber) 123
United Communist Party of Turkey v Turkey App no 19392/92 (European
Commission of Human Rights, 3 September 1996) 123
United Macedonian Organisation Ilinden – PIRIN v Bulgaria
(No 2) App no 41561/07 (18 October 2011) 127

Vámos v Hungary App no 48145/14 (17 February 2015) 182
Van Wambeke v Belgium App no 16692/90 (European Commission
of Human Rights, 12 April 1991) 217
Vejdeland v Sweden App no 1813/07 (2014) 58 EHRR 15 .... 100, 104
Vereinigung demokratischer Soldaten Österreichs and
Gubi v Austria App no 15153/89 (1995) 20 EHRR 26 75
VGT Verein Gegen Tierfabriken Schweiz v Switzerland App no 32772/02
(Grand Chamber, 30 June 2009) 112
Vgt Verein Gegen Tierfabriken v Switzerland App no 24699/94 (2002)
34 EHRR 4 111
Viola v Italy App no 7842/02 (8 January 2008) 188
Vogt v Germany App no 17851/91 (1996) 21 EHRR 205 217
Von Hannover v Germany App nos 40660/08 and 60641/08 (2012)
55 EHRR 15 90
Vona v Hungary App no 35943/10 (9 July 2013) 130

Table of Cases

W X Y and Z v Belgium 6746/74 App no 6745 (1975) 2 DR 114
(European Commission of Human Rights) 167
Wilson v United Kingdom App nos 30668/96, 30671/96 and 30678/96
(2002) 35 EHRR 20 137
Wingrove v United Kingdom App no 17419/90 (1997) 24 EHRR 1 97
Women on Waves v Portugal App no 31276/05 (3 February 2009) 85

X and Association Y v Italy App no 8987/80 (European Commission of
Human Rights, 6 May 1981) 173
X and Y v Netherlands App no 8978/80 (1985) 8 EHRR 235 76
X v Belgium App no 8701/79 (European Commission of Human Rights,
3 December 1979) 189
X v Federal Republic of Germany App no 530/59 (1960) 3 Yearbook 184
(European Commission of Human Rights) 167
X v Iceland App no 8941/80 (European Commission of Human Rights,
8 December 1981) 245
X v Netherlands App no 6573/74 (1975) 1 DR 87 (European
Commission of Human Rights) 189
X v United Kingdom App no 5155/71 (European Commission of Human
Rights, 12 July 1976) 153
X v United Kingdom App no 7140/75 (1976) 7 DR 96
(European Commission of Human Rights) 231
X v United Kingdom App no 7566/76 (1976) 9 DR 121
(European Commission of Human Rights) 167, 172–3
X v United Kingdom App no 8873/80 (European
Commission of Human Rights, 13 May 1982) 173
X,Z and Y v Belgium App no 1065/61 (1961) 4 Yearbook 260
(European Commission of Human Rights) 167

*Yabloko Russian United Democratic Party and Others v
Russia* App no 18860/07 (8 November 2016) 256
Yazar v Turkey App nos 22723/93, 22724/93 and 22725/93 (2003)
36 EHRR 6 122
Yumak and Sadak v Turkey App no 10226/03 (2008) 48 EHRR 4 2
Yumak and Sadak v Turkey App no 10226/03 (2008) 48 EHRR 4
(Grand Chamber) 237
Yumak and Sadak v Turkey App no 10226/03 (Chamber,
30 January 2007) 236

Zana v Turkey App no 69/1996/688/880 (1997) 27 EHRR 667 ....88, 93
Zdanoka v Latvia App no 58278/00 (2006) 45 EHRR 17 2
Zdanoka v Latvia App no 58278/00 (2006) 45 EHRR 17
(Grand Chamber) 72, 74
Zehra Foundation and Others v Turkey App no 51595/07
(10 July 2018) 122
Zevnik and others v Slovenia App no 54893/18
(5 December 2019) 220

xxiv *Table of Cases*

Zhechev v Bulgaria App no 57045/00 (21 June 2007) 135
Zhermal v Russia App no 60983/00 (28 February 2008) 147
Zornić v Bosnia and Herzegovina App no 3681/06 (15 July 2014) 149

OTHER COURTS AND TREATY-MONITORING BODIES

August v Electoral Commission CCT 8/99, [2000] 1 Law Reports of the
   Commonwealth 608 (South African Constitutional Court) 190

Judgment No. 12-П/2016 of 19 April 2016 of the Russian
   Constitutional Court. English translation at
   <www.venice.coe.int/webforms/documents/default.aspx?pdffile=CDL-
   REF(2016)033-e> accessed 14 August 2019 195

Mahuika v New Zealand Communication No 547/1993
   (Human Rights Committee, 15 November 2000) 60

*Opinion 2/13 on the draft agreement on the accession of
   the European Union to the European Convention for
   the Protection of Human Rights and Fundamental Freedoms*
   (Court of Justice of the European Union, 18 December 2014) 161

Poma v Peru Communication no 1457/2006, (Human
   Rights Committee, 27 March 2009) 60

Table of Treaty Provisions

Additional Protocol to the European Charter of Local Self-Government
  on the right to participate in the affairs of a local authority 2009 164
African Charter on Democracy, Elections and Governance 2007 61
African Charter on Democracy, Elections and Governance 2007,
  article 5 61
African Charter on Democracy, Elections and Governance 2007,
  article 14 61
African Charter on Democracy, Elections and Governance 2007,
  article 17 61
African Charter on Democracy, Elections and Governance 2007,
  article 29 61
African Charter on Democracy, Elections and Governance 2007,
  article 31 61
African Charter on Democracy, Elections and Governance 2007,
  article 33 61
African Charter on Democracy, Elections and Governance 2007,
  articles 23–26 61
African Charter on Democracy, Elections and Governance 2007,
  articles 37 to 43 61
African Charter on Human and Peoples' Rights 1981, article 13 61
American Convention on Human Rights 1969, article 23 61

Charter of Regional and Minority Languages 1992 58
Consolidated Treaty on the European Union, article 2 62
Consolidated Treaty on the European Union, article 6(2) 63
Consolidated Treaty on the European Union, article 7 62
Consolidated Treaty on the European Union, article 11 20
Consolidated Treaty on the European Union, article 12 63
Consolidated Treaty on the European Union, article 21 63
Consolidated Treaty on the European Union, articles 10, 14 63
Convention on Action against Trafficking in Human Beings 2005 58
Convention on Biomedicine and Human Rights 1997 58

xxvi   *Table of Treaty Provisions*

Convention on Preventing and Combating Violence against
Women and Domestic Violence 2011 58
Convention on the Elimination of All Forms of Racial
Discrimination 1965, article 4 100
Convention on the Elimination of Discrimination against
Women 1979 68
Convention on the Elimination of Discrimination against
Women 1979, article 7 219
Convention on the Participation of Foreigners in Public Life
at Local Level 1992 .... 58, 164
Convention on the Rights of Persons with Disabilities 2006 198
Convention on the Rights of the Child 1989 145

European Charter for Regional and Minority Languages 1992 174
European Charter of Local Self-Government 1985 163
European Convention for the Prevention of Torture 1987 58
European Convention on Human Rights 1950, article 3 70
European Convention on Human Rights 1950, article 8 70–1
European Convention on Human Rights 1950, article 9 71
European Convention on Human Rights 1950, article 10 70–1
European Convention on Human Rights 1950, article 10(2) 71
European Convention on Human Rights 1950, article 11 70–1
European Convention on Human Rights 1950, article 11(2) 71
European Convention on Human Rights 1950, article 12 69
European Convention on Human Rights 1950, article 15 74
European Convention on Human Rights 1950 article 24 (1950 version) ... 50
European Convention on Human Rights 1950 article 25 (1950 version) ... 50
European Convention on Human Rights 1950, article 27 56
European Convention on Human Rights 1950 article 28 (1950 version) ... 50
European Convention on Human Rights 1950, article 28 56
European Convention on Human Rights 1950, article 29 56
European Convention on Human Rights 1950, articles 30, 31, 43 56
European Convention on Human Rights 1950 article 31 (1950 version) ... 50
European Convention on Human Rights 1950 article 32
(1950 version) 50–1
European Convention on Human Rights 1950, article 33 55
European Convention on Human Rights 1950, article 34 55
European Convention on Human Rights 1950, article 35 56
European Convention on Human Rights 1950, article 36 57
European Convention on Human Rights 1950 article 46 (1950 version) ...51
European Convention on Human Rights 1950 article 48 (1950 version) .. 50
European Convention on Human Rights 1950 article 54 (1950 version) 51
European Convention on Human Rights 1950 articles 44, 48
(1950 version) 51
European Convention on Human Rights 1950, article 45 57
European Convention on Human Rights 1950, article 59(2) 63
European Convention on Human Rights, article 46 57

Table of Treaty Provisions

European Social Charter 1961 57
European Social Charter Revised 1996 58
European Union Charter of Fundamental Rights 2000, article 40 63
European Union Charter of Fundamental Rights 2000, article 44 63
European Union Charter of Fundamental Rights 2000, articles 41–43 63

Framework Convention on National Minorities 1995 58

Inter-American Convention on the Prevention, Punishment
   and Eradication of Violence against Women 69
Inter-American Democratic Charter 2001, articles 2, 3 and 4 62
Inter-American Democratic Charter 2001, article 10 62
Inter-American Democratic Charter 2001, article 19 62
Inter-American Democratic Charter 2001, article 4 62
Inter-American Democratic Charter 2001, articles 11–16 62
International Covenant on Civil and Political Rights 60
International Covenant on Civil and Political Rights 1966, article 1 60
International Covenant on Civil and Political Rights 1966, article 2 219

Protocol 1 to the European Convention on Human Rights, article 1 68
Protocol 1 to the European Convention on Human Rights, article 3 60
Protocol 11 to the European Convention restructuring the
   control machinery established thereby 1994 53
Protocol 15 to the European Convention on Human Rights 78
Protocol 2 to the European Convention on Human Rights 52
Protocol 9 to the European Convention on human Rights 1990 52

Statute of the Council of Europe 1949, article 14 42
Statute of the Council of Europe 1949, article 15 42
Statute of the Council of Europe 1949, articles 16–18 43
Statute of the Council of Europe 1949, article 19 43
Statute of the Council of Europe 1949, article 21 43
Statute of the Council of Europe 1949, articles 22, 23 43
Statute of the Council of Europe 1949, article 24 43
Statute of the Council of Europe 1949, article 25 43
Statute of the Council of Europe 1949, article 26 43

United Nations Charter 1945, article 2(7) 34
United Nations Charter 1945, article 13(1) 34
United Nations Charter 1945, article 52 36
United Nations Charter 1945, article 55 34
United Nations Charter 1945, article 62(2) 34
United Nations Charter 1945, article 68 34
United Nations Charter 1945, article 76(c) 34

Vienna Convention on the Law of Treaties 1969, article 31(1) 66
Vienna Convention on the Law of Treaties 1969, article 32 69

xxviii *Table of Treaty Provisions*

OTHER AUTHORITIES

European Commission for Democracy through Law (Venice Commission) *Report on Electoral Rules and Affirmative Action for National Minorities' Participation in Decision-making Process in European Countries* (Strasbourg: Council of Europe Pub., 2005) 262

European Commission for Democracy through Law (Venice Commission), 371/2006 *Referendum Guidelines* (Council of Europe Pub., Strasbourg 2006). 163

European Commission for Democracy through Law (Venice Commission), 488/2008 *Report on the Imperative Mandate and Similar Practices* (Council of Europe Pub., Strasbourg 2009) 244

European Commission for Democracy through Law (Venice Commission), *CDL-AD(2017)005-e Turkey - Opinion on the amendments to the Constitution adopted by the Grand National Assembly on 21 January 2017 and to be submitted to a National Referendum on 16 April 2017, adopted by the Venice Commission at its 110th Plenary Session (Venice, 10–11 March 2017)* (Council of Europe Pub., Strasbourg 2017) 148

European Commission for Democracy through Law (Venice Commission), *Code of Good Practice in Electoral Matters (Guidelines and Explanatory Report)* (Council of Europe 2002) 248

European Commission for Democracy through Law (Venice Commission), *Opinion No. 832/2015 Interim Opinion on the Amendments to the Federal Constitutional Law of the Constitutional Court of the Russian Federation* (Council of Europe Pub., Strasbourg 2016) 195

European Commission for Democracy through Law (Venice Commission), *Study no. 352/2005 Report on Electoral Law and Electoral Administration in Europe* (Council of Europe Pub., Strasbourg 2006) 229

Joint Committee on the Draft Voting Eligibility (Prisoners) Bill *Draft Voting Eligibility (Prisoners) Bill 2013* HL 103/HC 924 (18 December 2013) 201

Lund Recommendations on the Effective Participation of National Minorities in Public Life 1999 27

Universal Declaration of Human Rights 34–5, 48, 116, 144, 163

Abbreviations

AKP	Justice and Development Party (Turkey)
App no	Application number
BHRC	Butterworths' Human Rights Cases
CEC	Central Electoral Commission
CEDAW	Convention on the Elimination of Discrimination against Women
CERD	Convention on the Elimination of All Forms of Racial Discrimination
CET	Council of Europe Treaty Series
CHP	People Republican's Party (Turkey)
DR	Decisions and Reports
DSP	Democratic Left Party (Turkey)
DTP	Party for a Democratic Society (Turkey)
ECHR	European Convention on Human Rights
EHRR	European Human Rights Reports
EHRR SE	European Human Rights Reports Summaries and Extracts
ESC	European Social Charter
ETS	European Treaty Series
ICCPR	International Covenant on Civil and Political Rights
ILM	International Legal Materials
ILO	International Labour Organisation
MHP	Nationalist Movement Party (Turkey)
NATO	North Atlantic Treaty Organisation
NGO	Nongovernmental Organisation
ODIHR	Office for Democratic Institutions and Human Rights
OECD	Organisation for Economic Co-operation and Development
OSCE	Organization for Security and Co-operation in Europe

P1	Protocol 1
P1–1	Protocol 1, article 1
P1–3	Protocol 1, article 3
P12	Protocol 12
PACE	Parliamentary Assembly of the Council of Europe
PKK	Workers' Party of Kurdistan
RMT	National Union of Rail, Maritime and Transport Workers (UK)
SGP	Staatkundig Gereformeerde Partij (Netherlands)
UCP	United Communist Party (Turkey)
UDHR	Universal Declaration of Human Rights
UN	United Nations
Yearbook	Yearbook of the European Convention on Human Rights

Introduction

The European Convention on Human Rights 1950 (the Convention)[1] has long been associated with the idea of democracy. Its preamble speaks of the importance of an 'effective political democracy' while several articles refer to the ideal of a 'democratic society'.

During much of the history of the European Court of Human Rights ('the Court) and the European Commission of Human Rights, the Convention institutions have shown some timidity or deference in developing the content of this effective political democracy, but this has changed in the last thirty years or so. There are several reasons for this. First, Turkey decided to accept the Court's jurisdiction; this has led to many cases involving the Turkish Constitutional Court's proscription of various parties. Second, a large number of Eastern and Central European countries have ratified the Convention, bringing with them questions of how to manage the transition to democracy. Third, among the new members are countries with decidedly dubious democratic and human rights records (most notably Russia). Fourth, even among established members, there have been rumblings of concern about the quality of democratic practices; Italy is perhaps the best example, though by no means the only one. Fifth, changes in governance, including the possibility of a supranational organisation (the European Union) joining the Convention, create new questions for the Convention institutions.

Concerns about democratic practices in Europe have increased even more dramatically in the last ten years. There is concern about the increasing rise of populism in some countries (Hungary, Greece, Italy), with the term 'authoritarian' even used (Turkey). The far-right has undergone something of a resurgence, with a Le Pen once again challenging for the Presidency of

---

[1] European Convention on Human Rights, Rome, 4 November 1950, in force 3 September 1953, ETS 5.

2 *Introduction*

France. Europe itself in the form of the European Union still has to deal with criticisms of its democratic legitimacy, and this has only been exacerbated by multiple crisis and the Union's response to them – the financial crisis, the refugee crisis, the rise of populist anti-European parties, the crisis in Ukraine, Brexit.

For these reasons we have moved from a situation where Convention decisions on matters of electoral rights (unlike free expression and free assembly) were on the fringes of European jurisprudence to one in which the Grand Chamber has delivered a string of important decisions in this area. The Grand Chamber has found that prisoner disenfranchisement in the UK breaches Convention rights (*Hirst*),[2] and that the consociational arrangements in post-Dayton Bosnia and Herzegovina breach the non-discrimination rights in the Convention (*Sejdic and Finci*).[3] On the other hand it has also upheld Latvian lustration laws (*Zdanoka*),[4] the Turkish electoral quota for a party to be represented in the legislature (*Yumak and Sadak*)[5] and, perhaps most controversially of all, the Turkish Constitutional Court's proscription of the Islamist Welfare Party (*Refah Paritisi*).[6] The sensitivity of decisions in this area is made apparent by the strength of the dissenting opinions in some of these cases, most strikingly Judge Bonnello's dissent in *Sejdic*. This increased interest in political rights jurisprudence makes it urgent to interrogate the European Court's idea or ideas of democracy.[7]

This book explores the ideas of democracy which are implicit in the jurisprudence of the European Court of Human Rights. I do not claim that there is any one model of democracy which is explicitly and exclusively promoted in the text of the Convention or in the jurisprudence of the European Court of Human Rights – or indeed in the opinions of individual judges of the Court. Nevertheless, the text and the interpretation of the text may tend to reinforce the requirements of a particular model of democracy, even if this is not always consciously articulated. Or the text and its

---

[2] *Hirst v United Kingdom (No. 2)* App no 74025/01 (2006) 42 EHRR 41 (Grand Chamber).
[3] *Sejdic and Finci v Bosnia and Herzegovina* App nos 27996/06 and 34836/06 (2009) 22 BHRC 201 (Grand Chamber).
[4] *Zdanoka v Latvia* App no 58278/00 (2006) 45 EHRR 17.
[5] *Yumak and Sadak v Turkey* App no 10226/03 (2008) 48 EHRR 4.
[6] *Refah Paritisi (Welfare Party) v Turkey* App nos 41340/98 41342/98 41343/98 and 41344/98 (2003) 37 EHRR1.
[7] All civil, cultural, economic, social and political rights are interconnected, and so there are cases on the right to life, personal liberty, non-discrimination, religion, education and other rights which are also potentially relevant to the question of democracy, but this work focuses on the more narrowly conceived list of electoral and political rights.

Introduction 3

interpretation may ignore or fail to promote other models of democracy. Or they may even undermine other forms of democratic experiment.

This is possible because the text, the jurisprudence interpreting it and the rights protected therein are all 'abstract concepts' or even 'floating signifiers' whose meaning needs to be fleshed out in the process of interpretation. In interpreting the Convention rights, we can draw on other sources not usually considered formal legal sources, including normative ideals (whether we label these ideals of political morality, or background assumptions, or views about what is reasonable). This monograph will focus on normative ideals or models of democracy.

This exercise has a critical and an interpretive dimension.[8] The exercise of examining the jurisprudence through the lens of democratic theory becomes more practically useful if we can draw on political literature to identify flaws and benefits in different models of democracy. If the text and jurisprudence support a particular model of democracy and we know that there are flaws or dangers associated with that model (e.g. marginalisation of minorities or tending towards oligarchy), then we can be more alert to the menace that the jurisprudence might unwittingly ignore, reproduce or aggravate those flaws or dangers. If we can identify models of democracy which are more appealing than mainstream ones, we can see if there is scope to make arguments within the Convention system to promote elements of those more progressive models. The models of democracy discussed in the Chapter 1 therefore provide a critical tool to analyse the Court's jurisprudence but also to suggest how to interpret the Convention.

While the previous paragraph sets out the general approach, let me be more specific. My conclusions are that (unsurprisingly) the text and jurisprudence of the Convention and the Court tend to reinforce a model of democracy that is representative, liberal and often substantive. My concern is to see how the Court's jurisprudence may be 'democracy-enhancing'[9] and support or encourage democratic practices that are more inclusive, deliberative and participatory.

We will do this in the following way. First, Chapter 1 examines different theories of democracy and how they might relate to the Convention. The next two chapters continue the introductory work and examine the historical

---

[8] For more thorough critical readings of the Convention, see Marie-Bénédicte Dembour, *Who Believes in Human Rights? Reflections on the European Convention* (Cambridge University Press 2006) and Damian Gonzalez-Salzberg and Loveday Hodson, *Research Methods for International Human Rights Law: Beyond the Traditional Paradigm* (Routledge 2020).

[9] Robert Spano, 'Universality or Diversity of Human Rights? Strasbourg in the Age of Subsidiarity' (2014) 14 Human Rights Law Review 487.

origins of the electoral rights and the basic principles used by the European Court of Human Rights. Following these introductory chapters, Chapters 4 to 8 examine particular aspects of the Court's political and electoral rights jurisprudence. These chapters cover the rights of expression, assembly and association, the scope of the electoral rights, the right to vote, to run for election and the regulation of elections. In examining the jurisprudence of the Court in Chapters 4 to 8, each chapter considers whether the jurisprudence tends to reinforce any particular model of democracy. Each chapter presents a critical analysis of the relevant right and in particular its role in upholding a liberal representative model of democracy. Each chapter considers the scope for the right to promote deliberative, participatory, inclusive models of democracy. The final chapter summarises the potential for a jurisprudence that would further enhance deliberative, participatory and inclusive politics. To consider this, we first need to set out different models of democracy, and to this we now turn in the first chapter.

1

Theories of Democracy

This chapter introduces some of the different models of democracy discussed in politics literature.[1] 'Democracy' is a classic essentially contested concept. Trying to identify a common core to these diverse models is difficult, though perhaps Beetham's focus on the twin principles of popular control and equality may be useful.[2] Even these, though, are subject to interpretation. Popular control may slide from the chance to replace one set of leaders in an election every four or five years to everyone affected by a particular decision sitting in a room and thrashing it out. Equality may range from a formally equal chance to vote to ensuring relative economic equality and special representation for different groups.

Any effort to discuss models is necessarily a simplification for many reasons. First, it is unlikely that any political system is consciously designed from first principles to reflect a particular model. Therefore, it is quite likely that we will find elements of different models happily being employed within the same polity. Second, there may not even be any great paradox or tension in this – it may make perfect sense in both theory and practice for a polity to employ elements of different models. Third, there are porous boundaries between the requirements of the different models. Fourth, none of these models are presented as flawless ideals or panaceas.

The following discussion seeks to identify the key features of each model and the key flaws in each model, or at least the challenges facing the model.

---

[1] J. Morison, 'Models of Democracy: From Representation to Participation' in J. Jowell and Dawn Oliver (eds) *The Changing Constitution* (Oxford University Press 2007); Frank Cunningham, *Theories of Democracy* (Routledge 2002); David Held, *Models of Democracy* (Polity 2006).

[2] David Beetham, *Democracy and Human Rights* (Polity 1999).

6   Theories of Democracy

Finally, each section outlines some of the implications of this model for the European Convention and Court.

The Convention and the jurisprudence seem to align well with a mixed model of democracy that incorporates three key elements – a democracy that is liberal, representative and substantive. We will discuss some of the tensions involved in *liberal* democracy and then examine more closely different variants of representative democracy – classical, competitive elitist and pluralist. We will also note that liberal representative democracy may be substantive and not merely procedural; the Convention text and jurisprudence seems to support a model of democracy that is substantive to some extent. Then we will discuss three broad models of democracy which all offer critical commentary on the claims of liberal and representative democracy. These are the participatory, deliberative and egalitarian and inclusive models. A final section will consider the challenges that modern governance, particularly processes of globalisation and supranationalisation, poses for democracy.

LIBERAL DEMOCRACY

We will not start the discussion with a purely procedural model of democracy. A purely procedural model would concentrate on the procedures by which decisions are made (eg majority voting) and be unconcerned with the actual outcomes. It would be surprising if a human rights instrument associated itself with a purely procedural model of democracy. After all, human rights are typically seen as limits on state power, including the power of democratic authorities. Such a purely procedural democracy emphasises political representative procedures but does not include special protection for rights.[3] Being procedural and majoritarian in nature, it runs the risk of representing the 'tyranny of the majority'. In particular, there is a danger that the rights of minorities may be infringed in a majoritarian representative democracy. This may be particularly the case with permanent minorities who cannot realistically hope to exercise political power. This purely procedural vision of democracy is unlikely to be supported by the text of a human rights treaty.

It is more logical and likely that a human rights treaty would embrace a model of democracy in which democratic procedures were limited in some way. This is the central theme in liberal democracy. In a liberal democracy, the people should not inherit the absolute sovereign power associated with absolutist monarchs; rather there are limits on the sovereign power even when

---

[3] It is possible that a representative democracy without special protection for rights may in practice be more liberal than some liberal democracies which do offer special guarantees.

Liberal Democracy

exercised by the people (or their representatives).[4] This is the central theme in liberal democracy where democracy is seen as realising liberty or specific liberties. Indeed, we can be more specific and argue that the European Convention text (and the related jurisprudence) envisages a liberal representative democracy.

That the ECHR preferred model is liberal stems from its protection of largely classic civil and political rights – personal liberty, free expression, freedom of thought and religion, free association, (formal) equality in the enjoyment of rights, even the right to property[5] (a right that does not make it into either of the 1966 International Covenants). The very fact that the Convention establishes a Court where individuals can complain about state political decisions indicates its concern with ensuring there are limits on political power. That the Convention system is representative in character is evident from the text of article 3, Protocol 1 (P1–3), which speaks of elections by means of secret ballot to choose a legislature.

Liberal representative democracy has a considerable appeal. As well as allowing the participation of all in the political process (at least through their representatives), it also offers a guarantee that a range of rights will be protected. It avoids, therefore, the danger that certain vital interests are subject to a show of hands or a secret vote. However, liberal democracy does not just offer protection from abuse. More ambitiously, it may be seen as offering a zone of autonomy where the individual may develop and flourish.[6]

Liberal representative democracy also has benefits for the political system and society, not just the individual. It allows for the political system to be peaceful and stable; it takes the heat out of political disagreement – whatever may be the outcome of an election, it will not cost the losers their rights.

There are, of course, tensions and problems. In yoking together liberalism and democracy, there is the question of what weight to give to these values. Liberal democracy may seem an obvious, even the default, solution in the twenty-first century,[7] but it should not be forgotten that for many historic

---

[4] Benjamin Constant, *Principles of Politics Applicable to All Representative Governments* in Benjamin Constant and Biancamaria Fontana (eds) *Constant: Political Writings* (Cambridge University Press 1988 [1815]), 175–180.

[5] Compare this list of the Convention rights with the one Constant gives: 'individual freedom, religious freedom, freedom of opinion, ... the enjoyment of property.' Constant, *Principles of Politics Applicable to All Representative Governments*, 180.

[6] Benjamin Constant, *The Liberties of the Ancients Compared with that of the Moderns* in Benjamin Constant and Biancamaria Fontana (eds) *Constant: Political Writings* (Cambridge University Press 1988 [1820]), 327.

[7] Frank Cunningham, *Theories of Democracy*, 27.

8 *Theories of Democracy*

liberals, democracy was seen as an undesirable practice wherein the multitude brought ignorance, rapacity, fear and anger to the table, as well as numbers.[8] Some may put so much emphasis on liberal rights that it is difficult to see what is left of democracy.[9] Conversely, others, while defending the idea of rights, believe that ultimately some authority has to have the final say on what rights we have and that final say belongs with a representative assembly.[10] Whilst the tension between liberalism and democracy (or the rights of the moderns and the rights of the ancients) is a central concern of modern political theorising,[11] it is not clear that there is any definitive resolution of this tension. At some point, it seems any balancing act must come down on the side (at least temporarily) of either liberal rights or representative democracy.

The nature and content of the liberal rights protected is also a point of contestation. Do they include only a minimum core of civil and political rights (somewhat like the ECHR and P1 were originally intended to do), or do they run the gamut of civil, cultural, economic, social and political rights found in UN human rights instruments? Not to mention collective rights, minority rights, people's rights, environmental rights and so on.

Liberalism's history is even more deeply contested than this, and critics may argue that liberalism and liberal rights create an overly individualistic or atomistic approach to politics, one where individuals are encouraged to be self-regarding and indeed selfish.[12] The implicit liberal preference for liberty may favour leaving unchecked market forces while the liberal zone of autonomy may well be a cloak for private oppression, particularly in the home.[13] Thus a host of political theorists from different camps – conservative, socialist, communitarian, republican, feminist – have taken issue with liberal individualism.

---

[8] Constant typifies the fear that the poor are no fit to exercise political power and need to be restrained from using it in a selfish manner: Constant, *Principles of Politics Applicable to All Representative Governments*, 214–215.

[9] Dworkin is a prominent culprit here. See, for example, Ronald Dworkin, 'The Moral Reading and the Majoritarian Premise' in Harold Hongju Koh and Ronald Slye (eds) *Deliberative Democracy and Human Rights* (Yale University Press 2000).

[10] Jeremy Waldron, *Law and Disagreement* (Oxford University Press 2001). In the UK context, this provides a strong argument for the traditional doctrine of parliamentary sovereignty. See, for example, Jeffrey Denys Goldsworthy, *The Sovereignty of Parliament* (Clarendon 1999), 261–263.

[11] Constant, *The Liberties of the Ancients Compared with that of the Moderns*, 327.

[12] This is the criticism raised by (among many others) Marx, Macpherson and communitarians such as Sandel: Karl Marx, 'On the Jewish Question' in E. Easton and K. Guddat (eds) *Writings of the Young Marx on Philosophy and Society* (Doubleday Books 1967 [1843]); C. B. Macpherson, *The Theory of Possessive Individualism* (Oxford University Press 1962); Michael Sandel, *Liberalism and the Limits of Justice* (Cambridge University Press 1982).

[13] David Held, *Models of Democracy* (Polity 2006), 88.

Representative Democracy   9

Whilst liberal democracy addresses some of the problems about a majority oppressing a minority, it does not necessarily address all of the problems associated with representative democracy. The representative democratic element in liberal democracy is not without problems either. To look at these more closely, we must disentangle some of the different variants of representative democracy.

REPRESENTATIVE DEMOCRACY

For centuries, Western philosophical discussions on democracy considered the Athenian forum to be the paradigmatic example of democracy. Yet with the rise of the modern state as a large territorial entity, indeed sometimes on a continental scale, this was not a viable conception of democracy. Furthermore, the Athenian model depended on the existence of a body of men who could devote considerable time to political discussion. This was only possible in Athens thanks to the labour of slaves, foreigners and women. And it is hardly possible in modern societies when individuals must spend a large portion of their time working.[14] The solution to the practical problems posed by the Athenian model of democracy is to institute some system of representation.[15] Representative government is the only feasible way of protecting political liberty in the modern world; it enables the citizenry to hold the governors to account by subjecting them to scrutiny and to reject them at regular intervals by means of elections.[16]

Representation is more than just a practical response, however. Constant thought that the ancient model of democracy associated with Greek city states protects political participation *at the expense* of private autonomy;[17] any effort to pursue those ancient ideals in modern societies would collapse in terror and infringe the modern liberties. Madison argued that representation in large-scale societies introduces a qualitative change for the better. Madison was wary of small parochial communities and thought that considering views from a larger-scale organisation allowed for better decision-making.[18] Weber thought that the use of representatives allowed for the negotiation of the compromises necessary in modern complex industrial societies.[19]

---

[14] Constant, *The Liberties of the Ancients Compared with that of the Moderns*, 314.
[15] Thomas Paine, *Rights of Man* (Penguin 1984 [1791]), 180; Held, *Models of Democracy*, 129 citing Weber.
[16] Constant, *The Liberties of the Ancients Compared with that of the Moderns*, 326.
[17] Ibid., 311.
[18] Held, *Models of Democracy*, 73.
[19] Ibid., 130.

Liberal representative democracy solves (or at least offers a solution for) one of the problems associated with democracy – the danger of oppression by the majority. The problems with representative democracy, though, go beyond a failure to protect the rights of individuals. Even if individual rights are protected, there is much more to politics than just rights. There may still be difficulties if a minority or a section of the community fails to identify with the polity, perhaps because it is underrepresented or, if proportionally represented, is not able to influence policy (see later on egalitarian and inclusive models). Indeed, the danger is not just that a minority will fail to identify with the polity. The focus on procedures of representation, voting, the compromise and negotiation of interests may undermine any ideal of a 'common good' or other source of political integration. We shall return to the communitarian or civic republican critique in the section on substantive democracy; for now we will focus on the tendency towards elitism in representative democracy.

The process of representation may leave political power open to capture and monopolisation by a narrow elite or set of elites. This is particularly likely in large-scale[20] complex societies. Under such circumstances, it is not possible to participate in the political process without efficient and large organisations and financial resources. This leads to the dominance of political parties and professional politicians in the system. The dominance of political parties and professional politicians leads to a number of consequences. First, it may make it unlikely that the actual majority of the population will engage in political activity beyond voting. Second, the political process becomes dominated by political parties and professional politicians who may find it difficult to identify with the 'governed'. Third, the demands of organisation and financial resources may create a climate where wealth plays a significant role in politics. Indeed, the problem is not just that wealth can buy influence, but more fundamentally all governments depend on a successful private sector 'as the source of incomes, growth, jobs'.[21] Fourth, professional politicians seek power for its own sake, and in competing for electoral victory, parties and politicians may resort to a host of irrational stratagems, most notably personality politics and advertising techniques;[22] democracy on this model may involve nothing

---

[20] Bellamy examines how late nineteenth- / early twentieth-century theorists saw the rise of mass democracy as facilitating the advent of new elites either in the form of demagogues or more bureaucratic or technical elites: Richard Bellamy, 'The Advent of the Masses and the Making of the Modern Theory of Democracy' in Terence Ball and Richard Bellamy (eds) *The Cambridge History of Twentieth Century Political Thought* (Cambridge University Press 2001).

[21] Anne Phillips, *Which Equalities Matter?* (Polity 1999), 17.

[22] In short, the political sphere becomes a marketplace where consumers (voters) can be manipulated into choosing particular products. For a critique of the consumer or marketplace

Representative Democracy

'more thoughtful or authentic' than a choice 'between brands of soap or cigarettes'.[23] Fifth, the locus of power may shift from a representative assembly to the executive and expert bureaucracy.

In short, while some models of representative democracy (and even liberal representative democracy) appeal to a notion of a political marketplace, the danger is that marketplaces are open to manipulation and monopolistic or oligopolistic practices.[24] This could quickly lead to a 'low-intensity' model of democracy,[25] or a merely 'technocratic' vision of politics,[26] or even a sort of 'inverted totalitarianism'[27] or semi-authoritarianism where elections legitimate illiberal government.[28]

In painting this picture of the negatives of representative democracy, there are people who see these features of representative democracy and welcome them in different degrees. The classic representative government theorist JS Mill argued that there was a difference between the skill required to hold government to account and the skill required to govern.[29] Holding government to account was critically important given the vast powers invested in political and administrative institutions and the danger of the abuse of those powers; however, this does not mean that there should be no distinction between the governed and the governors. This interpretation has the appeal of being pragmatic and realistic; it recognises that government is a potential threat to liberty which must be controlled, but also that government is a complex demanding business and that most people have no time or

approach to democratic politics, see Bob Watt, *UK Election Law: A Critical Examination* (Cavendish 2005), 18.

[23] James S. Fishkin, *Democracy When the People Are Thinking: Revitalizing Our Politics through Public Deliberation* (Oxford University Press 2018), 21.

[24] Macpherson notes that such representative theories rely on the idea of responding to the power of citizens as consumers. The flaw is that consumers are not in equal positions. The unequal distribution of wealth is one inequality, but also the fact that some citizens or consumers are better able to make use of opportunities thanks to their occupation, education or other special advantage; Macpherson, *The Life and Times of Liberal Democracy*, 87–88.

[25] Susan Marks, *The Riddle of All Constitutions* (Oxford University Press 2000), 52.

[26] Held, *Models of Democracy*, 154.

[27] Sheldon S. Wolin, *Democracy Incorporated: Managed Democracy and The Specter of Inverted Totalitarianism* (Princeton University Press 2008).

[28] These possible flaws in representative democracy are especially important because they cast doubt on a rather too straightforward argument that the protection of rights by courts is a threat to democracy. If democracies in practice are only 'low-intensity' democracies, then that weakens the argument against rights. See Sandra Fredman, 'Scepticism under Scrutiny: Labour Law and Human Rights' in Tom Campbell, Keith Ewing and Adam Tomkins (eds) *Sceptical Essays on Human Rights* (Oxford University Press 2001).

[29] Held, *Models of Democracy*, 86.

inclination for it; however, people still know their own interests and can play a critical role in holding the government to account.

For some representative democrats, even Mill's version is far too optimistic and fails to understand the realities of democracy in large-scale complex societies. All that is left for representative democracy is to manage competition between different elites. Schumpeter is the most famous exponent of this view, labelled 'competitive elitism' by Held.[30] Schumpeter, like many representative democrats, is sceptical of notions like the 'common good', 'popular sovereignty' or even the idea of the 'people' as a collective actor. In avoiding relying on a notion of the common good, it is possible to argue that this is simply realistic – that after the Enlightenment, it is unrealistic to imagine that a single narrative can provide for a common good or other strong source of political integration. Notions of the common good may be ideological masks for sectional interests, and it is better to do without them.[31] Most notably, one may agree with Schumpeter:[32] one might deny that there exists any collective actor known as the 'people'[33] and doubt the ability of actual ordinary people to make intelligent policy choices. In such a framework, political quietism is a virtue. It is to be welcomed that the majority of people do not get actively involved in politics, but limit themselves to choosing between sets of rulers in periodic elections. This vision of democracy also has the merit of recognising the importance of political parties as central actors in politics. Even an advocate of more participatory democracy like Macpherson accepts that political parties are 'needed to allow issues to be effectively proposed and debated'.[34] The focus on the executive rather than a representative assembly again could also easily merit the accolade of realism. One should be wary of imagining a golden age of parliamentarism when representatives freely and rationally debated the issues of the day. The centrality of parliaments may well have ended decades before the Convention was drafted.[35]

---

[30] Held presents Weber and Schumpeter as advocates of this more pessimistic view: Held, *Models of Democracy*, 125, 137. Macpherson suggests the term 'pluralist elitist equilibrium' to cover both Schumpeter and the pluralists like Dahl: Macpherson, *The Life and Times of Liberal Democracy*, 77.

[31] Weber critiques socialism for a 'fictitious solidarity': Held, *Models of Democracy*, 133; see also Held's interpretation of Schumpeter at 143, 146.

[32] Joseph Alois Schumpeter, *Capitalism, Socialism, and Democracy* (5th edn, Allen and Unwin 1976).

[33] Not just Schumpeter; Thornhill notes the views of Durkheim and Weber that the idea of a 'subjectivised popular will' was 'illusory': Chris Thornhill, *The Sociology of Law and the Global Transformation of Democracy* (Cambridge University Press 2018), 94.

[34] Macpherson, *The Life and Times of Liberal Democracy*, 112.

[35] Thornhill, *The Sociology of Law and the Global Transformation of Democracy*, 54–55, 148.

This extremely pessimistic (or realistic) interpretation of representative democracy is not the only one. An alternative, which still emphasises its realistic and empirical bases, is the vision of interest group pluralism advocated at an early stage by Dahl.[36] Dahl labelled it 'polyarchy', as pluralist democracy required multiple centres of power rather than power residing in the one or the few or the many. While acknowledging the existence of political elites and administrative power, the pluralists also stressed the myriad interest groups in society and their relations of competition, negotiation and cooperation. This provides some indication of how accountability might function; again a realist might argue that accountability is the best that can be hoped for in modern complex states. The many different interest groups function as checks and balances on each other. This pluralism, though, does not require active citizen participation on the part of large numbers of people.[37] Furthermore, pluralists tend to avoid the issue of inequalities among individuals and groups.[38]

Held notes that pluralist theory has evolved, and that neo-pluralist theory sometimes overlaps with social democratic models of democracy.[39] The prominent pluralist Dahl is a good example here – he has addressed the issue of inequality more directly, devoting the entire of an admittedly short book to the topic.[40] Therein he identifies six factors which impede the realisation of political equality. These include the unequal distribution of political resources, skills and incentives; time; size; market economies; international but largely undemocratic systems; and the effects of severe crises.[41] In particular, market economies (which Dahl regards as inevitable) have the possibility to inflict serious harm on persons, can provoke further inequalities in resources and are linked to a consumerist ethos that undermines the ideal of citizens participating in collective self-government. Dahl even refers to Ancient Greek ideals of debate on the 'common good'.[42]

Dahl's mention of the common good suggests one further gloss on the idea of a liberal representative democracy that we must consider before moving on to discuss some models of democracy that go beyond the representative ideal.

---

[36] Held, *Models of Democracy* 159.
[37] Ibid., 162.
[38] Ibid., 165.
[39] Ibid., 170.
[40] Robert Alan Dahl, *On Political Equality* (Yale University Press 2006). Interestingly, Rawls also moves in the direction of greater political equality in his later writings.
[41] Ibid., chapter five.
[42] Ibid., 65–67, 87–91.

SUBSTANTIVE DEMOCRACY

The picture of liberal representative democracy drawn so far is largely about procedures and individual rights. A polity based on procedures and individual rights might aspire to liberal 'neutrality' – that is to say, the one that aspires to be neutral in debates about values, ethics, the good life. There is considerable debate as to whether a polity is viable or sustainable purely on the basis of a set of procedures and individual rights.[43] At the most basic level, what can a liberal neutral state argue when individuals seek to use liberal rights to undermine liberal democracy itself? Beyond this minimal question of the survival of liberal democracy, politics is not just about procedures and rights; do liberal democrats simply believe that voters and politicians vote their preferences or even prejudices within the constraint of fair procedures and individual rights? It is legitimate to ask whether there is there some need for an ideal of the common good (or common goods), or some set of shared values, or even a shared community identity.

Certainly many have argued that this is necessary. Some liberals, such as JS Mill or Joseph Raz, believe a liberal state must defend values such as creativity or autonomy and the social conditions that make these possible. Communitarians and civic republicans of various hues identify other common or collective goods that provide some integrating focus or force in a polity. These may indeed be deeply liberal values such as the ideals of equality discussed by Michael Walzer.[44] A shared national identity may be important for the practice of democracy – if 'we the people' are to govern, then there must be some shared understanding of just who the 'people' are and what they have in common.

Though the range of perfectionist liberals, communitarians and civic republicans is a broad one, in a sense they are all agreed that democracy is not (or at least should not be) merely procedural – there are substantive common values that stand behind it. Rather than borrow the term 'civic republican' or 'communitarian' or 'perfectionist' to describe this constellation of views critical of liberal democracy, I will borrow the term 'substantive' from the militant democracy literature[45] to highlight the importance of substantive values of whatever nature in such contributions.

---

[43] Michael Sandel, 'The Procedural Republic and the Unencumbered Self' in S. Avineri and A. De-Shalit (eds) *Communitarianism and Individualism* (Oxford University Press 1992).

[44] Michael Walzer, *Spheres of Justice* (Robertson 1983).

[45] Fox and Nolte use this term and explain its basis drawing on writings from the unlikely pairing of John Rawls and Carl Schmitt: Gregory Fox and Georg Nolte, 'Intolerant Democracies' (1995) 36 Harvard International Law Journal 1, 17–20.

Substantive conceptions of democracy avoid a tendency to excessive individualism. In avoiding an excessive individualism they allow for public discussion to result in limits being placed on individual rights in order to protect public interests. They also encourage more explicit discussion of the public goods or values that are necessary to secure benefits (including rights) for individuals. Substantive democrats have ambitions for a democratic culture that goes beyond formal elections and includes debate on shared values (and in this regard may be close to some deliberative democratic thinkers). A national identity in particular provides resources of solidarity that help to explain why persons in different regions of a country should be concerned about people in other regions, and this is especially important when it comes to the allocation and more precisely the redistribution of resources.

Yet substantive conceptions also have dangers. It is necessary to consider what values might be genuinely common to everyone. The achievement of the Enlightenment was to undermine, challenge and uproot many claims of tradition, religion or social order to provide some form of common or shared value or identity. At the same time national identity emerged as one possible source of common value or identity, yet this is also troubling. The sheer diversity of modern multicultural, sometimes even multilingual or multinational, societies makes it even more difficult to identify common values or identities. Furthermore, there are ideological criticisms of the possibility of a common good. As we have already noticed, the idea of a common good may serve as no more than an ideological fig leaf. And the ideas of the common good may well end up being exclusionary and anti-egalitarian. This is true even more so of claims about a common identity which suggest that the political community is based on a homogenous moral or ethnic community.[46] The challenges are even greater in the context of international or supranational organisations like the Council of Europe or the European Union.

THE CONVENTION, THE COURT AND LIBERAL REPRESENTATIVE SUBSTANTIVE DEMOCRACY

The Convention system itself has an affinity to the ideals of liberal representative, indeed substantive, democracy. As we will see repeatedly, the Court stresses the importance of the classic liberal rights in the type of democracy envisioned by the Convention; a party fundamentally opposed to these liberal

---

[46] Noel O'Sullivan, *European Political Thought Since 1945* (Palgrave 2004) 11. On the Second World War's fostering of relatively homogenous nations, see Tony Judt, *Postwar: A History of Europe since 1945* (Penguin Press 2005).

rights may legitimately be proscribed. Therefore, the question is not so much what are the implications of a liberal democratic vision for the Court as whether the Court's jurisprudence shows an awareness of the pitfalls of different variants of liberal representative democracy, whether it permits or requires or prohibits flaws in these variants. Does it reach decisions in such a way as to allow the creation or maintenance of a limited competitive, elitist-style (or even a technocratic or inverted totalitarian managed) democracy, or does it enable or require a more open pluralistic or social democratic variant of liberal democracy? Does the Court adopt a more substantive understanding of democracy?

It is possible that the protection of liberal rights alleviates some of the problems associated with some variants of representative democracy. This very much depends on what rights are protected and how they are interpreted. It is possible that freedom of expression and association, education, equality and so forth are understood in such a way that political debate is promoted, that no association or class of people has a stranglehold on political power and that the influence of money is kept from tainting the political system.

A set of liberal rights may well underpin the pluralist or polyarchical vision which after all is about different associations interacting in the political system. A classic, pluralist or polyarchical variant would presumably favour expansive notions of free expression and free association rights. Further the Court might take on itself the job of representation reinforcing suggested by J. H. Ely.[47] The flip side of this might be to suggest that there are some types of cases where the Court should be deferential. The suggestion was made some time ago that the Court's margin of appreciation doctrine has a role to play in this.[48] The margin of appreciation doctrine allows the Court to display a degree of deference to the national authorities in cases involving the distribution of economic resources, public morality, emerging technologies or national security. It would not be too difficult to suggest that deference is also due in cases where a measure has been approved by a vote in a democratic representative assembly.[49]

However, it is also true that these and other rights may be given such an interpretation that the Schumpeterian vision triumphs. It is important to remember that some of the early advocates of representative democracy saw

---

[47] John Hart Ely, *Democracy and Distrust* (Harvard University Press 1980).
[48] Conor Gearty, 'Democracy and Human Rights in the European Court of Human Rights: A Critical Appraisal' (2000) 51 (3) Northern Ireland Legal Quarterly 381.
[49] Ibid.

it as a bulwark to protect the *propertied* minority from the poor masses.[50] The liberal democratic emphasis on the rights of free and equal individuals may even highlight a particularly striking danger for liberal democrats. Whilst classic texts like the UDHR speak of persons being free and equal in rights, how feasible is it if one is not free and equal in society, in the home, in the workplace? A jurisprudence which accepted (perhaps only implicitly) the idea of competitive elitism would no doubt accept many of the traditional civil and political rights, but would not envisage especially radical versions of these. It might well accept more political institutions which ensure effective designation of governors rather than representation of popular (or populist views). Political parties would be important in such a framework, but a premium might be put on manageable numbers of political parties particularly in the centre of the political spectrum. Challenges to the role of political parties from grassroots activists or independents might not be regarded as important. The idea of the political sphere as a marketplace might lead to distinctive trends in free expression jurisprudence, which allow all ideas and speakers to compete in a formally equal setting but ignore inequalities of power and resources.

It is perhaps in a social democratic model of democracy that the Schumpeterian vision can be dispelled, by placing more emphasis on social and economic rights and substantive equality. This indeed was central to the post–Second World War political developments in Western Europe.[51] The Council of Europe's decision to split social and economic rights from civil and political ones, and to insert most of the former in a separate, oft-neglected European Social Charter, somewhat undermines the possibility of developing this response in the Convention system.[52]

The substantive ideal does have an interesting fit with the jurisprudence of the European Court of Human Rights. Substantive ideas of democracy figure in the jurisprudence in a number of ways. First, like most post–Second World War human rights texts, the Convention is avowedly substantive in prohibiting the use of human rights to attack the system of human rights and democracy. This is the so-called abuse of rights doctrine.[53] Yet the Convention and its

---

[50] See Held's interpretation of Madison: Held, *Models of Democracy*, 74.
[51] O'Sullivan, *European Political Thought since 1945*, 7–10.
[52] There is considerable scholarship now on the possibility of using the ECHR jurisprudence to offer indirect protection to social and economic rights, but there are limits on how far this may go. For analysis, see E. Palmer, 'Protecting Socio-Economic Rights through the European Convention on Human Rights: Trends and Developments in the European Court of Human Rights' (2009) 2 (4) Erasmus Law Review 397–425.
[53] Article 17 ECHR.

18   *Theories of Democracy*

jurisprudence are more substantive in nature than merely ruling out its use as a suicide pact.

Second, the Court actually identifies substantive values which underpin the convention's system of rights and may be thought of as common values – 'pluralism, tolerance and broad mindedness'[54] – and has specified that pluralism implies 'dialogue and a spirit of compromise'.[55]

Third, the Court is mindful of the importance of substantive values within the states party to the Convention. This is apparent when it alludes to the importance of various public interests or constitutional values in member states. The mantra of the Court, that the Convention strikes a balance between the interests of the individual and those of the community, resonates well with the substantive communitarian or republican ideal. Rights activists have certainly been critical of some Court decisions which permit limiting individual freedom in order to protect public interests in national security or public morality.[56]

The Court's jurisprudence, if read in a substantive light, may well indicate some of the dangers associated with substantive democracy. Most notably in cases involving Islam, the Court has upheld claims about state neutrality and secularism, and has made comments about Islamic law, that may make some Muslims doubt whether the Court's vision of common interests reflects their concerns.[57]

This section has discussed some of the key aspects of different variants of liberal representative democracy, and has mentioned some of the flaws in liberal representative substantive democracy. It has also noted how the Convention text and jurisprudence frequently offer some support to a model of democracy that is liberal, representative and substantive. The next section presents three models of democracy which seek to go beyond the representative model, emphasising ideals of participation, deliberation and equality.

BEYOND LIBERAL REPRESENTATIVE SUBSTANTIVE DEMOCRACY

PARTICIPATION

There are a range of democratic theories which decry the limited opportunities in liberal representative democracy for ordinary citizens to participate directly in the exercise of power. Representative democracy relies on political

---

[54] *Handyside v United Kingdom* (Little Red Schoolbook case) (1979) 1 EHRR 737, para 49.
[55] *Leyla Sahin v Turkey* App no 44774/98 (2005) 41 EHRR 8, para 108.
[56] *Otto-Preminger-Institut v Austria* App no 13470/87 (1994) 19 EHRR 34.
[57] *Refah Paritisi (Welfare Party) v Turkey* App no 41340/98 41342/98 41343/98 and 41344/98 (2003) 37 EHRR 1.

Participation

parties and in particular political elites; in so far as it treats the political system as a marketplace, it accepts certain inequalities that may reinforce political apathy.[58] Indeed, representative democrats may accept or even welcome such apathy. To the extent that this is an accurate description of liberal representative democracy, it is also an indictment of it. That is to say, the actual existing model of liberal representative democracy is troublesome for those who value participation.

Such participation theorists generally advocate that it is valuable for citizens to participate directly in the exercise of power. Frequently participation is seen as intrinsically valuable, though participation also has instrumental value. For participatory democrats even the more appealing versions of representative democracy offer only an anaemic political experience.

Participation comes in different forms, from the Athenian model of meetings in a public forum and choosing office holders by lot (sortition), through to direct democracy models where the people as a whole can make decisions, to electronic democracy initiatives and modern processes of participation and consultation.

A Western European almost inevitably thinks of the Athenian city state when considering models of democracy. The Athenian model eschewed for the most part the key tool of modern democracies, the election of representatives. Public decisions were taken by assemblies of the 'people' and by citizens who held office according to a system of lot or sortition. There were some elected officials, notably military experts.

The Athenian system is one which is often impracticable and undesirable in large complex societies. It is not practicable to have assemblies of all the people in any except perhaps the smallest of states. Selecting office holders by lot may also seem a random, even arbitrary procedure. More seriously perhaps, the Athenian system allowed for participation by citizens only by relying on exclusionary policies. Citizens by definition did not include women, slaves, children or foreigners. These exclusions did not just keep the number of citizens manageable; the citizens only had the time to participate in politics thanks to the (often literally slave) labour of the excluded. Political freedom for Athenian citizens depended on the enslavement of others. Even the most famous sons of Athens were sceptical of the democracy, Plato famously blaming the system for the death of Socrates.[59]

These concerns about the impracticability and undesirability of the Athenian solutions do not mean that they are irrelevant. For some, the Athenian

---

[58] Macpherson, *The Life and Times of Liberal Democracy*, 88.
[59] For most of the two millennia since then 'democracy' was a term of criticism.

model of active involvement in political self-government remains attractive. An impressively high percentage of Athenian citizens could actually participate in making political decisions in a way that was far more meaningful than the casting of a ballot. The lot has a special attraction in potentially breaking the stranglehold which a privileged elite may hold on political power. So occasionally there is a call for a return to Athenian innovations. It is of course possible to model local government (at the most local of levels) on the Athenian system. And sortition is feasible – and is indeed used for selecting lay juries in some European countries. Some argue that more use could be made of sortition in some contexts such as choosing members of a largely advisory legislative chamber.[60] Sometimes this is used in combination with a deliberative democratic model.[61]

While we have so far discussed direct democracy in the context of the Athenian model of face-to-face discussion in the agora and sortition, direct democracy in modern societies often takes the form of referenda or plebiscites whereby the people are asked directly to vote on certain issues. For a long time, such mechanisms were associated with the US or Switzerland. In European countries it has generally been associated with constitutional changes in some though by no means all European states. More recently, though, it has acquired a prominence by virtue of controversial referenda on European Union treaties (including negative votes on different aspects of European integration in Ireland, France, Netherlands and Denmark), the inclusion of a popular initiative clause in the EU Reform Treaty,[62] the Irish referendums on equal marriage, abortion and divorce, and debates about the role of referenda,[63] recall mechanisms[64] and the Brexit referendum in the quintessential representative democracy, the UK.

While such popular votes have a certain democratic appeal, they often trouble democrats who believe that negotiation by representatives or deliberation is the real hallmark of a democracy. Such preference counting mechanisms do not necessarily respect fundamental rights or the interests of minority

---

[60] Anthony Barnett and Peter Carty, *The Athenian Option: Radical Reform for the House of Lords (Sortition and Public Policy)* (Imprint Academic 2008).

[61] E. Ghosh, 'Deliberative Democracy and the Countermajoritarian Difficulty: Considering Constitutional Juries' (2010) 30 (2) Oxford Journal of Legal Studies 327.

[62] Article 11 Consolidated Version of the Treaty on European Union as amended by the Treaty of Lisbon.

[63] See Parliamentary Voting System and Constituencies Act 2011 (UK) providing for a referendum on the voting system and the European Union Act 2011 (UK) with its referendum requirement for the approval of certain European Union treaties.

[64] Recall of MPs Act 2015 (UK).

Participation

communities. It offers little reason to think of the impact on future generations. Whilst a transnational[65] or supranational plebiscite is possible, there are other reasons to doubt the democratic quality of a multinational vote. And of course, plebiscites or referendums may be manipulated, particularly by populist leaders, or may be carried out in wholly unpropitious circumstances, such as the referendum pursuant to the Russian occupation of Crimea.

How might sortition systems fare under the European Convention system? Given P1–3's obligation to hold elections for a legislature, sortition is ruled out as the main method of selecting a legislature. Whether it might be used to select part of a legislature or an upper chamber is more of an open question. Rules in a sortition system would presumably also escape ECHR scrutiny, except in so far as the freestanding equality clause in Protocol 12 applies.

The adoption of direct democracy mechanisms may have implications for the Convention. While voting in such procedures is presumably not caught by P1–3 (which speaks of elections for the legislature), P12 may be relevant; furthermore, the practice of recalling a sitting parliamentarian in the UK would have to be shown to be a justified restriction on the right to be elected.

Finally – and here we revert somewhat to the Athenian forum ideal – there are modern notions of participation. The ideal of participatory democracy reappears periodically, for example in Rousseau's writings in the eighteenth century, Marx's in the nineteenth century and again during the 1960s.[66] Recently indeed there are theorists who stress the role of participation in a deliberative democracy (though many deliberative democrats are wary of participation).[67] A participatory model of democracy avoids some of the flaws associated with representative democracy. Most notably it envisages people actually being directly involved in making decisions that affect them.

Despite its idealistic overtones, participatory democracy is somewhat in vogue again. For instance, participation is a key component of many UN human rights obligations (as interpreted by the respective expert committees)[68] and is frequently referred to by human rights academics.[69] Similarly

---

[65] Witness the simultaneous referendums on the 1998 Belfast or Good Friday Agreement in Northern Ireland and the Republic of Ireland.

[66] Carole Pateman, *Participation and Democratic Theory* (Cambridge University Press 1970).

[67] Held, *Models of Democracy*, 236–237.

[68] Rory O'Connell, Aoife Nolan, Colin Harvey, Mira Dutschke and Eoin Rooney, *Applying an International Human Rights Framework to State Budget Allocations: Rights and Resources* (Routledge 2014), 106.

[69] Sandra Fredman, *Human Rights Transformed: Positive Rights and Positive Duties* (Oxford University Press 2008).

Theories of Democracy

participation crops up in discussions of budgeting[70] and also equality main-streaming.[71] In a sense the use of electronic forms of democracy also are a means of enhancing communication and participation, though there are questions of access to such mechanisms, the quality of the participation they promote[72] and their susceptibility to interference including interference by foreign powers.

Participatory democracy advocates still face challenges. One advocate of participatory democracy stresses that preconditions for its realisation are a shift from the understanding of citizens as consumer, and a reduction in the levels of social and economic inequality.[73] These are not insignificant challenges. Some of the other challenges are the old ones of practicability, and the menace of participation actually fostering intolerance and extremism. Participation does not necessarily mean deliberation; indeed deliberation may be sidelined during a plebiscite, or ignored in some forms of electronic democracy. Similarly equality is not necessarily assured by participation, especially if it simply results in decisions by majority votes perhaps at a very local level (the iron law of oligarchy can apply at local level as well as national level). In addition there are also regular concerns about the quality of participation, with commentators frequently invoking Arnstein's ladder of participation, where participation ranges from forms of manipulation to genuine citizen control.[74]

The implications of participatory democracy for the European Court is that the Court would encourage procedures which facilitated participation. This could, for instance, be done by insisting that a right can only be limited when all those affected have had a chance to participate in the relevant decision.[75] Or it might involve a revivified freedom of association jurisprudence which envisioned a role for trade unions beyond merely making their views known. Or we might see it in jurisprudence that envisioned imposing duties on political parties to organise along participatory lines.[76] Conversely, we might

---

[70] See the Participatory Budgeting Unit at www.participatorybudgeting.org.uk/
[71] The Northern Ireland Act 1998 Section 75 statutory equality duty in Northern Ireland is one classic example of this.
[72] Macpherson, for instance, was sceptical of the possibilities of electronic democracy even in the 1970s: Macpherson, *The Life and Times of Liberal Democracy*, 95–98.
[73] Ibid., 99–100.
[74] Sherry Arnstein, 'A Ladder of Citizen Participation' (1969) Journal of American Institute of Planners 216.
[75] Rory O'Connell, 'Towards a Stronger Conception of Democracy in the Strasbourg Convention' (2006) European Human Rights Law Review 281.
[76] Macpherson, *The Life and Times of Liberal Democracy*, 112. The arguments about requiring parties to be internally democratic are explained in Yigal Mersel, 'The Dissolution of Political

Deliberative Democracy 23

see a rejection of participatory democracy if such national measures were ruled incompatible with freedom of association.

DELIBERATIVE DEMOCRACY

One of the key criticisms of the models of democracy discussed so far is that they make an assumption as to how people vote, whether they are expressing their views in the Athenian agora, in the election booth or indeed as a representative in an assembly. The assumption is that a person votes according to his or her preferences. That preference may be an expression of self-interest, an idealistic position, an altruistic position, an ill-informed one or even a prejudice. Democracy on this model is simply a method of aggregating preferences.[77] What this assumption ignores is the possibility that such preferences are not given but can be *transformed through deliberation*.

This is where deliberative democrats come in. Since the emergence of deliberative democratic theorising in the late twentieth century, this model has become one of the key, perhaps even the dominant model of democracy for political theorising. Deliberative democrats come in many different guises, and offer a varied bag of institutional suggestions, but what is central to them is the idea that the paradigmatic democratic act is not that of expressing one's preference through a vote. That aggregative model of democracy falsely treats preferences as 'given', has no distinctive conception of a public realm, promotes a 'thin and individualistic form of rationality' and does not take seriously notions of 'normative and evaluative objectivity'.[78] Rather, for deliberative democrats the paradigmatic democratic act is that of engaging in deliberation with others in a way that one's preferences may be transformed.

This difference is critical. A deliberative democrat would no doubt welcome the extension of formal political rights to all individuals, and also perhaps welcome extending political democracy into the social and economic spheres. However, this is not the key issue for deliberative democrats. Rather the key issue is the quality of the deliberation between those citizens in the political sphere or elsewhere[79] and the creation of institutions which foster deliberation.

Parties: The Problem of Internal Democracy' (2006) 4 International Journal of Constitutional Law 84.

[77] Iris Marion Young, *Inclusion and Democracy* (Oxford University Press 2000), 19. According to Habermas, this reflects a market logic based on strategic rationality: Jürgen Habermas, *The Inclusion of the Other: Studies in Political Theory* (Polity Press 1998), 243.

[78] Young, *Inclusion and Democracy*, 20–21.

[79] Held, *Models of Democracy*, 232.

Some deliberative democrats make strong claims for the theory. Habermas, for instance, believes that it overcomes many of the tensions in political theorising that we have discussed. He argues that his discourse theory of law and democracy successfully integrates both the liberties of the ancients and the liberties of the moderns, answering the challenge identified by Constant nearly two centuries ago. He also presents it as overcoming the tensions between liberalism and civic republicanism.[80] For Habermas this version of deliberative democracy also requires considering the threat of factual inequalities that undermine the equal exercise of rights; for this reason, 'rights to the provision of living conditions that are socially, technologically and ecologically safeguarded' are necessary for the equal enjoyment of civil and political rights.[81]

These are strong claims for deliberative democracy. However, once we get beyond this central core in deliberative democratic theorising, we discover a near-bewildering range of views as to what deliberative democracy entails. There are views that seem to be indistinguishable from idealised versions of the representative process (though perhaps no less valuable for that) to others which envisage more radical institutional innovation, even transformation, and much greater levels of substantive equality.[82] Some deliberative democrats take existing notions of equality, autonomy and reciprocity and explain how these can be understood in both a political sense and a deliberative sense; so political equality requires equal voting rights for all while deliberative equality refers to the 'equal representation of diverse positions, regardless of their numerical strength'.[83]

As with all theories, there are criticisms of deliberative democracy. The wide variety of implications (with some not very different from existing institutions) is one. However, there are also those who criticise the undoubtedly idealistic and perhaps even utopian elements of deliberative democracy. For those who defend the realistic version of representative democracy associated with a wide variety of thinkers, it is not plausible to imagine that persons have the time, inclination or even skills to engage in the wide-ranging debate envisioned by deliberative democrats. Even those sympathetic to the notion

---

[80] Jürgen Habermas, *The Inclusion of the Other: Studies in Political Theory* (Polity Press 1998), 248.

[81] Jürgen Habermas, *Between Facts and Norms* (MIT Press 1996), 123.

[82] Sandra Fredman, *Human Rights Transformed: Positive Rights and Positive Duties* (Oxford University Press 2008), 39.

[83] Michael Rabinder James, *Deliberative Democracy and the Plural Polity* (University of Kansas Press 2004), 9.

that it is necessary to debate, deliberate and shape preferences of voters express doubt as to the inclination or ability of political parties to do so.[84]

Deliberative democratic theorists envisage persons engaging in reasoned debate oriented towards the common good or at least an impartial position, but the very existence of a 'common good' or an 'impartial position' may be doubted. It does not seem plausible to exclude the role of interest from politics, and invocations of a common good or impartiality may simply be ideological. There are also critics who deplore the emphasis on one particular mode of debate, i.e. reasoned debate, which may deligitimise others who wish to use rhetoric, narrative, emotion,[85] arguments about identity (national or minority) or even religion in their public discourse. If some disagreements revolve around a simple value difference, it is not certain that deliberation will resolve matters. There is also the criticism alluded to above that deliberative democracy actually is in many ways only a supplement to representative democracy, and the supplements are themselves too easily open to elite manipulation. Some authors accept basic premises of deliberative democracy but recognise some of these problems propose more radical and inclusive models of deliberative democracy that recognise the importance of differences.[86]

Deliberative democrats also need to consider whether their model of democracy still requires some notion of substantive democracy, some common sense of identity and, if so, what might that be. Would a constitutional patriotism based on adherence to and acceptance of constitutional rights and procedures suffice, or is some deeper notion of 'solidarity'[87] required, and if so how is that to be generated without relying on problematic notions of identity and exclusion?

What are the implications of the deliberative democratic vision for the European Court of Human Rights? Some aspects of the Court's jurisprudence – notably the importance attached to political expression – resonate with deliberative democratic ideals. Yet this might be developed even more –

---

[84] Claus Offe, 'The Union Entrapped: Does the EU Have the Political Capacity to Overcome Its Current Crisis?' in Claus Offe and Ulrich K. Preuß (eds) *Citizens in Europe: Essays on Democracy, Constitutionalism and European Integration* (ECPR Press 2016), 483.

[85] Dahl offers a varied list of emotions that may play a role in struggles for political equality, including altruism, compassion, empathy, envy, anger, indignation and hatred. Dahl, *On Political Equality*, 36.

[86] Young, *Inclusion and Democracy*, 18.

[87] Habermas, addressing the crisis in the European Union, speaks of the need for solidarity within and across national boundaries: Jürgen Habermas, *The Crisis of the European Union: A Response* (Polity 2012), 21; also Jürgen Habermas, *The Lure of Technocracy* (John Wiley & Sons 2015), 3–28.

the strong utopian ideals of equality and inclusion in deliberative democracy may suggest the possibility of positive obligations to secure more egalitarian frameworks in which all can participate to public debate; on the other hand, the emphasis on equality and reasoned debate may suggest that expressions lacking civility or disrespecting equality need to be devalued in the Court's jurisprudence (as arguably they are). Fredman has suggested that human rights adjudication can enhance the quality of political debate by insisting on more accountable decision-making.[88] As a specific manifestation of this, the Court may defer to decisions made not by a representative political process but by a political process which demonstrates a high level of deliberative quality.[89]

EQUALITY, DIFFERENCE AND INCLUSION: PARITY DEMOCRACY, GROUP REPRESENTATION, CONSOCIATIONALISM

This is not really a model of democracy, but rather a category for those critics of the representative democratic model who latch on to similar criticisms, namely that the representative, participatory and deliberative models of democracy we have discussed do not do justice to the level of division and disagreement that exists in modern societies, and in particular do not recognise the importance of differences among various groups. This may be because a representative democracy relies on a vision of citizens as formally free and equal but ignores real differences of identity among the heterogeneous population; or it may be because language of impartiality and the common good obscures or even delegitimises differences. Representative democracy often takes for granted restrictions based on age, nationality, residence, but these have the effect of limiting or excluding many individuals from the political process.

The types of group differences at issue here vary enormously, as do the prescriptions. The failure of many countries to ensure equal representation of women in political institutions has provoked calls for what the Council of Europe calls 'parity democracy'. The Venice Commission recognises the legitimacy of parity laws in electoral matters in cases where they have a constitutional basis.[90]

---

[88] Fredman, *Human Rights Transformed*, 103–105.
[89] What counts as high-quality deliberation is itself open to interpretation. Held cites Offe and Preuß's criteria of 'fact regarding', 'future regarding' and 'other regarding': Held, *Models of Democracy*, 232.
[90] European Commission for Democracy through Law (Venice Commission), *Code of Good Practice in Electoral Matters (Guidelines and Explanatory Report)* (Council of Europe 2002).

There may also be instances of special procedures or representation for other groups, especially national ethnic, religious or linguistic minorities. Depending on questions of geography and demographics, these may take the form of regional autonomy stopping short of secession or powersharing (consociational) governments.[91]

In many cases these proposals do not represent an alternative theory of democracy to a representative or deliberative model, but rather seek to offer important correctives to an accepted model. This may be the case even where the relevant advocate makes sweeping claims about the radical nature of a new approach.

These issues of group representation are likely to pose some of the sharpest questions for the European Court's idea of democracy. Already the Court has faced a series of cases dealing with consociationalism and even some on minority representation. One of the cases on consociationalism (dealing with the institutions set up post Dayton in Bosnia-Herzegovina) indicates the potentially high stakes involved in the Court entering the political thicket, with one dissenting judge warning that the majority's judgment might sow the seeds of future bloodshed.[92]

Implications for the Court are myriad – so much so that one imagines a ready recourse to the margin of appreciation doctrine on the part of the Court. Parity laws or special representation laws can easily be represented as discriminatory restrictions on the right to vote or run for election. The formal freedom and equality of citizens in a liberal representative democracy might seem to preclude such measures, but the support of the Council of Europe and other European organisations for parity democracy and measures to promote participation in public life would probably lead the Court to the safety of the margin of appreciation. If the Court were to actually require such measures, or indicate that the de facto existence of inequality in participation is a violation, then we would have an indication of a support for more egalitarian and inclusive versions of democracy.

THE CHALLENGES OF GOVERNANCE

It is tempting to have a final section on global governance models of democracy, or cosmopolitan democracy or supranational democracy. This, however,

---

[91] The Lund Recommendations on the Effective Participation of National Minorities in Public Life 1999.

[92] *Sejdic and Finci v Bosnia and Herzegovina* App nos 27996/06 and 34836/06 (2009) 22 BHRC 201 (Grand Chamber). See the dissent of Judge Bonello.

does not do justice to the range of challenges to democracy that stem from changing patterns of governance in the late twentieth and early twenty-first centuries. Many of the classic models of democracy discussed above make assumptions that the locus of democracy is a state (not true, of course, for participatory democracy) – that is, a territorially bound entity with a central political authority that is capable of enforcing its sovereign will internally and resisting external pressures. In such a model there is a congruence[93] between the population which is affected by political decisions and the population which (through representatives elected to central political authorities) makes those decisions. Perhaps there is even an assumption that the population is to a large extent homogenous and forms a nation state. These assumptions are all seriously misplaced in the twenty-first century.

That states are affected by myriad problems and challenges beyond their ability to control is a commonplace. These include questions of environmental change, population movements, terrorism, technological change and social media, economic crises and international investment, and pandemics. The worldwide recession in the wake of problems in the housing market and financial services in the US is one marked example, as is the argument of some politicians to lower tax on companies to encourage inward investment.

It is not just an issue that the population of a territorially bound entity is affected by what populations in other territorially bound entities do. Some parts of the population may identify with the population in another territory. This may well be because a practice of large-scale emigration creates a significant diaspora (Ireland, Italy, Greece), or conversely because immigration policies foster a large immigrant or *gastarbeiter* population (UK, Germany). Or it may be because the historic process of boundary drawing has not created perfectly homogenous nation states (Northern Ireland, Basque country). This may lead to transnational or transfrontier political movements. We see this, for instance, in Basque and Northern Irish/Irish politics, and the Court has already addressed cases stemming from this. There are also other ethnic or religious groups which do not respect national borders but who may have political aspirations. These groups include the Roma of Europe. These issues of transnational politics, though, are not just about political movements or parties; there are also institutional manifestations. The clearest example of this is Northern Ireland, where the 1998 Belfast or Good Friday Agreement resulted in the creation of North South Ministerial Council and a British Irish

---

[93] Held, *Models of Democracy*, 290.

The Challenges of Governance

Council involving representatives from all the parliaments in the UK and Ireland.

We also see a shift from a focus on the central political institutions to more local ones. In Italy, Spain and the UK regional bodies and assemblies are granted executive and legislative powers. Such localism raises questions of the applicability of P1–3 rights, as well as about the unequal application of rights within a single state.

Most importantly – especially in light of the possible accession of the European Union to the European Court of Human Rights – there is the increasing power of international and supranational organisations. What is the significance of classic civil and political rights binding the state when so much power is exercised by supranational bodies? More challengingly perhaps, what effect will the classic civil and political rights have on a supranational organisation like the EU? Do the P1–3 rights apply to the European Parliament in the same way as to national legislatures? Do the P1–3 rights have any impact on the European Council and Commission which share legislative power with the Parliament? Do the weighted majority rules and rules on number of seats for states raise equality concerns? Will the EU have positive obligations in respect of civil and political rights?

These are also challenges for the models of representative, participatory, deliberative and inclusive democracy discussed above. How can representative democracy respond to changes in the locus and scope of political power? Can it deal with the transfer of power to international, transnational and supranational organisations or indeed the shift of political power away from formal political institutions and to actors in the economic sphere and civil society? How do we approach questions of representation in a supranational bicameral legislature such as the European Union, where even the basic representative principle of 'one person one vote of equal value' has to be modified? How does a representative model of democracy accustomed to dealing with matters in a single nation state cope with political parties or movements that organise on a transnational or multinational basis?

The continental scale as well as multilingual and multicultural nature of a supranational organisation also pose difficulties for different substantive (communitarian or republican), deliberative and participatory models of democracy. The scale of politics in a supranational system may pose difficulties for the search for common values on a continental scale, rational deliberation or any form of face-to-face participation.

Even more complex is the shift of power away from central formal political institutions to a range of non-state actors in the economic and civil society spheres. To some extent, the importance of economic and civil society (especially labour representatives) actors has frequently been recognised in various corporatist and 'social partner' programmes. Yet there is the possibility of more powers and responsibilities formally exercised by central political bodies being delegated to economic and civil society actors. These include indeed transnational economic and civil society actors. This 'hollowing out of the state' also implies changes in the borders between the formal political institutions and these non-state actors. Specifically, there may emerge public servants who are now new public managers, lobbyists and political advisors who muddy the boundary between political and state actors on the one hand and economic actors on the other. No doubt there are also some public bodies which ally themselves more naturally with civil society (e.g. independent state-created and -funded human rights and equality organisations). The implications raised by this aspect of governance are a pressing topic for the twenty-first century. If fundamental economic decisions over (e.g.) interest rates can be delegated away to independent central banks, and public services are privatised or handed over to an unfunded Big Society, then what value is left to the political rights in P1–3? Or, paradoxically, does P1–3 require that democratic accountability somehow be maintained, and if so, in what manner?

Several of these challenges have also, arguably, played a role in fostering different political trends variously described as illiberal democracy, populist[94] or autocratic legalist.[95] Certain political movements take issue in particular with the development of global, international or supranational political and economic institutions and reassert more traditional notions of national or popular sovereignty. This is seen in euro-scepticism in the UK which has given us the Brexit referendum as well as regular challenges to the role of the European Court of Human Rights. In other contexts, populist movements are even more clear about the ethnic nature of the identity they are concerned with protecting and much more direct in dismantling mechanisms of legal and political accountability (Hungary, Poland, Turkey).[96] The distinctive feature of populists in government is that they seek to colonise the state, support clientelism or corruption and repress civil society.[97]

---

[94] Müller argues that 'illiberal democracy' concedes too much to populist rulers who have no problem being described as illiberal as long as they can claim to be democrats. Jan-Werner Müller, *What Is Populism?* (Penguin 2017), 56.

[95] Kim Lane Scheppele, 'Autocratic Legalism' (2018) 85 University of Chicago Law Review 545.

[96] Bojan Bugarič, 'A Crisis of Constitutional Democracy in Post-Communist Europe: "Lands in-between" Democracy and Authoritarianism' (2015) 13 (1) International Journal of Constitutional Law 219.

[97] Müller, *What Is Populism?*, chapter two.

This is also in the new context that technology has created new means of political mobilisation through social media. This enables new alliances to be forged and provides low-cost platforms for groups to participate in politics. It is also, however, subject to manipulation by wealthy interests and even foreign governments.

CONCLUSION: TOWARDS DELIBERATIVE, INCLUSIVE AND PARTICIPATORY DEMOCRACY

This book will examine the political rights jurisprudence of the European Court. It seeks to show which models of democracy are supported or permitted or indeed ruled out by the European Court. With respect to those visions of democracy supported by the Court's jurisprudence, the work will be to consider whether the Court shows awareness of the flaws in the conception (even if it does not use the philosophical terms).

It should not be surprising that the Convention and jurisprudence support a liberal representative democratic structure. In the aftermath of the Second World War, and faced with socialist democracies to the East, this was the default choice. Yet it is important to understand that there are different variants even of liberal representative democracy. One can see the classic image but also more realistic images of representative democracy. Some of these more realistic images shade into rather elitist versions which may charitably be described as competitive elitist or can attract more negative sobriquets. Other realistic images stress the role of interest groups and different centres of power and hold out the possibility that political power can be controlled and held accountable though the interplay of these different groups. That the Court seems to reach decisions compatible with a substantive model of democracy, if unsurprising, is also not to be assumed.

These variants of liberal representative democracy are subject to many challenges, even when given a substantive dimension. Even writers associated with the pluralist variant of representative democracy increasingly worry about the effects of inequality on the democratic system. Deliberative democrats query the deliberative quality of discussion in such representative democracies, while egalitarian or inclusive democrats point to the dangers of exclusion or marginalisation of women and minority communities. Participatory democrats lament the formalism and lack of opportunity for people to actually take part in decision-making. Many or most of these critics worry about the tendencies to oligopoly and elitism in representative democracy. Other democratic theorists worry about whether any of these models of democracy can tackle changes in systems of governance and the challenge of long-term problems.

The deliberative, participatory and egalitarian critics of liberal representative democracy identify important criticisms. However, they also, despite tensions between them,[98] are potentially mutually supportive of a democratic vision that is closely suited to the ideals of human rights law. Human rights require that decisions about rights should be decided according to certain standards of rationality and not merely through a political log rolling or preference counting. That is to say, they require deliberation which takes seriously the interests of all. Furthermore, as noted in many UN human rights texts and human rights scholarly texts, public decision-making that respects rights must involve active participation by those affected. Finally, the realisation of inclusion and equality is essential both as a precondition for deliberation and to avoid the dangers of participation collapsing into tyranny.

Therefore, in what follows we will examine the jurisprudence to see if the Court shows an awareness of these flaws and what is the Court's response. In some cases, we can see that the Court has permitted or even required measures that ameliorate some of the flaws in representative democracy. We will consider whether there are other ways of addressing these flaws and whether indeed there is scope to promote not merely a reformed representative democracy but more deliberative, participatory and inclusive models of democracy. To do this we first need to understand how the Council of Europe envisioned the role of the European Convention on Human Rights; this is the subject of the next chapter.

---

[98] Fishkin notes there is an apparent trilemma in promoting political equality, inclusion and deliberation; it may not be possible to promote all three: Fishkin, *Democracy When the People Are Thinking*, 7.

2

Council, Convention and Court

Origins and Evolution

This chapter introduces the work of the Council of Europe and its most significant achievement, the European Convention on Human Rights. The chapter sets the context for the emergence of the Council of Europe in the aftermath of the Second World War; it then discusses the drafting of the European Convention on Human Rights. The original structure and subsequent evolution of the Convention institutions are outlined along with the modern competences of the European Court of Human Rights. The chapter concludes by situating the work of the Court in the wider context of the work of other Council of Europe, international and regional organisations.

The Council itself emerged in 1949 at a fraught time in European history. The Second World War had ended in 1945 and left much of the continent in ruins. European countries had been overrun, bombed and subjugated. Tens of millions had been killed; tens of millions more were displaced. Human rights violations had been committed on an unimaginable scale. The period after the Second World War also witnessed important demographic, social and political changes. Politically, the period saw the emergence of the Soviet Union as a major power in opposition to the US, and the consolidation of Soviet control of Eastern Europe.

This was also a time for important legal developments in international law, most notably the formation of the United Nations and the emergence of international human rights law. These events at the world level are the prelude to the formation of the Council of Europe and the Council's own distinctive contribution to human rights law.

THE UNITED NATIONS AND THE UNIVERSAL DECLARATION OF HUMAN RIGHTS

The end of the Second World War saw the impetus for the creation of international and regional organisations. At the world level, the United

34   *Council, Convention and Court*

Nations was the most significant, and in particular significant for the development of human rights law.

The 1945 Charter refers to human rights at several points, though there is a priority given to the maintenance of peace and security. There is also an important recognition of the principle of 'domestic jurisdiction', i.e. some matters remain within the national competences.[1] Its preamble declares the faith of the peoples of the United Nations in 'fundamental human rights, in the dignity and worth of the human person'. Article 1 declares as one of the purposes of the UN to promote and encourage 'respect for human rights and fundamental freedoms for all without distinction as to race, sex, language, or religion'. The United Nations will promote 'universal respect for, and observance of, human rights and fundamental freedoms for all without distinction as to race, sex, language, or religion'.[2] The General Assembly has competence to commission studies and make recommendations in the field of human rights.[3] The Economic and Social Council has a similar competence to make recommendations in this field[4] and to establish relevant commissions.[5] The trusteeship system shall also encourage respect for human rights.[6] These references do not define the terms 'human rights and fundamental freedoms'.

To better define these terms, the United Nations drafted the Universal Declaration of Human Rights (UDHR) and adopted it by a unanimous vote of the General Assembly on 10 December 1948.[7]

The UDHR is important as the foundational document of modern international human rights law.[8] There is much debate about when and where human rights emerge, and it is possible to trace its antecedents among ancient legal texts, religious and philosophical traditions, as well as to specific historical events like the US Declaration of Independence, the French Declaration of the Rights of Man and the Citizen 1789, and so on.[9] One can find arguments for international law precedents in the laws of war, the prohibition

---

[1] Article 2(7) United Nations Charter, San Francisco, 26 June 1945, in force 24 October 1945.
[2] Article 55.
[3] Article 13(1).
[4] Article 62(2).
[5] Article 68.
[6] Article 76(c).
[7] Universal Declaration of Human Rights 1948, A/RES/217 A (III), UN Doc A/810 at 71.
[8] For a history of the drafting, see Johannes Morsink, *The Universal Declaration of Human Rights: Origins, Drafting and Intent* (University of Pennsylvania Press 2000). The UDHR was not the first such postwar declaration: the Organisation of American States adopted the American Declaration of the Rights and Duties of Man on 2 May 1948.
[9] Paul Gordon Lauren, *The Evolution of International Human Rights: Visions Seen* (3rd edn, University of Pennsylvania Press 2011).

on the slave trade, and later the work of the International Labour Organisation and the interwar minority rights treaty system. However, it is with the United Nations and in particular the UDHR that we have definitive assertion of human rights as an aspect of international law at the world level. This is an important and striking departure from the position of classic international law which treated states as the only recognised legal subject.

The UDHR was impressive also for the range of the rights it included. The UDHR drew some inspiration from the model of the 1789 Declaration,[10] but was also influenced by other traditions including the socialist states and the Latin American countries. This is particularly evident in the inclusion of strong non-discrimination rights and social and economic rights.

Despite these important achievements of the UDHR, its deficits should not be ignored.[11] Most notably, it is a declaration and not a treaty. This means that its legal status is rather weak; as initially conceived, it is only a hortatory statement of rights and does not impose legally binding obligations even as a matter of international law.[12] Consequently, the UDHR provides no international mechanism to enforce the rights contained therein. Proposals to allow the Commission on Human Rights to hear petitions alleging breaches of human rights in national contexts were quickly denuded of value, while work on binding international treaties to give binding legal effect to the rights in the UDHR would not come to fruition at the international level until 1966.[13]

It is perhaps understandable that it should take so long to achieve agreement at the world level on legally binding human rights norms, especially if these were to be accompanied by actual remedies. Such innovations would be a major advance on a world legal system which had just recognised the principle of human rights. In that context, more might be done in the context of regional organisations. The UN Charter indeed envisaged the formation of regional arrangements for dealing with matters such as international peace

---

[10] Stephen Marks, 'From the "Single Confused Page" to the "Decalogue for Six Billion Persons": The Roots of the Universal Declaration in the French Revolution' (1998) 20 Human Rights Quarterly 459.

[11] An early advocate of an international bill of rights was scathing of flaws in the Declaration: Hersch Lauterpacht, 'The Universal Declaration of Human Rights' (1948) 25 British Yearbook of International Law 354.

[12] There are arguments that the Declaration has some indirect but binding force, either because it provides a definition of the rights in the legally binding Charter or because it contributes to international customary law.

[13] Roger Normand and Sarah Zaidi, *Human Rights at the UN: the Political History of Universal Justice* (Indiana University Press 2008).

36   *Council, Convention and Court*

and security.[14] A smaller number of states in a geographical area and presumably sharing some history, culture and values in common would be more likely to agree on legally binding obligations and perhaps even provide for collective international enforcement of human rights.[15]

EUROPEAN REGIONAL DEVELOPMENTS: INTEGRATION MOVEMENTS

In one sense, the Nazi war effort had been geared towards unifying Europe under Nazi rule and were thus a form of European integration. The postwar period saw Europeans respond with efforts to create very different forms of European integration. There were several movements for greater European cooperation, integration, even union, and specifically for organisations to promote human rights and democracy.[16] Among the numerous supporters of such integration were Winston Churchill, who called for European integration and greater protection for human rights,[17] and the US government which urged European states to form plans for a federation and even threatened to withhold Marshall Plan payments if no progress was made.[18] There were European integration movements on mainland Europe, particularly among the Benelux countries and the French leadership. Greater European integration was considered essential for several reasons.

First, for many it was necessary in order to prevent the outbreak of war, and more specifically it was necessary to restrain Germany. Three times in the period 1870–1940, the two most powerful nations on the Western European mainland had gone to war following German aggression against France and others; improving Franco–German relations would be a key priority for maintaining peace in Europe.

Second, it was also essential in order to prevent the massive human rights violations that states had perpetrated during the previous decade. The European leaders were aware that the national institutions in Europe had many

---

[14] UN Charter, article 52.

[15] Simpson's invaluable work includes a quote from a British official which makes this point: 'It should nevertheless be possible to produce a reasonably homogenous text and since France, Belgium and Holland are all colonial powers we should be able to see eye to eye on such vexed questions as individual petition and the like.' AW Brian Simpson, *Human Rights and the End of Empire: Britain and the Genesis of the European Convention* (Oxford University Press 2001), 614.

[16] Mark Mazower, *Dark Continent: Europe's Twentieth Century* (Allen Lane 1998), 202.

[17] AW Brian Simpson, *Human Rights and the End of Empire: Britain and the Genesis of the European Convention*, 605.

[18] Ibid., 618, 622, 626.

European Regional Developments: Integration Movements 37

deficiencies during the interwar period and the Second World War. The fascist states had systematically, ruthlessly violated human rights across the continent. Mass executions, slave camps, torture and censorship were some of the depredations of the times. One human rights violation – the systematic extermination of a group of people – did not even have a name until the term 'genocide' was coined by Raphael Lemkin.

It was not just the fascist states and their allies that had violated human rights. The Soviet Union had its own show trials and labour camps, while the Soviet army's advance across Eastern Europe was accompanied by war crimes including rape.[19] Western Europeans were not immune either. The governors of the occupied states themselves had collaborated with the Nazi machinery of oppression.[20]

Third, the Second World War also suggested that there were considerable problems with an international system overly focused on the claims of the nation state, and the unfettered exercise of state sovereignty.[21] International law in the 1930s could not address wrongs such as *Kristallnacht* or the Nuremberg laws: what a state did to its own population on its own territory was not a matter of international law.

Fourth, it was not only the nation states that were at fault. States had established a League of Nations after 'the war to end all wars'. The League of Nations proved to be impotent in the face of fascism; from Abyssinia to Sudetenland, the League was toothless. The minority rights treaty regime established after the First World War similarly had proven inefficacious; not only had it not stopped the descent into world war, but many observers found fault with the notion of group rights that it presupposed. In particular, the Nazi government of Germany had used minority rights as a cloak for its expansionist policies. These negative views on minority rights would cast a long shadow on European institutional developments.[22]

Fifth, even when the war was over, the effects of it were not. In particular, the rule of law was in jeopardy in the aftermath of the conflict. Across the continent, the entire system of respect for law was in peril not only under occupation but even afterwards as reprisals took the place of justice and property rights were ignored.[23]

---

[19] Mazower, *Dark Continent*, 220.
[20] Simpson, *Human Rights and the End of Empire*, 601.
[21] Ibid., 602.
[22] Mazower, *Dark Continent*, 202. It was not just at the European level. The UN General Assembly postponed any discussion of minority rights during the debate on the Universal Declaration, commenting that they raised complex issues.
[23] Ibid., 222.

38   *Council, Convention and Court*

Sixth, totalitarianism had not been banished from Europe. Fascist regimes remained in Spain and Portugal, while the Soviet Union was securing its hold on Eastern Europe. On 25 February 1948, the Communist Party of Czechoslovakia staged a coup with Soviet backing.

These motivations led to numerous plans for integration of one sort or another. The North Atlantic Treaty Organisation (NATO) treaty of 4 April 1949 and the Brussels Treaty union were adopted primarily for security purposes (the latter would become the Western European Union after 1954). Other plans addressed the need for economic cooperation, such as the Organisation for European Economic Cooperation which later became the Organisation for Economic Co-operation and Development (OECD) in 1960. Yet there were also movements for greater political integration even union. One such project would result in the Council of Europe.

A QUESTION OF DEMOCRACY?

These movements for integration, however, must also be set in the context of debates on the meaning of democracy. The experience of the previous decades raised questions about the nature of democracy.

This was hardly new. While modern Europeans may well take for granted the existence of liberal democratic regimes based on a parliamentary system of government, this had by no means been the default assumption of Europeans through the first half of the twentieth century. In many ways liberal democracy is a very young and possibly fleeting system of government; while the groundwork of liberal democratic regimes may have been laid in previous decades, even centuries, many regimes only became fully democratic after the end of the Second World War. France only enfranchised women in 1944; the UK abolished plural voting systems in 1945; the US faced up to the de facto exclusion of African Americans only in the 1960s.[24] And these successes for liberal democracy were by no means preordained.[25]

Liberal democracy was one of three major ideologies in Europe in the first half of the twentieth century, alongside fascism and communism. There were numerous critiques of liberal democracy, including most especially the

---

[24] On the late arrival of reasonably inclusive democratic systems, see Chris Thornhill, *The Sociology of Law and the Global Transformation of Democracy* (Cambridge University Press 2018), 154–156.

[25] 'Liberal democracy usually emerges only at the end of long, often violent, struggle, with many twists, turns, false alarms and detours'; Sheri Berman, *Democracy and Dictatorship in Europe: From the Ancien Régime to the Present Day* (Oxford University Press 2019), 406.

system of parliamentary government. Carl Schmitt most famously lambasted parliamentary government as inadequate.[26]

During the interwar period, both fascism and communism might have seemed more likely to survive in any struggle for survival when liberal principles and parliamentary discourse might hinder any war effort. For these reasons, numerous commentators spoke of the demise of liberal democracy and even expressed some admiration for fascist achievements or ideas;[27] fascism could reasonably have been presented as the 'wave of the future'.[28] In the event, the Second World War witnessed the defeat of fascism and the restoration, in Western Europe at least, of liberal democratic regimes.

Nevertheless, it was not simply a matter of turning the clock back to the interwar democratic experience. The end of the First World War saw a rapid expansion of democratic regimes across Europe, but only five functioned continuously through the period to 1945.[29] Many of the democracies in Europe had been overrun and their occupation governments proved supine. Hobsbawm identifies four weaknesses of the interwar democracies: many of them had not accumulated sufficient legitimacy; they included states with heterogeneous populations; the machinery of the classic night-watchman state was inadequate to the challenges of governing in the face of crisis; and the economic crisis overcame many of the democratic states.[30] For many, including De Gaulle,[31] Schmitt had been right to criticise the parliamentary model of democracy for being an endless talking shop that could not defend itself.

Perhaps the most serious accusation levelled at liberal democracies was that they gave too much opportunity to the enemies of democracy to undermine the democratic system. The menace was not just that a democratic regime would be weak in the face of invasion, but that a democratic (or at least formally democratic) regime might be undermined from within. Fascist movements might appeal to the masses[32] and avail of liberal freedoms like free expression and association to destroy democracy. This at least was one interpretation of how the Nazi regime came to power through constitutional

---

[26] Carl Schmitt, *The Crisis of Parliamentary Democracy* (MIT Press 1988, [1923]).
[27] Ambassador Joe Kennedy is one example of the former: Mazower, *Dark Continent*, 187. The novelist John Buchan described fascism as a 'bold experiment': Eric Hobsbawm, *Age of Extremes: The Short Twentieth Century, 1914–1991* (Michael Joseph 1994), 123.
[28] Hobsbawm, *Age of Extremes*, 112.
[29] Ibid., 111. These were the UK, Finland, Ireland, Sweden and Switzerland.
[30] Ibid., 111, 138–141.
[31] Mazower, *Dark Continent: Europe's Twentieth Century*, 187.
[32] Hobsbawm, *Age of Extremes*, 111, 117. This association of mass appeal with totalitarianism is not new: Aristotle and Plato had been sceptical of the merits of rule by the many.

forms[33] and precipitated the development of 'militant democracy' reforms. The lessons to be learned from the perceived weakness of interwar democracy still reverberate in twenty-first-century European jurisprudence.

The lessons of the interwar period were not just limited to this question of militant democracy. There were also important social[34] and economic dimensions.[35] The war had produced a levelling and equalising experience for many, had demonstrated the possibilities of the interventionist state and underlined the need to attend to social and economic rights. At the end of the First World War, the British prime minister had proclaimed a need to create a 'home fit for heroes'. The failure to address social and economic issues across Europe during the interwar period laid the seeds for the Second World War. The desire to address social needs produced many responses, from the various forms of the welfare state[36] to the rise of Christian Democratic parties in Europe[37] and, not least, the political enfranchisement of women.[38]

The postwar commitment to human rights and democracy may look less than thoroughgoing to modern eyes. The postwar context included massive and frequently involuntary population movements. In particular, in the aftermath of the war, German populations were frequently compelled to flee; these numbered perhaps 12–13 million people during 1944–1947.[39] While the example of the German population is the largest, other minorities were also expelled. In a sense, these population movements completed a process begun by the Nazi regime: states were increasingly 'nation' states having a major national population (there were exceptions, Yugoslavia being the most obvious).

Furthermore, the onset of the Cold War led to the adoption of numerous practices that offend sensibilities about human rights and democracy. In Eastern Europe, the last five years of Stalin's rule produced 'stalinism' in the form of 'show trials, police terror and forced industrialization'.[40] The violations of rights in the Soviet Union and Eastern Europe are unsurprising, but also in Western Europe, we have disturbing practices. The looming Cold War

---

[33] Both the Italian and German fascists came to power through the formal constitutional process: Hobsbawm, *Age of Extremes*, 127.
[34] Mazower, *Dark Continent*, 188–192.
[35] Hobsbawm, *Age of Extremes*, 140.
[36] Mazower, *Dark Continent*, 302.
[37] Ibid., 196.
[38] Ibid., 291. France recognised female suffrage with the 1946 Constitution of the Fourth Republic.
[39] Ibid., 217–221.
[40] Ibid., 267.

led to political intolerance and suppression of communists. There were initiatives against the Communist parties in Western Europe; in Greece, communist insurgents were bombed; across Europe, intelligence agencies established secret guerrilla groups to conduct warfare in the event of a communist takeover.[41] Many states adopted vetting practices and loyalty requirements.[42]

Finally, several of the victorious allied powers retained large empires in which political and other rights were regularly denied. Concern about the impact of emerging international human rights law on policies in the colonies frequently animated the public servants of the colonial powers. The newly liberated states of Western Europe had no qualms about crushing independence movements in their colonies.[43]

THE COUNCIL OF EUROPE

The Council of Europe thus emerged as a consequence of movements for European integration. The Council of Europe grew out of a series of compromises; some political leaders, notably in France, were in favour of integration even a 'European Union' while leaders in other European countries, notably the UK, favoured something looser, more of a talking shop than an actual union. The Council of Europe owes much to this compromise. Being a much weaker institution than pro-integrationists desired (Mazower describes it as a 'bureaucratic drone'[44]), it inspired the French to pursue other plans for economic and political integration without the British.[45] These other plans would later lead to the European Coal and Steel Community and gradually to the European Union of today.

The Council of Europe, however, was established to discuss matters of common concern, except for defence. The Council was established by the Statute of the Council of Europe 1949, sometimes called the Treaty of London.[46] This was opened for signature on 5 May 1949 and ratified by ten original founding members: Belgium, Denmark, France, Ireland, Italy, Luxembourg, Netherlands, Norway, Sweden and the UK.

---

[41] Daniele Ganser, NATO's Secret Armies: Operation Gladio and Terrorism in Western Europe (Frank Cass 2005).
[42] Mazower, Dark Continent, 293.
[43] The French killed some 40,000 people in Algeria in the aftermath of a 1945 rebellion; up to 100,000 were killed during a rebellion in the French colony of Madagascar in 1947: Mazower, Dark Continent, 213.
[44] Ibid., 213.
[45] Simpson, Human Rights and the End of Empire, 646.
[46] Statute of the Council of Europe, London, 5 May 1949, in force 3 August 1949, ETS 1.

In its Preamble, the Statute identifies the common heritage of the European countries participating: 'the spiritual and moral values which are the common heritage of their peoples and the true source of individual freedom, political liberty and the rule of law, principles which form the basis for all genuine democracy'. There is a close link here between democracy, the rule of law and freedom, though the term 'human rights' is not found in the Preamble. It is proclaimed prominently enough in article1(b), though, where it is indicated the Council will work for the 'maintenance and further realisation of human rights and fundamental freedoms'. By virtue of articles 3 and 4, European states may join the Council if they are committed to the rule of law, human rights and fundamental freedoms. Article 8 provides that the Council, through a two-thirds vote of the Committee of Ministers, may invite a state to withdraw from the Council, or may expel a state where it has seriously violated the principles of the rule of law, human rights and fundamental freedoms. This extreme sanction has rarely been seriously considered, though in 1969 the Greek Colonels' regime withdrew from the Council rather than face expulsion. For some states, the threat of expulsion may be effective by itself in securing compliance.[47]

The primary institutions of the Council of Europe are the Committee of Ministers, the Consultative Assembly (styed the Parliamentary Assembly since 1994) aided by the secretariat. These institutions are established by the Statute of the Council of Europe and again reflect a compromise – the French had favoured an elected assembly with some form of democratic legitimacy whereas British leaders preferred an intergovernmental meeting of ministers. The compromise was to adopt both, but with an attenuated Assembly.[48] The Council is based in Strasbourg, symbolically chosen for its Franco–German history.[49]

The Committee of Ministers consists of one minister from each state party, normally the foreign affairs minister.[50] The Committee has a remit to consider how the aims of the Council should be forwarded and may, for example, consider the drafting of conventions or issue recommendations to the states.[51] It decides upon the organisation of the Council, can establish advisory com-

---

[47] Oona Hathaway and Scott Shapiro, *The Internationalists: And Their Plan to Outlaw War* (Penguin UK 2017), 385.
[48] Simpson, *Human Rights and the End of Empire*, 630, 634–635.
[49] Ibid., 633.
[50] Statute of the Council of Europe 1949, article 14.
[51] Ibid., article 15.

mittees and determines its own internal procedure.[52] The Committee meets in private normally[53] and reports annually to the Assembly.[54]

The Assembly is described as the 'deliberative organ' of the Council: it debates matters of concern and can make recommendations to the Committee;[55] it can also establish its own committees.[56] The Assembly consists of representatives of the national parliaments chosen by either parliamentary election or appointment.[57] The number of representatives from each state is based on the state's population.[58] As Simpson describes it, this Assembly was a considerably weaker institution than that desired by European integrationists. Although intended to be deliberative and representative of parliaments, it was not directly elected, and stunningly there was a plan to exclude communists – then well represented in Italy and France – from the Assembly.[59]

The Council is not and certainly was not intended to be any sort of proto-federal or supranational body. Rather, the Council acts through fairly conventional international law mechanisms; thus, for example, its most significant task is the drafting of treaties which states are then free to adhere to. And among the very first of these treaties is the European Convention on Human Rights.

DRAFTING THE EUROPEAN CONVENTION ON HUMAN RIGHTS

The idea of a European treaty on human rights was frequently suggested in the period prior to the formation of the Council of Europe, and as we saw, the maintenance and realisation of human rights were specified in the aims of article 1 of the Statute of the Council of Europe.

The processes of drafting the Convention was somewhat involved, even if accomplished in a relatively short space of time. There were numerous parties involved. Among the earliest was a non-governmental organisation outside of the Council of Europe, the European Movement.[60] This organisation included a large number of UK representatives, including Sir David

---

[52] Ibid., articles 16–18.
[53] Ibid., article 21.
[54] Ibid., article 19.
[55] Ibid., articles 22, 23.
[56] Ibid., article 24.
[57] Ibid., article 25.
[58] Ibid., article 26.
[59] Simpson, *Human Rights and the End of Empire*, 635–636; Simpson speculates that the UK government might have been keen to exclude Churchill as well.
[60] Ibid., 649.

Maxwell-Fyfe, but also, importantly, Pierre-Henri Teitgen,[61] a French member of the Resistance and Minister of Justice in France. The European Movement drafted a number of policy documents and a draft convention.[62] Under Teitgen's leadership, a draft convention was submitted to the Council of Europe.[63] The drafts of the European Movement are included in the *travaux préparatoires* of the Convention, in light of their role in influencing the Consultative Assembly.

The Consultative Assembly (of which Maxwell-Fyfe and Teitgen were members) met on 10 August 1949 and set about trying to exert itself.[64] Among other matters, it decided to take up the issue of human rights. The Consultative Assembly considered the need for a convention and referred the matter to its Committee on Legal and Administrative Questions.[65] This resulted in a draft which the Assembly further considered before sending it to the Committee of Ministers on 5 November 1949.[66] The Committee of Ministers appointed a committee of experts to examine the draft.[67] The experts produced alternative drafts of articles on rights, a draft A with rights declared but not defined and a draft B with rights defined.[68] When it returned to the Committee of Ministers at the end of March 1949, the Committee appointed a conference of government officials to further examine the draft.[69] This conference produced a draft largely based on the B draft[70] which the conference submitted to the Committee, which referred it to a further subcommittee of experts.[71] The Committee approved a text on 7 August 1950; this draft was considered by the Assembly's Committee on Legal and Administrative Questions. The Assembly Committee was critical of the Committee of Ministers' text; the Assembly itself approved its own Committee's report and drafted a preamble for the Convention.[72] The Committee of Ministers eventually agreed on the final text based on the 7 August text but including the Assembly's preamble.[73]

---

[61] Ibid., 657. In 1976, Teitgen became a judge of the European Court of Human rights.
[62] Ibid., 652, 657.
[63] Ibid., 659–662.
[64] Ibid., 668.
[65] Ibid., 674.
[66] Ibid., 682.
[67] Ibid., 686, 690.
[68] Ibid., 696.
[69] Ibid., 703.
[70] Ibid., 712.
[71] Ibid., 731–735.
[72] Ibid., 738–739.
[73] Ibid., 752.

The aim of the Convention was to guarantee the basic rights essential for a democratic system; in this regard, it was looking to the past but also to developments in Eastern Europe. The *travaux* show a palpable fear about developments in Eastern Europe; Teitgen referred to an 'aggression ... being prepared against this unfortunate Europe of ours and all that it represents in the way of history, tradition and civilisation; an aggression that might sweep away for ever – or at least for decades – all that really makes life worth living'.[74] Thus, the Convention would serve to safeguard political liberty and to act as a warning system whenever any state was slipping into totalitarianism.[75]

The process of negotiating the Convention revealed several tensions and points of controversy. The key ones were: whether the Convention should declare rights in a very abstract or detailed way; whether the enforcement of the Convention would be mainly political (entrusted to the Committee and a Commission) or judicial (with a Court and petition);[76] how to deal with colonies; and finally, there were controversies over which rights to include. Overshadowing much of the discussion were larger political questions; these included colonial questions but even more so the political situation in Europe with the onset of the Cold War.

The debate over whether the rights should be abstract or detailed was also related to the perceived role of a court and whether its case law should play a dominant role in giving meaning to the rights. The end product adopts something of a mixed approach but tending more towards giving detail. Thus, several articles of the Convention have their own limitation clause, while some rights (notably article 5 on personal liberty) are quite detailed.

The debate over whether the enforcement of the Convention should be political or judicial saw a split between those who argued that political mechanisms of protecting rights had proved valueless during the European catastrophe and those who argued that in certain contexts (i.e. the Cold War) it was desirable for the final say on a violation to be a political one. The result was a series of compromises. Political mechanisms were included: there was a Commission which would consider petitions, try to find a friendly settlement and investigate. In some cases, the Commission report would go to the Committee of Ministers for further action. However, there would also be a Court and individual petition, albeit with numerous safeguards: the Commission would act as a filtering mechanism; only the Commission or states could

---

[74] Council of Europe, *Collected Edition of the Travaux Preparatoires, Volume 7* (Martinus Nijhoff 1985), 92–96.
[75] Simpson, *Human Rights and the End of Empire*, 681.
[76] Ibid., 678.

refer a case to the Court; the Court's jurisdiction would be optional; the individual petition would be optional; and the enforcement of the judgment would be left to the Committee of Ministers.

On the colonial question, there were contradictory positions over the need for a colonial clause and whether it should deal with extending the Convention to the colonies, or provide for a degree of deference for local contexts. The UK position was that it would be perceived as hypocritical if European states openly applied different standards in colonies than what they applied in Europe.

CONVENTION RIGHTS: INCLUSION AND DEFINITION

There was also disagreement about which rights to include and how to define the ones included. The Convention text includes far fewer rights than are found in the UDHR. It does not include minority rights (though neither does the UDHR[77]) and does not include most social and economic rights.

The intention was to include the most basic rights and in particular the rights which could be made legally enforceable because they were sufficiently defined.

From the early European Movement drafts to the final text of the Convention, certain classic civil and political rights were included. These included freedom of expression, freedom of association and assembly and non-discrimination rights. These rights underwent amendment in the course of the drafting process; in particular, the articles on expression, association and assembly became more detailed and accompanied with an exceptions clause. The non-discrimination clause in the final Convention text was somewhat narrower than early European Movement drafts which had envisaged a free-standing right to equality before the law[78] rather than the accessory non-discrimination principle in article 14 ECHR.

A small number of rights proved to be extremely controversial because there were arguments to include them, but other states were very nervous about their inclusion. These were property rights, education rights and rights relating to democratic institutions. Given the difficulties in reaching agreement on the content of these rights, it was necessary to address these rights in a separate protocol to the Convention.

---

[77] The International Covenant on Civil and Political Rights 1966 would later include a minority rights provision in article 27.

[78] Simpson, *Human Rights and the End of Empire*, 654, 660.

Convention Rights: Inclusion and Definition 47

For various reasons the drafting of these rights proved controversial. The right to property was unsurprisingly controversial[79] and in particular there were disagreements over any requirement of compensation. States disagreed on several matters concerning the right to education: whether it should be a positive or negative right; the role of private (primarily religious) schools; the role of parents; and the feasibility of providing education in colonial territories.

The drafting of the provision on democratic institutions was also controversial, though resolved somewhat more easily than the first. Still, in view of the entire purpose of the Convention, indeed of the Council system, to defend a Western European system of democracy, it is at least ironic that states found it difficult to agree on the content of this right and even more so that states thought it appropriate to distinguish between electoral and other rights. The point was made repeatedly in the Assembly that human rights, the rule of law and political democracy were interlinked and that it was meaningless to have human rights without democracy; such indeed was the practice of totalitarian Peoples' Democracies.[80]

Early on in the process, it was decided to write the article on elections somewhat differently from the other rights. According to a report by the Secretariat General for the Committee of Experts, this was because the section on elections concerned the 'direct functions of Government action' and so required a 'more solemn and more unequivocal commitment', but otherwise there was to be no difference between the individual rights and the political rights.[81]

Despite this assertion that these was no such difference in principle, several states, notably the UK, identified serious concerns about the article on democratic elections.

UK representatives argued that the very concept of democracy was variable and that no agreement was possible on what it meant,[82] and connected with this that this was too political for inclusion in a treaty on human rights.[83] There was a concern about the principle of 'universal suffrage'. even though

---

[79] The drafting of the right to property had also been the subject of major disagreement during the drafting of the UDHR; when the International Covenant on Economic Social and Cultural Rights and the International Covenant on Civil and Political rights were adopted in 1966, the right to property was included in neither.

[80] Teitgen, Council of Europe, *Collected Edition of the Travaux Preparatoires, Volume 5* (Martinus Nijhoff 1979), 286–294.

[81] Council of Europe, *Collected Edition of the Travaux Preparatoires, Volume 3* (Martinus Nijhoff 1976), 16.

[82] Ibid., 182 (Committee of Experts, views of the UK).

[83] Council of Europe, *Collected Edition of the Travaux Preparatoires, Volume 4* (Martinus Nijhoff 1977), 22–24.

48   *Council, Convention and Court*

this appears in article 21 of the Universal Declaration of Human Rights. The UK member of the Committee of Experts argued that suffrage was never truly universal; there were qualifications and exceptions.[84] The term 'universal suffrage' does not appear in the final text of the article. Early drafts of the article referred to the ideas that 'governmental action and legislation may accord with the expressed will of the people'[85] or that the government and legislature 'represent the people'.[86] While not expressly discussed in the published records, Simpson makes the point that states were also concerned about the implications for the colonies.[87] This was also the reason the UK representatives did not agree with proposals to limit the article to the 'metropolitan' or 'home' territories; this would emphasise rather too starkly the difference between the colonial powers and colonial territories.

During the drafting process, the idea was at one point adopted that the article on democratic elections should not fall under the Court's competence but only that of the Commission.[88] This suggestion found some favour with members of the Assembly who otherwise complained about the deletion of the article from the draft of the Convention.[89] This suggestion was reminiscent of the 'republican' guarantee clause in the US Constitution, but was dropped during the discussions on the Protocol.

The UK was not alone in its opposition, though its representatives articulated the concerns best. The opposition of other countries[90] to the inclusion of such an article led to it disappearing from the text of the Convention, notwithstanding the views of the Assembly.[91] The resulting compromise was that this right (along with property and education) would be dealt with in a separate protocol to the Convention.

---

[84] Council of Europe, *Collected Edition of the Travaux Préparatoires, Volume 3* (Martinus Nijhoff 1976), 182 (Committee of Experts, views of the UK).

[85] European Movement submission to Committee of Ministers, Council of Europe, *Collected Edition of the Travaux Préparatoires, Volume 1* (Martinus Nijhoff 1975), 298.

[86] Council of Europe, *Collected Edition of the Travaux Préparatoires, Volume 3* (Martinus Nijhoff 1976), 22.

[87] Simpson, *Human Rights and the End of Empire*, 758.

[88] Council of Europe, *Collected Edition of the Travaux Préparatoires, Volume 3* (Martinus Nijhoff 1976), 264.

[89] Council of Europe, *Collected Edition of the Travaux Préparatoires, Volume 5* (Martinus Nijhoff 1979), 274–278.

[90] Other countries opposed to its inclusion during the Conference of Senior Officials were Denmark, Greece, Netherlands, Norway and Sweden; Council of Europe, *Collected Edition of the Travaux Préparatoires, Volume 4* (Martinus Nijhoff 1977), 180, 214, 252, 254.

[91] See the views of Sir Maxwell-Fyfe, Teitgen and Others in Council of Europe, *Collected Edition of the Travaux Préparatoires, Volume 5* (Martinus Nijhoff 1979), 224–228, 274–278, 286–294.

Convention Rights: Inclusion and Definition   49

This protocol – the first protocol to the Convention – was elaborated largely by experts selected by the Committee of Ministers.[92] The Assembly attempted to influence the drafting, though most of the work was carried out by officials.

During the process of drafting the protocol, the controversies over the content of the article on democratic elections continued and new issues appeared. The wording of an Assembly proposal was queried because it was thought a literal reading of 'under conditions which will ensure that the government and legislature shall represent the opinion of the people' might commit a state to adopt proportional representation rather than (presumably) a majoritarian system.[93] The UK government proposed a change in this formulation to address the question of electoral systems: 'under conditions which will ensure the free expression of the opinion of the people in the choice of government and legislature'.[94] This language was also preferred in place of an Assembly proposal which might prohibit non-elective Chambers such as existed in the UK and Belgium.[95]

There was controversy over whether the wording being considered required the direct election of the government as opposed to just the legislature.[96] Finally, there was disagreement about including an introductory phrase referring more broadly to 'political liberty', with some states arguing this was a potentially wide term.[97]

The final text of article 3 of Protocol 1 provides that:

> The High Contracting Parties undertake to hold free elections at reasonable intervals by secret ballot, under conditions which will ensure the free expression of the opinion of the people in the choice of the legislature.

In addition, the Protocol has a colonial application clause – article 4 – which allows a state to extend the protocol or parts of it to its colonies; the article also permits the withdrawal of this extension.

Protocol 1 was opened for signature on 20 March 1952; it entered in to force on 18 May 1954 once the requisite ten states ratified it.

---

[92] Protocol to the Convention for the Protection of Human Rights and Fundamental Freedoms (Protocol 1), Paris, 20 March 1952, in force 18 May 1954, ETS 9.

[93] Council of Europe, *Collected Edition of the Travaux Preparatoires, Volume 7* (Martinus Nijhoff 1985), 130.

[94] Ibid., 192 and 194.

[95] Council of Europe, *Collected Edition of the Travaux Preparatoires, Volume 8* (Martinus Nijhoff 1985), 44–46.

[96] Council of Europe, *Collected Edition of the Travaux Preparatoires, Volume 7* (Martinus Nijhoff 1985), 210 and 212.

[97] Ibid., 248, 324, 326, 330.

THE CONVENTION INSTITUTIONS

For all the compromises and gaps, two features of this Convention stand out. First, it was an international treaty and so would create binding legal effects in international law once ratified and in force. Second, it created enforcement mechanisms, including a Court.

The primary focus of this book is on the work of the European Convention institutions and in particular the European Court of Human Rights. The Court has not been the only European Convention institution, though various reforms unquestionably make it the most important one in the twenty-first century.

As originally established, the Court was only one of three Convention institutions. The Committee of Ministers had an important role to play under the original Convention scheme (and still has a role to play), while the Convention established a European Commission of Human Rights.

The Commission was an extremely important institution under the original Convention. It was the Commission which received interstate complaints, i.e. complaints by one state that another had breached its obligations under the Convention.[98] In the original scheme, it was the Commission which received individual petitions alleging violations of the Convention rights, though this was optional, i.e. states had to specifically accept this possibility.[99] The Commission had the task of examining the petition and, if necessary, carrying out an investigation and then trying to facilitate a friendly settlement.[100] When there was no friendly settlement, the Commission produced a report on whether the Convention had indeed been violated.[101] At this point, the report could be referred to the Court, but if this was not done the Committee of Ministers would decide upon the report.[102] In the original Convention only certain parties could refer the case to the Court: the Commission, or a state that was involved (as complainant, respondent or because the victim was a national); the victim did not have the possibility to refer a case.[103]

The role of the Committee of Ministers under the original 1950 Convention was quite important. If the petition was not referred to the Court, then the Committee had the responsibility of deciding by a two-thirds majority whether

---

[98] European Convention on Human Rights 1950, article 24 (1950 version).
[99] Ibid., article 25 (1950 version).
[100] Ibid., article 28 (1950 version).
[101] Ibid., article 31 (1950 version).
[102] Ibid., article 32 (1950 version).
[103] Ibid., article 48 (1950 version).

there was a violation of the Convention.[104] Furthermore, the Committee had the responsibility to supervise the execution of the Court's judgments.[105]

The European Court of Human Rights was therefore a heavily circumscribed institution as originally established.[106] The Convention provided that the Court only had competence if a state recognised it;[107] even then there was a filtering mechanism in the form of the Commission, and the requirement that only the Commission or a state could refer a case to the Court.[108] As well as the possibility of an individual petition being referred to the Court after the Commission's report, the Court also had the competence to hear interstate complaints

The Convention was signed in Rome on November 1950 by thirteen states of the Council of Europe (two others signed later). The Convention entered into force in 1953 following ten ratifications.[109] France was notably tardy, ratifying the Convention only in 1974.

As noted above, the Convention bears the hallmarks of several compromises. One of these was whether to adopt a political or judicial mechanism for enforcement. The solution was to adopt both but make the judicial one optional. Under the original Convention, individual petition was optional and only came into effect when six states accepted the possibility under article 25 of the original Convention. The first states to accept this were Sweden (1952), Denmark, Ireland (1953), Norway, West Germany (1955), Austria and Luxembourg (1958). The UK only accepted petition in 1966 and France in 1981. As a further safeguard, the competence of the Court was also optional – states had the option to recognise its competence under article 46 of the original Convention.

EVOLUTION OF THE COUNCIL OF EUROPE AND THE CONVENTION INSTITUTIONS

The adoption of the European Convention on Human Rights and its First Protocol were among the earliest and most significant achievements of the

---

[104] Ibid., article 32 (1950 version).
[105] Ibid., article 54 (1950 version).
[106] See Stephen Greer, *The European Convention on Human Rights: Achievements, Problems and Prospects* (Cambridge University Press 2006) and Ed Bates, *The Evolution of the European Convention on Human Rights: From Its Inception to the Creation of a Permanent Court of Human Rights* (Oxford University Press 2010) on the evolution of the Court.
[107] European Convention on Human Rights 1950, article 46 (1950 version).
[108] Ibid., articles 44, 48 (1950 version).
[109] These were by Denmark, West Germany, Greece (renounced the Convention in 1970; ratified again in 1974), Iceland, Ireland, Luxembourg, Norway, Saarland (later merged with West Germany), Sweden and the UK.

Council of Europe. The Council of Europe has developed considerably since those early days: the Convention institutions have been amended, and the Council has created a vast architecture of human rights treaties and institutions (Other Council of Europe Institutions). Critical, and indeed fundamentally related to these developments, has been the development or more precisely the enlargement of the Council of Europe itself. From a small club of ten Western European states, the Council has expanded dramatically to encompass forty-seven states ranging from Iceland to Azerbaijan and even including the successor state of the Soviet Union, modern Russia.

This originally limited role for the Court has been considerably changed by subsequent amending protocols, several adopted to deal with the expanding case load consequent on the expansion of the Council.

Protocol 2 introduced an advisory competence for the Court.[110] It enabled the Committee of Ministers to ask the Court a legal question on the interpretation of the Convention or its protocols, provided the question did not relate to the interpretation of the rights in the Convention and could not relate to a case that might come before the Court. This protocol was opened for signature in 1963 but only acquired the required ratifications in 1970.

The 1980s saw important developments in the Convention machinery. In the first place, several states chose to adopt the principle of petition. This system was optional in the original Convention, and it was only in this period that some of the founder and early members of the Convention accepted the principle of petition. Notably the socialist government of France (a founder state) in 1981 and the Turkish government (a member of the Council since 1950) in 1987 accepted the principle of petition.[111] By 1990, all the states party to the Convention had accepted the right of petition.[112] In the second place, the fall of the Iron Curtain paved the way for expansion of Convention ratification as well as Council of Europe membership.

Protocol 9 to the Convention, opened for signature in 1990 and in force from 1994, provided that the petitioner could refer a case to the Court following the Commission's report.[113] This was an important step in transforming the system into a more judicial process aimed at securing individual justice. It recognised a role for the victim (individual or non-governmental

---

[110] Protocol 2 to the Convention for the Protection of Human Rights and Fundamental Freedoms, conferring upon the European Court of Human Rights competence to give advisory opinions, Strasbourg, 6 May 1963, in force 21 September 1970, ETS 44.

[111] http://conventions.coe.int/Treaty/en/Treaties/Html/005-1-bis.htm, accessed 6 August 2019.

[112] Greer, *The European Convention on Human Rights*, 37.

[113] Protocol 9 to the Convention for the Protection of Human Rights and Fundamental Freedoms, Rome, 6 November 1990, in force 1 October 1994, ETS 140.

Evolution of the Council of Europe and the Convention Institutions 53

organisation) in bringing a case to the Court and not just the Commission. This innovation triggered a new screening process whereby a panel of the Court had to confirm that a case referred by the victim raised a serious question about the interpretation of application or the Convention or otherwise warranted the attention of the Court. This was a more onerous requirement than merely passing the admissibility criteria.

In 1998, Protocol 11 came into force, radically restructuring the system.[114] In line with the trend towards a more judicial approach, this Protocol did away with the Commission entirely; it also did away with the adjudicative function of the Committee of Ministers; it made the right of application to the Court (symbolically, the language of 'petition' was changed to 'application') compulsory for states. It established a new permanent court and set out its formations and competences. Under the Protocol 11 reforms, the Court would sit in three-judge committees, seven-judge Chambers and a seventeen-judge Grand Chamber. The Court was given the competence to hear individual applications and interstate complaints, and to offer advisory opinions when requested by the Committee of Ministers.

The greater emphasis on the judicial nature of the process following the Protocol 11 reforms coincided with a considerably greater workload for the Court; this has led to a serious crisis of 'pandemic proportions'[115] in the Court system, with tens of thousands of cases on the Court's docket. The 2012 Annual Report of the Court reported that there were 128,100 cases pending before the Court; this astonishing figure was nevertheless an important improvement upon the figure of 151,600 for the previous year.[116] The Council of Europe and the Court have attempted to deal with this in various ways. The Court, for example, has developed a so-called pilot judgment procedure which enables it to process large numbers of similar cases through the prism of a single typical case.

The Council of Europe has adopted Protocol 14 to amend the Court's machinery.[117] This provides that the Court can sit in single-judge formations as well as committees, Chambers and Grand Chamber. Protocol 14 also reforms the admissibility criteria in order to provide for swifter processing of

---

[114] Protocol 11 to the European Convention restructuring the control machinery established thereby 1994, Strasbourg 11 May 1994, in force 1 November 1998, ETS 155.

[115] Greer, *The European Convention on Human Rights*, 38.

[116] Council of Europe, *Annual Report for 2012 of the European Court of Human Rights* (Council of Europe 2013) 'Statistical Information'.

[117] Protocol 14 to the Convention for the Protection of Human Rights and Fundamental Freedoms, amending the control system of the Convention, Strasbourg, 13 May 2004, in force 1 June 2010, ETS 194.

Council, Convention and Court

cases, introducing the 'no significant disadvantage' criterion. The adoption of Protocol 14 was seriously delayed by the refusal of Russia to ratify the Protocol; every other state ratified the Protocol by 2006 at the latest, but Russia delayed ratification until 2010. This led to the temporary use of Protocol 14bis procedures for those states that had accepted the Protocol until Protocol 14 came into force on 1 June 2010. The effect of the pilot judgment innovation and Protocol 14 has been significant. The Annual Report for 2018 of the Court indicates the backlog of pending cases is now at 56,350.[118]

Following the Brighton conference on the European Court system,[119] the Council of Europe has adopted Protocols 15 and 16. Protocol 16, which came into force in August 2018 and is in force for those countries that have ratified it, enables the Court to give advisory opinions at the request of domestic courts.[120] Protocol 15 is not yet in force, as only forty-five of the forty-seven states have ratified it, as of June 2020. This Protocol will amend the Convention by including explicit references to 'subsidiarity' and the 'margin of appreciation' doctrine in the Preamble, amending the criteria for becoming a judge of the Court, the process for relinquishing a case to the Grand Chamber, reducing the six-month time limit for bringing a case to four months and amending the 'significant disadvantage' admissibility criterion.

COMPETENCES OF THE MODERN COURT

The modern Court hears four types of cases: advisory opinions, interstate complaints, individual applications and referrals concerning execution of judgment. The individual applications form the bulk of the work of the Court.

Under article 47 of the Convention, the Committee of Ministers may request the Grand Chamber to issue an advisory opinion on the Convention's terms but not on any of the rights or freedoms in the Convention or even a matter which could arise in other proceedings before the Court. Advisory opinions of this sort are extremely rare: there have been only two such opinions. Both relate to the method for appointing judges to the European

---

[118] Council of Europe, *Annual Report for 2018 of the European Court of Human Rights* (Council of Europe 2019), 'Statistics'.

[119] Council of Europe, *Brighton Declaration: High Level Conference on the Future of the European Court of Human Rights* (2012), available at www.echr.coe.int/Documents/2012_Brighton_FinalDeclaration_ENG.pdf, accessed 20 August 2019.

[120] Protocol 16 to the Convention for the Protection of Human Rights and Fundamental Freedoms, Strasbourg, 2 October 2013, in force 1 August 2018, CETS 214.

Court of Human Rights;[121] an earlier request had been rejected as outside the scope of article 47.[122] As one of the Brighton reforms, the Court has received another, probably more onerous advisory competence. Protocol 16 to the Convention authorises the highest courts and tribunals in a state to refer a question on the interpretation of the rights and freedoms in the Convention to the Grand Chamber for an advisory non-binding opinion. The process is inspired by the preliminary reference procedure of the Court of Justice of the European Union and is intended to reduce the backlog in Strasbourg by providing guidance earlier on the Convention requirements.

In comparison to advisory opinions, there are rather more interstate complaints, though even so, these are rare. Under article 33 of the Convention, any state may make a complaint that any other state has breached one of the rights in the Convention. Interstate complaints are not subject to the same admissibility criteria that individual petitions must satisfy. More importantly, though, some of the interstate complaints have given rise to jurisprudentially important decisions. Indeed, one of the earliest of these – the Greek case – gave rise to a judgment directly concerning democratic rights, as it reviewed the violations of human rights, including the suspension of elections, in Greece under the Colonels' regime.[123]

The individual applications comprise the bulk of the Court's work, and they produce the vast caseload and consequent problems of delay facing the Court.

Article 34 provides that individual applications may be lodged against a state by anyone claiming to be a victim of a violation of a Convention right. Importantly, the victim need not be an individual – a non-governmental organisation or a group of individuals (a political party, for instance) can lodge a complaint. This is at least symbolically important, as it enables a political party or non-governmental organisation that has been the victim of a denial of political rights to make a complaint in its own name rather than rely on an individual member of the organisation to make a complaint.

Applications must satisfy certain criteria to be admissible and must be within the competence of the court. The applicant must allege to be a victim

---

[121] *Advisory Opinion on certain legal questions concerning the lists of candidates submitted with a view to the election of judges to the European Court of Human Rights* (12 February 2008); *Advisory Opinion on certain legal questions concerning the lists of candidates submitted with a view to the election of judges to the European Court of Human Rights* (22 January 2010).

[122] *Decision on the competence of the Court to give an advisory opinion on whether the CIS Commission could be regarded as 'another procedure of international investigation or settlement'* (2 June 2004).

[123] *Denmark and others v Greece (The Greek case)* App no 3321/67 (European Commission of Human Rights, 5 November 1969).

him- or herself; there is no right to bring an individual petition on behalf of a third party or an *actio popularis*.[124] It is true that states could bring such an action, as they do not need to claim to be victims or to have any interest whatsoever.[125] Article 35 lists the admissibility criteria: the applicant must have exhausted all domestic remedies; the applicant must be lodged within six months of a final national decision; the application must not be anonymous, or substantially the same as an application already examined in Strasbourg or before another international mechanism; the application must not be manifestly ill-founded, incompatible with the Convention, or an abuse of the right of petition. In addition, the application can be rejected as inadmissible if the applicant has not suffered a 'significant disadvantage' though this criterion can only be applied if the matter has been duly considered by national courts and respect for human rights does not require the Court to consider it (Protocol 15 will remove this requirement of domestic due consideration).

The Court at any stage may decide an application is inadmissible; in particular, after Protocol 14, a single judge can rule an application inadmissible under article 27. A committee can also rule on admissibility, but in addition can deliver a finding on the merits if the subject matter of the application has been the subject of well-established case law (article 28).

The Court may decide that an application is outside the competence of the Court because of questions of timing, subject matter or jurisdiction. Some of these issues of jurisdiction have produced important if complicated case law on the extent to which the Convention might apply to a state because of events which commenced prior to the state's ratification of the Convention,[126] or because the application concerns events occurring outside of the formal territorial jurisdiction of the state.[127]

As noted above, committees have the power to decide the merits of an application if it is the subject of well-established case law. It is the seven-judge Chamber which is the main body for deciding cases on the merits (article 29). The Grand Chamber exists to hear 'referrals' from chamber judgments or to decide cases which raise serious issues of Convention interpretation.[128]

---

[124] There is a limited exception in right-to-life cases for relatives.

[125] *Denmark and others v Greece (The Greek case)*.

[126] For example, one case concerned an effort to use the Convention to hold Russia accountable for the Katyn massacre in 1940: *Janowiec v Russia* App no 55508/07 and 29520/09, 58 EHRR 30 (Grand Chamber).

[127] This latter issue concerns cases about military action abroad, e.g. NATO's bombing of Serbia or UK action in Iraq: *Bankovic v Belgium and 16 other states* App no 52207/99, (2001) 44 EHRR SE5; *Al Skeini v United Kingdom* App no 55721/07, (2011) 53 EHRR 18 (Grand Chamber).

[128] Articles 30, 31, 43.

When considering a case, the Court may receive third-party interventions from a state whose national is an applicant or the Commissioner for Human Rights (article 36). In addition, the President of the Court may permit third-party interventions by other states or 'any person concerned.' The Court can carry out an investigation if required and may try to pursue a friendly settlement to the case. When delivering judgments, judges can deliver individual opinions if they disagree in whole or in part with the court judgment (article 45).

States are obliged to respect any judgment to which they are a party. The Committee of Ministers is in charge of supervising the execution of a judgment. As part of this role, the Committee of Ministers can refer certain questions back to a Grand Chamber: a two-thirds majority of the Committee can ask the Grand Chamber to clarify the interpretation of a judgment, or to rule on whether the respondent state has failed to abide by the court judgment.[129]

OTHER COUNCIL OF EUROPE INSTITUTIONS

While the focus of this work is on the Convention institutions and in particular the Court, these are only a part of the much more extensive Council of Europe architecture,[130] much of which is at least indirectly relevant to the work of the Court. The primary institutions of the Council – the Committee of Ministers and the Parliamentary Assembly – also play roles in protecting human rights, including the political and electoral rights discussed in this book.[131]

In addition to these primary Council and Convention institutions, the Council of Europe has created a host of other institutions relevant to the promotion of human rights and democracy. In some cases, these are the result of the Council's work in adopting and sponsoring treaties. Others, though, have been created outside of the treaty system.

Within the treaty system there are numerous treaties which address human rights, democracy or governance issues. Alongside the European Convention (which primarily considers civil and political rights) there is the European

---

[129] Article 46.
[130] Gauthier De Beco, *Human Rights Monitoring Mechanisms of the Council of Europe* (Routledge 2011).
[131] Chemavon Chahbazian, 'The Contribution of the Parliamentary Assembly of the Council of Europe to Soft Law in Electoral Matters' in Helen Hardman and Brice Dickson (eds) *Electoral Rights in Europe: Advances and Challenges* (Taylor & Francis 2017).

Social Charter 1961,[132] which addresses a range of social and economic rights. Other examples include the European Convention for the Prevention of Torture 1987,[133] the Charter of Regional and Minority Languages 1992,[134] Convention on the Participation of Foreigners in Public Life at Local Level 1992,[135] the Framework Convention on National Minorities 1995,[136] the Convention on Biomedicine and Human Rights 1997 (the Oviedo Convention),[137] Convention on Action against Trafficking in Human Beings 2005[138] and the Convention on Preventing and Combating Violence against Women and Domestic Violence 2011.[139]

Many of these treaties have themselves been amended on numerous occasions. The European Social Charter 1961 was amended in 1988 by an Additional Protocol and again in 1991. In 1995, an Additional Protocol provided for a system of collective complaints, while the entire system was overhauled with the European Social Charter Revised 1996.[140] This latter instrument considerably lengthened the list of social and economic rights protected in the Charter.

Many of these treaties create their own monitoring bodies with a range of different powers. None of them create a court (the European Convention remains unique in that regard). In some cases, the monitoring bodies receive state reports and comment on them, similar to the procedure in the UN treaty monitoring system. However, depending on the institution, they may also carry out visits and meet interested parties. The European Committee for the Prevention of Torture is empowered to visit places of detention. The European Committee of Social Rights (created by the European Social Charter)

---

[132] European Social Charter 1961, Turin, 18 October 1961, in force 26 February 1965, ETS 5.

[133] European Convention for the Prevention of Torture and Inhuman or Degrading Treatment or Punishment, Strasbourg, 26 November 1987, in force 1 February 1989, ETS 126.

[134] European Charter for Regional or Minority Languages, Strasbourg, 5 November 1992, in force 1 March 1998, ETS 148.

[135] Convention on the Participation of Foreigners in Public Life at Local Level, Strasbourg, 5 February 1992, in force 1 May 1995, ETS 144.

[136] Framework Convention for the Protection of National Minorities, Strasbourg, 1 February 1995, in force 1 February 1998, ETS 157.

[137] Convention for the Protection of Human Rights and Dignity of the Human Being with Regard to the Application of Biology and Medicine: Convention on Human Rights and Biomedicine, Oviedo, 4 April 1997, in force 1 December 1999, ETS 164.

[138] Convention on Action against Trafficking in Human Beings, Warsaw, 16 May 2005, in force 1 February 2008, 2005 ETS 197.

[139] Convention on Preventing and Combating Violence against Women and Domestic Violence, Istanbul, 11 May 2011, in force 1 August 2014, CETS 210.

[140] European Social Charter Revised, Strasbourg, 3 May 1996, in force 1 July 1999, ETS 163.

can hear collective complaints under the 1995 Additional Protocol. This makes it closest to the judicial European Court of Human Rights.

These treaty-based bodies by no means exhaust the resources of the Council of Europe. The Council has also created many institutions outside of the treaty system which are relevant for the promotion of human rights and democracy. These include the Commissioner for Human Rights who has a mandate to visit states and speak out on human rights issues, either thematically or on a country-specific basis. The Commissioner has addressed issues concerning democracy promotion, including, for example, the rise of far-right parties in Greece and the legitimacy of measures to tackle such parties. The Council has a European Commission against Racism and Intolerance (ECRI) and has also created the European Commission on Democracy through Law (the Venice Commission).

Some of these institutions work on human rights issues, but these may also overlap with concerns about democratic practice. The most obvious is the Venice Commission which produces important recommendations on democratic practice and sometimes on specific situations in individual countries. Furthermore, the European Court frequently refers to these statements in its judgments. The work of other institutions is also very relevant. Thus, the Advisory Committee of the Framework Convention on National Minorities has to consider issues under article 15 of the Framework Convention: this provides for the 'effective participation' in 'cultural, social and economic life and in public affairs'.

While the work of these organisations is only sometimes tied explicitly to issues of participation and democracy, this does not mean that their work has no relevance to the fostering of democratic practices. One of the clearest messages to come from the European Court, for instance, is that a democratic society presupposes a particular type of society, one which nourishes pluralism, tolerance and broadmindedness. The work of these other institutions should help to create that sort of society.

THE INTERNATIONAL LAW CONTEXT

In Chapters 4 through to 9 we will examine the jurisprudence of the Court, and in particular how it has deployed these principles in democratic rights cases, how it has upheld the notion of a liberal representative democracy, and whether it has the potential to further deliberative, participatory and egalitarian political practices. Before immersing ourselves in this jurisprudence it is helpful to briefly sketch the role of international and regional human rights standards in this area.

Several key actors have developed work on an international right to democracy. Much of this has taken place in the context of the United Nations, both in the Treaty and Charter mechanisms of the UN. However, the regional organisations such as the African Union, the Organisation of American States and the other European regional organisations have also been active. Other intergovernmental organisations (the Inter-Parliamentary Union and the Commonwealth) have also developed important standards or mechanisms.

Within the United Nations treaty-based system, the International Covenant on Civil and Political Rights (ICCPR) is most relevant and perhaps the treaty mechanism closest to the ECHR system.[141] It includes important democratic rights in article 25 and its monitoring body, the Human Rights Committee frequently deals with communications very similar to those heard in Strasbourg. However, it is worth highlighting some important differences. The ICCPR also includes a right to self-determination and minority rights (article 1 and article 27 respectively). These rights are relevant to the practice of democracy. While the Human Rights Committee cannot entertain communications about article 1, it has issued a general comment on the right to self-determination and can review state practice on this point as part of the state reporting mechanism. The Committee can receive communications in relation to article 27 and some of these raise important issues of democratic participation.[142]

It is interesting to compare the language of P1–3 with the terms of article 25 ICCPR:

> Article 25 Every citizen shall have the right and the opportunity, without any of the distinctions mentioned in article 2 and without unreasonable restrictions:
>
> (a) To take part in the conduct of public affairs, directly or through freely chosen representatives;
> (b) To vote and to be elected at genuine periodic elections which shall be by universal and equal suffrage and shall be held by secret ballot, guaranteeing the free expression of the will of the electors;
> (c) To have access, on general terms of equality, to public service in his country.

---

[141] International Covenant on Civil and Political Right, New York, 16 December 1966, in force 23 March 1976, UNTS, vol 999, p 171.

[142] *Mahuika v New Zealand* Communication No 547/1993 (Human Rights Committee, 15 November 2000) and *Poma v Peru* Communication no 1457/2006 (Human Rights Committee, 27 March 2009).

The ICCPR standards are interesting because they are expressed in wider and more detailed terms than P1–3. Article 25 speaks of the right to take part in public affairs; it provides for a right of access to the public service and it explicitly refers to the principle of 'universal and equal suffrage'. Article 25 is also different though in expressly limiting these rights to 'citizens'; P1–3 contains no such express limit. Article 25 is not limited to legislative elections. Finally, the ICCPR makes it clear these are subjective rights and not only a general undertaking to hold elections.

The major regional organisations have standards and case law on democracy rights; the main treaties (the American Convention on Human Rights 1969 and the African Charter of Human and Peoples' Rights 1981) include clauses on political participation rights very similar to article 25 ICCPR.[143] However, in some ways these organisations have gone beyond the ICCPR or ECHR examples. Both organisations have adopted specific regional charters on democracy, while the Inter-American system has also developed considerable case law on the participation rights of indigenous peoples.

The African Charter on Democracy, Elections and Governance 2007[144] includes obligations in relation to democracy, but also situates them within wider norms on respect for human rights, non-discrimination (with special recognition of the role of women,[145] the youth and people with disabilities[146]), the rule of law, human development,[147] good governance[148] and the fight against corruption. The Charter includes relatively detailed rules on the need for an independent electoral body and fair electoral processes.[149] The Charter emphasises the need for constitutional transfer of power[150] and civilian control of the armed forces.[151] It provides several articles detailing the sanctions that can be imposed following any unconstitutional change of power.[152]

The Inter-American Democratic Charter 2001 sets out the elements of a representative democracy, which requires a range of institutional practices,

---

[143] American Convention on Human Rights 1969, San Jose, 22 November 1969, in force 18 July 1978, 1144 UNTS 123, article 23; African Charter on Human and Peoples' Rights 1981, Banjui, 27 June 1981, in force 21 October 1986, 21 ILM 58 (1982), article 13.
[144] African Charter on Democracy, Elections and Governance 2007, Addis Ababa, 30 January 2007, in force 15 February 2012.
[145] Ibid., article 29.
[146] Ibid., article 31.
[147] Ibid., articles 37–43.
[148] Ibid., article 33.
[149] Ibid., article 17.
[150] Ibid., article 5.
[151] Ibid., article 14.
[152] Ibid., articles 23–26.

respect for human rights and participation.[153] The Charter emphasises the need for all state institutions to be subject to the legally constituted civilian authorities.[154] The Charter recognises the need for democracy to be based on the full respect of all human rights including social and economic rights, the fight against poverty and social and economic development.[155] The Charter condemns unconstitutional changes of power, describing them as 'insurmountable' obstacles to a government participation in the institutions of the Organization of American States.[156]

The other European regional mechanisms have increasingly addressed democracy and human rights in the past few decades. The Organisation for Security and Cooperation in Europe (OSCE)[157] played a critical role during the end of the Cold War and the transition to democracy in Eastern Europe. It adopted a number of public statements on the need for a democratic transition[158] and has also created new standards, institutions and mechanisms to promote democracy. These include important soft law principles on the rights of minorities, including the right to effective participation in public affairs,[159] and the creation of election monitoring, rule of law promotion and minority rights monitoring mechanisms.

The European Union has increasingly addressed issues of democracy and human rights. The Union is declared to be founded on the principle of democracy, along with human dignity, freedom, equality, the rule of law and human rights including minority rights.[160] Breach of these values may result in a state losing its voting rights.[161] The Union has developed its own system of democratic (or quasi-democratic) supranational governance, with a directly elected European Parliament, distinctive rights to vote in European

---

[153] Inter-American Democratic Charter 2001, Lima, 11 September 2001, articles 2, 3 and 4.

[154] Inter-American Democratic Charter 2001, article 4.

[155] Inter-American Democratic Charter 2001, article 10 emphasises workers' rights; articles 11–16 address development; poverty; illiteracy; social, economic and cultural rights; the environment and education.

[156] Inter-American Democratic Charter 2001, article 19.

[157] Originally the CSCE, the Conference on Security and Cooperation in Europe.

[158] See, in particular, the Vienna Concluding Document, the Copenhagen Concluding Document, the Charter of Paris for a New Europe and the Moscow Meeting on the Human Dimension of the CSCE.

[159] The Hague Recommendations regarding the Education Rights of National Minorities 1996; The Oslo Recommendations regarding the Linguistic Rights of National Minorities 1998; The Lund Recommendations on the Effective Participation of National Minorities in Public Life 1999; Warsaw guidelines: Recommendations to assist national minority participation in the electoral process, elaborating on the Lund Recommendations 2001.

[160] Consolidated Treaty on the European Union, article 2.

[161] Ibid., article 7.

Parliament elections across Europe,[162] principles on consultation and dialogue and a European initiative mechanism,[163] and processes of consultation with national parliaments.[164] This vision of supranational governance is also fleshed out in the European Union Charter of Fundamental Rights 2000 which has a chapter on Citizens' Rights. This includes the right to vote in and run for office in municipal elections across Europe;[165] the right to good administration, access to information and the Ombudsman;[166] and the right to petition the European Parliament.[167]

There is an important external dimension as well: the Union's external action is supposed to be guided by these principles including that of democracy.[168]

Of most direct relevance to this book, however, is the possibility for the actions of the Union to be the subject of litigation in the European Court of Human Rights. As the Union's twenty-seven members are all parties to the European Convention on Human Rights, this is, indirectly at least, already a possibility – indeed, a reality. The most striking example of this so far has been in the litigation on the right of Gibraltarian residents to vote for the European Parliament.[169] This will become even more important as the European Union itself becomes party to the Convention.[170]

CONCLUSION

The European Convention on Human Rights protects political rights within a constantly evolving political and institutional context. Shaped by the European catastrophe and the Cold War, the Convention drafters adopted a model of liberal and representative democracy. Even though the Convention is imbued with a concern for democracy, the drafters cautiously chose to include the provisions on electoral rights in a separate Protocol and drafted it in such a way as to allay concerns about excessive ('universal') suffrage demands or an end to unelected components of legislatures.

[162] Ibid., articles 10, 14.
[163] Ibid., article 11.
[164] Ibid., article 12.
[165] European Union Charter of Fundamental Rights 2000, article 40.
[166] Ibid., articles 41–43.
[167] Ibid., article 44.
[168] Consolidated Treaty on the European Union, article 21.
[169] *Matthews v United Kingdom* App no 24833/94 (1999) 28 EHRR 361 (Grand Chamber).
[170] Consolidated Treaty on the European Union, article 6(2); European Convention on Human Rights 1950, article 59(2).

The Convention drafters opted to create a Court, but initially at least it was a Court that was tightly circumscribed; concerns about state sovereignty were not simply jettisoned, even if drafters were aware of the dramatic failures of state sovereignty. The original text of the Convention clearly reflected a preference for more political means of protecting rights. Over the course of the system evolution, it become a much more judicialised process.

It also became bigger. The Convention system expanded dramatically at the end of the Cold War, creating new institutional challenges. The most striking of these was the dramatic expansion in the workload of the Court; by the end of the second decade of the twenty-first century the system has developed to meet or at least ameliorate this challenge. In the twenty-first century the situation continues to evolve with new challenges, many of which would have seemed unimaginable to the Convention architects or even those who oversaw the expansion in the 1990s. Meeting these challenges requires consideration of how the Court interprets and applies the Convention.

3

European Principles of Interpretation and Application

The previous chapter took us through the history of the Council of Europe's formation, the drafting the ECHR and the creation and evolution of the Council and the Convention institutions. It highlighted the Convention as one of the most important achievements of the Council, and it is the Convention that will be the focus of this book. However, if the Convention is the focus of the book, it only has meaning in so far as it has been interpreted by the Court; the case law of the Court, and the response of the states to that case law, makes the difference between a vacuous proclamation and a genuine effective mechanism for furthering human rights and democracy in Europe.

Later chapters will examine how the Court has given meaning to these textual provisions on political rights, but in this chapter, it is necessary to say a few words about the principles which guide the Court's work.[1] The chapter introduces the interpretive principles used by the Court; it then explains the Court's approach to limitations on rights and the doctrine of positive obligations. The controversial margin of appreciation doctrine is then discussed. Having introduced these general principles of the Court's approach, the following chapter examines the free expression jurisprudence of the Court.

THE INTERPRETATION OF THE CONVENTION

The Convention does not contain any clauses on how it should be interpreted, even though the drafters were well aware of the importance of judicial interpretation. The Vienna Convention on the Law of Treaties 1969 provides some guidance on the interpretation of treaties establishing as a principle that 'A treaty shall be interpreted in good faith in accordance with the ordinary

---

[1] For a more thorough examination, see Janneke Gerards, *General Principles of the European Convention on Human Rights* (Cambridge University Press 2019).

66 *European Principles of Interpretation and Application*

meaning to be given to the terms of the treaty in their context and in the light of its object and purpose.'[2]

While the Court has sometimes referred to the Vienna Convention, it has developed certain principles to guide the interpretation. Three are especially important and closely related: the principle of effective interpretation, the evolving interpretation principle and the autonomous meaning principle. Whilst these three do not exhaust the interpretive tools used by the Court, they are the most significant.

The most important interpretive principle is that of effective interpretation. The Court adopts the position that the rights in the Convention are not intended to be illusory or empty but rather they should be effective: 'the Convention must be interpreted in the light of present-day conditions . . . and it is designed to safeguard the individual in a real and practical way.'[3] This means that the Court interprets the Convention in such a way as to make the enjoyment of rights effective even if this means going beyond a strict literal reading of the text. Ensuring that the rights are effective in present-day conditions means that the Convention is seen as a 'living instrument'.[4]

The classic case here is the *Golder v UK* judgment, which concerned a UK rule requiring a prisoner to obtain the permission of the Secretary of State before beginning a court case.[5] The Convention contains a right to a fair trial but does not specify that there is any right of access to the courts. Nevertheless, the Court reasoned that the right to a fair trial would be nugatory ('of no value at all'[6]) if individuals could simply be denied access to the courts in an arbitrary manner. The Court said that this was not a case of an 'extensive interpretation forcing new obligations' on the states, but was rather an interpretation based on the text 'read in its context and having regard to the object and purpose of the Convention'.[7]

Since then the Court has had frequent recourse to the principle of effective interpretation. As we will see, it is one of the key justifications for the entire doctrine of positive obligations.

---

[2] Vienna Convention on the Law of Treaties 1969, Vienna, 23 May 1969, in force 27 January 1980, UNTS, vol 1155, p 331, article 31(1).

[3] *Airey v Ireland* App no 6289/73 (1979) 2 EHRR 305, para 26.

[4] Chris Thornhill, *The Sociology of Law and the Global Transformation of Democracy* (Cambridge University Press 2018), 248–261 on the notion of 'living constitutionalism'.

[5] *Golder v United Kingdom* App no 4451/70 (1975) 1 EHRR 524.

[6] *Golder v United Kingdom*, para 35.

[7] *Golder v United Kingdom*, para 36. The majority judgment provoked a lengthy dissent by Sir Gerald Fitzmaurice, the UK judge, objecting to the majority's approach to interpretation and urging a 'cautious and conservative interpretation' (section 39 of the dissent).

The Interpretation of the Convention   67

Allied to the idea of an effective interpretation is that of an evolving interpretation. If rights are to be effectively enjoyed in society, then they must evolve as society evolves. The Court indicated unequivocally in a series of landmark cases in the 1970s that the Convention 'must be interpreted in the light of present-day conditions'.[8] This entails that the interpretation of rights evolves as society evolves, and so it is not normally acceptable to argue that because a practice was familiar to the drafters of the Convention and acceptable in European societies in the late 1940s, it is still acceptable today. During the late 1940s, states might have practiced the judicial corporal punishment of children or discriminated against children born outside of marriage. Nevertheless, a 'present-day' interpretation of the Convention may prohibit judicial corporal punishment as a breach of article 3 (prohibition of degrading punishment)[9] and discrimination against children born outside marriage as a breach of article 14 non-discrimination in conjunction with article 8 (respect for private and family life) and Protocol 1, article 1 (property).[10] In particular, the Court has regard to how European societies evolve and whether there is a 'clear measure of common ground in this area among modern societies'.[11]

This 'present-day', 'evolutive' or 'evolving' interpretation is most evident in cases involving new technologies, though it is not unique to these sorts of cases. Gender reassignment surgery is a very clear example. When cases involving gender reassignment surgery first came before the Court in the 1980s, it adopted a very deferential approach to the decisions of states.[12] In the 1990s, the Court showed a more demanding approach, expecting states to, for example, modify identity card practices in order to respect the rights of persons who had undergone gender reassignment surgery.[13] By the early twenty-first century, the Court was prepared to find that states had to adapt practices on birth certificates and marriage law in order to protect the right to respect for a family and private life and the right to marry.[14]

The principle of evolving interpretation must always be borne in mind when interpreting the Convention. It means that political practices – for example the disenfranchisement of prisoners or bankrupts – that may once have been entirely acceptable and even common place must now be

---

[8] *Tyrer v United Kingdom* App no 5856/72 (1978) 2 EHRR 1 para 31.
[9] *Tyrer v United Kingdom*, para 31.
[10] *Marckx v Belgium* App no 6833/74 (1979) 2 EHRR 330.
[11] *Marckx*, para 41.
[12] *Rees v United Kingdom* App no 9532/81 (1987) 9 EHRR 56.
[13] *B v France* App no 13343/87 (1992) 16 EHRR 1.
[14] *Goodwin v United Kingdom* App no 28957/95 (2002) 35 EHRR 18.

68   *European Principles of Interpretation and Application*

subjected to more rigorous examination to determine their compatibility with the Convention in light of present-day conditions.

The third key principle, like the evolving interpretation principle, is again linked to the idea of an effective interpretation. This is the principle of the autonomous meaning of Convention terms, i.e. the terms in the Convention do not necessarily have the same meaning as in the domestic legal systems, but have their own, Convention-specific meaning. This is important, as otherwise states could evade responsibility simply by redefining the terms in national law. This principle is frequently employed in relation to procedural matters; thus, what is considered to be a criminal offence for the purposes of articles 6 and 7 is not a matter to be defined merely by reference to national law. Similarly, the definition of a 'court' is not purely for national law to decide. The principle, though, also extends to non-procedural matters; thus, the idea of 'property' in Protocol 1's right to property has been given extensive interpretation by the Court to include social security payments.[15]

The autonomous meaning principle may well be relevant in political rights cases. For example, P1–3 refers to the 'legislature'; does this include a body like the supranational European Parliament? What are the implications, if any, where the Executive has law-making powers? More generally, the political rights are subject to exceptions and limitations 'in accordance with law', but this does not refer merely to what is provided for in national legislation but has a Convention specific meaning (see the section 'Legality or Lawfulness' later in the chapter).

As well as these three principles, a number of others have been used in the Court's case law. One that has increasing importance is the willingness of the Court to interpret the Convention in the light of other international treaties. The Court, for example, invoked the Vienna Convention on the Law of Treaties in its *Golder* judgment. More interestingly, though, the Court frequently interprets the Convention in the light of other human rights treaties. For example, when deciding that discriminatory laws denying certain groups of people the right to work in the private sector violated article 14 in combination with article 8, the Court based its interpretation of these articles partly on the European Social Charter 1961 which explicitly protects the right to work.[16] More recently, the Court relied on the UN Convention on the Elimination of Discrimination against Women (CEDAW)[17] and the Organisation of

---

[15] *Andrejeva v Latvia* App no 55707/00 (2010) 51 EHRR 28.
[16] *Sidabras v Lithuania* App nos 55480/00 and 59330/00 (2006) 42 EHRR 6.
[17] Convention on the Elimination of Discrimination against Women, New York, 18 December 1979, in force 3 September 1981, UNTS vol 1249, p 13.

American States' Belém do Pará Convention[18] to conclude that domestic violence is a form of sex discrimination.[19]

As well as referring to other international treaties, the Court may refer to other international law sources. For example, in the domestic violence case just mentioned, the Court referred to a case before the Inter-American Commission on Human Rights and to a General Recommendation of the CEDAW Committee.[20] The Court has also relied on other international law sources that are even more clearly examples of 'soft law' rather than treaty-based obligations. In particular, it has relied on statements from the Venice Commission when interpreting some of the political rights in P1–3. The willingness of the Court to refer to such soft law sources may be seen as a means of enhancing the Court's own opportunities for creativity.

The Vienna Convention on the Law of Treaties specifies that regard may be had to the preparatory works of a treaty as a supplementary form of interpretation where there is ambiguity, obscurity or the danger of arriving at an absurd or unreasonable result.[21] The Court very rarely refers to the intention of the drafters or the *travaux préparatoires* of the Convention, though there are examples of it doing so.

While the Court frequently invokes the idea of an effective, evolving or autonomous interpretation of the Convention, there are also cases where it concludes the best reading of the Convention is the one offered by a more straightforward literal approach or even a historical interpretation, which refers to the conditions in Western Europe at the time of drafting the Convention. The clearest example of this is the Chamber judgment concluding that article 12 on the right to marry does not require states to recognise same-sex marriage. In reaching this conclusion, the Chamber explicitly referred to the terms of article 12 (which refer to 'men and women' rather than 'everyone') and to the 1950s understanding of marriage.[22] In reaching this conclusion, though, the Chamber did not exclude the possibility that a European consensus might emerge which would justify a different result.[23]

To sum up this section, the Court can have recourse to a range of interpretive tools, but places especial emphasis upon the ideas of effective interpretation, evolving interpretation and autonomous meaning. These principles

---

[18] Inter-American Convention on the Prevention, Punishment and Eradication of Violence against Women, *Belem do Para*, 9 June 1994, in force 5 March 1995.

[19] *Opuz v Turkey* App no 33401/02 (2010) 50 EHRR 28.

[20] *Opuz v Turkey* App no 33401/02 (2010) 50 EHRR 28, paras 74, 187, 190.

[21] Vienna Convention on the Law of Treaties 1969, article 32.

[22] *Schalk and Kopf v Austria* App no 30141/04 (2011) 53 EHRR 20, para 55.

[23] *Schalk and Kopf*, paras 58–61.

THE PRINCIPLES ON LIMITATIONS OF RIGHTS

come into play when determining the scope for limiting rights, the doctrine of positive obligation and the margin of appreciation.

THE PRINCIPLES ON LIMITATIONS OF RIGHTS

The early understanding of the Convention emphasised the importance of protecting human rights against arbitrary state interference, while also allowing the state to restrict rights when appropriate to do so. This is perfectly understandable in the context of the aftermath of the Second World War and the existence of totalitarian communist regimes in Eastern Europe. This emphasis implies a focus on the state's negative obligation not to interfere with or limit rights and consequently a focus on the criteria the state must satisfy to justify such interference or limitation. At least, this was a plausible way of conceptualising the Convention when originally drafted; as the section on 'Positive Obligations' demonstrates, the Convention must be understood more expansively today.

The Court has elaborated several principles that help it adjudicate cases on the limitation of rights. Most of the rights relevant to democracy in the Convention are so-called qualified rights, i.e. they are subject to qualification or limitation when necessary to serve a legitimate public interest. Qualified rights are distinguishable from the rights sometimes called absolute rights in that the latter are not subject to a general possibility of limitation.[24] An absolute right can only be limited, if at all, by pointing to a specific exception. Thus, a right like the prohibition on torture, inhuman or degrading treatment or punishment (article 3) is not subject to any sort of limitation: if conduct is proscribed under the terms of the article, its infliction cannot be justified. Similarly, article 2 provides for the right to life; no qualification is permitted except by reference to the terms of the article. Article 5 provides for the right to personal liberty; this cannot be limited unless the state can show that a specific exception provided for in article 5 has been satisfied.

The qualified rights are different from the absolute rights: these can be limited in order to satisfy a wide range of public interests. This is most clearly seen by examining the terms of article 8 (right to respect for private and family life) or article 10 (free expression) or article 11 (freedom of association and

---

[24] Similarly, the political rights are subject to derogation in times of national emergency under article 15; a small number of Convention rights – freedom from torture, inhuman and degrading treatment or punishment; the right to life; freedom from slavery and servitude and the principle that criminal punishments are not retrospective – are non-derogable under article 15.

assembly). Each of these articles sets out the right in broad terms but then provides a second clause which allows the right to be restricted. Take article 11 (2) as an example:

> 2. No restrictions shall be placed on the exercise of these rights other than such as are *prescribed by law* and are *necessary in a democratic society* in *the interests of* national security or public safety, for the prevention of disorder or crime, for the protection of health or morals or for the protection of the rights and freedoms of others. This Article shall not prevent the imposition of lawful restrictions on the exercise of these rights by members of the armed forces, of the police or of the administration of the State. [emphasis added]

These clauses introduce three key principles: the legality or lawfulness principle ('prescribed by law'), the legitimate aim principle ('in the interests of . . .') and the proportionality or necessity principle ('necessary in a democratic society'). These three principles are essential to understanding the Court's case law. Before discussing them in turn, we need to acknowledge that there are differences in how these principles apply.

First, even though articles 8, 9 (religion and conscience), 10 and 11 all have this same two-clause structure, the wording is somewhat different in each of them.[25] Article 10(2) for example alludes to the 'duties and responsibilities' that attach to free expression; there is no reference in the other articles to equivalent duties and responsibilities. Article 10(2) refers to 'formalities, conditions, restrictions or penalties' whereas article 11(2) uses the generic 'restrictions'. Article 11(2) includes a specific restriction for the armed forces, police and state administration, but there is no such explicit mention in article 10(2) even though any arguments in favour of specific limitations on these organisations in respect of association and assembly would also seem to apply to expression. Even the lists of legitimate public interests are different as between the articles. Article 10(2) refers to restrictions necessary to safeguard 'national security, territorial integrity or public safety' whereas article 11(2) refers to 'national security or public safety'. If the protection of territorial integrity requires and justifies limits on free expression, it is difficult to see why this does not apply to freedom of association and assembly.

Second, some of the qualified rights do not have the typical two-clause structure; article 14 (non-discrimination in the enjoyment of rights) and Protocol 1 article 3 (P1–3, the right to vote and run for elections) do not have

---

[25] The first clauses of each article also contain some divergences. Article 10(1) contains a specific saver for broadcasting rules; article 9(1) draws a distinction between freedom of conscience and religion and the manifestation of conscience and religion; only the latter can be restricted.

any sort of explicit limitations clause. This does not mean that they are absolute rights; rather, the Court has held that they are subject to implied limitations. In discussing the implied limitations in respect of these rights and especially the rights to vote and run for election, the Court has sometimes indicated that states are entitled to a wider discretion in determining the limitations on these rights or that the principles in relation to articles 8-11 do not necessarily also apply in P1–3 cases.[26] The exact difference, though, is not always clear, and even when discussing the rights to vote and run for election, the Court has often used similar language to that of the legality, legitimate aim and necessity principles.

Legitimate Aim

When it comes at least to those rights with the explicit two-clause structure, the state must be able to articulate a legitimate aim, and this legitimate aim should be one of those listed in the second clause of the relevant article. However, these clauses are broadly worded, and the Court has shown itself willing to defer to states on whether a legitimate aim is present. The Court's treatment, therefore, of the legitimate aim requirement is often brief, as the Grand Chamber has recognised.[27]

Occasionally it may happen that a state fails to adduce any aim at all; in this event the legitimate aim principle is not satisfied.[28] Or, the only conceivable aim may be a bare interest in harming someone or expressing prejudice – in that situation the Court has indicated it will be doubtful as to whether there is a legitimate aim.[29] In one article 11 case, *Navalnyy v Russia*, the Court has also said it could not discern any legitimate aim behind the decision of Russian police to detain a prominent political activist as he was walking away from a demonstration and again when he had turned up to a court hearing.[30] Indeed, in that case the Grand Chamber, unusually, found a violation of article 18 of the Convention. Article 18 prohibits states from using the possibility to restrict rights for purposes other than those prescribed in the Convention. The Grand

[26] *Zdanoka v Latvia* App no 58278/00 (2006) 45 EHRR 17 (Grand Chamber), para 115.
[27] *Merabishvili v Georgia* App no 72508/13 (Grand Chamber, 28 November 2017), para 297.
[28] This is unusual but has occurred: *Beian v Romania* App no 30658/05 (6 December 2007).
[29] In cases involving a prohibition on gay men and women serving in the armed forces, the Court indicated that to the extent the prohibition was based on prejudice, this could not be considered a legitimate aim, though the protection of military efficiency could be a legitimate aim: *Lustig-Prean v United Kingdom* App nos 31417/96 and 32377/96 (1999) 29 EHRR 548, para 90.
[30] *Navalnyy v Russia* App no 29580/12 and four others (Grand Chamber, 15 November 2018), paras 124–126.

Chamber concluded that the state authorities had been interfering with the applicant's article 5 and article 11 rights and targeting him as an opposition politician; such a purpose was to 'suppress that political pluralism which forms part of "effective political democracy" governed by the "rule of law"'.[31]

Apart from very rare instances, the Court is usually willing to accept that the state is pursuing one of the legitimate aims listed in the second clause, even if it has to give a broad meaning to the aim, or show some deference to the judgement of the state authorities. Looking at those rights which do not have the explicit two-clause structure then, it might sometimes be said that the category of legitimate aims extends beyond those listed in the ones with two clauses. In relation to P1-3, it may be legitimate to plead the need for a workable electoral system, though this aim does not appear explicitly anywhere in the Convention. This might imply that there is greater scope to limit these rights; in practice, though, the breadth and flexibility of the limitation clauses are such that the importance of this should not be exaggerated.

Legality or Lawfulness

The second criterion – that of legality or lawfulness – is much more demanding than the legitimate aim criterion. This requires legal authority for interference with a right. The Court is flexible on one important point; as part of the autonomous meaning approach, it does not insist that this legal authority be a statute. The legal authority might be found in secondary legislation, administrative regulations or (importantly for the common law jurisdictions) case law. While the Court is flexible on this point, it nevertheless insists that any legal authority have certain qualities, and this makes for a more rigorous principle that the legitimate aim one. In this sense, there is a Convention autonomous meaning of legality or lawfulness.

The legal authority must be accessible, and must allow for predictability and be reasonably detailed. Furthermore, some of the case law indicates the legal authority must contain appropriate safeguards (this is also relevant to the proportionality point).

Proportionality; or Necessity in a Democratic Society

The proportionality or necessity principle is potentially the most demanding of the three elements. While the Convention uses the term 'necessary', this

---

[31] *Navalnyy v Russia*, para 175.

does not mean literally that the limitation or restriction must be the only measure available to the state.

It is frequently subdivided into more specific questions: Does the restriction rationally relate to the legitimate aim? Does it correspond to a pressing social need? Is there a less restrictive means for achieving the same legitimate aim? Are there adequate safeguards? Does the restriction go too far and deny the essence of the right?

These are probing and often extremely useful questions to bear in mind when examining any restriction on a right. More important perhaps is to remember that the proportionality principle can be applied with varying levels of strictness. In particular, to reiterate the point, the language of 'necessity' can be misleading if it implies a restriction must be the least restrictive measure available. Whilst there are circumstances where the Court may insist on a showing of strict necessity, there are other cases where this is not so.

The text of the Convention itself supports this sliding scale. Thus, article 2 sets out the right to life but then indicates that force can be used provided that it is 'absolutely necessary'. Similarly, article 15 on derogations in times of public emergencies insists that measures derogating from Convention obligations must be 'strictly required by the exigencies of the situation.' Both these clauses envisage a strict version of necessity. At the other end of the scale is P1–1 on the right to property, which envisages 'the right of a State to enforce such laws as it deems necessary to control the use of property in accordance with the general interest'. This suggests a much looser requirement. Somewhere in between are the qualified rights such as free expression or the right to vote. And here the Court has sometimes used language which indicates that proportionality applies more strictly in relation to article 10 and 11 than P1–3. When it comes to the rights to vote and run for election, the Court has arguably applied a looser notion of proportionality than that found in the articles 8–11 case law.[32]

The variable nature of proportionality is not just between different articles but may also apply in respect of different situations engaging the same right. Even within the right to free expression, for instance, the Court is more demanding in political expression cases than in, say, artistic or commercial expression cases. At the lowest end of the scale are expressions endangering

---

[32] At the least, there is some inconsistency: thus proportionality is applied with different levels of scrutiny in the right to run for election cases of *Zdanoka v Latvia* App no 58278/00 (2006) 45 EHRR 17 (Grand Chamber) and *Ādamsons v Latvia* App no 3669/03 (24 June 2008); again the Court has adopted varying approaches to right to vote until the Grand Chamber judgment in *Scoppola v Italy (No 3)* App no 126/05 (Grand Chamber, 22 May 2012).

Positive Obligations 75

the values of the Convention, e.g. racist or other forms of hate speech, sectarian speech, Holocaust denial, etc.[33]

The notion of necessity is qualified by the phrase 'in a democratic society'. The Court does not simply treat this phrase as an empty formality, but rather gives it meaning. It identifies certain key values of a democratic society. These are 'pluralism, tolerance and broadmindedness'.[34] These values play a prominent role in the articles 10 and 11 case law.

POSITIVE OBLIGATIONS

The previous section has focused on the idea of the state limiting (i.e. interfering with) rights and the criteria the Court uses to assess the legitimacy of such interferences. It is now well established that the Convention is not just concerned with prohibiting state interference with rights: in some cases, it also requires state action to realise rights; this is the celebrated notion of 'positive obligations'.[35]

It is likely that the Convention drafters were focused on the dangers posed by state interference with rights; they were, after all, concerned with the threat posed by totalitarian states. Nevertheless, as we have seen, the interpretation of the Convention can evolve and is not limited to the original intention of the drafters. Starting in two seminal cases in the late 1970s (*Airey v Ireland; Marckx v Belgium*[36]), the Court has developed a hydra like doctrine of positive obligations.

Several justifications have been offered for the positive obligations doctrine. First, several articles of the Convention explicitly include positive obligations, demonstrating their consistency with the Convention system. Most notably article 3 of Protocol 1 (P1–3) is expressed purely as an obligation rather than a right: it imposes an obligation on the state to hold free and fair elections. P1–3 is not the only example; article 2(1) says that everyone's life 'shall be protected by law'; article 5(5) provides a right to compensation for those detained in breach of article 5; article 6(3)(c) provides for legal assistance in criminal cases where the interests of justice require it, and article 13 provides a right to a

---

[33] In some instances, such speech may trigger the abuse of rights clause in article 17.

[34] *Vereinigung demokratischer Soldaten Österreichs and Gubi v Austria* App no 15153/89 (1995) 20 EHRR 26, para 36.

[35] Alasdair Mowbray, *The Development of Positive Obligations under the European Convention on Human Rights by the European Court of Human Rights* (Hart 2004); Brice Dickson, 'Special Issue on Positive Obligations and the European Court of Human Rights' (2010) 61 (3) Northern Ireland Legal Quarterly.

[36] *Airey v Ireland; Marckx v Belgium.*

76   *European Principles of Interpretation and Application*

remedy where Convention rights have been violated. Other provisions may also imply positive obligations on the state; article 12 presupposes the state will have laws on marriage, for example.

In addition to these specific examples, the nature of the obligation in article 1 of the convention, at least in the English-language version, implies a wider obligation than non-interference on the part of the state. Article 1 says that the state shall 'secure to everyone within their jurisdiction the rights and freedoms in the Convention'. The use of the word 'secure' implies more than 'not interfere with', though admittedly the French text uses the term 'reconnaissent' (recognise), which is perhaps not as strong as the English term.

Apart from these textual arguments, the key argument in favour of positive obligations is the need to give the Convention an effective interpretation. According to the Court, contemporary conditions mean that the effective enjoyment of rights will sometimes require state action in various forms. In *Airey*, the state action envisaged was the provision of civil legal aid or some other mechanism to enable the applicant to vindicate her article 8 and article 6 rights. In *Marckx*, the state was obliged to reform its legal code to recognise the family relationships of a child, including a child born outside of marriage.[37]

These two early cases demonstrate that the doctrine of positive obligations can give rise to different implications. Since 1979, the Court has recognised several different types of positive obligation. It has recognised, for example, duties to investigate alleged violations of articles 2, 3, 4[38] and 14. It has recognised a duty on states to protect persons from violations of their rights by other private persons. Sometimes this duty to protect implies changes in the law;[39] but it can also require the state to take operational measures to protect rights.[40] Positive obligations may also include duties to provide information,[41] or even to provide resources as in the original case of *Airey*.[42]

The doctrine of positive obligations has two significant implications for the role of the Convention and Court in protecting human rights. First, the doctrine may entail the Convention giving indirect protection to social and

---

[37] *Marckx*, para 31.
[38] *Rantsev v Cyprus and Russia* App no 25965/04 (2010) 51 EHRR 1.
[39] *X and Y v Netherlands* App no 8978/80 (1985) 8 EHRR 235.
[40] This is the Osman duty: *Osman v United Kingdom* App no 23452/94 (1999) 29 EHRR 245 (Grand Chamber).
[41] *Guerra v Italy* App no 14967/89 (1998) 26 EHRR 357.
[42] For a rare example of a failure to provide civil legal assistance giving rise to a convention violation, see *Steel and Morris v United Kingdom* App no 68416/01 (2005) 41 EHRR 22.

Positive Obligations

economic interests or rights. The Court itself acknowledged this in the *Airey* case when it rejected Ireland's argument that the Court was straying illegitimately into the sphere of social and economic rights:

> the mere fact that an interpretation of the Convention may extend into the sphere of social and economic rights should not be a decisive factor against such an interpretation; there is no water-tight division separating that sphere from the field covered by the Convention.[43]

The second implication is that the Convention has an indirect horizontal effect, that is to say it offers protections not just against the state but also (indirectly) against private individuals. This protection is indirect because the Convention achieves this effect by imposing obligations on state. Still, this has an important effect in private law relationships, as seen in *Marckx* and more recent cases dealing with rights in the workplace[44] and domestic violence.[45]

This extension of the Convention into horizontal legal relationships is also a function of the fact that courts are seen as agents of the state and so court judgments even in private law matters can engage the state's responsibility under the Convention.[46] This aspect of the Convention is quite important to how the Convention relates to political democracy, as it enables the Court to set out standards in defamation and similar cases involving political figures or topics (see Chapter 4).

While this chapter's presentation has first examined the principles governing the limitation of rights before looking at the doctrine of positive obligations, it needs to be borne in mind that the Court does not draw a sharp distinction between these. Rather, it not infrequently states that the same principles apply in both sorts of case and that they stem from the basic idea of the Convention, the need to find a fair balance between the interests of the individual and the interests of the community. This often makes it unnecessary to decide whether a case involves a negative obligation or a positive obligation.[47]

---

[43] *Airey v Ireland*, para 26.

[44] *Fuentes Bobo v Spain* App no 39293/98 (2001) 31 EHRR 50.

[45] *Opuz v Turkey* App no 33401/02 (2010) 50 EHRR 28.

[46] *Sunday Times v United Kingdom* App no 6538/74 (1979) 2 EHRR 245.

[47] *Fuentes Bobo v Spain* App no 39293/98 (2001) 31 EHRR 50. On the other hand, in the Animal Defenders International case, one of the dissents warned that discussions of positive obligations could downplay the primary negative obligation in free expression cases: joint dissent of Ziemele, Sajó, Kalaydjieva, Vučinič, and De Gaetano para 12, *Animal Defenders International v United Kingdom* App no 48876/08 (2013) 57 EHRR 21 (Grand Chamber).

THE MARGIN OF APPRECIATION

There is a final important principle and one which is not so clearly signalled in the text of the articles: the 'margin of appreciation' principle. Although not found in the current text of the Convention, the margin of appreciation doctrine has some origin in the debates on the drafting of the Convention; during the debates, Teitgen spoke of a 'liberté d'appreciation' for the states in deciding how to regulate the rights.[48]

Article 1 of the Convention provides some textual basis for this when it puts the obligation on the High Contracting parties (i.e. the states) to 'secure to everyone within their jurisdiction' the Convention rights. The Court has indicated that this means the primary obligation to uphold rights is on states, not the Court; the Court's role is subsidiary though nevertheless important. This principle (along with that of subsidiarity) will be explicitly included in the Preamble to the Convention once Protocol 15 comes into force.[49]

The principle is based on the notion that it is the states' responsibility to protect the rights in the Convention; the Court merely exercises a supervisory role. In exercising that supervisory role, the Court remembers that it is a supranational court and that there are certain questions best decided by the relevant domestic authorities. This principle tends to appear most frequently in certain types of cases. Thus, in national security contexts, the Court often observes that the state authorities are best placed to decide if there is a threat to the life of the nation under article 15. When faced with cases involving planning decisions, the Court again says that these are issues where the local authorities are in a better position to assess competing needs. The margin of appreciation is also frequently mentioned in relation to public morality cases and issues raised by new technologies. These latter types of cases are typically though not necessarily ones where there is considerable divergence of opinion among the states and the Court does not believe there are appropriate European standards. Finally, and most directly relevant to us, the margin of

---

[48] A. W. Brian Simpson, *Human Rights and the End of Empire: Britain and the Genesis of the European Convention* (Oxford University Press 2001), 676.

[49] Protocol 15 will amend the Preamble to include the recital: 'Affirming that the High Contracting Parties, in accordance with the principle of subsidiarity, have the primary responsibility to secure the rights and freedoms defined in this Convention and the Protocols thereto, and that in doing so they enjoy a margin of appreciation, subject to the supervisory jurisdiction of the European Court of Human Rights established by this Convention.' Protocol 15 amending the Convention for the Protection of Human Rights and Fundamental Freedoms, Strasbourg, 24 June 2013, CETS 213.

appreciation is considered especially important in the type of political system chosen by each state.

The margin of appreciation is a controversial doctrine, and its implications should not be taken for granted. First, while there is a margin of appreciation in these types of cases, this does not mean the Court abandons its supervisory role; even in cases involving national security or public morality, the Court will not infrequently find that the state has exceeded its margin of appreciation.[50]

Second, the margin of appreciation (like much of the Court's jurisprudence of course) can evolve, and a practice deemed to be within the margin of appreciation may be judged to be outside it a few years later. This happened in relation to sexual orientation cases and the gender reassignment case law. Sometimes the 'evolution' of the margin of appreciation may be even more dramatic. Two cases from France demonstrate this vividly; both concerned adoption by a gay or lesbian applicant. In both cases, the applicant was denied prior authorisation to adopt a child. In the 2002 case in Strasbourg, the Court found this within the margin of appreciation;[51] in a 2008 case, this denial was found to be a breach of the Convention, with no mention made of any margin of appreciation.[52]

Third, the margin of appreciation is a controversial and somewhat slippery concept; while it rightly pays attention to legitimate concerns about the Court's competence and the respective competence and legitimacy of other institutions, it is difficult to avoid the conclusion that the Court deploys the term in a conclusory way. Thus, if the Court thinks there is a violation, it says the state has acted outside the margin, and if the Court thinks there is no violation it says the state has acted within the margin. But in this sort of situation, the 'margin of appreciation' language adds nothing and perhaps even worse serves to obfuscate any reasoning.

Fourth, the increased references to the concept of subsidiarity, may suggest new approaches to the margin of appreciation. The Council of Europe has indicated that the new reference to subsidiarity does not weaken human rights protection but rather highlights the states' responsibilities in this area.[53] Brems argues that 'positive' subsidiarity might require the Court to give more guidance to states or even to restrict the marign of appreciation.[54]

---

[50] *A v United Kingdom* App no 3455/05 (2009) 49 EHRR 29 (Grand Chamber).

[51] *Fretté v France* App no 36515/97 (2004) 38 EHRR 21.

[52] *EB v France* App no 43546/02 (2008) 47 EHRR 21.

[53] Council of Europe, *Copenhagen Declaration* (2018) available at <https://www.echr.coe.int/Documents/Copenhagen_Declaration_ENG.pdf>, accessed 16 June 2020, para 10.

[54] Eva Brems, 'Positive Subsidiarity and Its Implications for the Margin of Appreciation Doctrine' (2019) 37 (3) Netherlands Quarterly of Human Rights 210.

CONVENTION PRINCIPLES AND DEMOCRACY

Ensuing chapters will examine how the Court's interpretations of different rights promote particular conceptions of democracy – liberal, substantive, deliberative and so forth. Before moving on to that discussion, however, the Court's approach to the principles discussed in this chapter may also say something about ideas of democracy.

The use of these principles implicates questions of democracy in several ways; frequently this resolves itself into the classic questions of the legitimacy of judges reviewing decisions by politically accountable branches of government. These debates have been extensively explored particularly in national constitutional contexts.[55] In the Strasbourg context, we are dealing with an international court established by treaty agreed to by sovereign states. This international law context introduces a number of complicating factors in drawing on national constitutional debates about the legitimacy of constitutional review. For starters, we have to note that the European Court judges are not unelected as is sometimes said. Rather, the Parliamentary Assembly elects judges from short lists compiled by the national governments. Indeed, at one time, judges could be re-elected.[56] Second, the Court is necessarily a multinational court, representing all of the different legal traditions in the Council of Europe.

Third, and perhaps most importantly, the national law dichotomy between courts and democratically elected politicians is not necessarily perfectly analogous to the tension in the Strasbourg system between the Court and sovereign states. That is to say, we should not assume that the will of the sovereign state is necessarily identical to the expression of the democratic will.[57] Certain national decisions (democratically adopted legislation, measures approved by referenda) presumably bear the democratic imprimatur. However, in other cases, the state measure under review may simply be an administrative decision or a court decision or a piece of secondary legislation. In these cases, it is not so easy to accuse the Court of illegitimately interfering with the democratic will. It may even be the case that the measure under review is a statute adopted by an undemocratic legislature; again, in this situation it is not at all

---

[55] See for contrasting views the writings of Waldron and Dworkin: Jeremy Waldron, *Law and Disagreement* (Oxford University Press 2001); Ronald Dworkin, 'The Moral Reading and the Majoritarian Premise' in Ronald Dworkin (ed) *Freedom's Law* (Harvard University Press 1996).

[56] Protocol 11 provided for a six-year renewable term of office; Protocol 14 establishes a nine-year non-renewable term.

[57] Conor Gearty, 'Democracy and Human Rights in the European Court of Human Rights: A Critical Appraisal' (2000) 51 (3) Northern Ireland Legal Quarterly 381.

Convention Principles and Democracy

obvious that the Court's role is inimical to democracy.[58] Having made these qualifications, it should not be thought that the issue of how the Court's role relates to democratic practices is an uncontentious one.

Rather, indeed, the decisions made by the Court sometimes themselves show a tendency to reflect a tension between the different elements of the term *liberal democracy*. A choice for the evolving effective and autonomous interpretation of the Convention lays stress upon the *liberal* conception of democracy. Similarly, when the Court decides to adopt a strict notion of proportionality, and to subject state decisions to very close scrutiny, this again suggests an emphasis on the liberal dimension of the Convention. Whilst the use of an effective evolving and autonomous interpretive approach may sometimes lead the Court to conclusions not self-evidently justified by the text of the Convention, nevertheless there is strong support in both the history and text of the Convention for such an approach. In the aftermath of the Second World War, the drafters were aware that democratic legislatures were far from infallible. Rather, democratic legislatures might illegitimately trample on individual rights; in the most extreme circumstances the drafters were aware that democratic institutions might be subverted. This is precisely why the drafters adopted a Convention that included an enumeration of rights but more significantly a system of guarantee including a Court.

It would have been possible for the Court, or rather its judges, to adopt a more deferential attitude, to insist, for instance, on criticising only the clearest and most unambiguous breaches of the Convention. It would have been feasible to argue that the Convention was an agreement among sovereign states and so the Court should not interpret it to impose obligations beyond those contemplated by the sovereign states. This position was suggested, often with detailed argumentation, by the UK judge on the Court, Sir Gerald Fitzmaurice, in the 1970s; Sir Gerald had previously served as the senior judge on the International Court of Justice. As we saw above, this approach was rejected in decisions such as *Golder*.

However, the Court not infrequently pays tribute to this more deferential approach, which may sometimes mean it lays more emphasis upon the democratic element of liberal democracy, or at least indicate where it understands are the limits of the liberal dimension. The Court does not always embrace the principles of effective evolving and autonomous interpretation (witness the right-to-marry case); it frequently applies very deferential notions of legitimacy; it sometimes applies deferential notions of legality or

---

[58] This, for instance, is the situation when the Court finds that a nineteenth-century statute violates the rights of gay men, such as in *Norris v Ireland* App no 10581/83 (1991) 13 EHRR 186.

European Principles of Interpretation and Application

proportionality; and of course, there is the margin of appreciation doctrine. In some cases – indeed, many cases – the Court defers to the national authorities. Deference is frequently to the national authorities, but this sometimes overlaps with respect for democratic decisions.

The areas where the Court shows most deference – moral questions, national security, social and economic questions – suggest the dimensions of the liberal democracy envisaged by the Court. Indeed, the deference shown by the Court on social and economic matters indicates a distinctively liberal conception of democracy which focuses on traditional liberal rights and leaves questions of economic governance to the political process; on this view states may pursue free market or social democratic or socialist policies. It should be noted though there are some limits here; in particular, there is a right to property which presumably imposes some limits on steps to abolish private property. The liberal democracy envisaged by the Court does not require economic democracy, for instance (though it is probably compatible with it).

While the tendency to show some deference in social and economic cases reinforces the distinctively liberal nature of the Convention (and specifically in the protection of private property), the other areas where the Court speaks of a margin of appreciation suggest there are limits to the liberalism of the Court. Thus, in cases involving public morality, the court's judgments sometimes imply that a more substantive conception of democracy is compatible with the Convention. The relatively frequent recourse to the margin of appreciation in national security cases suggests a conception of democracy that is potentially illiberal.

Deliberative Democracy?

While much of the case law could be analysed in terms of whether the cases contribute to a liberal conception of democracy, or are compatible with a substantive (e.g. communitarian) conception of democracy, there is also another important aspect to the limitation principles. Arguably they contribute to a more deliberative conception of democracy.

Deliberative democracy, let us recall, requires that free and equal citizens debate issues with a view to finding a principled agreement. In this process, they exchange reasons and seek to rely on publicly available reasons and not prejudice, intolerance or violence, or indeed simple numbers. The Court's reasoning process arguably enhances the deliberative component of democracy. The systematic requirement that states explain their legitimate aim, identify the legal basis for a restriction and explain why it is necessary contribute directly to a deliberative system. States must offer reasonably detailed,

Conclusion

structured reasons. In doing so they must not rely on prejudice but must be able to articulate a legitimate aim, i.e. one that could in principle be accepted by anyone. The state must identify a legal basis, which avoids secret or incomprehensible regulations. Finally, the necessity test probes how well tailored a restriction is in order to satisfy a legitimate aim. The role of the margin of appreciation and the possibility to limit rights also fits well within a deliberative theory of democracy and rights: Habermas argues that 'popular sovereignty and human rights go hand in hand'; so, while constituent authorities and legislators have to respect a set of rights, they also play a role in democratically articulating more specific contents of those rights in concrete settings.[59]

CONCLUSION

This chapter has provided a brief but necessary introduction to the key institutions and principles which we will encounter in the analysis of the Court's jurisprudence on democratic rights in modern Europe. It has also presented briefly some of the other international institutions and standards in the area of the right to democracy, so that we can refer where appropriate to them later in order to better understand the Court's approach. The chapter discussed how the Court's approach to interpretation and the application of principles such as legitimacy, legality and proportionality may support varying models of democracy. It is time to consider these in more detail, and so we now turn to the classic example of a liberal and political right – free expression.

[59] Jürgen Habermas, *Between Facts and Norms* (MIT Press 1996), 125–127.

4

Freedom of Expression

This chapter considers the right to freedom of expression and what the European Court of Human Rights' jurisprudence in this area tells us about the type of political democracy envisaged by the ECHR. The chapter introduces the general approach that the Court takes to free expression before indicating examples where the Court's position may seem to support a more specifically liberal democratic, substantive or deliberative conception of democracy. The case law on political advertising highlights an important Grand Chamber judgment that demonstrates the potential for the Convention to support a deliberative democratic model, while recent cases also suggest a greater concern with access to state-held information.

GENERAL APPROACH

Article 10 contains the guarantee on freedom of expression in the Convention. It is in two paragraphs and in this regard exemplifies the idea of a qualified right – the first paragraph announces the right while the second envisages that it can be limited:

1. Everyone has the right to freedom of expression. This right shall include freedom to hold opinions and to receive and impart information and ideas without interference by public authority and regardless of frontiers. This Article shall not prevent States from requiring the licensing of broadcasting, television or cinema enterprises.
2. The exercise of these freedoms, since it carries with it duties and responsibilities, may be subject to such formalities, conditions, restrictions or penalties as are prescribed by law and are necessary in a democratic society, in the interests of national security, territorial integrity or public safety, for the prevention of disorder or crime, for the

General Approach

protection of health or morals, for the protection of the reputation or rights of others, for preventing the disclosure of information received in confidence, or for maintaining the authority and impartiality of the judiciary.

While article 10 is a paradigmatic example of a qualified right, resembling articles 9 and 11 in this regard, it also contains some distinctive features. The first paragraph includes a specific provision on broadcasting, television and cinema enterprise which has given rise to some debate about the doctrinally most logical way of considering the regulation of these media. The first paragraph also includes the right to receive and impart information, but the Court has shied away from interpreting this as a right of general access to information. Much of the right to information cases tend to fall under article 8 rather than article 10.

The second paragraph, unusually, refers to the 'duties and responsibilities' that accompany the right to free expression. It also includes a number of legitimate aims that are not found elsewhere in the Convention, i.e. relating to the protection of confidence and the protection of the authority of the judiciary; these relate to particular ways in which free expression may hamper other public values.

Generally, the Court has taken an expansive approach to what is included as expression under the first paragraph. Thus, it includes artistic expression,[1] symbolic expression and protest[2] as well as written and verbal communication. Animal rights and environmental activists who physically prevent or impede hunters and construction crews are engaged in expressive activity.[3] A public display of dirty clothes outside the Hungarian parliament similarly constitutes an exercise of expression.[4] A feminist group chartering a ship and conducting seminars on it to protest Portugal's restrictive abortion laws is an example of symbolic expression.[5] A wide range of expressive activities are covered by article 10. Nevertheless, not all activities that have an expressive content necessarily bring the case within the ambit of article 10. The Court has frequently held in cases involving the German authorities denying access to employment or promotion in the public service, that the cases did not involve

[1] *Müller v Switzerland* App no 10737/84 (1991) 13 EHRR 212, para 27.
[2] *Taranenko v Russia* App no 19554/05 (15 May 2014), para 71; *Açık and Others v Turkey* App no 31451/03 (13 January 2009).
[3] *Steel v United Kingdom* App no 24838/94 (1999) 28 EHRR 603 para 92; also *Hashman and Harrup v United Kingdom* App no 25594/94 (2000) 30 EHRR 241.
[4] *Tatár and Fáber v Hungary* App nos 26005/08 and 26160/08 (2014) 59 EHRR 8.
[5] *Women on Waves v Portugal* App no 31276/05 (3 February 2009).

86   *Freedom of Expression*

free expression even though the reason for the denial was related to the expression and associations of the person affected.[6] As discussed later, certain extreme forms of odious expression may also fall outside of article 10's scope due to the abuse of rights clause in article 17.

While the Court is generally inclusive in its approach to the first paragraph, it does not accord the same weight to all forms of expression. There is a hierarchy in the Court's approach, which accords primacy to political expression and expression on matters of public interest. Rather less importance is attached to artistic expression, at least in much of the older jurisprudence. Commercial expression is less favoured again, while the least important category of expression includes racist, sectarian, homophobic or similar language.

The doctrine of positive obligations is increasingly important in relation to free expression. This includes significantly the possibility for free expression to be relevant in private or horizontal relationships, and not just in vertical relations between public authorities and individuals. Thus, an individual can invoke free expression rights in the workplace against the state to argue that the state needs to protect the employee from an employer's violations of rights.[7] Even aside from the doctrine of positive obligations, the Convention has an impact in what might look like private law disputes, as judicial action in defamation, breach of privacy or confidence, or contempt of court cases,[8] will trigger the application of the Convention.

If expression has been interfered with, the Court examines the interference using the familiar tripartite structure: Is the interference prescribed by law? Is it for a legitimate aim? Is it necessary in a democratic society? It is the inquiry under the last limb of the test that is most significant; the question of a legitimate aim is usually straightforward (almost invariably there is a legitimate aim). The requirement prescribed by law has given rise to some interesting case law on the Convention's autonomous notion of legality. The Court requires that the law be 'foreseeable' but also recognises that the law must avoid 'excessive rigidity'; in this context it regards terms such as 'obscenity' as

---

[6]   David Harris, Ed Bates, Michael O'Boyle, Colin Warbrick and Carla Buckley, *Law of the European Convention on Human Rights* (4th edn, Oxford University Press 2018) 595, discussing *Glasenapp v Germany* App no 9228/80 (1986) 9 EHRR 25, *Kosiek v Germany* App no 9704/82 (1986) 9 EHRR 328, *Otto v Germany* App no 27574/02 (24 November 2005).

[7]   *Fuentes Bobo v Spain* App no 39293/98 (2001) 31 EHRR 50; this aspect of the right is by no means unlimited, and the Court has accepted restrictions where it was exercised in the form of a cartoon depicting fellow employees and a manager having oral sex: *Palomo Sanchez v Spain* App nos 28955/06, 28957/06, 28959/06 and 28964/06 (2012) 54 EHRR 24 (Grand Chamber).

[8]   *Sunday Times v United Kingdom* App no 6538/74 (1979) 2 EHRR 245.

satisfying the foreseeability criterion, especially where there is relevant case law that clarifies the meaning.[9]

THE IMPORTANCE OF FREE EXPRESSION

Freedom of expression is frequently cited as one of the most important of fundamental rights, even being described as 'iconic',[10] and certainly in US jurisprudence it is treated as a preferred freedom, the freedom essential to secure all others.

Numerous courts and philosophers identify a variety of frequently compatible reasons for assigning importance to free expression. Often the chief purpose is that it is seen as essential to any system of political democracy; democracy cannot exist without individuals and associations being able to express their feelings, opinions, judgements; they need to be able to debate, deliberate and protest in any system of democracy. The argument from democracy is not the only argument, though. Other oft-cited ones are that free expression is essential, a good in itself, as it is central to the idea of individual autonomy, which requires self-expression, the possibility to communicate, express feelings and emotions, to engage in artistic endeavour. A third argument is usually credited to John Stuart Mill, that free expression is essential for the pursuit of truth. This is tied up with the US concept of a 'marketplace of ideas', that everyone must be freely able to participate in such a marketplace, arguing or accepting what they will, and this is the best process for arriving at some reliable conception of the truth. Some argue for free expression on the pragmatic grounds that no one, and certainly no government, can be trusted with the power to censure.[11]

Within the European Convention system, the Court frequently gives pride of place to the political argument for free expression, though the other reasons also appear. The landmark *Handyside* judgment emphasises the role of freedom of expression in a democratic society, in an oft-cited passage:

> The Court's supervisory functions oblige it to pay the utmost attention to the principles characterising a 'democratic society'. Freedom of expression

---

[9] *Müller v Switzerland* App no 10737/84 (1991) 13 EHRR 212 para 29.

[10] Noel Whitty, Therese Murphy and Stephen Livingstone, *Civil Liberties Law: The Human Rights Act Era* (Butterworths 2001) 280.

[11] This last point is encapsulated in the joint dissenting opinion of Judges Palm, Pekkanen and Makarczyk in *Otto-Preminger-Institut v Austria* App no 13470/87 (1994) 19 EHRR 34, when they argue that the Court should not leave it to states to decide whether any particular act of expression contributes to progress, as this would depend entirely on what the state thought was 'progress'.

88 Freedom of Expression

constitutes one of the essential foundations of such a society, one of the basic conditions for its progress and for the development of every man. Subject to paragraph 2 of Article 10 (art. 10-2), it is applicable not only to 'information' or 'ideas' that are favourably received or regarded as inoffensive or as a matter of indifference, but also to those that offend, shock or disturb the State or any sector of the population. Such are the demands of that pluralism, tolerance and broadmindedness without which there is no 'democratic society'. This means, amongst other things, that every 'formality', 'condition', 'restriction' or 'penalty' imposed in this sphere must be proportionate to the legitimate aim pursued.[12]

This refers to the political argument for free expression, but also the argument that it is important for each individual's development or 'self-fulfilment'. Following this strong statement, the Court also alludes to the obligations – the 'duties and responsibilities' of persons exercising their free expression rights. Subsequent cases frequently refer back to this language in Handyside but often add that 'Freedom of expression, as enshrined in article 10 (art. 10), is subject to a number of exceptions which, however, must be narrowly interpreted and the necessity for any restrictions must be convincingly established'[13] or, more specifically, that the Court requires 'very strong reasons for justifying restrictions on political debate'.[14]

The Handyside case is also important for introducing the notion of a margin of appreciation in article 10 jurisprudence. The Court observed that the national authorities must make the 'initial assessment' as to the necessity for limiting the exercise of free expression.[15] However, this is not unlimited: the 'domestic margin of appreciation thus goes hand in hand with a European supervision.'[16]

The Court has also emphasised that this right is closely linked with the article 11 right of assembly and association, and so the values underpinning free expression frequently appear in article 11 case law, and vice versa. The Court observes that it interprets article 11 in the light of article 10[17] and also article 10 in the light of article 11.[18]

---

[12] Handyside v United Kingdom (Little Red Schoolbook case) App no 5493/72 (1979) 1 EHRR 737, para 49.
[13] Sunday Times v United Kingdom No 2 App no 13166/87 (1991) 14 EHRR 229, para 50; similar language is also seen in Zana v Turkey App no 69/1996/688/880 (1997) 27 EHRR 667, para 51.
[14] Taranenko v Russia, para 77.
[15] Handyside, para 48.
[16] Handyside, para 49.
[17] Nemtsov v Russia App no 1774/11 (31 July 2014) para 62.
[18] Taranenko v Russia App no 19554/05 (15 May 2014), paras 69–79.

LIBERAL DEMOCRACY

A dominant theme in much of the free expression literature is the commitment to a liberal democratic conception of free expression. The importance of this – in particular in relation to political expression – has frequently been a hallmark of the Court's jurisprudence. The liberal democratic commitment makes sense also in the historic context of the Convention's drafting, as a rejection both of the fascist regimes and of the contemporary communist dictatorships.

The *Lingens* case highlights the liberal democratic argument for freedom of expression and especially freedom of the press.[19] The case emerged in the context of a political controversy in Austria: it involved a lively debate in Austria on dealing with its legacy from the Second World War era; the case arose during political negotiations about the formation of a coalition government; furthermore, it concerned an effort by no less than the Federal Chancellor to stifle debate by means of the law of defamation. The applicant, Lingens, had been sued by the Austrian Chancellor Kreisky for defamation. Lingens had criticised the Chancellor for his attitude to politicians associated with Austria's Nazi past; in the course of this Lingens used the terms 'basest opportunism', 'immoral' and 'undignified' to describe the Chancellor's conduct. According to the domestic courts, these comments were defamatory; they fined Lingens and ordered confiscation of the publications.

The European Court of Human Rights repeated the language from *Handyside* on the importance of free expression. It went on to assert the importance of a free press in imparting 'information and ideas on political issues'; this is a matter not just of the rights of the press but also the public's right to receive such information.[20] More specifically,

> Freedom of the press furthermore affords the public one of the best means of discovering and forming an opinion of the ideas and attitudes of political leaders. More generally, freedom of political debate is at the very core of the concept of a democratic society which prevails throughout the Convention.[21]

For the Court this meant that politicians – who freely choose their profession – had to accept a degree of public criticism that would not be acceptable in the case of purely private citizens.[22] This is one of the key doctrinal elements

---

[19] *Lingens v Austria* App no 9815/82 (1986) 8 EHRR 407.
[20] *Lingens*, para 41.
[21] *Lingens*, para 42.
[22] *Lingens*, para 42.

introduced by the Court in this case. The Court also drew attention to the need to understand the comments in the wider context of a 'post-election political controversy'[23] and crucially stressed that the comments in question were value judgements and so not susceptible to being proved true. As Austrian law required Lingens to prove the truth of these statements – something impossible in the case of value judgements – the Court found a violation of article 10.[24] *Lingens* thus establishes the importance of the free press in a democratic society, and more specifically develops a number of doctrinal tools to protect the press in a democratic society. Subsequent cases develop the important role of the press as a 'watchdog' in a democratic society.[25]

Lingens demonstrates the Court's willingness to defend political expression in the context of a defamation case. Other private law remedies have the potential to curtail political expression, and so the Court has addressed these sorts of disputes in relation to privacy claims. In the course of these cases, the Court has articulated criteria in order to help balance the interest in free expression with the interest in privacy or reputation. The Court has listed these criteria in *Axel Springer AG v Germany* and *Von Hannover v Germany*, both cases concerning claims by celebrities that their privacy rights had been interfered with.[26]

These factors include: the contribution of the expression to a debate of general interest; whether the person is well known, and the subject of the report; the prior conduct of the person; method of obtaining the information and its veracity; content, form and consequences of publication; and finally the severity of the sanction.[27] The notion of a debate of general interest is a wide one – it can include sporting issues or art, but probably not marital difficulties of the head of state.[28] Also significant is whether the individual is in the public eye. This is directly related to the role of free expression in a political democracy and in particular the role of the press. It is a variable standard; politicians have to accept that they are open to criticism, but public servants to a lesser degree.[29] This does not mean, though, that politicians have no protection from objectionable expression.

---

[23] *Lingens*, para 43.
[24] *Lingens*, para 46.
[25] *Bladet Tromso and Stensaas v Norway* App no 21980/93 (2000) 29 EHRR 125, paras 59–62.
[26] *Axel Springer AG v Germany* App no 39954/08 (2012) 55 EHRR 6 and *Von Hannover v Germany* App nos 40660/08 and 60641/08 (2012) 55 EHRR 15. Reputation is considered to be an aspect of the right to respect for private life: *Axel Springer AG*, para 83.
[27] *Axel Springer*, paras 89–95.
[28] *Axel Springer*, para 90.
[29] *Pedersen and Baadsgaard v Denmark* App no 49017/99 (2004) 42 EHRR 24.

Liberal Democracy 91

While much of the case law concerns such efforts to use private law remedies such as defamation or breach of privacy to restrict political expression, the Court has also considered specific legal prohibitions on criticising the state, fundamental principles of the state or state officials. Unsurprisingly in light of the importance of political expression, the Court tends to find such rules and practices a breach of the Convention. In so holding, the Court frequently alludes to the centrality of political expression, and the principle that the

> limits of permissible criticism are wider with regard to the government than in relation to a private citizen, or even a politician. In a democratic system the actions or omissions of the government must be subject to the close scrutiny not only of the legislative and judicial authorities but also public opinion.[30]

In the Court's view, the government should refrain from using criminal law measures even when responding to unjustified criticism.

The Court requires tolerance for political expression even where it is accompanied by 'unlawful conduct involving some degree of disturbance of public order', as highlighted in *Taranenko v Russia*.[31] In this case, protesters had sought to deliver a petition critical of Russian leader Putin at a public building, but instead of complying with procedures had occupied one of the rooms of the building. The Court reprised its case law on article 10 in the context of protest, and emphasised that while the state could punish illegal activity, its discretion to do so was not unlimited. The Court emphasised that persons who took part in a demonstration but who did not themselves cause any violent or otherwise 'reprehensible' action could not be prosecuted simply for taking part in a demonstration which resulted in damage.[32] The Court also made clear that damage to property was of less concern than violence against the person in judging whether conduct was reprehensible. In *Taranenko*, the applicant had endured approximately twelve months of pre-trial detention and had been sentenced to three years imprisonment (suspended). This, the Court concluded, was a disproportionate restriction, being considerably in excess of penalties in similar cases before.[33] Several judges issued a concurring opinion

---

[30] *Okçuoğlu v Turkey* App no 24246/94 (8 July 1999), para 46. The Court found violations both of article 10 and article 6 following the conviction of the applicant before a National Security Court for the offence of spreading propaganda aimed at undermining the territorial integrity of the state.

[31] *Taranenko v Russia*, para 82.

[32] *Taranenko*, para 88.

[33] See similarly *Murat Vural v Turkey* App no 9540/07 (21 October 2014). Thirteen-year imprisonment for vandalizing a statue of Atatürk was excessive.

92 *Freedom of Expression*

in which they criticised the Russian law on public disorder as being both severe and unclear.[34]

THE LIBERAL DEMOCRATIC STATE AND NATIONAL SECURITY

Perhaps more critical are those cases where the state relies on notions of national security or the threat of violence or similar concepts to justify censorship. Where the concern is about the prevention of violence, the Court may find that the state is entitled to a wider margin of appreciation.[35] It is understandable that the Court gives greater weight to the state's arguments when the threat is one of actual violence. However, the Court, and earlier the Commission, may sometimes be too readily persuaded by the state arguments in such cases.

Earlier petitions before the Commission on admissibility in cases involving the censorship of expressions by representatives of the Sinn Fein political party in Ireland and the UK had been dismissed as manifestly ill-founded: *Purcell v Ireland, Brind v UK*.[36] The Irish legislation and implementing measures were especially severe, prohibiting any interview with any spokesperson, including elected representatives, of Sinn Féin on any topic (the broadcaster's internal guidance specified nature programmes as one example to indicate the breadth of the ban), whether of general public interest or not, at any time.

In *Purcell*, the Commission gave explicit weight to the national security argument, noting that the 'defeat of terrorism is a public interest of the first importance' and that it was difficult to find a balance between the different legitimate interests in a society threatened with political violence. The Commission characterised the Irish legislation as being about denying to the supporters of terrorism the possibility of promoting illegal activities and undermining the state. The application was dismissed as manifestly ill-founded. The decision is a particularly surprising one given the over-breadth of the Irish position. In *Brind*, the Commission was faced with a significantly narrower British restriction on Sinn Féin and other organisations; the British restriction did not apply to expression during electoral contests, nor did it apply when a member of the organisation was acting in a capacity other than that of representative of the organisation. As might be expected in light of *Purcell*, the Commission also dismissed this as manifestly ill-founded.

---

[34] Joint concurring opinion of Judges Pinto de Albuquerque, Turković and Dedov.
[35] *Okçuoğlu v Turkey* App no 24246/94 (8 July 1999), para 46.
[36] *Purcell v Ireland* App no 15404/89 (European Commission of Human Rights, 16 April 1991); *Brind v United Kingdom* (1994) 77 DR 262 (European Commission of Human Rights).

The Liberal Democratic State and National Security

At the level of the Court itself, *Zana v Turkey* is an example of this tendency to accord the state some deference in national security cases on the part of the Court.[37] The applicant was a former mayor of the largest city in south-east Turkey. While serving a prison sentence, he gave an interview in which he expressed support for the PKK (Workers' Party of Kurdistan) liberation movement; he condemned massacres but also indicated that the PKK killed women and children only by mistake. He was prosecuted for defending a serious crime. He was in prison for being a member of a different, non-violent organisation.

The Court reiterated the standard position on the importance of free expression; it then stressed, however, that the words had to be understood in the context of a violent conflict in south-east Turkey.[38] The Court considered that Zana's language had been 'contradictory and ambiguous'[39] and was 'likely to exacerbate an already explosive situation'.[40] The Court found no violation of article 10 but did find a violation of article 6.

Judge Van Dijk dissented, joined by six other judges.[41] He referred to the classic position on free expression (that it covers ideas that offend, shock and disturb) to argue that expressing support for a political organisation like the PKK by itself did not justify a restriction. He contended that the majority did not give enough importance to the applicant's history of rejecting violence. He accepted the comments were contradictory and ambiguous but suggested that the failure of the domestic courts to allow Zana to explain the comments indicated a violation of article 10 as well as article 6. He also suggested that the majority should have given more consideration to the fact that these were the words of a former mayor who was in jail. Judge Thór Vilhjálmsson also dissented; he argued the applicant's language suggested a rejection of violence and that it was difficult to see how words published in an Istanbul newspaper could enflame the situation.

Some of the later case law demonstrates a significantly greater toleration of free expression. Not long after *Zana*, the Court found a breach of article 10 in *Okçuoğlu v Turkey*.[42] The applicant had been convicted of spreading separatist propaganda on the basis of comments made in a round-table debate and subsequently published in a low circulation journal.[43] The separate opinions

---

[37] *Zana v Turkey* App no 69/1996/688/880 (1997) 27 EHRR 667.
[38] *Zana*, para 56.
[39] *Zana*, para 58.
[40] *Zana*, para 60.
[41] Judges Palm, Loizou, Mifsud Bonnici, Jambrek, Kūris and Levits.
[42] *Okçuoğlu v Turkey* App no 24246/94 (8 July 1999).
[43] *Okçuoğlu*, para 48.

94 *Freedom of Expression*

in *Okçuoğlu* suggest that the Court should give more attention to the context in which controversial expression occurs to determine whether there is a 'real and genuine risk' of violence.[44] The separate opinion of Judge Bonello goes further and endorses the use of the clear and present danger test developed in US constitutional law, replying on the thought of Justice Brandeis.

Even more strikingly, the Court's Second Chamber has affirmed the importance of protecting even extremist speech in *Nedim Şener v Turkey*.[45] The applicant in this case was a prize-winning investigative journalist; he was interrogated, held in pre-trial detention for a year and charged in connection with providing assistance to a criminal organisation. The Court indicated its doubt that it was reasonably foreseeable that the crime of belonging to or assisting a criminal organisation could include preparing and publishing a book, but focused on the proportionality inquiry.[46] Strikingly the Court indicated that free expression also included expression by illegal organisations provided the expression did not constitute incitement to commit terrorist crimes or apologies for violence: the public had a right to be informed of the different views on a situation of conflict or tension.[47] Unless there was incitement to violence, justification of terrorist acts or incitement to hatred, the state could not justify restrictions on free expression; furthermore, merely abstract advocacy of violence is protected if it is not likely to lead to violence in the actual circumstances.[48]

Much of the case law demonstrates a commitment to liberal democratic conceptions, and even demonstrates an increasingly robust approach to claims of national security since the turn of the century. Nevertheless, the Court has frequently indicated that free expression can be legitimately restricted in order to protect other interests. Sometimes, as the subsequent sections will demonstrate, this unveils a different conception of democracy, one with a more majoritarian, substantive or deliberative turn; on other occasions it may bespeak a less than rigorous commitment to free expression. The next two sections consider case law suggesting a commitment to a more substantive conception of democracy, though there are at least two different substantive conceptions: one based on a notion of a communitarian basis to a democratic

---

[44] *Okçuoğlu v Turkey* separate concurring opinion of Judges Plm, Tulkens, Fischbach, Casadevall and Greve.

[45] *Nedim Şener v Turkey* App no 38270/11 (8 July 2014). See also the companion case *Sik v Turkey* App no 53413/11 (8 July 2014) as well as the cases of *Gül and Others v Turkey* App no 4870/02 (8 June 2010), *Gözel and Özer v Turkey* App no 43453/04 (6 July 2010).

[46] *Nedim Şener*, para 102.

[47] *Nedim Şener*, para 115.

[48] *Nedim Şener*, paras 116–117.

SUBSTANTIVE CONCEPTION I

While much of the case law shows a commitment to a liberal democratic conception of free expression, there is also some that shows a commitment to a more substantive and specifically somewhat communitarian notion of democracy. This line of case law stresses more the limitations that can be placed on individual expression in order to protect certain public values where those public values represent a particular idea of social value. These are most apparent in those cases dealing with the relationship between free expression and either public morals or religion.

The Court has frequently shown a willingness to allow public morality restrictions on free expression, dating back even to the early *Handyside* decision on the 'Little Red Book' in the UK. The applicant had sought to publish a reference book for young people which included a chapter on sex. The domestic courts had convicted him of publishing obscenity, on the grounds the book contained passages that would tend to deprave or corrupt their readership. Copies of the book were seized and destroyed. A subsequent, revised version of the book was published without giving rise to any prosecution.

The Court set out some of the key principles in regards to the importance of free expression but also the margin of appreciation. Critically, the margin of appreciation was particularly relevant to a case involving public morals:

> In particular, it is not possible to find in the domestic law of the various Contracting States a uniform European conception of morals. The view taken by their respective laws of the requirements of morals varies from time to time and from place to place, especially in our era which is characterised by a rapid and far-reaching evolution of opinions on the subject. By reason of their direct and continuous contact with the vital forces of their countries, State authorities are in principle in a better position than the international judge to give an opinion on the exact content of their requirements as well as on the 'necessity' or a 'restriction' or 'penalty' intended to meet them.[49]

The European Court of Human Rights, having set out the notion of the margin of appreciation and the value of free expression in a democratic society, agreed that this decision was for the legitimate aim of protecting

---

[49] *Handyside*, para 48.

96   *Freedom of Expression*

public morality, particularly because the book was aimed at children and young people.[50] The Court also agreed that the measure had been necessary notwithstanding that there had not been any conviction in any part of the UK other than England and Wales, that the book was subsequently published without prosecution or that it freely circulated in many European countries.[51] On this last point, the Court reiterated that views differ about public morality.[52]

This early judgment demonstrates an acceptance of the notion of public morality, which may differ from country to country and thus calls for a margin of appreciation to be shown by the international court sitting in Strasbourg.

The later *Müller* case concerned artistic displays including explicit sexual depictions.[53] The display was open to the public without any charge or age limitation. Accordingly, children could wander in, and one had a violent reaction to the display. The Swiss courts found the applicants guilty of obscenity; they ordered confiscation of the painting. The Court agreed that the conviction (and also the confiscation) was necessary in order to protect public morals, having regard to the possibility anyone could enter the display and come across the crude sexually explicit depictions.[54] Judge Spielmann, in his dissent, drew attention to the need for states to have regard to the 'relativity of values' in this area, and for the need not to simply allow each local sub-state entity to exercise its own judgement.

These cases on public morality are frequently associated with the case law on blasphemy and more broadly protection of religious sensibilities, where the Court has also accepted limitation on free expression.[55] The Court refers to the obligations on persons exercising that right not to use expressions that are 'in regard to objects of veneration, gratuitously offensive to others and profane'.[56] In this analysis, there is a balance to be struck between the article 10 right to free expression and the article 9 right to freedom of religion.[57] This requires tolerance of criticism but not necessarily an abusive attack on a key

---

[50] *Handyside*, para 52.

[51] *Handyside*, paras 53–59.

[52] *Handyside*, para 57. Judge Mosler issued a separate opinion doubting the necessity of a measure which only affected 10% of the published run of the work.

[53] *Müller v Switzerland* App no 10737/84 (1991) 13 EHRR 212.

[54] *Müller*, para 36. Judge De Meyer's separate opinion particularly emphasised the facts of the case referring to this paragraph in the majority judgment.

[55] The Danish cartoon debate nearly ended up in the Court, but the case was declared inadmissible, as the applicants were not within the jurisdiction of the state: *Ben el Mahi and others v Denmark* App no 5853/06 (11 December 2006).

[56] *Klein v Slovakia* App no 72208/01 (2010) 50 EHRR 15, para 47. Also *IA v Turkey* App no 42571/98 (2007) 45 EHRR 30, para 24.

[57] *Kokkinakis v Greece* App no 14307/88 (1993) 17 EHRR 397, *Otto-Preminger-Institut v Austria* App no 13470/87 (1994) 19 EHRR 34, *IA* para 27.

religious symbol or figure.[58] According to the Court, certain portrayals can be 'provocative' and a 'malicious violation of the spirit of tolerance'.[59]

The landmark case is *Otto-Preminger-Institut v Austria*, which involved showings of a film containing satirical images of God, Christ and Christ's mother Mary; in the film they are shown asking the Devil for assistance in punishing the human race by visiting syphilis upon them.[60] The advertisement for the film alluded to the satirical depictions and noted that young people were prohibited by law from viewing it. The film was to be shown in an art-house cinema in Innsbruck. The local prosecutor, at the request of the local Catholic church, sought an order to seize the film before its first showing; this was granted. Subsequently the court ordered the film's forfeiture. The Court found that the state's actions could be justified as necessary, alluding to the high levels of Catholic observance in the locality. Strikingly the Court found this even though the applicant had sought to limit the display of the film in several significant respects: it was displayed in a particular cinema, for a fee; people under seventeen were prohibited; the nature of the film was described in its literature.[61]

This approach of the Court to the protection of religious sensibilities has the potential to offer particular protection for the adherents of the majority faith of a country (or a sub-state district[62]) or even to protect the perceived interests of a powerful group in society.[63] In *Wingrove* the Court upheld a blasphemy law that only protected the Christian faith.[64] The applicant had been denied a certificate for a short video *Visions of Ecstasy*, which figured sexual images of a saint and Christ; this denial of a certificate effectively amounted to a ban on the video. The Court found no violation and decided not to address the issue of the law only protecting one faith, as this aspect of the case was not before it.[65] More recently the Court has indicated a Muslim country can punish blasphemy against Islam. In *IA*, the Court (by a narrow majority) found that Turkey could punish the publisher of a novel which referred to the Prophet Muhammed not forbidding bestiality or necrophilia.[66]

---

[58] *Wingrove v United Kingdom* App no 17419/90 (1997) 24 EHRR 1, para 60.

[59] *Otto-Preminger-Institut v Austria* App no 13470/87 (1994) 19 EHRR 34, para 47.

[60] *Otto-Preminger-Institut v Austria*.

[61] *Otto-Preminger-Institut*, para 53.

[62] This is referred to as the idea of a 'federal margin of appreciation' in the joint dissenting opinion of Tulkens, Sajó Lazarova Trajkovska, Bianku, Power-Forde, Vučinić and Yudkivska in *Mouvement raëlien suisse v Switzerland* App no 16354/06 (2013) 56 EHRR 14, para 7.

[63] *Otto-Preminger-Institut* joint dissenting opinion of Judges Palm, Pekkanen and Makarcyzk.

[64] *Wingrove v United Kingdom* App no 17419/90 (1997) 24 EHRR 1.

[65] *Wingrove*, para 50.

[66] *IA*, para 29.

98 *Freedom of Expression*

The dissenters in this case accepted that the language was 'insulting and regrettable' but also noted that this was a novel with a relatively small circulation; furthermore, they argued a novel was likely to have less impact than a video or film. They called for the *Otto-Preminger-Institute* and *Wingrove* case law to be re-examined.[67]

While any blasphemy law has the potential to offer special protection to the majority faith in a country, what is striking about the laws in both the UK and Turkish cases was that they explicitly only protected the majority faith. It is remarkable that a human rights court would uphold restrictions on free expression that only protect the majority.

Some of the Court's case law on public morals and religion therefore offers some support for a communitarian conception of a political democracy, one which recognises that the community shares certain moral, ethical, even religious sensibilities.

It is worth sounding a note of caution; the case law in these areas (when it does not consider the issue of hate speech to be addressed in the next section) is somewhat dated. Cases like *Müller* and *Wingrove* are still good law, but these issues do not occupy much of the Court's workload. Furthermore, more recently, the Court seems to be alive to the dangers that public morals or blasphemy legislation might stifle free expression on matters of public interest. The use of vulgar or sexual language in an article criticising a public figure (an archbishop who had called for censorship of an allegedly blasphemous film and associated poster) does not amount to a pressing social need to punish the author of the article.[68]

Having expressed these words of caution, one of the most controversial of Grand Chamber judgments in relation to free expression seems to tolerate majoritarian restrictions on free expression at least in the specific context of poster campaigns on publicly regulated billboards. The case, *Mouvement raëlien suisse v Switzerland*, concerned a request by the Raelien movement to put posters up which referred to their belief in aliens and included a link to their website.[69] The Swiss authorities upheld a decision not to allow this, and a Chamber of the Court and the Grand Chamber (split 9–8) agreed that this was compatible with the Convention. The Grand Chamber judgment is somewhat brief in its main part dealing with the necessity of the restriction,

---

[67] Joint dissenting opinion of Judges Costa, Cabral Barreto and Jungwiert.

[68] *Klein v Slovakia*, paras 49, 54. See also *Giniewski v France* App no 64016/00 (2007) 45 EHRR 23.

[69] *Mouvement raëlien suisse v Switzerland* App no 16354/06 (2013) 56 EHRR 14.

and certainly does not elaborate any clear message as to the possibility for regulating such public fora.

SUBSTANTIVE CONCEPTION II

While there is much in the case law of the court that suggests a deference to communitarian conception of democracy, a somewhat different substantive conception also appears in the case law of the Court. This is a conception which is based on the notion of a democratic society that is committed to notions of pluralism tolerance and broadmindedness but which is avowedly not neutral on these issues. In this conception of democracy, expression which rejects the notions of pluralism, tolerance and broadmindedness is itself considered of lesser value in the hierarchy of the Convention.

This substantive conception is reflected in article 17 of the Convention, the abuse of rights clause. This is a clear expression of the militant democracy principle in the Convention, prohibiting the use of the Convention rights and freedoms in order to carry out acts aimed at the 'destruction' of Convention rights and freedoms or indeed their limitation beyond that permitted by the Convention.

Norwood v United Kingdom demonstrates an application of article 17.[70] The applicant, a member of the far-right British National Party (BNP), had displayed a poster in the months after 9-11 which implicated all Muslims in the attacks on New York and the Pentagon, and suggested all Muslims should be removed from Britain. He was convicted of an offence under public order legislation; this, he argued, breached his rights under article 10. In a short decision, the European Court rejected the complaint as inadmissible: the expression fell within article 17. This article sought 'to prevent individuals or groups with totalitarian aims from exploiting in their own interests' the Convention principles. The Court described the poster as an attack on a religious group, linking the group to an act of terrorism. Such a message was 'incompatible with the values proclaimed and guaranteed by the Convention, notably tolerance, social peace and non-discrimination'.

While article 17 provides a commitment to the ideal of a democratic society founded on certain values, the Court has more frequently considered this issue as part of the balancing exercise in deciding whether free expression has been limited compatibly with convention principles. Thus, the inquiry is considered in the context of article 10(2) rather than article 17. This is an

---

[70] *Norwood v United Kingdom* App no 23131/03 (2005) 40 EHRR SE 11.

approach which pays much more attention to the liberal democratic core of the Convention. Rather than ruling out any protection for the expression, it recognises it as entitled to some protection under article 10(1) and then considers whether the criteria for limiting free expression have been met. This still allows for the recognition that certain types of expression are less favoured. Examples of the type of expression the Courts sees of limited value include racist, xenophobic and sectarian expression and more recently homophobic expression.[71]

Hate speech is a controversial topic because of the conflicting values in play. Not infrequently the Court is divided on this issue, and this is seen in the first Grand Chamber ruling in this area, *Jersild v Denmark*.[72] The applicant was a journalist working for Danish TV. In this role he interviewed a number of young disaffected men who expressed blatantly unreconstructed racist remarks, praising the Ku Klux Klan and describing Africans as resembling gorillas. During the interview the applicant asked questions which challenged the young men's views, e.g. drawing attention to successful African Americans. These remarks were broadcast on Danish TV, and as a consequence the young men were successfully prosecuted. So was the applicant, for aiding and abetting in spreading such remarks. All were convicted, although the applicant repeatedly argued that his position was in no way comparable to the others: he had been trying to present a news story on a matter of general interest. Following his conviction, he took a case to Strasbourg.

The Court accepted 'the vital importance of combating racial discrimination in all its forms and manifestations'.[73] It drew attention to the UN Convention on the Elimination of All Forms of Racial Discrimination (CERD).[74] Article 4 CERD contains a strong condemnation of racist propaganda and requires states to take steps to combat such propaganda; in particular, having due regard to a list of principles that includes freedom of expression, states

> shall declare an offence punishable by law all dissemination of ideas based on racial superiority or hatred, incitement to racial discrimination, as well as all acts of violence or incitement to such acts against any race or group of persons of another colour or ethnic origin, and also the provision of any assistance to racist activities, including the financing thereof;[75]

---

[71] *Vejdeland v Sweden* App no 1813/07 (2014) 58 EHRR 15.

[72] *Jersild v Denmark* App no 15890/89 (1994) 19 EHRR 1.

[73] *Jersild*, para 30.

[74] Convention on the Elimination of All Forms of Racial Discrimination, New York, 7 March 1966, in force 4 January 1969, UNTS vol 660, p 195.

[75] Article 4(a).

Substantive Conception II

Both the applicant and the respondent state referred to CERD, the applicant emphasising the need to have due regard to freedom of expression.[76] The European Court accepted that article 10 should be interpreted 'to the extent possible' to be compatible with the obligations under CERD, without though the Court becoming an interpreter of CERD.[77]

For the Court, it was important that the applicant was not the author of the racist remarks, but was acting as a journalist. The court recognised that journalists were best placed to decide how to report; in this regard the Court noted that free expression applied to both the substance and the form of expression.[78] The Court acknowledged that there were relevant reasons favouring the applicant's conviction, but considered these were outweighed by other factors: the applicant was addressing a matter of public discussion; the programme sought to analyse the group of youths; it was broadcast as part of a serious TV programme aimed at a well-informed audience; and the applicant made comments which distanced himself from the interviewees.[79] Overall, the Court thought the key question was whether the purpose was to propagate racist views.[80]

A significant minority of judges dissented. According to the joint dissenting opinion of Judges Ryssdal, Bernhardt, Spielmann and Loizou, the Court should have accorded more weight to the feelings of those whose human dignity had been attacked; they thought that the domestic courts had thoroughly considered all the relevant factors, and were not disposed to disagree with them. The joint dissenting opinion of Judges Gölcüklü, Russo and Valticos expressed concern that the majority were over optimistic about the contemporary human condition; they expressed concern that many people, especially young people, affected by unemployment and poverty, would be only too willing to blame scapegoats; accordingly, the applicant should have challenged the racist expressions more emphatically.

The case of *Féret v Belgium* highlights a stark tension between the Court's commitment to political expression on the one hand and opposition to racist and similar expression on the other.[81] The case concerned a criminal prosecution of a political party leader – an elected politician – for disseminating political tracts and publishing material on websites, resulting in the loss of the right to run for election for a period of ten years. While this might normally

---

[76] *Jersild*, para 28.
[77] *Jersild*, para 30.
[78] *Jersild*, para 31.
[79] *Jersild*, paras 32–35.
[80] *Jersild*, para 31.
[81] *Féret v Belgium* App no 15615/07 (16 July 2009).

resemble a core example of the need to protect political expression, in this case the party was the Belgian National Front, and the expression included xenophobic comments.

The applicant, as party leader, had overseen the dissemination of a range of electoral literature and other party messages. These generally contained messages about the party's position on immigration. As such, they included numerous proposals in relation to immigration matters. These included legislating for a preference for Belgian and European employees, changing refugee facilities into homeless shelters, repatriation of immigrants and restricting property rights of immigrants. The material included warnings about conquering Islam. There was also a pamphlet claiming that refugees in one centre had 'poisoned' the lives of local residents, subjecting them to property degradation, waste, noise and altercations.[82] A number of parties complained about these and other statements, and the prosecutor's office successfully sought the removal of the applicant's parliamentary immunity. The domestic courts ultimately convicted the applicant, noting that the material constituted incitement to discrimination, segregation and hatred. He was sentenced to do community work in the immigrant integration sector, and denied the right to be eligible for election for ten years.[83] This was pursuant to a change in Belgian law to facilitate such prosecutions in light of international obligations.

The European Court was thus faced with a case which clearly put in play the tension between principles of respecting political expression and repressing racist and similar expression. Perhaps appropriately the Court split, narrowly finding by 4 votes to 3 that there was no breach of article 10.

The majority acknowledged the fundamental importance of political expression, which normally called for a narrow margin of appreciation; the free expression of an elected politician was especially precious.[84] It continued, however, to assert that tolerance and respect for the equal dignity of all humans constituted the foundation of a democratic and pluralist society; this meant that a democratic society might have to punish expression which propagated, encouraged, promoted or justified hatred based on intolerance.[85] The applicant's language had portrayed certain communities as criminally inclined and motivated by a desire to exploit their position in Belgium; the language lacked nuance, was unsupported by documented evidence and

[82] *Féret*, paras 8–13.
[83] *Féret*, para 34.
[84] *Féret*, paras 63, 65.
[85] *Féret*, para 64.

Substantive Conception II

created irrational associations; some passages likened Muslims to terrorists.[86] The majority held that incitement to hatred did not necessarily require a call to violence or other unlawful act.[87] Accordingly, there was an obligation on politicians to avoid language which nourished intolerance.[88] Racist or xenophobic language tended to harm political discourse and reasonable arguments.[89] While political parties had a right to put forward immigration policies, even ones that were controversial, they were obliged to refrain from language that was humiliating, that risked harming the public peace and damaging confidence in democratic institutions.[90] This can be seen as some of the duties and responsibilities that accompany the exercise of free expression rights.

Judge Sajó issued a lengthy and strongly argued dissent, in which he was joined by Judges Zagrebelsky and Tsotsoria. He rejected the idea that restrictions on expression could be based on their incompatibility with the 'spirit' of the Convention; such an approach did not provide clear standards by which to assess cases. Judge Sajó characterised the impugned language as largely consisting of vague statements addressed to the government, rather than calls to action by the people. He argued the respondent government should have shown that there was a practical risk of rights being violated, not merely a potential impact on rights. Judge Sajó argued that free expression was protected in a democracy as an expression of the belief that reasonable people could make informed choices; according to him, however, the majority rejected this vision; rather, they feared that people were incapable of responding to arguments and counterarguments because of the effect of irrational emotions. The majority ignored the importance of counterarguments and the exercise of independent judgement. Analogies from the Hitlerian regime were misplaced; rather, the experience of post-war democracy was that allowing doubtful political parties to participate actually diminished the risk of extremism and did not threaten democracies. He was sharply critical of the notion that hate speech could include mere disagreeable sentiments rather than a call to violence or other unlawful act.

The judges in this case – very narrowly split – evince different ideas of free expression in a democracy. The dissent of Judge Sajó articulates a conception of political democracy in which everyone is allowed to express themselves

---

[86] *Féret*, paras 69, 71.
[87] *Féret*, para 73.
[88] *Féret*, para 75.
[89] *Féret*, para 76.
[90] *Féret*, para 77.

because this is how democracy works: people put forward arguments and counterarguments. In post-war democracies, this process allows for extremist views to be managed. It is an optimistic view of humanity in democratic societies. It allows for limitations on free expression certainly, but only in more narrowly defined circumstances and certainly not on the basis that some sentiments are disagreeable or go against the spirit of the Convention.

The majority, by contrast, have a substantive conception of democracy which is founded on tolerance and respect for the equal dignity of all. Language which threatens to undermine this – even if it does not entail a direct call to an unlawful act – is dangerous. It threatens to undermine social peace and stability; it undermines political discourse itself by appealing to emotions and irrational instincts. Politicians indeed have a duty to abstain from language that nourishes intolerance. In the scheme of values of this substantive conception of democracy, such language can be prohibited and politicians using it banned from running for office for a lengthy period (in this case, until the applicant turned seventy).

M Féret is not the only prominent National Front leader who has failed in efforts to justify spreading xenophobic and sectarian comments using the Convention; in 2004, Jean-Marie Le Pen, then leader of the French National Front, was convicted in France for provoking hatred against a group of persons defined by their religion. He had been quoted in interviews stirring up differences between the French and Muslims in France. The European Court of Human Rights dismissed his complaint as manifestly ill-founded.[91]

In *Vejdeland v Sweden*, the Court considered a successful prosecution in Sweden for agitation against a national or ethnic group.[92] The applicants had distributed leaflets in the lockers of schoolchildren; the applicants themselves were not schoolchildren, nor did they have any link with the school. The leaflets denounced 'homosexual propaganda' and the 'morally destructive effect' of homosexuality; they also blamed homosexuality for AIDS and associated homosexuality with paedophilia.[93] The Swedish courts found the applicants guilty and imposed sanctions including probation, suspended sentences and fines up to 2,000 euros.[94]

The Court considered the cases primarily in relation to the necessity element of the limitations test; the prescribed by law and legitimate aim elements were easily met. The Court noted that freedom of expression extends

---

[91] *Le Pen v France* App no 18788/09 (7 May 2010).
[92] *Vejdeland v Sweden* App no 1813/07 (2014) 58 EHRR 15.
[93] *Vejdeland*, para 8.
[94] *Vejdeland*, para 17.

Substantive Conception II

to comments that 'offend, shock or disturb'[95] but also categorised the applicants' statements as 'serious and prejudicial allegations' even if they did not 'recommend individuals to commit hateful acts'.[96] The Court then indicated the scope of 'inciting to hatred' as not being limited to calling for violence or the commission of a crime:

> Attacks on persons committed by insulting, holding up to ridicule or slandering specific groups of the population can be sufficient for the authorities to favour combating racist speech in the face of freedom of expression exercised in an irresponsible manner.[97]

While this passage referred to racist speech, the Court noted that discrimination based on sexual orientation was as serious as racist discrimination. Combined with several other factors – the targeting of schoolchildren on school grounds, the careful consideration of the domestic courts and the minor nature of the penalties – the Court concluded that limitation on free expression was compatible with the Convention.

Several judges lodged concurring opinions which highlight a bit more clearly the attitude of the Court to the values underpinning the democratic society envisaged by the Convention. Judge Yudkivska, joined by Judge Villiger, had no hesitation about joining the judgment. Judge Yudkivska drew attention to the destructive potential of hate speech for democratic society, citing the well-known *Keegstra* judgment of the Supreme Court of Canada.[98] Her opinion emphasised the historical lessons of Europe's 'tragic experience' in the twentieth century. She warned against the US approach to hate speech as setting 'a very high threshold, and for many well-known political and historical reasons today's Europe cannot afford the luxury of such a vision of the paramount value of free speech'.[99] The allegations in the applicants' leaflets were not compatible with the values of the Convention.[100]

Two other judges issued concurring opinions, which, however, indicated they placed somewhat greater value on free expression. Nevertheless, they agreed with the finding in the specific circumstances of the case. Judge Spielman, with Judge Nussberger concurring, warned that the decision of the Swedish Supreme Court was based on vague reasoning inconsistent with the Strasbourg Court's jurisprudence; the Swedish Court had put some

---

[95] *Vejdeland*, para 53.
[96] *Vejdeland*, para 54.
[97] *Vejdeland*, para 55.
[98] Concurring opinion, para 9.
[99] Concurring opinion, para 6.
[100] Concurring opinion, para 8.

106 *Freedom of Expression*

emphasis on the obligations of those exercising expression rights to avoid 'unwarrantably offensive' speech.[101] Judge Zupančič also issued a concurring expression which warned that this case seemed to go too far in limiting free expression.

These cases demonstrate a different substantive conception of democracy to that discussed in the previous section. While some of the public morality cases suggest that a European democracy (or European democracies) may rest on a shared conception of an ethical or good life, and some shared understanding of communal and religious values, the cases in this section highlight a different set of values. While the more communitarian cases may highlight an incompatibility with the notion of liberal democracy, these cases suggest that a liberal democracy may have its own set of values to uphold, and these values are different from the communitarian ones. These are values that emphasise diversity and tolerance of difference rather than a shared identity. If there is a shared identity in this, it is one that rests on the acceptance of difference. This substantive conception, like the communitarian one, endorses greater limits on free expression than may be thought legitimate in a classic liberal democratic paradigm. However, the justification for defending these values is different. Rather than being exclusive and exclusionary, this substantive conception welcomes difference. There is a limit to the tolerance, though, and the limit expresses itself in rejection of those values that themselves reject diversity and tolerance.

Most of the case law in this area so far has concerned instances where the state imposed some sanction on expression in order to protect values like equality, diversity and tolerance. The Court, though, has more recently indicated that the Convention may require states to take action against expression that itself attacks the values underpinning the Convention. The vehicle for this jurisprudential development has been the ever-capacious article 8 which the Court deployed in *Aksu v Turkey*.[102] This is an instance of the positive obligations doctrine in the Convention.

In *Aksu*, the applicant sought domestic legal remedies in respect of two publications, an academic work on *The Gypsies of Turkey* [sic] and a pair of dictionaries. The book included a small number of passages describing the typical activities of Roma in different regions of Turkey. In some instances, they were described as engaging in criminality.[103] The dictionaries contained definitions of 'Gypsy' and included some 'metaphorical' uses of the term or

---

[101] Concurring opinion, paras 5–6.
[102] *Aksu v Turkey* App no 4149/04 and 41029/04 (2012) 56 EHRR 4 (Grand Chamber).
[103] *Aksu*, para 12.

similar terms. These metaphorical usages were typically pejorative, e.g. associating miserliness with Gypsies, defining 'Gypsy wedding' as a 'crowded and noisy meeting'.[104]

The applicant sought remedies in the domestic courts and also made representations to the Ministry of Culture, which had published the book and partly financed the dictionaries. The domestic courts found that there was no breach of the law.

The European Court set out the importance of rejecting discrimination in the European democracy envisaged by the Convention:

> Racial discrimination is a particularly invidious kind of discrimination and, in view of its perilous consequences, requires from the authorities special vigilance and a vigorous reaction. It is for this reason that the authorities must use all available means to combat racism, thereby reinforcing democracy's vision of a society in which diversity is not perceived as a threat but as a source of enrichment...[105]

This is an explicit affirmation that European democracy requires respect for diversity and must take a stance against racist discrimination. The Grand Chamber goes on though to treat the case under article 8 rather than article 14, on the grounds there was no evidence of a discriminatory effect or intent, and so the case was not similar to some of the article 14 cases involving Roma.

The reasoning under article 8 involved two key steps. First, the Grand Chamber argued that the private life of members of defined groups can be affected by negative stereotyping:

> [A]ny negative stereotyping of a group, when it reaches a certain level, is capable of impacting on the group's sense of identity and the feelings of self-worth and self-confidence of members of the group.[106]

The second key step was to invoke the positive obligations doctrine: the Grand Chamber chose to analyse the applicant's case in terms of whether the state had complied with its positive obligations to protect his article 8 rights including from actions of private parties. In determining this, the Grand Chamber recognised the importance also of the article 10 rights of the other parties, and the need for the domestic courts to balance these rights.[107] The Grand Chamber concluded the domestic courts had struck a reasonable balance in respect of the book; their reasoning was compatible with the Convention,

[104] *Aksu v Turkey*, para 28.
[105] *Aksu*, para 44.
[106] *Aksu*, para 58.
[107] *Aksu*, para 66.

108 *Freedom of Expression*

including the emphasis on protecting academic freedom.[108] Similarly the Grand Chamber also found the decision regarding the dictionaries to be compatible, though noting that the objectionable definitions would be better described as 'pejorative' or 'insulting' rather than merely 'metaphorical'.[109]

Judge Gyulumyan dissented, pointing to the difference in approach of the domestic courts in this case compared with cases concerning criminal proceedings for insulting Turkishness. She attached greater importance to the 'violations of Roma dignity, intolerance and a lack of respect for a culture that is different from the majority of society'.[110]

Notwithstanding that the Court found no violation in *Aksu*, the case signals an important shift in this area. It includes an explicit reaffirmation of the value of diversity in a democracy, and thus strengthens the idea that the Court's vision of democracy is a substantive one. Further, the Court lays the basis for an argument that states must take steps to combat anti-egalitarian expressions like racist hate speech which denigrates members of a defined group in such a way as to damage their feelings of self-worth and self-confidence.

DELIBERATIVE AND PARTICIPATORY DEMOCRACY

There is a final conception of democracy which appears in the case law on free expression. This is a more deliberative conception, which emphasises the importance of the process of reasoned deliberation among equals.

A more deliberative and participatory conception of democracy may explain the prominence attached to political expression but also provides a basis for not limiting free expression concerns to the narrowly defined political sphere. The deliberative and participatory model of democracy recognises that free expression cannot be left to an unregulated marketplace of ideas.

The notion of rational deliberation may provide an explanation for some of the case law where the Court has stressed the obligations and duties that accompany the exercise of free expression. For instance, journalists may not simply say or imply whatever they wish; when their comments have the potential to injure an individual's reputation or privacy, they are expected to show good faith and a conscientious application of journalistic standards.[111]

---

[108] *Aksu*, para 71.
[109] *Aksu*, para 85.
[110] Dissenting opinion, para 5.
[111] *Pedersen and Baadsgaard v Denmark* App no 49017/99 (2004) 42 EHRR 24.

Free Expression during Campaigns and Political Advertising   109

It is in the realm of the regulation of diversity in the media and the regulation of political advertisement that the strongest arguments for a specifically deliberative conception of democracy can be seen.

FREE EXPRESSION DURING CAMPAIGNS AND POLITICAL ADVERTISING

The state's role in regulating political expression in the context of elections, and political advertising more generally, is sensitive. There is a manifest risk that the state could curtail expression and in particular manipulate public media to support governing parties. On the other hand, the absence of state regulation might mean that private wealth determines the publicity each party or candidate might receive and so deform the political discussion.[112] And there are numerous practical considerations – it is improbable that every single candidate in an election could be offered airtime on television for instance.[113] Also challenging is defining what is political expression in this context – is it advertising by political parties? What about advertising by NGOs seeking to highlight issues of public concern? If NGO expression can be limited as political advertising, what of consumer-oriented commercial advertising? Should all media be treated equally, or do we need to differentiate across state broadcasters, private broadcasters, streaming services, social media, print media? How to deal with technological changes which raise difficulties in controlling broadcasting at national boundaries (or conversely where states may exercise excessive control at digital boundaries)? Is it possible to devise general schemes that avoid hard cases, or alternatively, do targeted measures leave themselves open to evasion?

The starting point is that the state is the 'ultimate guarantor of pluralism'; this requires the state to ensure that television and radio services provide the public with 'impartial and accurate information and a range of opinion and comment', and that those working in the media industry are not impaired from offering this content.[114] These principles were stated in *Manole v Moldova*, where journalists at the state-owned broadcaster complained they had

---

[112] Dickson argues, for instance, that the Court should ensure there is a fair political process when considering issues of electoral finances: Brice Dickson, 'Electoral Finances, Human Rights and Fairness' in Helen Hardman and Brice Dickson (eds) *Electoral Rights in Europe: Advances and Challenges* (Taylor & Francis 2017).

[113] A point made by the BBC in *Huggett v United Kingdom* App no 24744/94 (European Commission of Human Rights, 28 June 1995).

[114] *Manole v Moldova* App no 13936/02 (17 September 2009), paras 99–100. See also *Centro Europa 7 srl v Italy* App no 38433/09 (Grand Chamber, 7 May 2012), para 134.

been subjected to editorial control and censorship. They were not allowed to discuss sensitive subjects like human rights abuses during the Soviet era and were required to give priority to covering the actions of the ruling political party. For much of the country this station was the sole media resource which made it all the more imperative for the state to ensure it offered impartial information and a diversity of views. The state regulation, however, did not insulate the broadcaster from political influence; in particular, the governing party could appoint the vast majority of the individuals charged with regulating the broadcaster. This was a violation of article 10.

The same issue came up in a very different context in the *Communist Party of Russia and others v Russia* case. Here the applicant political parties claimed that the state broadcasters had devoted more, and more favourable, coverage to the governing party, United Russia. The context was quite different in that there were multiple sources of information, and Russia did have legislation which seemed to address the issues of neutrality and pluralism during election campaigns; the applicants complained not about the legislation but about the diverse practices which led to the difference in coverage. In this context the Court, considering the issue of alleged manipulation, constrained itself to reviewing whether the Russian Supreme Court had reviewed the complaint adequately, and found that it had.[115] On the separate issue as to whether Russia had discharged its positive obligations to ensure that media coverage was balanced and respected the notion of free elections, the Court again found no violation. Russia did have legislation on neutrality and seeking to ensure a degree of pluralism, and the parties did have access to appreciable amounts of airtime, as well as the possibility to spread their message on other media outside the state broadcasters.

The case involved a very different context from the one in *Manole* and so perhaps the different conclusion is unsurprising. Deciding on effective regulations to secure impartiality and neutrality while also protecting the independence of broadcasters is also a difficult challenge, and one of the reasons for the Court to show deference in this area.

The tensions involved in regulating free expression during elections were seen clearly in the 14–6 judgment in *Bowman v UK*. The applicant, an antiabortion activist, had circulated leaflets outlining the views of candidates on the topic of abortion and experimentation on embryos. She was prosecuted under the Representation of the People Act 1983 which prohibited third

---

[115] *Communist Party of Russia and Others v Russia* App no 29400/05 (19 June 2012), paras 114–122.

Free Expression during Campaigns and Political Advertising

parties spending more than 5 pounds to support or oppose a candidate in a constituency during an election.

The majority acknowledged that the aim of the measure was to promote equality in the political process and that it was but one part of an ensemble of measures designed to ensure free and fair elections.[116] In this sense the article 10 rights and the P1–3 rights might sometimes conflict.[117] The majority concluded, though, the measure was disproportionate in that the 5-pound limit effectively prevented the applicant from seeking to influence how people voted for candidates; the majority was not persuaded that other means of expressing her views were readily available (e.g. writing letters to papers); the majority also found the measure disproportionate given that no such restrictions applied to the media.[118]

Six judges dissented, arguing that the measure was in fact narrowly tailored, and left the applicant many other opportunities to express her views outside of the election period or indeed during it as long as she did not contravene this narrow restriction.[119] Judge Freeland in his dissent pointed out that the rationale for the measure required a low limit of the type the majority found problematic; further, the exemption for the media simply reflected the importance attached to the media in a political democracy.[120] Judge Valticos expressed incredulity at the idea of giving the 'British government lessons in how to hold elections and run a democracy'.[121] Academic commentators also highlighted the 'depressing' nature of the majority's reluctance 'to recognise the debilitating effect of disproportionate financial resources'.[122]

The difficulties of striking a balance in this area is also apparent in the case law on political advertising. The Court's initial case law in this area has generally upheld the free expression arguments in cases involving bans on political advertising. *Vgt Verein Gegen Tierfabriken v Switzerland* concerned a group which wanted to run an advert on cruelty in animal farming.[123] The commercial could not be shown because of its political character. The Court acknowledged the legitimacy of seeking to protect public opinion from being

---

[116] *Bowman v United Kingdom* App no 141/1996/760/961 (1998) 26 EHRR 1, paras 38, 41.

[117] *Bowman*, para 43.

[118] *Bowman*, paras 46–47.

[119] Joint dissent of Judges Loizou, Baka and Jambrek, dissent of Judge Freeland (joined by Judge Levits).

[120] Judge Freeland, paras 10–11.

[121] This was years before the 2016 Brexit referendum and subsequent debates after the UK's 2017 General Election.

[122] Conor Gearty, 'Democracy and Human Rights in the European Court of Human Rights: A Critical Appraisal' (2000) 51 (3) Northern Ireland Legal Quarterly 381, 394.

[123] *Vgt Verein Gegen Tierfabriken v Switzerland* App no 24699/94 (2002) 34 EHRR 4.

influenced by wealthy actors but found the measure disproportionate: it applied to some media and not others; the applicant was not a powerful financial group; the broadcaster was the only one who could disseminate the applicant's message throughout the country.[124] The Court unanimously found a violation of article 10.[125] In *TV Vest v Norway*, the Court considered a ban on political advertising on television in Norway; the applicant was a very small party, the Pensioners' Party, which had difficulty getting its message heard on the mass media. The Court noted the ban applied at all times, i.e. not just during elections, and so disagreed that the wide margin of appreciation called for in P1–3 cases applied.[126] The Court noted the relevant reasons put forward by the government to support the ban; these centred around protecting the quality of political debate and protecting political pluralism from the threats posed by unequal financial resources. However, the Court concluded the ban was not proportionate. The Pensioners' Party was not the type of wealthy party supposedly targeted by the ban; there was nothing in the content of the advertisements that would lower the quality of debate or inflame social tensions.[127] It is true that in *Murphy v Ireland* the Court found that Ireland's ban on religious advertising was not a breach of article 10, but this seemed to be because of the sensitivity of religious discussions.[128]

In a case from the UK, the Grand Chamber finally indicated it would not always strike the balance in favour of free expression in political advertising cases. *Animal Defenders International* is unusual in any number of respects.[129] The respondent state adopted a ban on political advertising (broadly understood as including issue advertising by non-governmental organisations) at any time, i.e. not limited to elections. It did this being aware of the *VgT* judgment and having considered the implications of *VgT* in some depth. At domestic level, a challenge to the convention compatibility of the legislation was dismissed, unanimously, in both the High Court and House of Lords.

Unlike the domestic courts, the Strasbourg Court itself split 9–8, the Grand Chamber finding no violation. The issue before the Grand Chamber focused on the proportionality of the legislation; all parties accepted that the restriction

---

[124] *Vgt Verein Gegen Tierfabriken*, paras 74–77.

[125] The Court would unusually revisit the case and affirm a violation of article 10 in *VGT Verein Gegen Tierfabriken Schweiz v Switzerland* App no 32772/02 (Grand Chamber, 30 June 2009).

[126] *TV Vest AS & Rogaland Pensjonistparti v Norway* App no 21132/05 (2009) 48 EHRR 51, para 66.

[127] *TV Vest AS & Rogaland Pensjonistparti*, paras 72–78.

[128] *Murphy v Ireland* App no 44179/98 (2004) 38 EHRR 13.

[129] *Animal Defenders International v United Kingdom* App no 48876/08 (2013) 57 EHRR 21 (Grand Chamber).

Animal Defenders International *and Deliberative Democracy*   113

was prescribed by law and for a legitimate aim. The Grand Chamber majority highlighted the 'exceptional examination by political bodies of the cultural, political and legal aspects of the prohibition' and the careful analysis of the issues in the domestic courts.[130] The majority agreed the measure was carefully targeted to include advertising that was paid and disseminated by the broadcasting media of television and radio.[131] The majority agreed that the broadcasting media remained extremely influential notwithstanding the growth in the importance of the internet and social media.[132] The majority also noted that broadcast media continued to offer advantages and hence commanded rates which many in the non-governmental sector could not afford.[133] The state had special rules to permit political parties access to the broadcasting media during election times, which the majority found an important mitigation.[134] Adopting a rule with exceptions would leave open the possibility of abuse and arbitrariness, while the applicant also retained access to numerous other avenues for their expression.[135]

That the regulation of political advertising is a contested issue (though apparently not so in the UK at the time) is indicated by the narrow majority judgment in the Grand Chamber, with several prominent judges included among the dissenters. One joint dissent pointed out the evident incompatibility with the *VgT* judgment which had stood for a decade and objected to an approach which levelled the playing field by excluding everyone from accessing one form of political expression.[136] Another dissent disputed the necessity of a measure which targeted broadcasting but not the increasingly important arena of the internet and social media.[137]

ANIMAL DEFENDERS INTERNATIONAL
AND DELIBERATIVE DEMOCRACY

The *Animal Defenders International* case gives us an actual example of how deliberative democratic principles might play a role in Convention jurisprudence. The case is a split one, the court ultimately deciding by a 9–8 vote that the UK's ban on political (and religious) advertising was not in breach of the

---

[130] *Animal Defenders International v United Kingdom*, paras 114–116.
[131] *Animal Defenders International v United Kingdom*, para 117.
[132] *Animal Defenders International v United Kingdom*, para 119.
[133] *Animal Defenders International v United Kingdom*, para 120.
[134] *Animal Defenders International v United Kingdom*, para 121.
[135] *Animal Defenders International v United Kingdom*, paras 122–124.
[136] Judges Ziemele, Sajó, Kalaydjieva, Vučinič, and De Gaetano.
[137] Judge Tulkens joined by Judges Spielmann and Laffranque.

right to free expression. The dissenters take a strong view on free expression rights, insisting on an adherence to the earlier *VgT*[138] ruling on paid political advertising (and also *TV Vest*[139]). This gives quite strong protection to individual free expression rights and fits in neatly with a liberal democratic conception of democracy, with the emphasis on liberal.

The majority judgment (and the concurring opinion of the UK judge, Judge Bratza) could be characterised as emphasising a more procedural conception of democracy, perhaps a more majoritarian or a deliberative conception of democracy. Much of the judgment (this is a focus of the majority judgment and a critique in the dissenters) is taken up with the process by which the UK authorities decided to maintain this long-standing ban. On balance, the majority judgment might be best understood as a deliberative conception of democracy.

There are two key themes in the majority judgment which stand out as deliberative. First, there is the careful process of public scrutiny and debate by which the UK authorities decided to continue this ban. This decision was based on a careful consideration of the Convention and a realisation that there was a problem here, but one where the government was prepared to defend its position; advice from expert commissions on standards in public office and electoral bodies recommended the ban; the expert joint committee on human rights offered advice; Parliament debated and maintained the ban without dissent. This seems to embody the deliberative democratic ideal that even fundamental rights are subject to articulation and definition through a process of democratic debate.

Second, a key justification for the ban was the need to maintain political equality. The ban is largely motivated by a concern that if political advertising was left unregulated, this would allow inequalities in the economic sphere to infect the public and political sphere. Deliberative democracy depends on deliberation among free and equal participants. To be meaningful, this equality must not be merely formal. Those with greater wealth must not be able to use that wealth without restriction to secure greater avenues for expression on matters of public interest. It is true that in several of these cases the applicants were not necessarily wealthy and powerful actors themselves. The difficulty in designing a more targeted measure that was not open to abuse leans in favour of a general measure designed to ensure that wealth does not deform public debate on what remain the influential broadcasting media.

---

[138] *Vgt Verein Gegen Tierfabriken v Switzerland.*
[139] *TV Vest AS & Rogaland Pensjonistparti v Norway.*

While *Animal Defenders International* suggests some support for more deliberative models of democracy, another recent case provides support for more participation by developing the article 10 free expression right to include access to state-held information.

PARTICIPATION AND FREEDOM OF INFORMATION

Central to any notion of effective participation in government must be the principle of access to information. It is impossible to imagine how representative democracy can be held to account unless journalists, non-governmental organisations and concerned individuals have access to state-held information. Historically the European Court of Human Rights has been reluctant to engage in this area. Even though article 10 refers to the right to 'receive' 'information and ideas without interference by public authorities', the traditional interpretation was to see this as a negative obligation rather than a positive obligation to provide information.[140]

There was piecemeal identification of specific circumstances where individuals succeeded in arguing that they had a right to information. Typically this was in cases involving article 8 where they could claim access to information of personal interest to themselves, or cases where the domestic courts had already ordered disclosure and another arm of the state refused to comply. Some of the cases, though, seemed to hint at a more expansive notion of a right to receive information.[141]

The Grand Chamber finally 'clarified' the position in *Magyar Helsinki Bizottság v Hungary*.[142] In this case the applicant non-governmental organisation had sought information from police departments concerning the appointment of defence lawyers. While most police departments provided the information (in some cases after domestic court challenges), two refused. On this occasion the domestic courts ultimately agreed disclosure was not permitted. The Grand Chamber reviewed the case law on freedom of information to date and heard from several third parties, including the UK government (which argued for the traditional restrictive interpretation of article 10). The Grand Chamber noted the international trends: the free expression clauses in the ICCPR and the American Convention especially had been interpreted to include a right of access to information.[143] Furthermore, this

---

[140] *Leander v Sweden* App no 9248/81 (1987) 9 EHRR 433.
[141] *Társaság a Szabadságjogokért v Hungary* App no 37374/05 (14 April 2009).
[142] *Magyar Helsinki Bizottság v Hungary* App no 18030/11 (Grand Chamber, 8 November 2016). It is difficult to disagree with the dissenting opinion of Judge Kjølbro that the Grand Chamber in effect overruled the earlier, more restrictive interpretation.
[143] *Magyar Helsinki Bizottság*, paras 140, 146.

116 *Freedom of Expression*

was overwhelmingly the consensus among the thirty-one Council of Europe states it surveyed.[144] The argument based on the drafting of the Convention wording was not conclusive and did not prevail against the effective interpretation principle. The Grand Chamber concluded article 10 required disclosure of information where a domestic court ordered it or if its denial was an interference with the article 10 right.[145] In applying this second obligation, the Grand Chamber identified four criteria to apply: the purpose for which the information was sought and whether it was necessary for the applicant's free expression rights, the nature of the information as touching on the public interest, the role of the applicant and whether the information was readily available.[146] In this regard the Grand Chamber identified journalists and non-governmental organisations as having a watchdog role, though it specified that academics, authors and potentially bloggers might also exercise such a role. Applying these criteria, the Grand Chamber concluded that the applicant was entitled to receive the information and the government's arguments for non-disclosure did not satisfy the proportionality requirements, and thus there was a violation.

This Grand Chamber case demonstrates again how the Court uses the principle of effective interpretation, in this case aided by a convincing record of parallel developments in other human rights systems and among the Council of Europe states themselves, in order to provide effective protection of rights in a democracy.

CONCLUSION

Freedom of expression is frequently considered a cornerstone of the human rights architecture; it (or more specifically 'freedom of speech') is one of the four fundamental freedoms identified in Franklin Roosevelt's State of the Union speech, and this is echoed in the preamble to the Universal Declaration of Human Rights. The agreement on the fundamental importance of free expression does not preclude considerable disagreement on what weight to accord it in the human rights system and how to interpret its scope.

Free expression is a classic example of a liberal right, a right to be free from government interference or censorship in expressing opinions, disagreement, criticisms. The case law offers support for a liberal democratic conception of free expression, in particular in the much-quoted lines from *Handyside* that

[144] *Magyar Helsinki Bizottság*, para 139.
[145] *Magyar Helsinki Bizottság*, para 156.
[146] *Magyar Helsinki Bizottság*, paras 158–170.

Conclusion 117

article 10 protects expression that shocks, offends and disturbs. In later cases, this language is frequently joined to language which speaks of the need for any restrictions on this right to be 'convincingly established', and in political expression cases the Court puts special emphasis on the importance of free expression. Indeed, this is all in the context of understanding this right in a 'democratic society'.

Despite agreement on these principles, the Court's jurisprudence shows some disagreement on how they are applied in particular contexts, and this sheds some light on the particular type of democratic society envisaged. At least four key different models, diverging to an extent from what might be expected in liberal democracy, appear.

The earlier case law often appears to put a premium on state concerns about security. This is most evidently the situation with some of the political censorship cases from Ireland and the UK, but also Turkey. While the liberal right is given some recognition, it is frequently outweighed in the balance of interests by majoritarian concerns about public order and national security. Arguably this highlights a difference of opinion as to the balance between the 'liberal' and the 'democratic' elements of liberal democracy. The Court (and Commission) tend to show considerable deference to the judgements of the representatives of the democratic state in these cases, notwithstanding that they frequently clearly concern political expression, sometimes indeed expression by political party members. This tendency to show deference to the judgements of representative and presumably majoritarian institutions has some defects. It is precisely the situation that human rights are meant to redress, to avoid the danger of oppression even by a democratic majority. This is a concern that is only heightened when facing a situation where the state's general liberal democratic credentials are open to question, either because the state is facing a security threat or perhaps because the state's liberal democratic credentials have burnished brightly only recently, intermittently or even rarely. This highlights a concern that according considerable weight to majority political judgements of relatively youthful democracies like Turkey and Hungary, or even more seriously states that still retain significant authoritarian characteristics (Russia), might be to put too much faith in the outcomes of the domestic political structures. It is a welcome initiative, therefore, that the Court is increasingly sceptical of claims to restrict expression based on the demands of national security.

A second model, differing from what might be expected in a liberal democracy, arises from the public morality cases, those concerning matters like obscenity or blasphemy. Again, many of the early cases, including indeed *Handyside*, seem to accept limitations on free expression that reflect the importance of communitarian values. That is to say that when the Court spoke of the importance of free expression in a democratic society, it was understood that a democratic society needed to include some element of consensus, however minimal on ethical standards. This entailed corresponding obligations not to offend or undermine these standards. This suggests a substantive conception of democracy along communitarian lines, recognising that a political community needs to rest on community foundations that do not simply relate to political procedures, but also reflect a certain way or life or ethical commitment.

Other models diverging from liberal democracy are more recent and more telling. They concern the issues of hate speech and the scope for promoting deliberation and participation in the polity.

Hate speech is a typical test case for democracy and liberal democracy. At what point does expression that shocks, offends or disturbs cross the line into impermissible incitement to hatred? The European Convention on Human Rights does not address this expressly unlike the Convention on the Elimination of All Forms of Racial Discrimination 1965 (article 4) and the International Covenant on Civil and Political Rights (article 20). While both these other instruments expressly address hate speech, they also embrace the protection of free expression, and so the balance is not necessarily always clear in those instruments. In the case of the ECHR, it is for the Court to elaborate on that balance, and in so doing the Court has come down in favour of a view that hate speech can be banned, even in the absence of immediate threats of violence, discrimination or other unlawful activity. This is a different standard from that increasingly seen in the national security cases, where general or abstract language cannot be censored unless there is a real risk of violence in the actual circumstances. The differing standard suggests a type of democratic society which has (as in the discussion on political morality) a substantive component, but the substantive component are those values associated with liberal democracy, e.g. tolerance, respect for diversity. This is a substantive conception which rejects the implication that liberalism implies complete neutrality on all ethical questions. A neutral position would insist on stricter requirements before hate speech could be banned, and this is seen indeed in the splits in the Court's judgments on this topic (*Jersild, Féret, Vedjeland*). The recent case law comes down in favour of the substantive commitment, but there are important concurring or even dissenting opinions. The overall trend, though, seems to support the substantive conception, and this is reinforced in the *Aksu* case which lays the basis for positive obligations to provide remedies for offensive racial comments.

Conclusion

The fourth model is the possible recognition of a greater commitment to deliberation and participation in the case law. Participation is enhanced by recent decisions developing the free expression right to include, to a degree, the right to receive information. A deliberative and participatory conception of democracy needs to address issues that might affect the possibility for all concerned to contribute to public debate and participate in decision-making on a basis of equality. The commitment to equality may also require hate speech to be tackled as a form of speech with the potential to exclude some groups on discriminatory grounds from public debate. This suggests an emphasis on deliberation, especially in the public sphere and the need to tackle inequality. Some of the case law shows a striking concern with the quality of deliberation. Similarly, there is also a concern that the operation of a free marketplace of ideas in a liberal democracy might lead to imbalances in the way public affairs are debated, thus supporting the idea that the broadcast media must be supported by principles such as pluralism to ensure that all viewpoints are represented.

The role of the state as the ultimate guarantor of pluralism is important. The state is one of the few actors that can counter the influence of private wealth and ensure this does not deform political debate. The Court's case law in this area is still developing. Recognising that the state must ensure respect for pluralism by a state broadcaster and that it may legislate to ban political advertising if necessary to ensure political equality are important issues. But there are other possible positive obligations to consider here. Diversity among privately owned print media, for instance, is also an issue in some countries, and it seems likely that paid use of social media will come to be as important as broadcasting in the future. The role of private wealth in these media is one aspect of the threat posed by economic inequality to political democracy.

There are limited explicit textual resources in the Convention to address the role of economic inequality. After all, it protects mainly civil and political rights. One explicit textual resource is the mention of unions in article 11, and this will form part of the discussion in the next chapter on free assembly and association.

5

Association, Assembly and Political Parties

This chapter considers the freedom of association and assembly in article 11, a right closely related to article 10 on freedom of expression. The chapter gives particular attention to the role of political parties as the form of association most directly related to the political process, as well as the role of trade unions as a specific form of association mentioned in article 11. The role of unions is especially significant in what it may tell us about the Court's approach to concerns about economic inequality in a political democracy.

The article 11 case law represents different models of democracy. There is considerable case law supporting the liberal democratic model, often emphasising the close link before the article 11 and the article 10 rights. As with article 10, there is also a line of case law supporting substantive models of democracy; here there is a concern the Court may sometimes veer to too substantive a model. Finally, the chapter considers how the article 11 case law might support more deliberative and participatory models of democracy.

LIBERAL DEMOCRACY

Like the other qualified rights, Article 11 is well expressed to forward the liberal representative vision:

1. Everyone has the right to freedom of peaceful assembly and to freedom of association with others, including the right to form and to join trade unions for the protection of his interests.
2. No restrictions shall be placed on the exercise of these rights other than such as are prescribed by law and are necessary in a democratic society in the interests of national security or public safety, for the prevention of disorder or crime, for the protection of health or morals or for the protection of the rights and freedoms of others. This Article shall not

prevent the imposition of lawful restrictions on the exercise of these rights by members of the armed forces, of the police or of the administration of the State.

There are some points to note about the text. Article 11 protects two closely related but distinct rights: assembly and association. The right of assembly is limited to 'peaceful assembly'. Trade unions are given explicit protection, but other forms of association are not mentioned (not even political parties). The right to form and join trade unions is expressed to be for the protection of the right holders' interests. The second clause includes familiar language permitting limitation of the rights; additionally, though, it includes explicit recognition of the possibility of restrictions on three groups of public servants.

Given the importance of article 11 to the political democracy envisaged by the Convention, any exceptions must be interpreted strictly.[1] Article 11 includes the same key principles of legitimate aim, legality and proportionality that we find in the article 10 jurisprudence. Where there is no lawful basis for interference with a right, the Court finds a violation of the legality principle.[2]

Like article 10's freedom of expression, article 11 rights appear to be classic liberal rights. But it is worth remembering that they are somewhat different from article 10 in that they are almost inevitably collective in nature – assemblies and associations by definition require more than one person. This may be why they do not appear in one early classic statement of liberal rights, the 1789 French Declaration of the Rights of Man and the Citizen; early liberals were often scathing of the danger of 'factions'. The nineteenth century, with the rise of socialism and the labour movement in particular, has changed that, and today we tend to see these rights as typical civil and political rights. Even so, the tension between individual and collective rights sometimes reasserts itself.

A liberal representative approach to association and assembly tends to emphasise the freedom or liberty aspect of these rights. As with free expression, the key point is one of non-interference, or at least any interference must be rigorously justified, and here again we encounter the core principles of legitimate aim, legality and proportionality. We may find, though, that the balance between the liberal and representative elements of the democratic conception are sometimes in tension here, and that the Court sometimes favours freedom and sometimes gives deference to the democratic authorities. It is important that the Court frequently links article 11 to article 10's free

---

[1] *Herri Batasuna v Spain* App nos 25803/04 and 25817/04 (30 June 2009), para 77.
[2] *Djavit An v Turkey* App no 20652/92 (2005) 40 EHRR 45, para 66.

Association, Assembly and Political Parties

expression values,[3] and examines article 11 cases in the light of article 10.[4] In some instances, protest cases might be decided under article 10 rather than article 11.

The case law on free assembly shows a general and arguably increasing level of protection for peaceful assembly. The concept of assembly covers a wide range of activities – marches, demonstrations, counter-demonstrations,[5] public meetings, even private meetings.[6] Assemblies are protected even if they have the possibility to lead to tensions – in the Court's view, a democratic exchange of views includes the need to contemplate some level of public tension and heated exchange.[7] The Court has made clear that even unlawful demonstrations are entitled to the protection of the Convention. When dealing with demonstrations which are not an example of the core article 11 right and which involve some disruption, authorities must show a 'necessary tolerance'.[8] Where a criminal sanction may be justified, the Court has examined the proportionality of the sanction. Importantly, the free assembly right also requires positive obligations to protect a peaceful assembly.[9] While the Court has been generally solicitous of free assembly rights, it also indicates there are limits – this is inherent in the concept of a 'peaceful' assembly. In upholding limits, the Court may be swayed by the egregious nature of the demonstration[10] and the moderation of the state response.

The Court's case law on free association also demonstrates a commitment to a liberal democratic defence of association rights. The Court has stressed that democracy requires respect for pluralism, tolerance and broad-mindedness: freedom of association protects all sorts of associations, including those formed to protect a cultural or spiritual heritage, for socio-economic reasons, for religious reasons and to support an ethnic identity or minority consciousness.[11] Pluralism in a democratic states entails 'genuine recognition of, and respect for, diversity and the dynamics of cultural traditions, ethnic and

---

[3] *Yazar v Turkey* App nos 22723/93, 22724/93 and 22725/93 (2003) 36 EHRR 6. In *Djavit An v Turkey* the Court said that the article 10 and article 11 issues could not be separated: para 39.

[4] *Rai and Evans v United Kingdom* App nos 26258/07 and 26255/07 (17 November 2009).

[5] *Ollinger v Austria* App no 76900/01 (2008) 46 EHRR 38.

[6] *Djavit An v Turkey*, para 56.

[7] *Ollinger v Austria*, para 36. *Ouranio Toxo v Greece* App no 74989/01 (2007) 45 EHRR 8, para 40.

[8] *Tuskia v Georgia* App no 14237/07 (11 October 2018), para 79.

[9] *Ollinger v Austria*, para 39; David Harris, Michael O'Boyle, Ed Bates and Carla Buckley, *Law of the European Convention on Human Rights* (Oxford University Press 2018), 686–688.

[10] *Cisse v France* App no 51346/99 (18 January 2001).

[11] *Gorzelik v Poland* App no 44158/98 (2005) 40 EHRR 4 (Grand Chamber) para 92, reaffirmed in *Zehra Foundation and Others v Turkey* App no 51595/07 (10 July 2018), para 50.

Political Parties 123

cultural identities, religious beliefs, artistic, literary and socio-economic ideas and concepts'.[12]

The free association and assembly rights are particularly important in relation to political parties and associations; this is most clearly seen in a string of cases in the 1990s and early twenty-first century, primarily from Turkey but also from other states.

POLITICAL PARTIES

The Turkish Constitution adopts the German innovation of giving a monopoly on the power to disband political parties to a constitutional court as a neutral guardian of the constitution. In these cases, the Turkish Constitutional Court had formally banned certain parties because their programme or activities were contrary to constitutional principles or they indicated a support for violence. The effects of the ban were serious: the party was disbanded, its assets seized and its leading political officers prohibited from holding office in other political parties, to prevent them simply carrying on disfavoured activity in a different guise. It is a striking feature of the cases that the bans were frequently sought very soon after the formation of the political party – in some cases weeks – and before they had the opportunity to engage in any political activity. In the initial set of cases – prior to the *Refah Paritisi* case – the Court unanimously found violations of article 11 and gradually developed a more robust approach to dealing with the infringements of article 11 rights.

The initial and still critically important case is the Grand Chamber judgment in the *United Communist Party* case.[13] This involved a ban based purely on the programme of the party as it was instituted before the party had any opportunity to carry out its activities. The Constitutional Court imposed the ban because of the use of a proscribed word – 'Communist' – in the title of the party, and more substantively because the party's programme threatened the territorial integrity of the state by its support for Kurdish self-determination and regional autonomy.[14] The applicants applied to Strasbourg where the Commission concluded unanimously that there was a violation.[15] The Commission referred the case to a Chamber of the Court, which itself relinquished the case in favour of the Grand Chamber.

---

[12] *Gorzelik v Poland*, para 92.
[13] *United Communist Party of Turkey v Turkey* App no 19392/92 (1998) 26 EHRR 121 (Grand Chamber).
[14] *United Communist Party of Turkey v Turkey*, para 10.
[15] *United Communist Party of Turkey v Turkey* App no 19392/92 (European Commission of Human Rights, 3 September 1996).

124 *Association, Assembly and Political Parties*

The Court dealt with numerous important issues of principle. First, it had to establish that political parties were a type of association protected by article 11. The Turkish government disputed this; article 11 indeed refers explicitly to trade unions but not other associations; even more importantly, according to the government, political parties were not ordinary associations but needed to be seen as part of the political structures of a state. The government argued that there was no justification for the Court to get involved in these questions of political design. Furthermore, the government invoked article 17, the abuse of rights clause.

The Court rejected this argument decisively. Partly this was because the language of article 11 envisaged that trade unions were simply one type of association protected by article 11, not the only one.[16] But more important was the Court's conception of the role of political parties in a democracy as envisaged by the Convention: they are 'essential to the proper functioning of a democracy'.[17] That any particular state might treat of political parties in its constitution does not immunise those provisions from Convention scrutiny.[18] The Court dismissed even more briskly the claim that the Convention only guaranteed the right to form associations, and not a right against dissolution of those associations.[19]

Having established admissibility, the Court had little difficulty concluding that the ban was a breach of the Convention. Considering the legality, legitimate aim and proportionality principles, the measure complied with the legality or prescribed by law principle. As regards the legitimate aim, the Court noted that the Commission had rejected the notion that banning a party for calling itself 'Communist' satisfied the legitimate aim criterion. The Court was prepared to accept that national security in the form of territorial integrity was in play. The crucial issue, therefore, was one of proportionality.

During the proportionality discussion, the Grand Chamber developed its views on the importance of political parties in a European democracy. The Grand Chamber reiterated that the state was the 'ultimate guarantor of the principle of pluralism' and that this required the organisation of free elections pursuant to P1–3 to ascertain the free expression of the will of the people.[20] The Grand Chamber went on:

---

[16] *United Communist Party of Turkey v Turkey*, para 24.
[17] *United Communist Party of Turkey v Turkey*, para 25.
[18] *United Communist Party of Turkey v Turkey*, para 30.
[19] *United Communist Party of Turkey v Turkey*, para 33.
[20] *United Communist Party of Turkey v Turkey*, para 44.

Political Parties

Such expression is inconceivable without the participation of a plurality of political parties representing the different shades of opinion to be found within a country's population. By relating this range of opinion, not only within political institutions but also – with the help of the media – at all levels of social life, political parties make an irreplaceable contribution to political debate, which is at the very core of the concept of a democratic society.

Democracy is without a doubt a fundamental feature of the European public order.[21]

And even more strongly:

Democracy thus appears to be the only political model contemplated by the Convention, and accordingly the only one compatible with it.[22]

This is a strong statement of the Court's commitment to the principle of pluralist democracy, and the description of the role of political parties fits very well with the liberal democratic model of democracy. The Grand Chamber based this position both on the explicit reference to democracy in the Preamble and on the repeated reference to 'democratic society' in articles 9 through to 11 of the Convention.

The implication for the Grand Chamber is that any restrictions on a political party required 'convincing and compelling reasons', that states have only a 'limited' margin of appreciation and there must be 'rigorous European supervision embracing both the law and the decisions applying it'.[23]

Applying these principles, the Grand Chamber rejected the notion that the use of the word 'Communist' in the title could justify the extreme step of dissolution, absent 'relevant and sufficient circumstances' showing the party constituted a threat to the state. The Grand Chamber explicitly rejected the analogy with the 1956 *German Communist Party* case before the German Constitutional Court.[24] On the more substantive point that the party programme encouraged separatism, the Grand Chamber examined the programme carefully. It read the programme more generously than the Turkish Constitutional Court had, noting that while it referred to the Kurdish 'people' and 'nation', it did not refer to 'minority', nor did if call for any special rights or treatment or secession; the programme explicitly endorsed peaceful political change. The Grand Chamber indicated that the party's programme was typical of democratic politics:

---

[21] *United Communist Party of Turkey v Turkey*, paras 44–45.
[22] *United Communist Party of Turkey v Turkey*, para 45.
[23] *United Communist Party of Turkey v Turkey*, para 46.
[24] *United Communist Party of Turkey v Turkey*, para 54.

The Court considers one of the principal characteristics of democracy to be the possibility it offers of resolving a country's problems through dialogue, without recourse to violence, even when they are irksome. Democracy thrives on freedom of expression. From that point of view, there can be no justification for hindering a political group solely because it seeks to debate in public the situation of part of the State's population and to take part in the nation's political life in order to find, according to democratic rules, solutions capable of satisfying everyone concerned.[25]

The Grand Chamber acknowledged that sometimes covert action might belie public statements, and also that decisions had to be understood in their particular contexts, especially when that context is the fight against terrorism. But in this case the party was faced with an application for dissolution shortly after its formation, and so there was no party action which would change the assessment.

This was a welcome and powerful decision, with its language on the role of political parties in a democracy especially welcome and much cited since. In some ways, though, the decision appears a relatively easy one, and in particular the Court was quick to accept claims that the UCP was not promoting separatism. Furthermore, the fact that the UCP had had no time in which to engage in any activities made it more straightforward for the Court; it was difficult to see how a written programme without supporting speech or action could imperil national security.

Subsequent judgments in this line of cases demonstrate a gradually more rigorous approach to defending freedom of association. In addition to closely scrutinising party dissolutions, the Court will examine temporary restrictions carefully, especially when imposed by a government on an opposition party.[26] While the *United Communist Party* case stressed the negative aspect of freedom of association, the Court has also moved to assert the positive obligation on the state to protect associations and political parties even when they offend other members of the public.[27] The article 11 protection covers not just decisions to dissolve a party but also decisions about the registration or re-registration of a party.[28]

The article 11 rights do know limits. For instance, when it comes to political party registration, states can insist on reasonable formalities for the registration

---

[25] *United Communist Party of Turkey v Turkey*, para 57.
[26] *Christian Democratic People's Party v Moldova* App no 28793/02 (2006) 45 EHRR 13.
[27] *Ouranio Toxo v Greece*, para 37.
[28] *Republican Party of Russia v Russia* App no 12976/07 (2015) 61 EHRR 20.

Political Parties

of a political party.[29] Textually, article 11 only applies to peaceful assembly. While this is not explicit in article 11, the Court regards associations organised for violent purposes as liable to restriction, even prohibition. This means more than an organisation declares itself to be revolutionary in nature;[30] there must be evidence of a real threat to the state. This may be straightforward in some cases. *Hizb Ut-Tahrir and Others v Germany* concerned an association which was founded in the Middle East with the intention of overthrowing governments in the Muslim world and establishing a caliphate; some of its publications denied the right of Israel to exist (advocating its destruction) and called for the killing of Jews. Germany prohibited the activities of this association and ordered the seizure of its assets. The Court concluded that the aims of the organisation were contrary to international peace, based on explicit statements and concluded that article 17 applied – the organisation was attempting to 'deflect' article 11 from its purpose. In this case the issue was straightforward, as the statements in the organisation's publications were explicit.

The difficulty arises where the association being banned is not explicitly a violent organisation but is alleged to be covertly supportive of violence, perhaps supportive of an armed organisation. This takes the Court into difficult factual territory: it must recognise that an organisation may have covert violent aims or activities, but must also be vigilant that the state does not too readily invoke evidence of violence.

These principles are discussed in *Herri Batasuna v Spain*, where a special chamber of the Spanish Supreme Court had ordered the dissolution of three Basque parties on the grounds that they were really part of the ETA terrorist campaign.[31] The applicant parties complained to Strasbourg. The Court outlined the key principles on article 11 and highlighted that a party supporting a programme of violence or the destruction of democracy and flouting of rights could be restricted.[32] In determining the existence of a threat, one could look not just to the official programme but the actions and words of the party leaders and members; furthermore, the state is not required to wait till a party has actually won power before intervening.[33] The Court noted that the parties had used language which created a 'climate of confrontation'; that the language used by the parties was close to condonation of terrorism; and that the parties' refusal to condemn ETA violence in the context of a thirty-year

---

[29] *United Macedonian Organisation Ilinden – PIRIN v Bulgaria* (No 2) App no 41561/07 (18 October 2011).
[30] *Tsonev v Bulgaria* App no 45963/99 (2008) 46 EHRR 8, para 59.
[31] *Herri Batasuna v Spain*, para 30.
[32] *Herri Batasuna v Spain*, para 79.
[33] *Herri Batasuna v Spain*, paras 80–81.

terrorist campaign all meant that the Spanish court's judgment had been reasonable.[34] Having found that there was a pressing social need justifying the interference with article 11, the Court concluded very briskly that the measure of dissolution was necessary.

The case demonstrates the Court's approach to parties linked to violence. It was reviewing a national decision that had been made by the Supreme Court and subject to examination by Spain's Constitutional Court, and especially in the aftermath of 9/11, the Court's approach is understandable (and the conclusion unanimous). The failure to probe the necessity of the drastic step taken, however, in particular whether any other steps were appropriate, is troubling, as is the willingness to rely on silence (a refusal to condemn) and language bearing 'a strong resemblance' to the commendation of terrorism. The scrutiny in these regards could have been more intense. Intriguing also in this case was the insistence of the Spanish courts that the Spanish model was not one of 'militant democracy'; in this regard the case focused on the link to violence. Other cases, though, are more firmly in the arena of militant democracy and tell us more about the model of democracy the Court envisages.

SUBSTANTIVE DEMOCRACY

As discussed in the previous chapter, notions of substantive democracy – as opposed to the liberal representative model – may be discerned in different ways.

First there may be cases where the Court permits restrictions on associations and assemblies in order to respect a communal value. There is one communal value which merits considerable respect in the case law of the Court – this is the interest in protecting territorial integrity. Thus, in the *United Communist Party* case, the Grand Chamber agreed that 'openly pursuing the creation of a separate Kurdish nation and consequently a redistribution of the territory of the Turkish State' engaged national security even in the absence of any support for terrorism.[35] However while protecting territorial integrity is a legitimate aim, this does not make it legitimate to ban separatist parties. Provided a separatist party does not intend to use violence or other undemocratic means or intend to harm democracy itself, it is entitled to advocate for changes to the national constitutional structure. This includes advocating for separatism.[36]

---

[34] *Herri Batasuna v Spain*, paras 86–91.
[35] *United Communist Party of Turkey v Turkey*, para 40.
[36] *United Macedonian Organisation Ilinden – Pirin and others v Bulgaria* App no 59489/00 (2006) 43 EHRR 52.

Unsurprisingly, then, the Court has also found that states cannot ban regional political parties. This was the conclusion of the Court in the *Republican Party of Russia* case. Russia had required political parties to have branches with more than 500 members in 45 districts, effectively banning regional parties.[37] The Court found the effective ban on regional parties a breach of the Convention and used strong language to underline the rights of people and associations to contest the existing constitutional order provided they did not threaten democracy itself. The mere fact that an association's members make 'shocking and unacceptable' statements and have 'illegitimate demands' does not justify dissolution, unless the threshold of threatening democracy itself is reached.[38]

The second and more important example concerns the 'militant democracy' strand in the case law of the Court. On one reading, a liberal representative democracy cannot be neutral and liberal on all questions – such a democracy cannot extend these rights to those who would use violence as above, but more substantively cannot accept claims from those who seek to destroy the rights in the Convention or the vision of pluralism on which it depends.

The militant democracy type cases give clear expression to a substantive conception – a democratic society founded on the principles of pluralism, tolerance and broad-mindedness. In this way it does not adopt a strictly content-neutral approach. This expresses itself in positive and negative ways. Pluralism requires 'the genuine recognition of, and respect for, diversity and the dynamics of traditions and of ethnic and cultural identities'.[39] In one article 11 case, the Court had occasion to comment on the purpose of education in the Convention system and outlined its purposes as including the promotion of religious peace, public order and tolerance in a democratic society; this implies the state must ensure education is delivered in an objective, critical, pluralist manner.[40]

There is also a negative or defensive aspect. In many of its judgments the Court accepts that the state has a right to protect its institutions and thus 'some compromise between the requirements of *defending democratic society* and individual rights is inherent in the system of the Convention'.[41] This has the

---

[37] *Republican Party of Russia v Russia* App no 12976/07 (2015) 61 EHRR 20.
[38] *Republican Party of Russia v Russia*, para 123.
[39] *Ouranio Toxo v Greece*, para 35.
[40] *Zehra Foundation and Others v Turkey*, para 51.
[41] *United Communist Party of Turkey v Turkey*, para 32 (emphasis added).

130 Association, Assembly and Political Parties

potential to raise 'fundamental questions about the organization of European political democracy'.[42]

In many cases this approach is apparent when the Court is dealing with extremist parties or associations founded on racist[43] or sectarian principles. In another case involving the organisation Hizb ut-Tahrir, the Court commented more extensively on the notion that certain political activities or goals were incompatible with the Convention. This case involved criminal prosecutions of Hizb ut-Tahrir members by Russia.[44] The case mainly turned on an argument that there was a breach of the non-retrospectivity principle in article 7, but the Court also considered whether article 17 precluded the organisation from relying on article 9, 10 and 11 rights. The Court reiterated that parties were free to advocate for changes to the law or constitution of a state, on two conditions. The first was that the means used must be legal and democratic; the second that the intended change must itself be compatible with human rights.[45]

Applying these standards, the Court found that the organisation's commitment to violence meant the means it proposed were not legal and democratic. Moreover, the aims of the organisation were not compatible with the Convention: Hizb ut-Tahrir wanted to establish a regime where political freedoms would be repressed, non-Islamic parties banned, apostasy punished by death, sex discrimination would be condoned, and personal laws and Sharia law would be applied.[46] Given the extreme views of the organisation on multiple issues and its advocacy of violence, the Court's decision is a relatively unproblematic example of the substantive democracy principle that the freedoms in the Convention cannot be invoked to destroy the system of rights and democracy.

Yet in some of these cases, the militant democracy approach may lead to a worryingly richer conception of what the democratic society envisaged by the Court might look like. The most serious instance of this is the *Refah Partisi* case. This concerned the decision of the Turkish Constitutional Court to

---

[42] David Harris, Michael O'Boyle, Ed Bates and Carla Buckley, *Law of the European Convention on Human Rights* (Oxford University Press 2018), 733.

[43] *Vona v Hungary* App no 35943/10 (9 July 2013).

[44] *Kasymakhunov and Saybatalov v Russia* App nos 26261/05 and 26377/06 (14 March 2013).

[45] *Kasymakhunov and Saybatalov v Russia*, para 105. In *Refah Partisi*, two concurring judges emphasised that both of these statements were too general – not every illegality or every proposal to change human rights would permit drastic restrictions on article 11: concurring opinion of Judge Rees joined by Judge Rozakis in *Refah Partisi (Welfare Party) v Turkey* App nos 41340/98 41342/98 41343/98 and 41344/98 (2003) 37 EHRR 1 (Grand Chamber).

[46] *Kasymakhunov and Saybatalov v Russia*, paras 109–111.

Substantive Democracy 131

dissolve the Welfare Party in Turkey. The case of Refah was significantly different from the other cases involving bans on organisations because of either a commitment to violence or to undemocratic aims; Refah was the largest party in Turkey with more than one-third of voters supporting it and was a member of a coalition government. This was not a regional party, much less a small violent extremist organisation. The Constitutional Court of Turkey ordered its dissolution and removed several of its members from Parliament, on the ground that the party's advocacy of sharia law was incompatible with the principle of secularism.[47] In the European Court of Human Rights, a Chamber found by a 4–3 majority that this dissolution was compatible with article 11. The case went to the Grand Chamber.

The Grand Chamber rejected claims that the measure was not prescribed by law; it also rejected an argument that the measure was for an impermissible purpose. The case turned on the necessity of the dissolution. The Grand Chamber outlined the general principles to be applied in cases like this. The Court reiterated the 'primordial' role of political parties in a democracy,[48] highlighting that they contribute to political pluralism and this must include the right to put forward ideas that offend, shock or disturb.[49] The Court also emphasised the importance of religious rights and the role of the state as the 'neutral and impartial organizer' with a 'duty of neutrality and impartiality'.[50] The role may mean that the state can limit the possibility for civil servants to participate in Islamic fundamentalist movements, or may restrict the possibility for fundamentalist members of a majority religion to exert pressure on others in a university setting.[51] The Court noted again the freedom of political parties to organise provided they used legal and democratic means and pursued aims compatible with human rights, reflecting the principle that 'no one must be authorized to rely on the Convention's provisions to weaken or destroy the ideals and values of a democratic society.'[52] This means the Court must be wary of the threat posed by 'totalitarian movements, organized in the form of political parties', but must also protect the article 11 rights, in particular respecting the notion that 'a political party animated by the moral values imposed by a religion cannot be regarded as intrinsically inimical to the

---

[47] *Refah Partisi (Welfare Party) v Turkey* App nos 41340/98 41342/98 41343/98 and 41344/98 (2003) 37 EHRR 1, paras 23–42.
[48] *Refah Partisi*, para 87.
[49] *Refah Partisi*, para 89.
[50] *Refah Partisi*, para 91.
[51] *Refah Partisi*, paras 94–95.
[52] *Refah Partisi*, para 99.

132 *Association, Assembly and Political Parties*

fundamental principles of democracy.'[53] The Court also underlined that authorities cannot rely solely on explicit programmes, as parties may conceal their ultimate plans; and furthermore the state was not required to wait until a party had actually seized power and begun implementing its programme.[54]

Applying these principles, the Grand Chamber unanimously upheld the Chamber finding that there was no violation of article 11. The Grand Chamber supported each of the three elements of the reasoning of the Constitutional Court in dissolving Refah. It held that the party had insufficiently distanced itself from the language of members who had endorsed violence as a means.[55] This, though, was not the main crux of the Grand Chamber discussion. Of greater weight was the view that the party was committed to two reforms that were incompatible with the Convention: the introduction of pluralist systems of law and the introduction of sharia law. The Grand Chamber endorsed the Chamber view that a plurality of systems of law would offend against the Convention on two grounds. First, such a system would end the state's role as guarantor of rights and favour a system where individuals were bound to respect 'static rules of law imposed by the religion concerned'; furthermore, it would infringe the non-discrimination principle.[56] The Grand Chamber also agreed that sharia law was 'incompatible with the fundamental principles of democracy'; the Grand Chamber quoted with approval the Chamber's findings that sharia was a form of divine rule that was 'stable and invariable', which had no place for 'pluralism in the public sphere or the constant evolution of public freedoms', and which on matters of criminal law and procedure and women's rights was inconsistent with the democratic vision in the Convention.[57] In this context the Grand Chamber unanimously found that the restriction met a pressing social need.

The Grand Chamber judgment is unusual for the rather sweeping approach to defining important concepts, in this case pluralist systems of law and sharia law. One of the concurring judgments, by Judge Kovler, draws attention to this, while not disagreeing with the finding. The judgment deserves rather more criticism on this ground than Judge Kovler offers. The discussion of both pluralist legal systems and sharia law is brief and includes assumptions about the nature of the legal system the Refah party would pursue, as well as assuming the Turkish constitutional system (and European

[53] *Refah Partisi*, paras 99–100.
[54] *Refah Partisi*, paras 101–102.
[55] *Refah Partisi*, para 131.
[56] *Refah Partisi*, para 119.
[57] *Refah Partisi*, para 123.

human rights system) would lack the resources to tame any excesses. There is an assumption that certain practices are compatible with the convention (e.g. recognition of religious marriages by the state[58]) but that the form of pluralist and sharia law that would be introduced by Refah would not. But it is not especially clear from the judgment precisely what reforms would be introduced or why they necessarily would go beyond what might be introduced by other political parties inspired by religious motivations. The approach seems somewhat different from that in the *Republican Party of Russia* case where the Court said that even statements that appear shocking and unacceptable or involve illegitimate demands do not justify dissolution unless the party threatens democracy itself. The poor reasoning on these major concepts leaves room for the criticism that Christian democracy and Islamic democracy are treated differently in Strasbourg.

The ultimate effect of the *Refah party case* is somewhat unclear. The party was dissolved; one of its members went on to join the Justice and Development Party (AKP) and become prime minster and later president (Erdogan). The AKP initially seemed to introduce reforms when in power, and some might have welcomed this as a vindication of the outcome of the *Refah case*. However, more recently President Erdogan has been accused of tendencies to authoritarianism, involving crackdowns on protest, purges following a coup attempt and changes to the Turkish constitution leading to a more presidentialist system of government.

DELIBERATIVE AND PARTICIPATORY DEMOCRACY

The aim of this work is to identify the possibilities and prospects for the Convention to support models of democracy which go beyond the liberal representative model and embody more participatory and deliberative modes of democratic politics. It is helpful then to think about what this might look like in the context of free association and assembly. There is necessarily a large overlap with liberal representative approaches – participation and deliberative democracy will also require freedom for individuals to converge freely around issues and controversies. A society committed to participation and deliberation would perhaps facilitate the formation of groups through support, might adopt mechanisms to facilitate participation by all elements of society, empower these associations to make their voice heard in politics, and support mechanisms which promote deliberation as free and equal citizens; such measures in

[58] *Refah Partisi*, para. 127.

134   Association, Assembly and Political Parties

a deliberative vision should be adopted themselves through democratically legitimate modes of lawmaking. In a participatory society it might be expected that groups like trade unions and non-governmental organisations would receive especial protection.

There is language in some of the Court's article 11 case law which supports an explicitly deliberative model of democracy. Let us return to the language of the Grand Chamber in the *United Communist Party* case:

> The Court considers one of the principal characteristics of democracy to be the possibility it offers of resolving a country's problems through *dialogue, without recourse to violence*, even when they are irksome. Democracy thrives on freedom of expression. From that point of view, there can be no justification for hindering a political group solely because it seeks to debate in public the situation of part of the State's population and to take part in the nation's political life in order to find, according to democratic rules, *solutions capable of satisfying everyone concerned.*[59]

The language here is compatible with a liberal democratic conception of democracy but also uses terms familiar to deliberative democrats. There is the use of the term 'dialogue' which is central to democratic deliberation and the rejection of violence. And strikingly, the quote finishes with a (presumably unintentional) paraphrase of the goal of a Habermassian ideal speech situation.

The role of civil society is also central to a deliberative and participatory democracy. 'Civil society' is usually used to refer to a realm of free associations operating distinct from the economy and state.[60] In particular, civil society contributes criticisms and new ideas in the public sphere,[61] and from the public sphere these criticisms and ideas can influence the official political institutions. A free and vibrant civil society and public sphere is thus critical to many deliberative and participatory democrats. At the same time, it has to be recognised that civil society is not a utopia; it may support hierarchical associations,[62] can contain uncivil elements[63] and is open to manipulation by governments.[64]

---

[59] *United Communist Party of Turkey v Turkey*, para 57 (emphasis added).
[60] Iris Marion Young, *Inclusion and Democracy* (Oxford University Press 2000), 157–159.
[61] Jürgen Habermas, *The Inclusion of the Other: Studies in Political Theory* (Polity Press 1998), 251.
[62] Young, *Inclusion and Democracy*, 164.
[63] James, *Deliberative Democracy and the Plural Polity*, 109.
[64] Kateryna Pishchikova, 'Between Democracy and Authoritarianism: The Hybrid Nature of Post-Soviet Political Transformation' in Seyla Benhabib, David Cameron, Anna Dolidze, Gábor

The Court has frequently recognised the importance of a diverse and vibrant civil society as an avenue for people to engage in collective action and contribute more broadly to democratic processes:

> While in the context of Article 11 the Court has often referred to the essential role played by political parties in ensuring pluralism and democracy, associations formed for other purposes are also important to the proper functioning of democracy. For pluralism is also built on the genuine recognition of, and respect for, diversity and the dynamics of cultural traditions, ethnic and cultural identities, religious beliefs, artistic, literary and socio-economic ideas and concepts. The harmonious interaction of persons and groups with varied identities is essential for achieving social cohesion. It is only natural that, where a civil society functions in a healthy manner, the participation of citizens in the democratic process is to a large extent achieved through belonging to associations in which they may integrate with each other and pursue common objectives collectively.[65]

A key part of deliberation is about offering opportunities for – at the minimum - consultation. This reflects the reality that the regulation of rights issues in modern democracies is often complex and involves competing rights and finding a fair balance between the individuals and the common interest in the Court's language. Some rights issues may be relatively clear-cut or amenable to resolution by applying familiar principles. Others though are not – these are the types of cases where the Court might deploy the notion of a wide margin of appreciation. It could also, though (or as an aspect of the margin of appreciation doctrine), look to the process behind a decision to see if it allowed for adequate deliberation and participation. The Court does draw attention to deliberative and participatory practices in its case law. For instance, in *UNITE the Union v UK*, the Court had to consider a claim that the UK's decision to abolish a board which set wages for agricultural labourers breached article 11 rights of the applicant trade union.[66] The trade union had an entitlement to seats on the board and saw it as a mechanism to ensure collective bargaining with agricultural employers. The Court dismissed the application as inadmissible, concluding that there was no requirement to make collective bargaining mandatory in the agricultural sector; the union was free to try and persuade employers to engage in collective bargaining.[67]

Halmai, Gunther Hellmann, Kateryna Pishchikova and Richard Youngs (eds) *The Democratic Disconnect* (Washington, DC: Transatlantic Academy 2013), 52.

[65] *Zhechev v Bulgaria* App no 57045/00 (21 June 2007), para 35.

[66] *UNITE the Union v United Kingdom* App no 65397/13 (3 May 2016).

[67] *UNITE the Union v United Kingdom*, para 65.

Among the factors relevant in coming to this decision was the fact that there had been a consultation exercise and published research into the issue. The UK had included an impact assessment and a human rights memorandum as part of the process in deciding to abolish the board. While brief, this is an indication that the Court attaches some importance to the process behind a decision.

The *UNITE the Union* case, though, also highlights another important participatory aspect of the Convention, or at least participatory potential. This is the role of trade unions. As noted above, the Court recognises a very wide range of associations as falling under the umbrella of article 11; this is necessary for the vibrant civil society and public sphere envisaged by the Convention. Among those associations, certain attract special attention, most notably political parties. Similarly, trade unions also require distinctive attention, as they represent an important civil society association. In important ways, trade unions can widen and deepen the participatory nature of modern liberal democracy. They offer a route to extend democratic practices into the economic sphere. The default democratic model of the Convention is the ideal of a liberal representative democracy with free and fair elections, liberal rights (expression, religion, association, etc), traditional civil and political rights including the right to property. This model of democracy assumes that the formal political institutions (especially parliament) are the main focus of democratic practice. This ignores claims by participatory democrats that the economic sphere also needs attending to. In part this is because of the potentially limited scope for participation offered by the formal political institutions – the caricature of voting once every four or five years is not much of a caricature. Moreover, while the formal political institutions regulate considerable portions of society, for many people a significant portion of their lives is spent in work, and many of the factors affecting their life chances and opportunities are shaped by decisions in the workplace. So the economic sphere is relevant to peoples' opportunities for participation. Further, the economic sphere is not carved off from the political sphere. The Convention provides institutional protection for economic actors through property rights, fair trial rights, etc. Economic actors have the possibility to influence political decisions, and this is arguably more prevalent under conditions of globalisation. Inequalities of wealth and resources in the economic and private spheres have the possibility to corrupt or deform debate in the public sphere and politics. Protecting participation in the employment sphere through protecting union rights is an avenue to widen the democratic potential of the Convention.

It is also an avenue, more indirectly perhaps, to deepen the practice of democracy. Trade unions regularly invoke their free expression and free association rights to advocate for their members. In some countries this makes them a target for violence and assassination. Even more importantly, though, they are concerned typically to advocate for the economic and social rights and interests of their members. The Convention, with its focus on civil and political rights, may lead to an unbalanced political system.[68] The European Social Charter and other treaties deal with economic and social rights, and the Convention cannot replace them.[69] But it can support them by ensuring those associations interested in economic and social rights can effectively exercise their own rights.

This takes us to the article 11 jurisprudence on trade unions, which has undergone considerable change since the end of the twentieth century. Early cases on trade union rights seemed limited in the protection offered to trade unions – they had the right to exist, to act on behalf of their members and to be heard. This right to 'strive for the protection of their members' interests' and thus to 'be heard' was based on the last words of article 11(1), recognising the 'right to form and to join trade unions for the protection of his interests'.[70] This, however, did not entail recognition for any particular form of collective action, bargaining or strike. The right to be heard did not even extend to a right to be consulted.[71] The jurisprudence was lacklustre. This changed in the early twenty-first century.

In *Wilson v UK*, the applicants were employees and members of trade unions in different firms. Their employers had written to them to ask them to accept a variation in contract whereby if they renounced certain union rights, they would receive more favourable pay. The employers also derecognised the trade unions for the purposes of collective bargaining. The House of Lords reversed lower court judgments finding the employers' actions unlawful; Parliament passed a law further protecting the employers' actions. The case, therefore, raised two questions: whether there should be an obligation on employers to engage in collective bargaining with a trade union, and whether the employers could offer better pay and conditions to employees if they

---

[68] K. D. Ewing, 'The Unbalanced Constitution' in Tom Campbell, Keith Ewing and Adam Tomkins (eds) *Sceptical Essays on Human Rights* (Oxford University Press 2001).

[69] Though there are numerous important ways in which the Convention can offer indirect protection to a range of economic and social rights including the rights to health, work and social security.

[70] *National Union of Belgian Police v Belgium* App no 4464/70 (1979–1980) 1 EHRR 578.

[71] See the concurring opinion of Judge Jörundsson in *Wilson v United Kingdom* App nos 30668/96, 30671/96 and 30678/96 (2002) 35 EHRR 20.

renounced their trade union rights. The European Court of Human Rights rejected an argument that the Convention required the recognition of trade unions for collective bargaining purposes.[72] On the second point, however, it found for the applicants. The Court noted that accepting the UK position would mean that employees had a right to be a member of a union but no right to enjoy the benefits of being in the union; this would make the right 'illusory'.[73] The European Court of Human Rights held that national law could not permit an employer to effectively bribe employees to renounce trade union rights.[74] This followed criticism by the body monitoring the European Social Charter.

More drastic anti-union activity was considered in *Danilenkov v Russia*.[75] Here the applicants were members of the TUR trade union in a seaport company. Following an unsuccessful strike, the applicants complained that they were the victims of numerous acts effectively penalising them for their union membership. This included being put in special teams which worked fewer hours, undergoing dubious tests and being punished for allegedly being absent from work. In many instances they succeeded in obtaining individual victories in the courts. However the courts refused to consider the specific claim of anti-union discrimination, arguing this was a matter for the criminal law, where the burden of proof was higher and there was a requirement to show an intention to directly discriminate. The actions continued, and the union membership dwindled from nearly 300 to about 20.[76] The International Labour Organisation (ILO) criticised the situation. Before the European Court of Human Rights, the Court considered the issue on the basis of article 11 in combination with article 14's prohibition of discrimination. The Court noted that the ILO had held that anti-union discrimination was an especially serious violation of freedom of association. It concluded that the existence of a criminal remedy was insufficient; not only was it not effectively used, but the higher burden of proof and requirement to show an intention to directly discrimination were inadequate to offer protection against discrimination. The Court concluded there was a failure by Russia in terms of its positive obligations to protect union members from discrimination.[77]

---

[72] *Wilson v United Kingdom*, para 45.
[73] *Wilson v United Kingdom*, para 46.
[74] *Wilson v United Kingdom*, para 47.
[75] *Danilenkov v Russia* App no 67336/01 (2014) 58 EHRR 19.
[76] *Danilenkov v Russia*, para 130.
[77] *Danilenkov v Russia*, paras 134–136.

Even more significant was the judgment in *Demir and Baykara v Turkey*.[78] Here, the applicants' trade union of municipal workers was not recognised as a trade union; Turkey applied a wide ban on trade unions in the public service at the time. The trade union had in fact negotiated a collective agreement with the municipal employer and even seen it implemented for two years, but it was ruled void by the Turkish courts. The Grand Chamber found this violated article 11 on two grounds. First, the Grand Chamber ruled that the refusal to recognise the public sector trade union was itself a breach of article 11. While states might impose some restrictions on the activities of the armed forces, police and administration of the state, the complete non-recognition was not necessary in a democratic society. Second, and somewhat unusually, the Court explicitly stated it was changing its jurisprudence on article 11 dating back to the 1970s and now recognising that the right to bargain collectively was an essential part of the article 11 trade union rights.[79]

While these cases demonstrate an increased sensitivity to the importance of trade union rights and specifically the possibility of collective action, including collective bargaining, more recent cases suggest there are limits to this evolution. As already noted, in the *UNITE the Union* case the Court refused to find that the Convention required a mandatory process of collective bargaining in the agricultural sector. Even more significant and surprising is the *National Union of Rail, Maritime and Transport Workers v UK* case (*RMT case*).[80]

This case concerned the general ban in UK law on secondary or sympathy strikes.[81] The applicant union had organised a strike at one place of work where there were only a small number of employees (Hydrex); previously they had been part of a bigger workforce with an employer called Jarvis, but Jarvis had transferred the Hydrex operation. The union's strike action in Hydrex was unsuccessful, and they argued that the ban on secondary strike action meant they could not launch strike action at the Jarvis workplace. The applicant and third parties noted that the ban on secondary strike action had been criticised by ILO and ESC organs, and that the changing nature of labour practices meant that it had a more severe effect. They also noted that the UK appeared to be among a small number of European states to adopt such a restrictive approach. The UK government pointed to the wide margin of appreciation

---

[78] *Demir and Baykara v Turkey* App no 34503/97 (2008) 48 EHRR 54 (Grand Chamber).
[79] *Demir and Baykara v Turkey*, para 154.
[80] *National Union of Rail Maritime and Transport Workers v United Kingdom* App no 31045/10 (2015) 60 EHRR 10 (*RMT case*).
[81] There was also a complaint about the procedural requirements for holding a strike, but this was declared inadmissible.

available when deciding social and economic issues and stressed the harmful wider ramifications of secondary strike action which could inconvenience others not involved in a dispute.[82] The government disputed the exact findings and authority of the ILO and ESC organs.

The European Court of Human Rights held that secondary strikes fell within the scope of article 11, and so the article was applicable; in this regard it said that the article should not adopt a much narrower approach than was apparent in other international instruments.[83] The issue became whether the ban was prescribed by law, for a legitimate aim and necessary in a democratic society. The Court relatively briefly accepted that the first two requirements were met, and at more length considered whether the measure met the necessity requirement. The Court noted that strike action was covered by article 11 but did not decide whether it was one of the essential elements of the right; in this case the applicant had enjoyed some of the essential aspects of the right and there was no Convention requirement of successful strike action.[84] In this case the Court thought that the claims involved a secondary rather than a core aspect of the article 11 right, and so a wider margin of appreciation was justified.[85] The Court largely dismissed the government's efforts to undermine reliance on the ILO and ESC organs – since the Court often relies on these, this is unsurprising. However, the Court then found another reason for it not to follow the views of the ILO and ESC bodies on this occasion. This was down to the different role of the Court as a court; its role was not to examine the law in abstraction from the facts of the case but to decide whether the applicant's rights had been restricted in the actual case.[86] The Court repeatedly stressed the wide margin of appreciation and also noted the broad democratic consensus given that this ban had been maintained by governments of different parties over some twenty years.[87]

The *RMT case* indicates there are limits to the Court's willingness to expand the interpretation of collective action in article 11, and limits on how far it will go in pursuing a harmonious interpretation with other human rights instruments.

---

[82] At different points referring to possible threats to the right to make one's living (para 82), property rights and apparently the right to life (*RMT case*, para 64).

[83] *RMT case*, para 76.

[84] *RMT case*, paras 84–85.

[85] *RMT case*, paras 87–88.

[86] *RMT case*, para 98.

[87] *RMT case*, para 99.

CONCLUSION

The Court's case law on article 11 strongly supports the liberal representative model of democracy. It has been relatively assiduous in protecting the rights of political parties and other associations as well as many forms of assembly, including protecting to some extent unlawful assemblies.

The Court's case law also reiterates its consistent support for a substantive model of democracy at least to the extent of defending the principles of pluralism, tolerance and broad-mindedness. This substantive conception justifies restrictions on associations that reject these values and indeed seek to use Convention rights to destroy the system of rights and democracy. Yet there is a danger that this substantive model could become rather too thick. The *Refah party case* demonstrates this risk; at the very least, the simplistic treatment of concepts like plural legal systems and sharia law needs to be avoided in future judgments.

The Court's jurisprudence on article 11 offers some scope to further a more deliberative and participatory model of democracy, though it has to be said this to date is somewhat limited. Some twenty-first-century case law on trade union rights (*Wilson, Danilenkov, Demir and Bakaya*) demonstrate the Court being more alive to the needs to support this important element of civil society. More recent cases, however, such as the *RMT case*, show that the Court is cautious in further expanding this line of cases. This is especially disappointing given the risk that the Convention may protect civil and political rights without always giving due regard to their equally important social and economic counterparts. Even if there is some scope for protecting social and economic rights indirectly in the ECHR system,[88] there is little scope to use it to argue directly or indirectly for more substantive economic equality, of the sort necessary for an effective deliberative democratic system.[89] As Phillips puts it, 'So long as large sections of the citizenry are constrained in the exercise of their political rights by lack of money, education, contacts, or time, declarations of basic equality will always ring rather hollow.'[90] The failure to address claims of social and economic rights or even equality could have serious consequences. As Roosevelt explained in a State of the Union address,

---

[88] Eva Brems, 'Indirect Protection of Social Rights by the European Court of Human Rights' in A. Barak-Erez and A. Gross (ed) *Exploring Social Rights* (Hart 2007); Ellie Palmer, 'Protecting Socio-Economic Rights through the European Convention on Human Rights: Trends and Developments in the European Court of Human Rights' (2009) 2 (4) Erasmus Law Review 397–425.

[89] Anne Phillips, *Which Equalities Matter?* (Polity 1999), 123.

[90] Phillips, *Which Equalities Matter?*, 130.

'People who are hungry and out of a job are the stuff of which dictatorships are made.'[91] Economic inequality has been tied to the rise of populist political actors in contemporary Europe.[92]

If the Convention does not provide a clear avenue to argue for economic equality or equality or resources, its case law on trade unions does provide an avenue to strengthen one form of association often (if not always or perfectly) concerned with issues of workers' rights and equality. The Court's approach runs the risk of envisaging a rather narrow understanding of political equality, despite important language about the role of civil society and trade unions.

While civil society and the public sphere are important for a deliberative model of democracy, deliberative democrats also recognise the basic limitations of civil society and the public sphere. Civil society and the public sphere can be freer and more inclusive than narrow political institutions, but they lack the ability of political institutions to achieve certain goals and in particular to deploy power in such a way as to create institutions and control important private actors.[93] For this reason the role of official political institutions remains critical. It is at this point that we turn to the political rights concerned explicitly with the electoral process, where we find that even these are very narrowly conceived as regards their scope.

---

[91] Franklin Delano Roosevelt 'State of the Union Address' (1944) <www.presidency.ucsb.edu/node/210825> accessed 7 August 2019.

[92] Roger Eatwell and Matthew Goodwin, *National Populism: The Revolt against Liberal Democracy* (Penguin UK 2018).

[93] Iris Marion Young, *Inclusion and Democracy* (Oxford University Press 2000), 186.

6

Scope of the Electoral Rights

While the previous two chapters have examined the key liberal rights in articles 10 and 11, this chapter moves the focus of the book to the electoral rights. This chapter focuses on the scope of article 3 of Protocol 1 (P1–3) which concerns the right to free elections. P1–3 reads as follows:

Right to Free Elections

The High Contracting Parties undertake to hold free elections at reasonable intervals by secret ballot, under conditions that will ensure the free expression of the opinion of the people in the choice of the legislature.

This text is somewhat unusual in not expressly identifying rights (apart from in its title). It includes implicitly the right to vote and to run for election as participation rights, and these are considered in the next two chapters. Increasingly it is also concerned with how elections are regulated, to which we return in Chapter 9. This chapter focuses on the scope of P1–3 – to what sort of elections it applies.

The chapter necessarily focuses on the nature of representative democracy as envisaged by the Convention and Court, and some of the concerns about substantive democracy or the role of deliberation may recede. The chapter, therefore, gives some more space to considering the limits and potentials for the Convention's model of democracy to address new challenges of participation: How does the Convention deal with referendums, for instance, or the scope for participation at levels that regulate day-to-day life in devolved or local administrations? How does it deal with the transfer of powers to international and supranational institutions such as the European Union? How indeed might the Convention deal with the Union's possible accession to the Convention? Does P1–3 have any application beyond the spheres of formal political institutions? How does P1–3 compare to other guarantees of political participation?

144   *Scope of the Electoral Rights*

LEGISLATURE

The text of P1–3 is more limited than some other texts on political rights. For instance, article 21 of the Universal Declaration of Human Rights (UDHR) protects the 'right to take part in the government' of the country; the notion of free elections is only one part of this broader right.[1] The broader rights include the right to take part not only through representatives but also directly. It also includes the right of equal access to public services. Article 21(3) UDHR is the closest to P1–3 in referring to periodic and genuine elections though spelling out specifically that there must be 'universal and equal suffrage' and 'secret vote' or 'equivalent' procedures. With some adjustment in language, article 25 of the International Covenant on Civil and Political Rights (ICCPR) reflects this broader understanding of political participation. Article 20 of the American Declaration of the Rights and Duties of Man speaks of the right 'to participate in the government of his country, directly or through his representatives'. Similarly, the American Convention on Human Rights includes a 'right to take part in the conduct of public affairs' and reflects the substance of the broader right in the UDHR.[2] The African Charter of Human and Peoples' Rights also guarantees the broader right to 'participate freely' and access to public service; it adds a reference to access to public property also, but it lacks a specific reference to the nature of elections.[3] Both the Organisation of American States and the African Union have adopted Charters on democracy.[4]

The European Convention, however, is much more circumspect than the UN and other regional instruments: there is no broad right to participation, the right is not really expressed as such, it is hived off into a separate protocol, and the right textually only applies to the 'legislature'.

This represents a particularly limited form of representative democracy – there is no right to vote in other forms or elections, no requirement for elections other than for a legislature. If representative democracy is open to criticism as a narrow form of democracy, then this is an especially narrow protection for it, at least as expressed in the text. As will be seen, the Court has interpreted it in such a way as to extend the rights to vote and run for election

---

[1] Article 21, Universal Declaration of Human Rights.
[2] Article 23.
[3] Article 13.
[4] African Charter on Democracy, Elections and Governance 2007; Inter-American Democratic Charter 2001.

Legislature 145

to certain other fora, though it has resisted efforts to extend P1–3 to cover presidential elections, referendums or municipal elections.

The limitation of P1–3 to certain voting processes also means that other avenues of participation are excluded from Convention protection. This is especially problematic when the involvement of certain groups may require participatory and consultative measures alongside or instead of formal voting processes to ensure their participation in society and politics. Children and adolescents, for instance, may not be able to vote or run for election, but it is perfectly possible to have formal processes of consultation and participation to ensure that their voice can be heard. The Convention on the Rights of the Child requires such mechanisms,[5] but the Convention offers no protection through P1–3 for these processes.

The textual reference to 'legislature', limiting as it is, does have at least one important implication: it requires that a legislature exist. This was established in the early Greek case, one of the rare but important interstate cases in the history of the Convention.[6] The Greek government had been overthrown in a military coup, and the military authorities had violated numerous Convention rights, seeking to invoke article 15's derogation clause. The regime abolished the old parliament and adopted a new constitution but did not implement legislation to establish the new parliament envisaged by this constitution. The Commission concluded the P1–3 requires the existence 'of a representative legislature, elected at reasonable intervals, as the basis of a democratic society'.[7] In this regard the Commission also referred to the impossibility for political parties to be formed as part of the breach of P1–3. The Commission dismissed the idea that any national emergency justified this breach, noting that even during the Greek civil war, the Greek parliament had functioned.[8]

The Greek case is an exceptional one in the European context, concerning the military overthrow of a government. While P1–3 requires that a legislature exists, does it require that there be one effectively functioning?[9] Does it have anything to say about situations where the legislature exists but is effectively

---

[5] Committee on the Rights of the Child, *General comment No 20 (2016) on the implementation of the rights of the child during adolescence* (United Nations 2016), Committee on the Rights of the Child, *General comment No 12 (2009) The right of the child to be heard* (United Nations 2016).

[6] *Denmark and others v Greece* (The Greek case) App no 3321/67 (5 November 1969) (European Commission of Human Rights).

[7] *Denmark and others v Greece* (The Greek case), para 319.

[8] *Denmark and others v Greece* (The Greek case), para 321.

[9] In a case concerning the 1973 Northern Ireland Assembly, the Commission expressed some doubt in 1984 whether it could be considered a legislature. It did not elaborate on the reason why, but this may have been because the Assembly had been suspended since 1974 and not

146   *Scope of the Electoral Rights*

stripped of powers? Does P1–3 imply anything about the power of other institutions? For instance, if an authority (presumably a president) had extensive rule-making powers of his or her own, or extensive powers to veto legislation or refuse to implement legislation, would this violate P1–3?

Do the P1–3 rights apply to all parts of the legislature or only one in the case of a bicameral parliament? In *Mathieu-Mohin and Clerfayt v Belgium*, the Court briefly indicated that it applied to one of the chambers of a legislature, referring to the *travaux préparatoires*.[10] At the time of the drafting of the Convention there existed, and exists today, a body like the unelected House of Lords in the UK, and the Convention text is, for now, interpreted to permit this. The House of Lords is unusual but there are other parliaments which have a number of unelected, usually appointed members (eg the Irish Senate).

Where both chambers are elected, the state may provide for different voting or candidacy rights in respect of them according to the European Commission of Human Rights. In *WXY and Z v Belgium*, the Commission found that different age limits for candidates – twenty-five and forty – for the two chambers of parliament were compatible with the Convention.[11]

This does not mean, though, that if a state has a bicameral parliament, it can adopt any rules on elections to one of them. In *Sejdic and Finci v Bosnia Herzegovina*, the Grand Chamber indicated that P1–3 applied to any chambers that were directly elected.[12] It then proceeded to apply it also to an indirectly elected chamber. In that case, the applicants complained that they were ineligible to run for the upper house of the legislature, the House of Peoples. This was an indirectly elected chamber comprising five representatives from each of the three constituent peoples. The applicants did not self-identify as one of the three constituent peoples and so were ineligible. The Court concluded that the P1–3 requirements did apply to the House of Peoples. It was elected, albeit indirectly, and decisively it played a major role

---

    exercised any legislative role notwithstanding the original intention that it should: *M v United Kingdom* App no 10316/83 (European Commission of Human Rights, 7 March 1984).

[10] *Mathieu-Mohin and Clerfayt v Belgium* App no 9267/81 (1987) 10 EHRR 1, para 53. Judge Pinheiro Farinha strongly disagreed with the Court expressing a view on this point given it was not in issue. He nevertheless added some important qualifications as to the issue of elections for a two-chamber legislature: the majority of the members of the legislature should be elected, and the unelected chamber should not have greater powers than the elected chamber.

[11] *W X Y and Z v Belgium* App nos 6745/74 and 6746/74 (1975) 2 DR 114 (European Commission of Human Rights, 30 May 1975).

[12] *Sejdic and Finci v Bosnia and Herzegovina* App nos 27996/06 and 34836/06 (2009) 22 BHRC 201 (Grand Chamber), para 40.

Other National Political Institutions 147

in the legislative process – its approval was required for legislation and for treaty ratification, and it played a major role in financial matters.[13]

The nature of a second chamber was also at issue in a Russian case, *Zhermal*. Here the applicant had sought election to the post of regional governor. As well as being an executive office, regional governors are also members of the upper house of the Russian parliament, the Federal Council. The Russian government argued that this was not an elected body (unlike the Duma) but consisted of appointees representing the federal states; this did not seem to carry any weight with the Court.[14] This is not the same as the UK House of Lords situation (where there are no elections apart from elections of hereditary peers), and so there may be no implications for that constitutional rarity.

OTHER NATIONAL POLITICAL INSTITUTIONS

The text of P1–3 implies that the rights therein do not apply to other national political institutions such as presidencies. In 1998, the Commission dismissed a complaint about a denial of the right to run in the Lithuanian Presidential election, merely noting that P1–3 did not apply to the election of a head of state and that there was no indication that the president exercised legislative power; this was despite the fact that the president could sign and initiate laws and had a power to refer legislation back to the parliament.[15]

A few years after this the Court considered this question in *Boskoski v Former Yugoslav Republic of Macedonia*.[16] The Court concluded that P1–3 did not apply to the election of the president. However, it added an important qualification. It explained that this would not necessarily always be the case. Given the need to interpret the right in light of the Convention's notion of an 'effective political democracy', if the president exercised 'the power to initiate and adopt legislation or enjoyed wide powers to control the passage of legislation or the power to censure the principal legislation-setting authorities', then the conclusion may be different. In *Boskoski*, the president had some powers, but these were not sufficient to trigger P1–3 rights. There was no power to initiate or adopt legislation, no wide-ranging powers to control the legislative process, no absolute right of veto or unlimited power of dissolution,

[13] *Sejdic and Finci v Bosnia and Herzegovina*, para 41.
[14] *Zhermal v Russia* App no 60983/00 (28 February 2008).
[15] *Baškauskaitė v Lithuania* App no 41090/98 (1999) 27 EHRR CD 341 (European Commission of Human Rights).
[16] *Boskoski v FYRM* App no 11676/04 (2 September 2004).

148 *Scope of the Electoral Rights*

no unlimited power over government appointments. The subsequent case of *Krivobokov v Ukraine* confirmed this approach. The Ukrainian president did not exercise sufficient legislative power for P1–3 to apply; while there was a power to initiate legislation, there was no power to adopt it; there was no absolute veto power; and there was no unlimited power to dismiss the government or dissolve parliament.[17]

This qualification was not discussed in the Russian prisoner voting case, *Anchugov and Gladkov v Russia*.[18] There the applicant prisoners had complained of not being allowed to vote in parliamentary or presidential elections. The Russian government did not raise the issue that P1–3 did not cover presidential elections, but the Court examined this of its own motion and concluded that this part of the complaint was inadmissible.[19] It did not discuss the qualification in the earlier cases about legislative powers of the president or examine the nature of the presidential office in Russia.

The qualification is important. There are presidents who do have much more extensive powers than primarily ceremonial heads of state – the presidents of France and Turkey, for instance. The powers of the Turkish president following the 2017 referendum have been considerably increased: the referendum ended the political neutrality of the post, abolished the post of prime minister, enhanced the veto powers, allowed the president extensive powers to appoint and dismiss ministers and vice-presidents, enhanced the powers of the president to appoint members of the Council of Judges and Prosecutors, and permitted the president to declare an emergency and to adopt even more wide-ranging decrees affecting fundamental rights during an emergency. The reforms were rushed through parliament during a state of emergency when several members of parliament had been detained. Political and legal accountability were diminished. The Venice Commission severely criticised the reforms, noting that they offered the potential for slipping into a system of authoritarian or personal rule.[20]

---

[17] *Krivobokov v Ukraine* App no 38707/04 (19 February 2013). In *Zhermal v Russia*, the Court did not examine the question whether the regional governor was part of the regional legislature, since the governor was also a member of the Federal Council, part of the federal legislature.

[18] Similarly, the Grand Chamber did not discuss the issues of P1–3's applicability to the Presidency in Bosnia and Herzegovina, as Protocol 12 was available: *Sejdic and Finci v Bosnia and Herzegovina*, para 54.

[19] *Anchugov and Gladkov v Russia* App no 11157/04 (4 July 2013).

[20] European Commission for Democracy through Law (Venice Commission), *CDL-AD(2017) 005-e Turkey – Opinion on the amendments to the Constitution adopted by the Grand National Assembly on 21 January 2017 and to be submitted to a National Referendum on 16 April 2017, adopted by the Venice Commission at its 110th Plenary Session (Venice, 10–11 March 2017)* (Council of Europe Pub., Strasbourg 2017), para 133.

Other National Political Institutions 149

The case law certainly leaves open the possibility that the right to vote and run for election would apply to these office-holders. The Court examined this issue in *Boskoski* and *Krivobokov*; unfortunately it did not examine it in the Russian case. Given the changes in the Turkish constitution since 2017, the Court may have the opportunity to consider this qualification in relation to that jurisdiction.

While the extension of the participation rights to vote and run for office would be welcome, caution is also needed about seeing this as sufficient for the effective enjoyment of P1–3. While the national legislature is not the only entity exercising legislative powers, there is reason to be concerned about the expansion of executives into the legislative arena which cannot be cured simply by free and fair elections for elected executives. If the default position of the Convention is a liberal representative regime with the focus in P1–3 on the legislature, then this should suggest some concern if the powers of the democratically elected legislature are hollowed out by transfer to other institutions. The approach of the Court is to recognise that the Convention is compatible with a wide range of democratic systems, and presumably this includes presidential and semi-presidential systems as well as classic parliamentary ones. But given the centrality of the legislature to P1–3 and the reluctance of the Court to extend voting and candidacy rights to other offices, there is scope to argue that the legislative powers of the legislature should be protected. If a representative assembly has minimal effective legislative power, then the value of the P1–3 rights seems limited.

The failure to extend the P1–3 rights to presidential offices also means it is quite important which states have ratified Protocol 12 on discrimination. Challenges in relation to the election to the Presidency of Bosnia-Herzegovina have been heard, for instance, but these have been decided on discrimination grounds under the free-standing right in Protocol 12 rather than under P1–3 alone.[21] Only twenty states have ratified Protocol 12, however, fewer than half of the Council of Europe membership.[22]

The other key national 'election' or at least voting exercise is a referendum. The language of P1–3 clearly implies that the rights do not apply to other votes in national politics such as referenda, initiatives and plebiscites. Despite important recent challenges, the Court has hewn closely to this position.

In an early case on the 1975 UK referendum on staying in the European Economic Community, the Commission rejected the notion that P1–3

---

[21] *Sejdic and Finci v Bosnia and Herzegovina, Zornić v Bosnia and Herzegovina* App no 3681/06 (15 July 2014), *Pilav v Bosnia and Herzegovina* App no 41939/07 (9 June 2016).

[22] As of 14 August 2019.

150 *Scope of the Electoral Rights*

applied to referendums.[23] The Commission noted that the referendum was not an election for the choice of a legislature. It then made a brief comment to the effect that the referendum was 'of a purely consultative character and there was no legal obligation to organise such a referendum'. Subsequently the institutions were even more lapidary in dismissing claims about referendums[24] and did not pick up on the language about 'consultative' character[25] and the optional nature of the referendum. In *McLean v United Kingdom*, the Court confirmed the view that P1–3 did not cover referendums in a case about the denial of prisoners' rights to vote in the Alternative Vote referendum in the UK. The Court did briefly say that there was 'nothing in the nature of the referendum at issue' which would suggest some other conclusion. Given that the vote in that referendum had a legally binding result about the coming into force of legislative provisions, it is not that straightforward to imagine what else might have been different about the referendum that might have brought it within the scope of P1–3 unless it were that the referendum was constitutionally required (not easily possible in the UK).

The reasoning of the Court in these cases about referendums was brief, but two more recent cases required the Court to consider more seriously the argument for extending P1–3 to at least some referendums. In *Moohan and Gillon*, the Court considered a claim (by prisoners) that P1–3 should cover the Scottish Independence referendum. In the UK courts, the Supreme Court had split 3–2 on the applicability of P1–3, the majority holding it inapplicable to the referendum. The applicants sought to rely on the reasoning of the dissenters in the Supreme Court, noting that the European Court of Human Rights had never given detailed reasons for the interpretation, that the language in P1–3 was not clear and that an effective political democracy required extending the article to cover such an important decision. The European Court of Human Rights responded with more detailed reasoning than it had hitherto provided, but still concluding (unanimously) that the article did not cover referendums, even one such as this. The Court noted that the lack of reasoning in earlier cases reflected the view that this was a clear interpretation.[26] While this was the first secession

---

[23] *X v United Kingdom* App no 7096/75 (European Commission of Human Rights, 3 October 1975).

[24] The P1–3 obligations 'are limited to the field of elections concerning the choice of the legislature and do not extend to referenda' is the brief discussion in *Bader v Austria* App no 26633/95 (European Commission of Human Rights, 15 May 1996). See also the Court in *Hilbe v Liechtenstein* App no 31981/96 (7 September 1999); *Niedzwiedz v Poland* App no 1345/06 (2008) 47 EHRR SE 2.

[25] The effects of the 23 June 2016 vote in the UK on leaving the European Union do highlight the difference between being legally and politically compulsory.

[26] *Moohan and Gillon v United Kingdom* App nos 22962/15 and 23345/15 (13 June 2017), para 40.

referendum, the Convention institutions had considered a number of accession referendums, and this was not a significant difference.[27] The Court did not attach importance to the language about the consultative and optional nature of the referendum in *X v UK*; it did note, though, that there was still the possibility that something described as a referendum might fall under the scope of P1–3.[28] The Court rejected the application as inadmissible, being incompatible with the provisions of the Convention under article 35.

Again the Court had the opportunity to review its case law on referendums in a significant case concerning Turkey's 2017 omnibus constitutional referendum making sweeping changes to the powers of the president. The applicant party complained of procedural flaws in the voting process, but had to persuade the Court that P1–3 was applicable in the first place. The applicant argued primarily about the nature of the referendum proposal: it would expand the president's powers to appoint and dismiss vice-presidents and ministers, to dissolve parliament, to issue decrees, to veto legislation, to make appointments to judicial bodies, to declare a state of emergency; it would also end the apolitical nature of the presidency. The proposals indeed had been severely criticised by the Venice Commission.[29] The Court rejected the argument for a living instrument or purposive interpretation in this case.[30] It noted that the language of P1–3 clearly envisaged regular elections for the choice of a legislature; referendums were not regular, but on a special issue and did not involve electing representatives.[31] The clear wording of the article did not permit the expansive interpretation urged by the applicant.[32] The Court held the application inadmissible as being incompatible with the provisions of the Convention. Interestingly, though, this is described as a majority decision, indicating this is not the unanimous view of all the judges.

This exclusion of referendums from the protection of P1–3 is troubling. It is odd that elections to the legislative body attract the protections of the right to vote and the right to run for election, but referendums do not. It is odd because in the first place a referendum may itself be a legislative act or part of a legislative act. Second, it may well be even more important than the ordinary process of legislation. While referendums take place on relatively trivial issues, others are clearly of significant importance to individual rights (e.g. the marriage or abortion referendums in Ireland, the legislation on the

---

[27] *Moohan and Gillon*, para 41.
[28] *Moohan and Gillon*, para 42.
[29] *Cumhuriyet Halk Partisi v Turkey* App no 48818/17 (21 November 2017), paras 27 and 21.
[30] *Cumhuriyet Halk Partisi v Turkey*, para 35.
[31] *Cumhuriyet Halk Partisi v Turkey*, para 33.
[32] *Cumhuriyet Halk Partisi v Turkey*, para 38.

152   *Scope of the Electoral Rights*

'erased' in Slovenia[33]), to major constitutional decisions (Brexit or other votes on European Union membership or treaties, the Greek bailout referendum of 2015) or even the fundamentals of constitutional design (Turkey's 2017 referendum). That voting rights apply to the election of the legislature but not these issues is at first glance paradoxical. Third, there is also a risk that referendums may be used to sidestep the processes of liberal representative democracy as envisaged in the Convention. This is a contemporary threat given the rise of populist political parties and the historical use of referendums by such leaders and parties. Extending voting rights to referendums would not prevent this but would allow for supervision over the participation process in the referendum itself.

FEDERAL, DEVOLVED AND LOCAL INSTITUTIONS

The text of the Convention refers to the 'legislature', and this in the singular. This might be interpreted as applying to a single national parliament. The Court, however, has adopted a much more purposive interpretation, and the P1–3 rights can extend to other legislative bodies at federal, devolved and local levels.

In its first case on P1–3 the Court explained that:

> The word 'legislature' does not necessarily mean only the national parliament, however; it has to be interpreted in the light of the constitutional structure of the State in question.[34]

The legislatures of federal entities, such as the German Lander, are treated as falling within P1–3.[35] The Court has also held that the St Petersburg Legislative Assembly, as a subject of the Russian Federation, constitutes a legislature for the purposes of P1–3.[36] Legislative bodies in systems that are not classic federal states are also covered by P1–3 – these include the autonomous communities in Spain.[37]

In *Mathieu-Mohin and Clerfayt v Belgium*, the Court recognised that several of the bodies in the complex consociational system in Belgium were part of the legislature given the powers they possessed; this included the

---

[33] On a turnout of only 31.54%, 95.59% of those voting opposed legislation intended to address the position of the 'erased': *Makuc v Slovenia* App no 26828/06 (31 May 2007), para 26.

[34] *Mathieu-Mohin and Clerfayt v Belgium* App no 9267/81 (1987) 10 EHRR 1, para 53.

[35] *Timke v Germany* App no 527311/95 (1995) 20 EHRR CD 133 (European Commission of Human Rights).

[36] *Davydov and Others v Russia* App no 75947/11 (2018) 67 EHRR 25, para 279.

[37] *Federación Nacionalista Canaria v Spain* App no 56618/00 (7 June 2001).

Community Councils and Regional Councils. These included powers to issue decrees with the force of law, and competence in the case of Regions covering a wide range of social and economic matters, with Communities having competence in cultural matters, education and certain other areas.[38]

In *Py v France*, the Court considered the Congress of New Caledonia which had been reformed in the light of an agreement to develop the territory's self-determination. The French government denied that the Congress had acquired sufficient powers to count as part of the legislature. The Court noted that it had to examine the question in terms of not just strictly legislative powers but the body's overall role in the legislative process.[39] The Congress had power to initiate legislation and adopt territorial laws (within defined fields), including criminal laws and possessed fiscal powers (approving the budget and accounts). This was sufficient to satisfy the Court that the Congress had become part of the legislature.[40]

Municipal bodies are generally not covered by P1–3, as made clear in another Belgian case where the Commission rejected as inadmissible P1–3 complaints in relation to municipal councils and also Public Social Assistance Centres. The Commission reached this conclusion noting how the Constitution conferred legislative powers on the Crown, Chamber of Representatives and Senate as well as regional and community bodies. The Commission also found that the power to issue by-laws was not sufficient to be said to be exercising legislative power.[41]

The exclusion of municipal bodies from the scope of P1–3 has been fairly consistent, and reaffirmed in *McLean v United Kingdom* in 2013.[42] The Court reiterated that the power to pass by-laws did not make local authorities part of the legislature for the purposes of P1–3, alluding to the fact that these generally apply only in the local area and were strictly controlled by statute; in addition most of the work of authorities was administrative in nature and concerned the delivery of services subject to regulation in primary and secondary legislation.[43]

---

[38] *Mathieu-Mohin and Clerfayt v Belgium*, paras 24–25, 36, 53.

[39] *Py v France* App no 66289/01 (2005) 42 EHRR 26.

[40] *Py v France*, para 43.

[41] *Clerfayt and Legros v Belgium* App no 10650/83 (European Commission of Human Rights, 17 May 1985). See also *X v United Kingdom* App no 5155/71 (European Commission of Human Rights, 12 July 1976), *Gorizdra v Moldova* App no 53180/99 (2 July 2002), *Uçar v Turkey* App no 4692/09 (24 June 2014).

[42] *McLean v United Kingdom* App nos 12626/13 and 2522/12 (2013) 57 EHRR SE 8.

[43] *McLean v United Kingdom*, para 29. Similarly, see *Molka v Poland* App no 56550/00 (11 April 2006).

154 *Scope of the Electoral Rights*

Some bodies may fall between the municipal level and that associated with devolved or federal legislatures. The Commission considered the claims of the now abolished metropolitan county councils in Britain in *Booth-Clibborn*. While these bodies had extensive powers, they were primarily of an administrative nature and largely circumscribed by statute or secondary legislation, or subject to approval by a higher authority. For these reasons they were not part of the legislature.[44] However, in *Santoro v Italy*, the Court found that Italian regional councils did exercise sufficient powers to fall within the scope of P1–3; while these laws were limited to the territory of the relevant council, they included 'pivotal areas in a democratic society, such as administrative planning, local policy, public health, education, town planning and agriculture'.[45]

Elections to regional or local executive posts such as governors or mayors fall outside P1–3.[46] There is language in the case law that this will be the position unless the office (similar to the qualifications in the presidential cases) exercised significant legislative power.[47] The issue was raised in relation to the election of regional governors in *Zhermal*, but the Court found it unnecessary to decide this point in that case.[48]

The exclusion of municipalities, though logical given the language of P1–3, is unfortunate in that it means the Court is unable to consider cases where there may be serious problems affecting the operation of an effective political democracy. There may be allegations that municipal reform is tied to a partisan political agenda, but this could not be examined in Strasbourg.[49] The failure of P1–3 to include municipal elections (like certain other forms of election) highlights some other important deficits in the Convention system which could only be partially remedied by wider ratification of Protocol 12. Given the judgment that municipal or presidential elections or referendums do not fall within P1–3, this means that article 14 does not apply in these cases. Not merely does the Court leave open the possibility that states might inadequately protect the right to vote or to be a candidate; this also leaves open for

---

[44] *Booth-Clibborn v United Kingdom* App no 11391/85 (1986) 8 EHRR CD 99 (European Commission of Human Rights).

[45] *Santoro v Italy* App no 36681/97 (2004) 42 EHRR 38, para 52.

[46] *Cherepkov v Russia* App no 51501/99 (25 January 2000).

[47] *Krasnov and Skuratov v Russia* App nos 17864/04 and 21396/04 (2007) 47 EHRR 46.

[48] *Zhermal v Russia*.

[49] See the allegations that reform to local municipalities was intended to support the governing party in *Uçar v Turkey*.

GLOBALISATIONS

most states the possibility of discriminatory laws or practices. This might take the form of voting booths inaccessible for wheelchair users, for instance.[50]

Multilevel governance requires consideration of the local and other subnational institutions. It also, however, requires consideration of the increased role played by international organisations and more especially supranational organisations such as the European Union.

Since the nineteenth century there has been an expansion of international organisations with administrative, judicial or legislative powers and with competences ranging from fairly specific ones (e.g. telegraphs, coffee) to fundamental ones such as economic regulation and political cooperation and integration. These include world-level organisations like the League of Nations and the United Nations with their associated judicial bodies the Permanent Court of International Justice and the International Court of Justice. They also include important organisations dealing with economic matters, such as the World Bank, International Monetary Fund and World Trade Organisation (replacing the General Agreement on Tariffs and Trade). They include important regional organisations such as the African Union, Organization of American States, European Union, Council of Europe, Organisation for Security and Cooperation in Europe and Arab League. A number of these have legislative powers, most notably the Security Council of the United Nations and the European Union.

The expansion of international organisations since the nineteenth century reflects the phenomenon of globalisation in different spheres and for different reasons. They respond to technological changes such as the creation of the telegraph, broadcasting or later the internet. They respond to economic challenges and environmental threats. They also, of course, represent political choices by states, laudable or otherwise. Two world wars shattered any belief in the stability of a world dominated by (European) nation-states and gave rise to universal initiatives as well as regional ones. Perhaps unsurprisingly the region which produced these conflicts gave birth to some of the most important efforts at regional economic and political cooperation and integration.

The phenomena of globalisation and the considerable expansion in international organisations create challenges and opportunities for human rights and in particular democratic rights. Globalisation phenomena through

---

[50] *Molka v Poland.*

technological and cultural changes and economic developments can create social and economic challenges. They can sunder established conceptions of identity and community, while at the same time creating a large underclass of people who lost out in the global marketplace.[51] The communications technology which enables almost instantaneous communication across the globe and allows networks to form independent of state control (the Arab Spring) can also foster hate speech and incivility, while not being immune to state manipulation within the borders of the state (China, Turkey) or state manipulation in another state (Russian interference in Western elections).

The role of international organisations in this is also important. They regulate important areas of activity, especially in the economic sphere and also more broadly in the social sphere, but often are only tenuously linked to democratic processes. Deliberative democrats bemoan the absence of transparency in critical institutions like the International Monetary Fund or the World Trade Organisation.[52] International organisations for the most part do not resemble the institutions of national democratic politics with representative institutions democratically elected on a regular basis and subject to the same mechanisms of political accountability to the people. For many they resemble international unaccountable technocratic elites that may offer technically sound outcomes but cannot provide any sense of democratic accountability.[53]

The problem is not only that they do not but that it is possible they cannot. Just as the direct democratic model of the city-state cannot be scaled up (at least easily) to the nation-state, the representative democratic model cannot easily be scaled up to large-scale, multilingual transnational, much less worldwide polities.

This gives rise to democratic paradoxes or tensions – in the European region this affects the European Union, but also the Council of Europe to a degree. The awareness of the democratic tensions is no doubt healthy, but the lack of solutions may give rise to worrying trends. This is seen in resistance to implementing some European Court of Human Rights judgments (e.g. the prisoner voting saga in the UK) and both right-wing and left-wing scepticism about the European Union (the 'take back control' motif in the Brexit referendum). The tension and paradox may also feed a potentially unhealthy

---

[51] Hauke Brunkhorst, *Solidarity: From Civic Friendship to a Global Legal Community* (MIT Press 2005).

[52] Iris Marion Young, *Inclusion and Democracy* (Oxford University Press 2000), 270.

[53] Roger Eatwell and Matthew Goodwin, *National Populism: The Revolt against Liberal Democracy* (Penguin UK 2018), 96–106.

paradox within liberal representative democracy itself: Müller argues that it is possible to present these disagreements as those between 'liberal' supranational institutions and 'democratic' national ones.[54] Schmitt's prediction of a necessary contradiction between liberalism and democracy comes to fruition a century late.

The role of the state in this trajectory is challenged and diminished but not to be underestimated either. State action or coordinated state action is still important and effective. The international protection of human rights ultimately happens when states implement international decisions. Restrictions on trade are eased because states make this possible.

Political theorists have proposed various responses to these challenges. Some argue for developing global democratic institutions. Others suggest we need a different model of democracy – that a deliberative or, more precisely, discursive model of democracy that focuses on democratic discourses is required and suited to globalisation and international institutions.[55] Others suggest accepting that democratic principles not only must be updated to deal with globalisation and international organisations but must be understood differently in relation to different parts of the global system.[56]

The European Union – generally considered the most developed regional system of political and economic integration – has responded with a number of innovations. One of these is the evolution of the Parliamentary Assembly of the European Economic Community. Renamed the Parliament in 1961, in 1979 this became a directly elected institution and in 1981 exercised its powers to reject the Commission's budget. From the Single European Act 1987 through the Maastricht 1993, Nice 2003 and Lisbon 2009 treaties, its power in the legislative arena was gradually increased, as were its powers over the Commission. The Maastricht Treaty, for instance, removed the description of Parliament's powers as 'advisory and supervisory'. More recently the European Union has adopted the European Citizens' Initiative whereby one million EU citizens can require the Commission to consider a response to a particular issue.[57]

How has the European Convention system evolved to respond to these important changes in global governance?

---

[54] Jan-Werner Müller, *What Is Populism?* (Penguin UK 2017).

[55] John S Dryzek, *Foundations and Frontiers of Deliberative Governance* (Oxford University Press 2012).

[56] Gunther Teubner, 'Quod omnes tangit: Transnational Constitutions without Democracy?' (2018) 45 Journal of Law and Society S5.

[57] http://ec.europa.eu/citizens-initiative/public/basic-facts.

158 — *Scope of the Electoral Rights*

THE CONVENTION AND INTERNATIONAL INSTITUTIONS

The Convention institutions have, somewhat slowly perhaps, tracked the developments in relation to the European Parliament.

There were regular efforts to argue that the European Parliament was a legislature in respect of which the P1–3 rights applied, even though it was not a national legislature. In 1979, applicants from Northern Ireland challenged the arrangements for the UK European Parliament elections, specifically the adoption of a different system of election (single transferable vote) in Northern Ireland from that in the rest of the UK (simple plurality). The Commission rejected the complaint as inadmissible. On the scope of P1–3, the Commission noted that the article seemed to apply to the national legislature but, importantly,

> This does not exclude, however, the possibility that developments in the structure of the European Communities require the High Contracting Parties to grant the right protected under Article 3 of Protocol 1 in respect of new representative organs partly assuming the powers and functions of national legislatures.[58]

The Commission went on to explain that at the time the Parliament was almost purely consultative, although it did have some budgetary and supervisory powers. The Commission also said that even if the Parliament were a legislature, it would find the argument manifestly ill-founded.[59]

The Commission had occasion to revisit the issue in a 1987 case after the Single European Act, *Tete v France*. This time the Commission made an important preliminary observation. It recalled earlier Commission jurisprudence that if a state adopts a treaty which prevents it from discharging its Convention obligations, then it will be liable for any resulting breach, bearing in mind the Convention reflects the 'public order of Europe'. The implication according to the Commission was that 'It cannot therefore be accepted that by means of transfer of competence the High Contracting Parties may at the same time exclude matters normally covered by the Convention from the guarantees enshrined therein. What is at stake is respect for fundamental rights.'[60] The Commission reiterated the earlier view that developments in the Community legal order might mean that the P1–3 rights should be

---

[58] *Lindsay v United Kingdom* App no 8364/78 (1979) 15 DR 247 (European Commission of Human Rights).

[59] See also *Alliance des Belges de la Communauté Européenne v Belgium* App no 8612/79 (1979) DR 259 (European Commission of Human Rights).

[60] *Tete v France* App no 11123/84 (1987) 54 DR 52 (European Commission of Human Rights) 67.

The Convention and International Institutions

extended to new representative bodies. However, it concluded that the change in the European Parliament's competences made by the Single European Act were still too slight.

The turning point came after the Maastricht Treaty changes, though not without twists and complications. The Maastricht Treaty, as noted above, removed the reference to the Parliament's 'advisory and supervisory' role and introduced a new co-decision procedure which required legislative measures in certain areas to require the consent of the Parliament.

The complication stemmed partly from the jurisdiction at issue in *Matthews v United Kingdom*.[61] While the case was against the United Kingdom, it concerned the territory of Gibraltar. Gibraltar was a dependent territory of the UK and not part of the United Kingdom, though the UK had ultimate responsibility for it. The 1976 EC Act on Direct Elections provided for elections only in respect of the UK and so did not cover Gibraltar. For some purposes European legislation applied to Gibraltar, including free movement of persons, services and capital, health, the environment and consumer protection; however, it was not part of the customs territory, free movement of goods did not apply, and neither did the common market in agriculture, VAT rules, etc.[62]

The European Commission of Human Rights concluded that there was no violation on the merits of the application. This was a majority vote of 11–6 and on a slightly unexpected basis. The majority noted the comments in the earlier Commission decision and highlighted that it had never decided whether P1–3 could apply to a supranational body. The Commission now decided that irrespective of the developments of the Parliament towards becoming a legislature, it could not be a legislature for the purposes of P1–3 – the purpose of that article was to protect the voting and candidacy rights in respect of the national parliament, or regional (sub-state) bodies, not a supranational representative body.[63] The Commission's reasoning was not detailed and did not persuade the Grand Chamber.

The Grand Chamber concluded (15–2) that the applicant's P1–3 rights had been violated; indeed, their 'very essence' had been violated.[64] The reasoning was detailed and addressed several important arguments. The Grand Chamber first rejected the argument that the UK could not be held liable for the situation, as it was a matter of European Community law. The Grand

---

[61] *Matthews v United Kingdom* App no 24833/94 (1999) 28 EHRR 361 (Grand Chamber).
[62] *Matthews v United Kingdom*, para 12.
[63] *Matthews v United Kingdom*, para 63.
[64] *Matthews v United Kingdom*, para 65.

Chamber noted that EC acts could not be challenged in the Convention institutions, but also that state responsibility to secure rights continued even after a transfer of competences.[65] In this particular case the 'Act' on Direct Elections and the other measures (e.g. the Maastricht Treaty) were treaties which the UK freely entered into, and the UK could be held responsible on that basis.[66]

The Grand Chamber then considered the argument that prevailed with the Commission, that P1–3 applied to the national legislature and could not apply to a supranational body. This the Grand Chamber rejected with a robust application of the 'living instrument' doctrine and the Convention goal of providing for an 'effective political democracy'. If the Convention states create, including by treaties, new bodies, then the Court must interpret the Convention and Protocols in the light of these.[67]

The Grand Chamber then turned to the critical point, whether the evolution in the role of the Parliament was such that it could not be considered a legislature under P1–3. The UK argued that the Parliament did not have the power to initiate and adopt legislation and these were requisites of a legislature. The Grand Chamber explained that it could consider the 'sui generis' nature of the Community institutions and look not just at the 'strictly legislative powers' of a body but also its 'role in the overall legislative process'.[68]

The Grand Chamber did not attach much importance to the removal of the 'advisory and supervisory' language by itself; what mattered were the actual powers. The Maastricht Treaty included different legislative routes; on some topics the Parliament could still be overruled by a unanimous Council, but on others its agreement was required. The Parliament also had other attributes of a legislature: it could censure the Commission; its consent was needed for the appointment of the Commission; it approved the budget. It could request the Commission to submit proposals even if it had no power of initiation. Being the only elected Community institution, it was the element which best secured the notion of an effective political democracy.[69] These elements were sufficient for the Parliament to be deemed a legislature for the purposes of P1–3, although Judges Freeland and Jungwiert strongly dissented. The Grand Chamber dismissed the arguments of the UK that from the viewpoint of

[65] *Matthews v United Kingdom*, para 32.
[66] *Matthews v United Kingdom*, para 33.
[67] *Matthews v United Kingdom*, para 39.
[68] *Matthews v United Kingdom*, paras 48–49.
[69] *Matthews v United Kingdom*, para 33.

electoral design it would be difficult to include Gibraltar in the UK's elections for the Parliament.[70]

The *Matthews* judgment was not obvious at the time – as noted, the Commission reached a different conclusion, and the Grand Chamber view was not without dissent. Since then, though, it has been applied consistently and uncontroversially in cases involving the European Parliament.[71] The judgment is interesting in a number of regards. To qualify as a legislature in the Grand Chamber's view, it is not essential that the body have the power to initiate and adopt legislation, but it must have a significant role in the legislative process, potentially along with certain other supervisory and budgetary powers. Also interesting is the range of issues over which the Parliament had jurisdiction – this was not the plenitude of jurisdiction associated with national parliaments, nor was it even the full range of areas which the European Community or Parliament had competence over. The range of issues in Gibraltar was relatively narrow but still sufficient to significant to trigger P1–3.[72]

Under the Treaty of Lisbon, the European Union has an obligation to accede to the European Convention on Human Rights. Negotiators have drafted a treaty to enable this to happen, but the Court of Justice of the European Union has given its opinion that parts of this treaty are incompatible with EU law.[73] The draft treaty addresses mainly the procedural and institutional aspects of the Convention system that would need to be modified to address the special circumstances of a supranational organisation (including a majority of Council of Europe states) joining the Convention. There is no consideration whether rights such as the P1–3 rights are suitable to be applied to the European Union in their current guise. There may be tensions, as 'democracy was not part of the DNA of European integration'.[74] Certain questions might arise about the EU's observance of P1–3 that have not had to be considered hitherto – for instance, that the Parliament's composition is not exactly based on population size or that different electoral systems are

---

[70] *Matthews v United Kingdom*, para 64.

[71] E.g. *Kulinski and Sabev v Bulgaria* App no 63849/09 (21 July 2017).

[72] This raises the issue of its application to the special arrangements for Northern Ireland adopted in the Ireland/Northern Ireland Protocol of the Withdrawal Agreement.

[73] *Opinion 2/13 on the draft agreement on the accession of the European Union to the European Convention for the Protection of Human Rights and Fundamental Freedoms* (Court of Justice of the European Union, 18 December 2014).

[74] Joseph Weiler, cited in Claus Offe and Ulrich K Preuß, 'The Union's Course: Between a Supranational Welfare State and Creeping Decay' in Claus Offe and Ulrich K Preuß (eds) *Citizens in Europe: Essays on Democracy, Constitutionalism and European Integration* (ECPR Press 2016), 14.

permitted in different countries. The elections to the European Parliament are based on 'universal and direct but unequal suffrage'.[75] It is unequal in being based on 'degressive proportionality' which limits the number of seats larger states can claim. Offe notes that the rules on European Parliament representation would be incompatible if applied in national legal systems.[76]

The composition of the European Union legislature is also potentially problematic. As discussed above, the European Parliament is the sole directly elected component of the EU institutions. And its role in legislation has significantly increased due to treaty changes. However, it remains only one part. The Commission retains effectively the sole right of initiative, albeit that it has to consider requests and directions from other bodies. The Council (representatives of member-state governments) is the other part of the 'legislature'.[77] Neither of these is directly elected.

Similarly questions might be raised about the way in which the Parliament has been sidelined in relation to European responses to the debt crisis, responses which have prioritised the role of the Commission, Council and European Central Bank leaving the Parliament only an advisory role.[78] Even more dramatic was the manner in which the democratic wishes of the Greek people and legislature were overridden in 2015 – a 'brutal act of overpowering the will of the Greek people'.[79]

Can the *Matthews* judgment be generalised to other supranational or international institutions? This seems possible but unlikely. One weakness in the line of cases including *Matthews* is that there is no suggestion that where legislative power is exercised at a supranational level, there must be some form of elected representative institution. The European Community created the directly elected Parliament, and it was some twenty years before the European Court of Human Rights concluded P1–3 applied to its election.

---

[75] Judge Wojtyczek in dissent in *Firth and others v United Kingdom* App nos 47784/09, 47806/09, 47812/09, 47818/09, 47829/09, 49001/09, 49007/09, 49018/09, 49033/09 and 49036/09 (2016) 63 EHRR 25.

[76] Claus Offe, 'The Union Entrapped: Does the EU have the Political Capacity to Overcome Its Current Crisis?' in Claus Offe and Ulrich K Preuß (eds) *Citizens in Europe: Essays on Democracy, Constitutionalism and European Integration*, 484.

[77] Judge Wojtyczek draws attention to this and other specific EU issues in his dissent in *Firth and others v United Kingdom*.

[78] Michaela Hailbronner, 'Beyond Legitimacy: Europe's Crisis of Constitutional Democracy' in Mark A Graber, Sanford Levinson and Mark Tushnet (eds) *Constitutional Democracy in Crisis* (Oxford University Press 2018), 284.

[79] Claus Offe and Ulrich K Preuß, 'The Union's Course: Between a Supranational Welfare State and Creeping Decay' in Claus Offe and Ulrich K Preuß (eds) *Citizens in Europe: Essays on Democracy, Constitutionalism and European Integration* 5.

Conclusion 163

There was no argument in the Commission or Court that the European Parliament should be given more powers because it was the directly elected component of the European Union system. Nevertheless, there is an argument based on the *Greek case* and the language in the case law on creating new international institutions and delegating powers to them that there must be an elected representative element in any such supranational institution. For a second reason, though, this is more likely to be theoretical than realistic. While there are many other international organisations, few of them have the range of competences and the distinctive legal doctrines of direct effect and supremacy associated with them that the European Union's legal order possesses.

CONCLUSION

The European Court of Human Rights has been relatively cautious in developing the scope of P1–3, largely thanks to the limitations of the language of the article itself. It has extended the scope of the article to cover substate legislatures including in certain cases bodies like regional or community councils where they share in legislative power. It has also rather importantly understood the article to cover the elected institution of the European Union, the European Parliament.

It has, however, declined to interpret the article to cover municipal elections, elections to advisory or consultative bodies, elections for presidents or referendums. The scope of the Convention, therefore, is limited in some important regards, and this raises some problems. It means the level of protection of political rights offered by the Convention is less than that offered by other regional systems in their main human rights treaties (never mind dedicated charters) and less than that in the Universal Declaration of Human Rights and the International Covenant on Civil and Political Rights.

Furthermore, the scope of the protection offered by the Convention is less than that suggested by other Council of Europe institutions. The Venice Commission (European Commission for Democracy through Law) has elaborated standards or at least guidelines for the conduct of referendums.[80] The Council of Europe has a treaty specifically on local self-government, the 1985 European Charter of Local Self-Government[81] which has been ratified

---

[80] European Commission for Democracy through Law (Venice Commission), 371/2006 *Referendum Guidelines* (Council of Europe Pub., Strasbourg 2006).
[81] European Charter of Local Self-Government, Strasbourg 15 October 1985, in force 1 September 1999, ETS 122.

by every Council of Europe state and provides for universal suffrage at the local level, though there is no enforcement mechanism in this Charter. This last has been supplemented by the 1992 Convention on the Participation of Foreigners in Public Life at Local Level and the 2009 Additional Protocol to the European Charter of Local Self-Government on the right to participate in the affairs of a local authority.[82]

This means that certain practices, e.g. denial of voting rights on grounds of prisoner status or mental capacity, might be found to be a breach of the Convention if they apply to national legislative or European Parliament elections, but bizarrely not if they apply to consultative bodies, municipal bodies, presidential elections or referendums. States would even be free to adopt discriminatory legislation in these voting processes unless they have ratified Protocol 12 with its freestanding non-discrimination right.

The challenge is all the more serious given concerns about the rise of populist, far-right or semi-authoritarian regimes. Hallmarks of these types of regimes include a strong executive figure. Such regimes have used referendums and plebiscites in the past to consolidate power and undermine rights and democracy. This is a historical fear in Europe dating at least to the use by Napoleon of a plebiscite to establish an Empire.[83] More recently there are concerns over how the Hungarian and Turkish governments have used public votes to approve constitutional change. Of course, other countries – Ireland and Switzerland most obviously – regularly use referendums too. Participation in these referendums is not subject to any human rights scrutiny by the European Court.

There is language in the case law which leaves open the possibility in certain circumstances for presidential elections and referendums to be brought within the scope of P1–3. The Court has not yet given serious consideration to the possibility for the powerful Russian, Turkish or French presidencies to be considered part of the legislature. The Court has recently rejected strong arguments for including referendums both in relation to the Scottish independence referendum and the Turkish 2017 reforms, but those cases also highlighted strong reasons (not least in the dissenting opinions in the UK Supreme Court) for a change in direction.

---

[82] Additional Protocol to the European Charter of Local Self-Government on the right to participate in the affairs of a local authority, Utrecht, 16 November 2009, in force 1 June 2012, ETS 122.

[83] Napoleon's nephew similarly consolidated his rule by means of a plebiscite in 1851: Sheri Berman, *Democracy and Dictatorship in Europe: From the Ancien Régime to the Present Day* (Oxford University Press 2019), 379.

The language of P1–3 may indeed support this – in focusing on the role of the legislature, the Convention drafters were highlighting the centrality of a democratically elected plural body which can represent a wide spectrum of views and which would function as the lawmaking body. The Convention may well be compatible with presidential or semi-presidential systems, but this cannot mean that the centrality of the legislature is denuded of significance. This is particularly concerning from a deliberative democratic point of view. An elected plural legislature offers a forum for representatives of different viewpoints, interests and discourses, to deliberate. A more presidential system of government does not facilitate this sort of deliberation. A referendum risks democracy being reduced to vote-counting rather than deliberation.

The implication is that the Court should include these other bodies within the guarantee of electoral rights, or consider whether P1–3 implicitly prohibits certain measures which would weaken the legislature as a central figure in the effective political system envisaged by the Convention. The former is the more manageable approach and would enable the Court to ensure that people could participate whether as voters or (for offices) as candidates. We now turn to how the Court deals with the right to vote and the right to run for office.

7

The Right to Vote

This chapter considers the right to vote in article 3 of Protocol 1 (P1–3). This is one of the two subjective rights identified by the Court in P1–3, along with the right to run for election. The chapter focuses on this element of representative democracy, and so issues about some of the more deliberative and participatory elements may recede.

It is important, though, that the right to vote be inclusive and effective and respect the principles of political equality. The right to vote is symbolically important as an indicator that one is an equal member of the political community. From the viewpoint of deliberative democratic theory, the exercise of the right to vote is also crucially the formal part of the exercise by which individuals can understand themselves as the authors of the laws enacted.

The history of the right to vote is one of the expansion of the franchise to include ever more people within the political community. Early democratic regimes accepted numerous restrictions on voting and other rights, and denied voting rights on grounds such as sex, property, race, nationality or mental capacity. Some democratic regimes and theorists endorsed the view that votes need not be equal – that heads of family or property owners or even people with university degrees might have special additional voting rights.

The chapter considers the basic principles which apply in relation to the right to vote in P1–3 – including the establishment of the view that this is a right, and then considers questions about how the Convention secures the formal inclusion of persons in the political process. This addresses a variety of issues that the Convention institutions have dealt with including age, nationality and residence-based conditions as well as issues of race, mental capacity, prisoner status and bankruptcy. The chapter concludes by discussing the potential for the Convention to address issues beyond formal inclusion in the electoral process and to promote deliberative democracy.

IDENTIFYING THE RIGHTS IN P1–3

The Convention institutions took some time to decide that the wording of P1–3 protected subjective rights. Originally the Commission adopted the position that it was only a requirement on states to hold elections using the modalities specified in P1–3 and did not create any individual rights such as a right to vote; states were free to exclude certain groups from elections (such as overseas residents) provided it did not impair the free expression of the will of the people.[1] In a later case these early cases were approved though the Commission indicated that P1–3 implied the principle of universal suffrage.[2]

Subsequently the Commission decided that P1–3 included not just the principle of universal suffrage but also individual rights. It revised its earlier case law in recognition that the clear purpose of Protocol 1 was to confer individual rights, in line with the nature of the Convention system as a whole. Specifically, the article was held to include the right to vote and the right to stand for election.[3] The Commission specified that these rights were not unlimited: 'states may impose certain restrictions on the right to vote and the right to stand, provided they are not arbitrary and do not interfere with the free expression of the people's opinion.'[4]

Being implicit rights, the Commission indicated that they were subject to limitations. Given the wording of P1–3, they may be subject to limitations according to standards laxer than the necessity inquiry in the qualified rights of the Convention. The Convention institutions have specified that the 'active' aspect of the right (the right to vote) is not subject to the same level of limitations as the 'passive' aspect (the right to run for election).

The European Court of Human Rights consolidated and glossed this jurisprudence in its first-ever judgment on P1–3, *Mathieu-Mohin and Clerfayt v Belgium*. The Court contextualised the P1–3 rights in the context of the Convention's reference to an 'effective political democracy'; this allowed the

---

[1] *X v Federal Republic of Germany* App no 530/59 (1960) 3 Yearbook 184 (European Commission of Human Rights), *X, Z and Y v Belgium* App no 1065/61 (1961) 4 Yearbook 260 (European Commission of Human Rights), *ADQ v Belgium* App no 1028/61 (1961) 4 Yearbook 324 (European Commission of Human Rights).

[2] *X v Germany* App no 2728/66 (European Commission of Human Rights, 6 October 1967), confirmed in *X v Netherlands* App no 6573/74 (1975) 1 DR 87 (European Commission of Human Rights, 19 December 1974).

[3] *W X Y and Z v Belgium* 6746/74 App no 6745 (1975) 2 DR 114 (European Commission of Human Rights).

[4] Ibid. Confirmed in *X v United Kingdom* App no 7566/76 (1976) 9 DR 121 (European Commission of Human Rights).

168   *The Right to Vote*

Court to say that P1–3 was of 'prime importance' in the Convention system.[5] The Court referred to the unusual manner in which P1–3 was phrased – seemingly in terms of state obligations rather than individual rights. This, however, was misleading; it was clear from the text of Protocol 1 (the Preamble and article 5) that it was intended to recognise individual rights; similarly, the *travaux préparatoires* supported the view that it was intended to allow individual petition in respect of the P1–3 rights.[6] The unusual phrasing was intended 'to give greater solemnity to the commitment' in P1–3 and recognise that such political rights required primarily positive action on the part of the state rather than a negative obligation not to interfere with freedoms.[7]

The Court recognised the evolution in the Commission jurisprudence, towards protecting the individual rights to vote and stand for election. In later cases, the Court has come to refer to these as the active and passive aspects of the P1–3 rights. It noted that these rights could be subject to limitations and that the states subjected these rights to a variety of conditions that were not prohibited by the Convention. Indeed,

> They [the states] have a wide margin of appreciation in this sphere, but it is for the Court to determine in the last resort whether the requirements of Protocol 1 (P1) have been complied with; it has to satisfy itself that the conditions do not curtail the right in question to such an extent as to impair their very essence and deprive them of their effectiveness; that they are pursued in pursuit of a legitimate aim; and that the means employed are not disproportionate ... In particular, such conditions must not thwart 'the free expression of the opinion of the people in the choice of the legislature.'[8]

This language deploys much more the language of qualified rights than had appeared in the tentative Commission jurisprudence – there are the references to proportionality and legitimate aim, as well as the essence of the right. These are, however, to be considered bearing in mind the wide margin of appreciation.

The Court was also careful to stress the wide margin of appreciation available to states in designing an electoral system, especially given the often competing, almost incompatible aims of electoral systems which have to both 'reflect fairly faithfully the opinions of the people' and 'promote the emergence of a sufficiently clear and coherent political will'.[9] In particular, while

---

[5] *Mathieu-Mohin and Clerfayt v Belgium* App no 9267/81 (1987) 10 EHRR 1, para 47.
[6] *Mathieu-Mohin and Clerfayt v Belgium*, para 49.
[7] *Mathieu-Mohin and Clerfayt v Belgium*, para 50.
[8] *Mathieu-Mohin and Clerfayt v Belgium*, para 52.
[9] *Mathieu-Mohin and Clerfayt*, para 54.

any elections must be free, at reasonable intervals, secret and assure the 'free expression of the opinion of the people', the Protocol said nothing about whether majoritarian or proportional systems should be used.[10] The reference to 'free expression of the opinion of the people' referred primarily to freedom of expression and equality.[11] The Court concluded its general statement of principles by stressing that these principles must be understood in a context sensitive manner:

> For the purposes of Article 3 of Protocol No. 1 (P1–3), any electoral system must be assessed in the light of the political evolution of the country concerned; features that would be unacceptable in the context of one system may accordingly be justified in the context of another, at least so long as the chosen system provides for conditions which will ensure the 'free expression of the opinion of the people in the choice of the legislature'.[12]

This last comment appears as part of the same discussion as that about electoral systems generally, rather than the discussion about the rights to vote and run for election. Nevertheless, it has been cited in later cases dealing with limitations on these rights.

Some of the comments in *Mathieu-Mohin* suggest that a different approach should be taken by the Court to limitations of the right to vote and the right to stand for election than is taken in cases assessing the necessity of restrictions on the rights in articles 8–11 ECHR. Indeed, the Court has said that this is so.[13] The oft-cited quote on the role of the Court in P1–3 cases, for instance, does not even refer to the principle that any restriction on these rights must be in accordance with law (legality or lawfulness). Further, it refers to the idea of not depriving rights of their effectiveness or thwarting the free expression of the opinion of the people. However, one should not exaggerate this. Of course, the Court reviews the legality or lawfulness of restrictions. The reference to depriving the rights of their effectiveness and most especially not thwarting the free expression of the people might be considered as aspects of proportionality (which the Court does mention). In particular, they may appear as the essential minimum of these rights.

---

[10] *Mathieu-Mohin and Clerfayt*, para 54.

[11] *Mathieu-Mohin and Clerfayt*, para 54. In particular, the Court did not believe 'that all votes must necessarily have equal weight as regards the outcome of the election or that all candidates must have equal chances of victory. Thus no electoral system can eliminate "wasted votes".' Para 54.

[12] *Mathieu-Mohin and Clerfayt*, para 54.

[13] The conditions regarding limitations on P1–3 are 'less strict' than those for articles 8–11: *Ādamsons v Latvia* App no 3669/03 (24 June 2008), para 111.

THE RIGHT TO VOTE

Much of the right to vote case law, and this chapter, concerns the question of who is entitled to vote. Apart from such exclusions, other violations of the right to vote are possible. For instance, if a Court quashes the results of an election in certain districts, then this means the votes in those districts do not contribute to the formation of the legislature in any way. The Court regards this as an interference with the right to vote, which requires justification.[14]

The Court has also drawn attention to the importance of an accurate electoral register. In the *Georgian Labour Party v Georgia* case, the Court was faced with a highly unusual situation in the wake of Georgia's Rose Revolution. The November 2003 election had been annulled because of major problems with the electoral register, and the Georgian authorities had to arrange for a new electoral register before the March 2004 election. The authorities adopted an active registration model whereby voters had to register themselves and confirm their registration. The Court highlighted the importance of an accurate electoral register: anything else might 'taint the effectiveness and practicability' of the P1–3 rights, both the right to vote and to run for election on an equal and fair basis.[15] The Court saw nothing objectionable about an active system of voter registration and concluded that in the special circumstances of 2003 and 2004 the authorities were making every effort to respect voting rights.[16]

The right to vote does not mean one is entitled to find on a ballot paper the party or candidate for which one intends to vote. This is clear from the *Russian Conservative Party of Entrepreneurs v Russia* case. The applicant party had been denied registration to compete in Russian elections (in breach of the Convention); as a consequence, one of the applicants in the case claimed that his right to vote had been violated, as he had intended to vote for this party. The European Court of Human Rights rejected this argument – normally the intention to vote for any particular party is not protected. The notion of a voting intention was too difficult to operationalise.[17] The Court did go on to say that this had to be considered in the overall political context – the P1–3

---

[14] *Riza and DPS v Bulgaria* App no 48555/10 (13 October 2015). While not strictly a right to vote case, see also *Georgian Labour Party v Georgia* App no 9103/04 (2008) 48 EHRR 14 where the Court found the Central Electoral Commission's decision to annul all votes in two districts due to alleged irregularities had the hallmarks of arbitrariness.

[15] *Georgian Labour Party v Georgia*, paras 82–83.

[16] *Georgian Labour Party v Georgia*, paras 92–93.

[17] *Russian Conservative Party of Entrepreneurs v Russia* App nos 55066/00 and 55638/00 (2007) 46 EHRR 39, para 76.

The Right to Vote

rights required there to be 'a plurality of political parties representing the different shades of opinion to be found within a country's population'.[18] In that particular case the Court was satisfied that there were a plurality of parties representing different opinions and that the elections had been regarded favourably by international observers.[19]

Before turning to the issue just who is included in the 'people' for the purposes of P1–3 – that is to say who is entitled to vote, it is worth noting that there are several issues raised by P1–3's voting rights that the Court has not yet engaged with.

The text of P1–3 expressly refers to the 'secret ballot'. The European Court of Human Rights does not seem to have considered any case law concerning the secrecy of the ballot and whether this is an absolute principle or one subject to certain safeguards in order to deal with electoral fraud. Another important issue that the Court does not seem to have dealt with is the practice of compulsory voting. Some democracies, indeed some Council of Europe states, provide that some level of participation in the electoral process is mandatory.[20] This is an issue that may become more relevant in different ways given frequent concerns about voter apathy and abstention in elections.[21]

The text of P1–3 raises an important issue of principle in its text. It refers to the 'free expression of the opinion of the people in the choice of the legislature', but just who counts as part of the 'people' for this right? This is indeed a notorious question in political theory and one which supposedly gives rise to claims of circularity – who precisely are the people who are the subject of democracy? Is this a group predefined in terms of some thick conception of identity as an ethnic, linguistic or other people? Or does it refer simply to all citizens or nationals? Does it reflect the democratic principle that that which touches all must be decided by all? But if so, common practices in democracies exclude certain categories, notably foreigners. And it ignores the feature of modern globalisation, that frequently people beyond a state's borders (and not just non-resident nationals) will be affected by state decisions.

The early cases of the Convention institutions tended not to problematise these issues but to accept the 'conditions commonly imposed in Convention

---

[18] *Russian Conservative Party of Entrepreneurs v Russia*, para 79.
[19] *Russian Conservative Party of Entrepreneurs*, para 80.
[20] Anthoula Malkopoulou, *The History of Compulsory Voting in Europe: Democracy's Duty?* (Routledge 2014).
[21] Voter turnout for European Parliament elections declined, for instance, even as the European Parliament was given more powers in the European Union legislative process.

172   *The Right to Vote*

countries on the possession or exercise of a right to vote' such as citizenship, residence or age.[22]

Age

The Convention institutions have not given detailed consideration to age-based restrictions on voting rights. In the prisoner voting case, *Hirst*, the Grand Chamber alludes briefly to the position that age restrictions are intended to ensure the 'maturity' of those voting.[23]

Discrimination based on age was briefly considered in the *Shindler* case (see below on residence-based restrictions). *Shindler* concerned the UK's rules providing that non-resident UK nationals could vote in UK elections if their length of time since leaving the UK was no more than fifteen years. Shindler had moved to Italy in 1983 following his retirement, and he sought to invoke article 14. He claimed the rule was discriminatory because statistics might show that the rule affected people who moved abroad due to retirement. The Court, however, treated this as speculative – there was no evidence before it of a difference of treatment based on age.[24] The case, though, does indicate the possibility at least to make an argument that voting restrictions may be facially neutral but nevertheless have a disproportionate impact on certain groups based on protected characteristics.

Residence

The Convention institutions have had to deal more extensively with residence-based restrictions on the right to vote. Residence requirements might affect people living in a territory but who do not meet the relevant residence requirement. Or residence may be an issue because a country's national is not resident at all on the territory of the state.

Early cases of the Commission and Court established the general principles, demonstrating an acceptance of residence-based restrictions. Subsequently the institutions had to deal with a number of cases raising more challenging questions in relation to minority rights and post-colonial matters. More recently, the Court has dealt in detail with arguments about residence

---

[22] *X v United Kingdom* App no 7566/76 (1976) 9 DR 121 (European Commission of Human Rights); *X v United Kingdom* App no 8873/80 (European Commission of Human Rights, 13 May 1982).
[23] *Hirst v United Kingdom (No. 2)* App no 74025/01 (2005) 42 EHRR 41 (Grand Chamber), para 62.
[24] *Shindler v United Kingdom* App no 19840/09 (2014) 58 EHRR 5, para 121.

The Right to Vote 173

including in a surprising case where the Court found a violation, only for this to be reversed by the Grand Chamber.

From an early period, the Commission recognised that there were several reasons justifying a residence requirement for the exercise of the right to vote, in particular where the voter lived outside the national territory. The Commission identified several reasons which meant this was not an arbitrary restriction: the non-resident is not as familiar with the daily affairs of the state; the difficulty for candidates to address non-residents; the risk of electoral fraud in postal votes; and the link with taxation.[25] The Commission did not require states to adopt a blanket policy: granting voting rights to certain non-residents such as diplomats or soldiers was not discriminatory according to the Commission, as there were significant differences in the situation of such persons.[26] This acceptance of residence-based restrictions applied to European Parliament elections (assuming these were within scope) and notwithstanding the variety of approaches across the European Community on the question.[27]

The Commission also accepted that states could allow non-resident nationals to vote but expect them to return to the national territory in order to do so; it was not a breach of P1–3 or article 14 to fail to provide for postal voting or some other mechanism for non-resident nationals.[28] According to the Commission, states could adopt general rules on this question, i.e. it was not necessary to take into account every individual circumstance.[29]

In a case involving Jersey, the Commission considered an argument that Jersey residents could only vote for the local legislative assembly and not the UK Parliament, even though the UK was responsible for the external affairs of Jersey and the UK Parliament possessed parliamentary sovereignty. The Commission accepted that Jersey residents were not residents of the United Kingdom, and that they had the opportunity to vote for their own legislature with competence in domestic affairs. The unusual constitutional tradition, long predating the Convention, was not upset by P1–3's requirements.[30]

In its first case on this issue, *Hilbe,* the Court endorsed the approach of the Commission in regards to the residence issue and in particular reiterated the

---

[25] *X v United Kingdom* App no 7566/76 (1976) 9 DR 121 (European Commission of Human Rights).

[26] *X v United Kingdom.*

[27] *Alliance des Belges de la Communauté Européenne v Belgium* App no 8612/79 (1979) DR 259 (European Commission of Human Rights).

[28] *X and Association Y v Italy* App no 8987/80 (European Commission of Human Rights, 6 May 1981).

[29] *Luksch v Germany* App no 35385/97 (European Commission of Human Rights, 21 May 1997).

[30] *X v United Kingdom* App no 8873/80 (European Commission of Human Rights, 13 May 1982).

174   *The Right to Vote*

reasons why such restrictions are justified: non-resident nationals are not as directly affected by the state's affairs and are less familiar with them, the interaction between candidates and non-residents is problematic, there is a close link between voting in a parliamentary election and being affected by the political body elected, and finally there was a legitimate interest in limiting the influence of non-resident nationals in relation to issues which 'primarily affect people living in the country'.[31]

While many of the cases hitherto had been relatively straightforward, the Commission and the Court started to deal with more complex issues and arguments from the 1990s onwards. One intriguing case involving residence was *Polacco and Garofalo v Italy*. The applicants had lived in Trento for most of their lives except for a period from 1984 to 1991 when they lived in Rome. They moved back to Trento in 1991 but could not participate in regional Trento elections due to a four-year residence requirement. The Commission noted that the residence requirement was adopted to protect the linguistic minority of the region, and this was a legitimate aim given both the need to protect 'stability, democratic security and peace' as well as 'cultural wealth and traditions'.[32] The Commission referred to what was then (1997) a growing trend towards recognising the importance of minorities witnessed in the OSCE (e.g. the Copenhagen Document) and the Council of Europe (referring to the European Charter for Regional and Minority Languages 1992 and the Framework Convention on National Minorities 1995). On the proportionality point, the Commission noted that four years was a lengthy requirement, but given the special circumstances of the region, the long period might be necessary for electors to have an understanding of the local context. Further, while the applicants were from the region, they did not belong to the relevant (German and Ladin) minorities.

An even more unusual case raised issues of decolonialisation and the rarely invoked 'local requirements' clause referring to overseas territories in the Convention.[33] The case, *Py v France*, concerned processes designed to end a conflict in New Caledonia and establish its relationship with metropolitan France. As part of the Noumeá Accord, the local Congress had its powers expanded (discussed in the Chapter on Scope), and a ten-year residence requirement was introduced for votes to this body. This reflected concerns that the electoral process might be unduly influenced by persons who were

---

[31] *Hilbe v Liechtenstein* App no 31981/96 (7 September 1999).

[32] *Polacco and Garofalo v Italy* App no 23450/94 (European Commission of Human Rights, 15 September 1997).

[33] Article 63, now article 56.

The Right to Vote 175

relatively recent immigrants to New Caledonia and who might not intend to remain for a lengthy period. The residence requirement meant that the applicant, a French national who had moved to New Caledonia when he obtained a lecturing post there, could not vote.

The Court set out the principles on the right to vote, noting the wide margin of appreciation available to states; the Court explained that voting regulations were designed to 'ensure both citizen participation and knowledge of the particular situation of the region'; furthermore, in assessing the compatibility of any such regulations with the Convention, the Court must consider the 'political evolution of the country concerned'.[34] The Court held that there was a legitimate aim for the restriction. On the issue of proportionality, the Court referred to the Commission's decision in *Polacco and Garofalo*, upholding a four-year residence requirement in the special circumstances of the Italian region concerned. The Court however indicated that the ten-year limit in *Py* might normally be thought disproportionate under the Convention.[35] What swayed the Court to find no violation was the Convention clause on having 'due regard' to 'local requirements' in respect of overseas territories. In this regard the Court noted that the reforms were part of an ongoing self-determination process, and that the Accord had ended a bloody conflict; the issues were even more complex than in the Belgian and Italian cases dealing with linguistic differences; furthermore, the Human Rights Committee of the United Nations had already found similar rules acceptable in the special context of New Caledonia.[36]

Sevinger and Eman v the Netherlands also concerned some of the aftereffects of European colonialism.[37] The applicants were residents of Aruba, one of the constituent parts of the Kingdom of the Netherlands, along with the Netherlands itself and the Netherlands Antilles. As part of the Kingdom of the Netherlands, each entity had its own local parliament while the Netherlands Parliament also functioned as the Kingdom Parliament for certain purposes. There existed dedicated arrangements for members of the Aruba and Antilles parliaments to make their voices heard in the Netherlands Parliament in respect of any bills concerning them. The applicants complained that they were not allowed to vote in elections for the Netherlands Parliament even though it functioned as a Kingdom Parliament and other Dutch nationals outside the Netherlands were allowed to vote. The Court rejected their

---

[34] *Py v France* App no 66289/01 (2005) 42 EHRR 26, para 46.
[35] *Py v France*, para 57.
[36] *Py v France*, paras 61–63.
[37] *Sevinger and Eman v Netherlands* App nos 17173/07 and 17180/07 (2008) 46 EHRR SE 14.

complaint – they had a right to vote for the Aruba Parliament in elections that satisfied P1–3 while there was a procedure for the Aruba Parliament to make representations in the Netherlands Parliament if its interests were affected; given the relatively small number of bills in the Netherlands Parliament which would actually affect Aruba, this fell within the margin of appreciation.[38] The Court also rejected the article 14 argument; while it was true the Netherlands allowed Dutch nationals to vote if they were outside the Dutch territory, the applicants were in a different position, since they could vote for the Aruba Parliament and therefore had an indirect possibility to influence deliberations in the Netherlands Parliament.[39]

Many countries provide that nationals residing abroad have the right to vote in certain circumstances and using specific modalities. The principles seemed relatively settled, so much so that in 2007, the Court was able to reject as inadmissible for being manifestly ill-founded a claim about the UK's rules on non-resident voters in *Doyle v United Kingdom*.[40] The applicant had moved to Belgium in 1983, and in 2006 inquired about voting in UK elections. At the time the UK laws provided that non-resident voters could only register to vote if they had left the UK within the previous fifteen years. The Court reiterated the reasons why the Convention institutions had always held that residence-based restrictions were generally acceptable:

> Residence requirements have previously found to be justified by the following factors: firstly, the assumption that a non-resident citizen is less directly or less continually concerned with his country's day-to-day problems and has less knowledge of them; secondly, the fact that it is impracticable for the parliamentary candidates to present the different electoral issues to citizens abroad and that non-resident citizens have no influence on the selection of candidates or on the formulation of their electoral programmes; thirdly, the close connection between the right to vote in parliamentary elections and the fact of being directly affected by the acts of the political bodies so elected; and, fourthly, the legitimate concern the legislature may have to limit the influence of citizens living abroad in elections on issues which, while admittedly fundamental, primarily affect persons living in the country. Even where it may be possible that the applicant has not severed ties with his country of origin and that some of the factors indicated above are

---

[38] *Sevinger and Eman v Netherlands.*

[39] Elections to the European Parliament were not at issue in the Strasbourg case, but the Court of Justice of the European Union had ruled in their favour in a separate case, *Eman and Sevinger v Netherlands* Case 300/04 (Court of Justice of the European Union, 12 September 2006).

[40] *Doyle v United Kingdom* App no 30158/06 (2007) 45 EHRR SE 3.

The Right to Vote

therefore inapplicable to this case, the law cannot always take account of every individual case but must lay down a general rule (*Hilbe*, cited above).[41]

The Court in *Doyle* thought that it was reasonable to believe that someone absent for fifteen years was likely to have weakened ties with the UK and would not be as affected by UK legislation as someone residing there. He had other opportunities to participate democratically – in European Parliament elections, in Belgian elections if he nationalised and by returning to reside in the UK. In these circumstances the Court found the application manifestly ill-founded.

Soon thereafter the Court found that it had to give more detailed substantive consideration to these issues. This may well reflect the appreciation that state provision for non-resident voting was expanding rapidly throughout Europe; indeed, the Court even had to revisit the UK rules. Four cases in particular required more detailed consideration of this issue: *Sitaropoulos and Others v Greece*, *Shindler v UK*, *Oran v Turkey* and *Vámos v Hungary*.[42]

Sitaropoulos was the subject of Chamber and Grand Chamber judgments where the Grand Chamber reversed the Chamber. The case concerned Greek nationals who were Council of Europe employees and lived in Strasbourg. The Greek Constitution of 1975 provided that the legislature could establish the conditions for voting of nationals residing abroad; a 2001 amendment affirmed this and introduced a requirement for a two-thirds majority in the legislature to approve such a measure. More than three decades later the legislature had not enacted implementing legislation regarding national elections, though it had enacted legislation with respect to the European Parliament elections. The applicants could have exercised their right to vote if they had physically returned to Greece, but as they pointed out, this would have financial and other impacts on their lives.

The Chamber noted that P1–3 did not itself require states to grant voting rights to nationals residing abroad, but that it could tell states not to allow a constitutional provision on the right to vote to fall into 'disuse'.[43] The Chamber noted that the Greek legislature had considered one initiative to implement the constitutional provision but this had not succeeded in the legislature; the situation was even more difficult for other Greek citizens living

---

[41] *Doyle v United Kingdom.*

[42] Elections outside the territory of the state were also at issue in *Riza*, but this was not the central issue: *Riza and DPS v Bulgaria* App no 48555/10 (13 October 2015). Riza did highlight again the disparity of approaches to non-resident voting. Non-residents could vote for parties but not individuals in the mixed majoritarian / proportional system in Bulgaria.

[43] *Sitaropoulos and Others v Greece* App no 42202/07 (Chamber, 8 July 2010), para 41.

abroad who might not have the resources or live as close as the applicants did, and amounted to 'unfair discrimination'.[44] The Chamber buttressed its reasoning by referring to the evolution in European practice since the 1980s, and the number of Council of Europe documents which urged state to facilitate external voting by their citizens.[45] The Chamber found a violation of the right to vote by a majority of 5–2.

It is notable that the Chamber felt the need to identify a number of different mutually supporting arguments that applied in the particular case, presumably believing there was not a clear compelling argument that supported the conclusion; it is also notable that the judgment does not engage with the reasons identified earlier in the jurisprudence as to why restrictions on residence can be valid. The majority did not discuss some key arguments raised in the dissent and notably the point that where a country, like Greece, has a large diaspora, the European Court of Human Rights should be reluctant to intervene on this issue (dissents of Judges Vajič and Flogaitis). This indeed was one of the reasons the Greek legislature had not passed a bill on the topic.[46] Unsurprisingly, the Grand Chamber reversed the judgment.

The Grand Chamber noted the general principles from the case law, including the principle that the Convention requirements could evolve in light of emerging consensus on European standards; it also noted the specific reasons Convention institutions had accepted residence-based limits in the past.[47] The Grand Chamber read the comparative evidence somewhat differently from the Chamber. It noted that none of the major human rights instruments at UN or regional level provided for a right to vote for nationals absent from the territory of the state; while different Council of Europe documents referred to the possibility, it was as a possibility to be considered rather than an obligation.[48] Furthermore, even though the majority of European states allowed nationals to vote from abroad, they did so using very different systems, e.g. having different voting mechanisms, different rules on length of time spent abroad before the right was lost, registration requirements, and some states allowed nationals abroad to elect their own delegates.[49] The Grand Chamber did not consider that it could tell the Greek legislature

---

[44] *Sitaropoulos and Others v Greece* (Chamber), paras 42–43.
[45] *Sitaropoulos and Others v Greece* (Chamber), paras 44–45.
[46] *Sitaropoulos and Others v Greece* App no 42202/07 (Grand Chamber, 15 March 2012), para 20.
[47] *Sitaropoulos and Others v Greece* (Grand Chamber), paras 67–69.
[48] *Sitaropoulos and Others v Greece* (Grand Chamber), paras 72–73.
[49] *Sitaropoulos and Others v Greece* (Grand Chamber), para 74.

The Right to Vote   179

how to implement the provision of the Greek constitution.[50] The Grand Chamber unanimously found there was no violation.

The judgment is also unusual in that the arguments of a third-party intervener featured an explicit quote from Habermas: the quote was that democracy 'required[d] that those who [were] subject to the law and those to whom the law [made] reference should consider themselves to be the creators of the law'.[51] This the intervenor interpreted not merely to refer to persons on the territory of the state, but also alluded to others not so resident.

Sitaropoulos was something of an unusual case given the significance attached to the constitutional provision by the Chamber and its reference to the concept of desuetude. Yet it also highlighted the increase in non-resident voting provision, the complexities that raised for some states with large diaspora, and the varied ways in which European states addressed this issue. This last point became even more apparent in the UK case of *Shindler*.

In *Shindler*, the applicant had moved to Italy in 1982 and by the time of his application (2009) no longer met the fifteen-year rule. The case highlighted the frequent changes in UK legislation on the topic of non-resident voting since the 1980s. Apart from specific groups of people, the UK did not permit non-resident nationals to vote until 1985. It then provided that non-resident nationals who had resided in the UK in the previous five years could register to vote. In 1989, the residence requirement was extended to twenty years. In 2000, legislation reduced this to fifteen years. Even more striking were the diversity of views expressed in Parliament and committees about the appropriate residence requirement, with some calling for a return to the earlier five-year rule and others calling for the time limit to be eliminated entirely.[52]

The judgment provides lengthy details on the comparative practice regarding non-resident voting and details on the evolving position of other Council of Europe institutions, including the Parliamentary Assembly, Committee of Ministers and the Venice Commission. As part of its review of the general principles relevant to the case, the Court reiterated the view that it must 'have regard to the changing conditions within the respondent State and within Contracting States generally and respond to any emerging consensus as to the standards to be achieved'.[53] Even more importantly, patterns of migration, new technologies and cheaper transport had changed the context dramatically since the Convention principles on residence-based restrictions had

---

[50] *Sitaropoulos and Others v Greece* (Grand Chamber), para 76.
[51] *Sitaropoulos and Others v Greece* (Grand Chamber), para 61.
[52] *Shindler v United Kingdom* App no 19840/09 (2014) 58 EHRR 5, paras 15–28.
[53] *Shindler v United Kingdom*, para 102.

180   The Right to Vote

first been developed, and therefore it was appropriate to re-examine the arguments in light of these developments.[54]

The Court reviewed the fairly extensive documentation from the Parliamentary Assembly, the Venice Commission and the Committee of Ministers. These clearly indicated that the Council of Europe was giving more attention to the issue of non-resident voting and the first two institutions used language encouraging states to create or expand non-resident voting rights for nationals. But there were also some words of caution from those bodies, while the Committee did not see the need to look into creating a binding legal instrument. The Venice Commission acknowledged that there was no obligation to extend voting rights to non-resident nationals. The Court agreed that there was no evidence of an obligation to extend unrestricted voting rights to non-resident nationals.[55] The Court saw that there was still a great deal of variety even within the Council of Europe institutions on how to approach the issue of migrant participation rights. This reflected the different approaches by the states to non-resident voting. While there was a strong majority of states which imposed no time limit of the sort used by the UK, states nevertheless implemented non-resident voting in different ways – whether by proxy, postal voting, in person at an embassy abroad or in person on the national territory.[56]

The applicant had indicated that he retained close ties with the UK and was affected by UK legislation in different ways, especially as regards taxation and pensions. The Court, however, accepted that the state could adopt a general policy on the residence requirement; this would avoid the risk of arbitrariness and inconsistency and promote legal certainty.[57]

The case of *Oran v Turkey* did not require as much detailed consideration of the principle and practice of non-resident voting, and indeed raises several other issues.[58] However, it usefully demonstrates again the variety of approaches taken to non-resident voting. The applicant was a candidate for office who ran as a non-party-affiliated independent in Istanbul. He complained that he was disadvantaged because of the manner in which non-resident voting was organised. Turkish rules permitted nationals who had been resident abroad to vote at polling stations established at customs posts. Their votes were not assigned to a particular constituency. Crucially, from the applicant's perspective, such non-resident voters could only vote for political

---

[54] *Shindler v United Kingdom*, para 110.
[55] *Shindler v United Kingdom*, para 114.
[56] *Shindler v United Kingdom*, para 76.
[57] *Shindler v United Kingdom*, para 116.
[58] *Oran v Turkey* App nos 28881/07 and 37920/07 (15 April 2014).

The Right to Vote

parties and not for independents. The Turkish government pleaded practical necessity for this distinction: there were over 700 independent candidates across the country, and they could not produce ballot papers listing all of them.[59]

The Court noted that different practices existed as regards non-resident voting rights and states had to weigh different competing interests in deciding how to implement them; the Court accepted that the national legislature had sought to balance competing interests.[60] The Court alluded indirectly to the difficulties of registering non-resident voters in specific constituencies, and to the legitimate concern in limiting the influence of non-resident voters on issues that primarily affected those resident.[61] The Court also referred to the aim of avoiding 'excessive and dysfunctional fragmentation of candidacies' as a justification for the measure.[62]

This was a 4–3 majority judgment in the Chamber, and the three dissenters (Sajó, Keller and Lemmens) unpicked the reasoning of the majority on several important points. They acknowledged that there were difficulties with non-resident voting but that the Venice Commission had given general guidance pointing to two possible solutions: either associating the non-resident voter with a specific constituency or creating a special constituency for non-residents. They argued that preventing certain electors from voting for independents prevented the 'free expression of the opinion' of the people. The dissenters also took issue with the majority's reference to the legitimate aim of limiting the influence of non-resident voters – the government had not actually put forward this aim, and in any event, it was irrelevant. The dissenters accepted the importance of political parties but pointed out the Turkish system already accepted the legitimacy of independent candidates, except for the non-resident voters. Similarly they were unconvinced by the claims about avoiding excessive fragmentation – preventing the category of non-resident voters from voting for independents would not achieve this.

The Court rejected as inadmissible a similar application from Hungary complaining about discrimination in how non-resident voting was organised. In that case, *Vámos v Hungary*, the legislature had decreed that non-resident voters fell into different categories. If they did not have a permanent residence in Hungary, they could use a postal vote; voters in this category could only

---

[59] *Oran v Turkey*, para 46.

[60] *Oran v Turkey*, paras 60–63.

[61] *Oran v Turkey*, para 63.

[62] *Oran v Turkey*, para 65. *Oran* was applied in *Timurhan v Turkey* App no 28882/07 (16 December 2014).

vote for the party list component of the election. If the non-resident voter had a permanent residence in Hungary, then they had to either return home to vote or could vote in a Hungarian embassy or consulate. Voters in this second category could vote for both parties and individuals in constituencies. The complaint turned not on the inability to vote for individuals, but on the fact the second category of voters could not use postal voting.

Considering the complaint under P1–3 alone, the Court had little difficulty in deciding that there was no violation. It followed from cases like *Sitaropoulos* and *Oran* that this did not impair the essence of the right and fell within the margin of appreciation. The Court considered the fact that the distinction between the two categories of non-resident voters raised problems under article 14. It concluded that there was an objective difference between the two categories, and the legislature was entitled to make distinctions based on which group might have closer links with the country. While in one sense postal voting might seem preferable, the Court noted that short-term non-residents were more likely to return to the country and so could more easily do so, and they could vote for individuals in constituencies as well as for party lists.[63]

The decision underlines again the heterogeneity of approaches taken to non-resident voting in Europe, the rapidly changing context (the law was only reformed in 2013) and the Court's reluctance to get too involved in how states regulate this issue. The deference shown so far on some of the issues of principle – whether non-resident nationals should be allowed a vote; should non-resident voting be limited to persons who have lived outside the country for no longer than a set period, and if so, what that period should be; what voting arrangements should be used (postal, electronic, return to country, voting in consulates, by proxy) – seems justified in view of the legitimate reasons the Court sees as justifying treating non-residents differently and in view of the different regulations across Europe. However, the case law does suggest that more scrutiny may be required to assess apparently arbitrary differences as between different types of non-resident voters (*Vámos*) or resident and non-resident voters (*Oran*). Similarly, frequent changes in the rules (as in the UK) or late changes before an election suggest concerns. Whilst there is no suggestion in these cases that rule distinctions or changes were being employed to advantage a governing party, there is a potential there. Certainly if arbitrary or late changes appear to benefit the government of the day, a heightened proportionality test would be justified when dealing with

---

[63] *Vámos v Hungary* App no 48145/14 (17 February 2015), paras 19–20.

The Convention institutions have accepted, unreflexively, nationality-based requirements in voting rules.[64] This is seen in *Luksch v Italy*, where the applicant was a German national but had been born in Venice and lived in Italy a long time and paid taxes in Italy. The Commission dismissed his application based on P1–3, noting very briefly that age, residence and nationality requirements were 'commonly imposed in Convention countries'. Strikingly the Commission did not feel the need to discuss the reasons why such restrictions on nationality were justified or whether they were appropriate in the specific case. Not only had the applicant been born in Italy, paid taxes there and lived there a long time, but he was also not allowed to vote in Germany.[65]

The Court had the opportunity to revisit this issue in the Slovenian 'erased' cases. These cases concerned the Kafkaesque situation in which a significant number of persons found themselves in the years following Slovenian independence in 1991. Under the Yugoslavian regime, individuals had citizenship of the federation and one of the individual republics. Slovenia provided that non-Slovenian Yugoslavian citizens could become Slovenian citizens if they were residing in Slovenia, had permanent resident status in Slovenia and applied for citizenship. For numerous reasons – lack of documents, the short time scale for applications, lack of education, confusion about the legal rules – some persons in this category did not apply. As a consequence, they did not obtain Slovenian citizenship and were removed from the Register of Permanent Residents. They became known as the 'erased'. The persons affected were not notified of these changes in status. During the post-independence period, efforts were made to address the problem, often thanks to Constitutional Court judgments, but still several thousand people lacked Slovenian citizenship or permanent resident status.

---

[64] Ruth Rubio-Marin and Rory O'Connell, 'The European Convention and the Relative Rights of Resident Aliens' (1999) 5 European Law Journal 4.

[65] *Luksch v Italy* App no 27614/95 (European Commission of Human Rights, 21 May 1997).

The consequences were severe – they could not vote or run for election, they could not access healthcare or social security, their workplace protections were diminished, their property rights affected and their ability to move within Slovenia or to leave Slovenia was impaired.[66] Some people were made homeless.[67] Some were rendered stateless. Some were deported. In some cases, these were people who had lived in Slovenia for their entire adult lives and had paid into the Slovenian social security system for years.[68]

In *Makuc v Slovenia*, the Court dealt very briefly with a claim by the applicants that their P1–3 rights were violated. The Court noted that there was an admissibility query due to non-exhaustion of domestic remedies but, rather than deciding on that basis, referred to the nationality issue. Noting that the applicants were not Slovenian citizens, it concluded that they could not invoke P1–3 rights. This part of the complaint was inadmissible as manifestly ill-founded.[69]

The Court indeed decided that many of the complaints were inadmissible; it ruled that certain complaints based on articles 6, 13 and 14 were admissible. The Chamber subsequently found violations of article 8 and article 13 on the grounds that significant interference with private and family life could not be said to be in accordance with law.[70] The Grand Chamber agreed but went further, finding this interference was not necessary in a democratic society – the Slovenian legislature could have provided a mechanism to regularise the situation of non-Slovenian Yugoslavians.[71] Furthermore, the Grand Chamber found a breach of article 14.[72]

In *Shindler*, the Court noted that one of the reasons for finding there was no obligation in the Council of Europe for states to extend voting rights to non-resident nationals was because there were ongoing debates over the best way to protect migrant rights and whether this might be done in the host country or in the country of residence.[73]

The failure to engage in detail with the justification for nationality-based restrictions is one of the major flaws in the Convention's approach to

---

[66] One applicant could not leave Slovenia to attend family funerals for fear he would not be allowed back into Slovenia: *Makuc v Slovenia* App no 26828/06 (31 May 2007), para 55.

[67] *Makuc v Slovenia*, para 41.

[68] This was the case with *Makuc*: *Makuc v Slovenia*, para 30.

[69] *Makuc v Slovenia*, para 208. Similarly, article 14 in combination with P1–3 was not applicable: para 215.

[70] *Kurić v Slovenia* App no 26828/06 (Chamber, 26 June 2012).

[71] *Kurić v Slovenia* App no 26828/06 (Grand Chamber, 12 March 2014), para 357.

[72] *Kurić v Slovenia* (Grand Chamber), para 394.

[73] *Shindler v United Kingdom*, para 114.

democracy. It is particularly striking given the cogency of the reasons generally offered to accept restrictions on non-resident nationals. Consider them one by one. First, it is said that non-resident nationals are less directly concerned with the country's day-to-day affairs and have less knowledge of them. This does not apply to non-national residents if they are in the country for a period of time. While tourists or short-term visitors might not be significantly affected by a country's legislation, this would not be the case for long-term workers, refugees or other residents. Similarly, short-term visitors might not have much understanding of a country, but the longer the period of residence, the less true this is.

Second, in the residence cases, the Court refers to the difficulty of political candidates interacting with nationals abroad and the difficulty for non-resident nationals to be involved in selection of candidates. Again this may apply to short-term visitors, but the longer the period of residence a non-national has in a country, the less likely these would be problems.

Third, the Court refers to the close relationship between being affected by legislation and voting for a parliamentary candidate. It is difficult to see any difference between a long-term resident non-national and a resident national on this ground.

Finally, in the residence cases, the Court refers to the legitimate interest in limiting the influence of nationals living abroad given that national legislative decisions will primarily affect persons living in the territory.

Furthermore, while the Court frequently alludes to difficulties of a practical nature in relation to non-resident voting, these practical issues are not so apparent in relation to non-national residents voting. Special poling votes or extra postal voting arrangements would not be required. There would be some difficulties about determining which non-nationals in particular would be allowed to vote, but many states (at least those in the European Union) manage to deal with the issue in relation to European Parliament elections.

Considering each of these issues, it is apparent that they operate as arguments for recognising the right to vote of at least some categories of non-national residents.

The *Makuc* and *Kurič* cases demonstrate the vulnerable position of one type of non-national, those persons who, living in Slovenia in 1991, found themselves rendered aliens unlawfully on the territory of the state. They had previously enjoyed social, economic and political rights and found themselves stripped of these. This had dramatic effects on their private and family life and indeed their homes, health and work. These were individuals who were directly and continuously affected by legislative decisions both on their status and their rights; they were excluded from the ordinary political process, and

186   *The Right to Vote*

one assumes a special referendum on legislation to determine their status. They were the subject of inflammatory and divisive rhetoric from some politicians. It is disappointing that the Court found the P1–3 simply inadmissible on the basis of a laconic reference to the fact these persons were not nationals.

Mental Capacity

There is little case law relating to voting rights and mental capacity, and we have to wait until a 2010 case involving Hungary for the European Court of Human Rights to pronounce on this.

In *Alajos Kiss v Hungary*, the applicant suffered from manic depression and had been placed under partial guardianship.[74] Even though this was done mainly because of financial irresponsibility and occasional aggressive behaviour, according to the Hungarian Constitution, this imposition of partial guardianship resulted in the automatic loss of voting rights.

The European Court of Human Rights accepted that the Hungarian measure had a legitimate aim, that of 'ensuring that only citizens capable of assessing the consequences of their decisions and making conscious and judicious decisions' could participate in public affairs.[75] It then turned to the proportionality question. Here the Court indicated that, in principle, there was a wide margin of appreciation available to states to decide how to pursue such a legitimate aim and what processes to use when doing so. However, there were two key indications as to why the measure was disproportionate. In the first place it was an indiscriminate ban on anyone subject to partial or full guardianship and irrespective of any individual assessment of the faculties of the person concerned. In this regard the ban was similar to the 'all-embracing' one in *Hirst*.[76] Furthermore, this particular ban applied to a vulnerable group, the mentally disabled, and one which had experienced discrimination in the past. This situation called for 'strict scrutiny', as the historical discrimination may give rise to 'lasting consequences, resulting in their social exclusion'; this prejudice could include 'legislative stereotyping'.[77] In line with the Court's case law under article 14 and vulnerable and disadvantaged groups, a state would need to show very weighty reasons to justify such a ban.

---

[74] *Alajos Kiss v Hungary* App no 38832/06 (20 May 2010).
[75] *Alajos Kiss v Hungary*, para 38.
[76] *Alajos Kiss v Hungary*, para 42.
[77] *Alajos Kiss v Hungary*, para 42.

The Court has reaffirmed this approach in subsequent cases involving Hungary[78] and is also considering a similar application from Bulgaria.[79] *Alajos Kiss* is important in indicating that a general ban on people for mental disability reasons will be a breach of the Convention; it indeed indicates that an 'individualised judicial evaluation' is required in such cases.[80]

Language

The Convention institutions have been relatively reluctant to intervene in issues involving language matters. In Belgian cases, for instance, the Court and Commission have noted that French-speakers living in the Dutch region had the same rights to vote as Dutch-speakers in the (formally monolingual, Dutch-speaking) region, even though they could only vote for candidates willing to take a parliamentary oath in Dutch and speak in Dutch in the elected body.[81] In the Court judgment there was a five-judge minority which dissented from this view.

National Origin

The case of *Aziz v Cyprus* presented the Court with an unusual situation stemming from the history of a divided society (and later partially occupied territory) in Cyprus. In 1960, Cyprus had adopted a consociational model of legislature. A majority of seats (70%) represented Greek Cypriots elected by person on the Greek Cypriot electoral register, while a minority (30%) represented Turkish Cypriots elected by person on the Turkish Cypriot register. The system had ceased to operate in 1963 following communal unrest; with the Turkish invasion, very few Turkish Cypriots remained in the unoccupied territory – just over one thousand. These Turkish Cypriots, of which the applicant was one, were effectively disenfranchised. The Cypriot government argued that they could not restore the consociational system as it was supposed to operate. The Court concluded that there was a violation of the right to vote. Indeed the 'very essence' of the right to vote was being denied, as the applicant, a Cypriot national, was denied an opportunity to vote in elections

---

[78] *Gajcsi v Hungary* App no 62924/10 (23 September 2014); *Harmati v Hungary* App no 63012/10 (21 October 2014).

[79] *Marinov v Bulgaria (communicated)* App no 26081/17.

[80] *Alajos Kiss v Hungary*, para 44.

[81] *Mathieu-Mohin and Clerfayt v Belgium*, para 57; *Clerfayt v Belgium* App no 27120/95 (European Commission of Human Rights, 8 September 1997).

188   *The Right to Vote*

for the national legislature.[82] In a rare move, the Court went further, also finding a violation of article 14, the right to non-discrimination. The Court frequently does not examine an article 14 case if there is already a violation of another right in the Convention, but can do so if the discrimination issue is a fundamental aspect of the case.[83] In this case that criterion was met given the exclusion in practice of Cypriots of Turkish origin. The Court dismissed the government's arguments for any possible justification and found a violation.

Bankruptcy

The European Court of Human Rights has dealt with a long series of cases from Italy on the effects of being declared bankrupt. Under laws dating back to the Middle Ages, persons declared bankrupt in Italy faced numerous privations of rights, including, in the Middle Ages, criminal law punishments.[84] Italy also provided, by laws passed as recently as 1992, that persons declared bankrupt could not vote for a period lasting up to five years after the bankruptcy order.[85] The Court rehearsed the general principles that applied in relation to the rights in P1–3, including that the state could invoke a wide range of legitimate reasons to justify limiting the rights; for instance, it cited the *Hirst* case which indicated the reasons for prisoner disenfranchisement including preventing crime, enhancing civic responsibility and respect for the rule of law. Rather remarkably, the Court found that the state had failed to put forward any acceptable legitimate aim for the restriction on voting rights. The Court identified the aim of the measure as being 'an essentially punitive measure designed to belittle and punish the persons concerned, demeaning them as individuals for no other reason than their having been the subject of civil bankruptcy proceedings'.[86] This was in the context that the proceedings were civil in nature and there had not been any issue of criminal wrongdoing. The Court has reiterated this finding in other Italian cases.[87]

The finding is rare; states usually manage to find a credible legitimate aim, and the Court is usually deferential in accepting the state's claimed aims as legitimate. Remarkably in this case, the Court accepted that the aim of the measure was no more than to 'demean' individuals, and this could not be said to be a legitimate aim. It is important that the Court demonstrates that there

---

[82] *Aziz v Cyprus* App no 69949/01 (2005) 41 EHRR 11 (22 June 2004), para 30.
[83] *Aziz v Cyprus*, para 35.
[84] *Campagnano v Italy* App no 77955/01 (2006) 48 EHRR 43, para 22.
[85] *Campagnano v Italy*, para 45.
[86] *Campagnano v Italy*, para 48.
[87] E.g. *Viola v Italy* App no 7842/02 (8 January 2008).

are limits to what it will accept as a legitimate aim, even in cases under P1–3 where it has held that states have a wide scope to put forward legitimate aims. The judgment implicitly ties the right to vote to notions of dignity – being stripped of this right demeaned the applicants.

Prisoner Status

The issue of prisoner disenfranchisement has, somewhat surprisingly perhaps, turned into one of the major sagas, indeed challenges, facing the European Court of Human Rights system. Even more remarkable, though, is the fact that this difficult saga involves a state generally well regarded in terms of respect for political democracy and its obligations under the Convention; yet the manner in which the United Kingdom has responded to the prisoner disenfranchisement case law has had important ramifications for the protection of human rights and international systems of law both in the UK and arguably further afield. And while much of the discussion focuses on the UK, the Court's prisoner disenfranchisement case law stretches much further across Europe, from the UK to Turkey and Russia.

The early cases give no hint of the turmoil to come. Several of the early Convention cases deal with lengthy, sometimes life-time restrictions on political rights as a result of collaboration with occupying powers during the Second World War. These the Convention institutions upheld with little discussion.[88] In one 1979 case, dealing with a life-time ban on voting imposed on the applicant in 1948 as part of his conviction for collaboration during the Second World War, the Commission briefly noted:

> The purpose of legislation depriving persons convicted of treason of certain political rights and, more specifically, the right to vote, is to ensure that persons who have seriously abused, in wartime, their right to participate in the public life of their country are prevented in future from abusing their political rights in a manner prejudicial to the security of the state or the foundations of a democratic society.[89]

An argument based on article 14 in combination with P1–3 was even more curtly rejected in the same application.

The Commission, in line with its general approach in early cases, accepted that states could deprive prisoners of the right to vote for a time, and this penalty could last after any period of imprisonment. It accepted, for instance, a

---

[88] *X v Netherlands* App no 6573/74 (1975) 1 DR 87 (European Commission of Human Rights).
[89] *X v Belgium* App no 8701/79 (European Commission of Human Rights, 3 December 1979).

Dutch disenfranchisement rule imposed on persons sentenced to a period of one year's imprisonment where the disenfranchisement lasted three years after the imprisonment. The Commission held that there was no need to make an exception for persons who were punished as conscientious objectors to military service. The Commission supported this position by referring to the practice of states in imposing such a penalty, which reflected a sense of 'dishonour' that attached to certain convictions.[90] The Commission also considered the position in Ireland whereby, although there was no legislative ban on prisoner voting, the state had not created any mechanisms to permit it, so in practice prisoners in jail could not vote. The Commission again referred to the notion of 'dishonour' that accompanied some offences and said that the policy was not arbitrary and did not affect the expression of the opinion of the people in the electoral process.[91]

The Court itself rejected as inadmissible a complaint from an Italian applicant who had been given a two-year ban on carrying out public functions by a court, supplementary to a conviction and three-year jail sentence for financial crimes.[92] The Court did find a violation of P1–3 in the case of an Italian who had been removed from the electoral role after his acquittal of Mafia-related crimes. The Court accepted that there was a legitimate aim to justify temporarily suspending political rights of someone suspected of being in the Mafia, but in the specific case the individual had already been acquitted.[93]

These early cases suggested that restrictions on prisoner voting were likely to be accepted in Strasbourg. But none of them considered a formal legislative ban on prisoner voting, and in most cases the discussion of the P1–3 issue was fairly brief. The first case where a formal legislative ban on prisoners voting was subjected to detailed scrutiny was *Hirst v United Kingdom*. This judgment marks the start of the prisoner voting saga in Strasbourg and the UK; the initial judgments themselves contain a number of different propositions, some of which remain controversial and some apparent arguments have been disavowed or clarified in later cases. The core principles, though, have now been applied to several other Council of Europe states with similar bans.

---

[90] *H v Netherlands* App no 9914/82 (European Commission of Human Rights, 4 July 1983).

[91] *Holland v Ireland* App no 24827/94 (European Commission of Human Rights, 14 April 1998). The case can be contrasted with the South African Constitutional Court judgment in *August v Electoral Commission* CCT 8/99, [2000] 1 Law Reports of the Commonwealth 608 (South African Constitutional Court).

[92] *MDU v Italy* App no 58540/00 (European Commission of Human Rights, 28 January 2003).

[93] *Labita v Italy* App no 26772/95 (2008) 46 EHRR 50.

The Right to Vote   191

Meanwhile it is only more than a decade after the *Hirst* judgment that the UK has developed a plan to implement the judgment.

Hirst had been convicted of manslaughter and received a discretionary life sentence; he was still being detained at the time of the case due to the risk he posed to others. Under the Representation of the People Act 1983, a convicted person detained in a penal institution was not allowed to vote. The prisoner voting ban did not apply to persons in jail for contempt, in default for non-payment of a fine or, after the Representation of the People Act 2000, persons on remand prior to conviction. Once released, convicted persons were free to vote. The voting ban had been found in earlier legislation in the nineteenth and twentieth centuries and ultimately could be traced to medieval notions of 'civic death'.[94]

In light of the furore to follow, it is noteworthy the Chamber of the European Court of Human Rights unanimously found a violation of P1–3. The Chamber noted that European countries had varied approaches to prisoner disenfranchisement – eighteen had no restrictions, thirteen did not allow prisoner voting and the remainder adopted an intermediary position.[95] The Chamber then indicated that the margin of appreciation was not appropriate when a state had not deliberated on a restriction but had passively adhered to it in the light of tradition; the Chamber also underlined that the right to vote was the 'indispensable foundation of a democratic system'.[96] The Chamber then considered the legitimacy and the proportionality of the measure. As regards a legitimate aim, the government suggested two: the prevention and punishment of crime; and the enhancement of civic responsibility and respect for the rule of law. The Chamber expressed considerable doubt about both aims, examining them especially in the light of the Canadian case on prisoner voting restrictions.[97] However the Chamber refrained from formally pronouncing on the legitimacy of the aims, as it found the measure disproportionate. The Chamber acknowledged that the ban was not as extensive as in some jurisdictions, but nevertheless found that it was 'indiscriminate', 'a blanket restriction on all convicted prisoners', that applied automatically and 'irrespective of the length of their sentence and irrespective of the nature or gravity of their offence'.[98] Further, the ban in the applicant's case was inappropriate, as he had entered a phase of imprisonment based not

---

[94] *Hirst v United Kingdom* (2004) 38 EHRR 825 (Chamber), para 17.
[95] *Hirst v United Kingdom* (Chamber), para 40.
[96] *Hirst v United Kingdom* (Chamber) para 41.
[97] *Hirst v United Kingdom* (Chamber), paras 44–47. As the five-judge dissent in the Grand Chamber mentioned, the Convention institutions usually avoid challenging the governments' aims in reviewing restrictions.
[98] *Hirst v United Kingdom* (Chamber), para 49.

192 *The Right to Vote*

on punishment but on his risk to society. The Chamber went on to note it was for the legislature to determine the exact parameters of any ban; it was struck by the fact that the UK legislature had apparently never 'sought to weigh the competing interests or to assess the proportionality of the ban'; the Chamber was careful, however, to indicate that an absolute ban was always outside the margin of appreciation.[99]

Unsurprisingly, the case went to the Grand Chamber, which also found a violation by a 12–5 vote; the majority also included a number of concurring opinions. The Grand Chamber indicated that the right to vote was a right and not a privilege, and that the presumption must be in favour of inclusion in a democratic society.[100] The Grand Chamber also acknowledged the wide margin of appreciation in this area given that 'There are numerous ways of organising and running electoral systems and a wealth of differences, inter alia, in historical development, cultural diversity and political thought within Europe which it is for each Contracting State to mould into their own democratic vision.'[101] Nevertheless there was still a European supervision and the Grand Chamber warned that 'any departure from the principle of universal suffrage risks undermining the democratic validity of the legislature'.[102]

The Grand Chamber went on to reiterate the principle that prisoners did not simply forfeit all their rights – any restrictions beyond imprisonment would have to be justified; furthermore, it was clearly inappropriate to adopt a general disenfranchisement policy 'based purely on what might offend public opinion'.[103] Further, as disenfranchisement was a 'severe' measure, there had to be a 'discernible and sufficient link between the sanction and the conduct and circumstances of the individual concerned'.[104]

The Grand Chamber was willing to accept the legitimate aims proffered by the government (not expressing the reticence shown in the Chamber). On the proportionality aspect, the Grand Chamber found the measure in breach of P1–3. It applied to offenders irrespective of the length of sentence or the gravity of the offence; it was arbitrary in that a judge might decide not to impose a custodial sentence in a particular case; the courts did not refer to disenfranchisement when sentencing.[105] Furthermore, neither the courts nor the

---

[99] *Hirst v United Kingdom* (Chamber), para 51.
[100] *Hirst v United Kingdom* (No. 2) App no 74025/01 (2005) 42 EHRR 41 (Grand Chamber), para 59.
[101] *Hirst v United Kingdom* (Grand Chamber), para 61.
[102] *Hirst v United Kingdom* (Grand Chamber), para 62.
[103] *Hirst v United Kingdom* (Grand Chamber), para 70.
[104] *Hirst v United Kingdom* (Grand Chamber), para 71.
[105] *Hirst v United Kingdom* (Grand Chamber), para 77.

The Right to Vote 193

legislature had sufficiently considered the proportionality of the ban in the light of Convention rights.[106] The Grand Chamber declined the invitation to give more guidance as to what measures might be acceptable – it was for the state to devise measures and the European Court's role to review those.[107]

The Grand Chamber judgment had a significant majority but was not without problems. Several prominent judges included concurring opinions pointing out flaws in the majority reasoning, and there was a trenchant five-judge dissent including the then President of the Court and a future President of the Court. The majority judgment included some comments which could be interpreted more or less strictly.

Within a few years, different chambers of the Court found violations of prisoners' right to vote in Austria (*Frodl*),[108] Romania (*Calmanovici*),[109] Italy (*Scoppola No 3*)[110] and the UK again (*Greens and MT*).[111] The finding of a violation in *Scoppola* gave rise to a hearing in the Grand Chamber. Part of the reason for this was that in at least the *Frodl* case, the Court seemed to read the *Hirst* judgment widely; the other reason was the reaction in the UK to the *Hirst* judgment. In *Frodl*, the Court considered an Austrian law which disenfranchised prisoners who had been sentenced to jail for more than one year. The Court held this breached the *Hirst* principle because it was an automatic rule without the opportunity for an individualised judicial assessment; the Court based this on several passages in the *Hirst* judgment including the reference to a need for 'discernible and sufficient link between the sanction and the conduct and circumstances of the individual concerned'.[112]

The Grand Chamber considered the *Hirst* and post-*Hirst* case law in *Scoppola No 3*. The UK intervened in this case, sending its Attorney General to make the case that *Hirst* was wrong. The Italian law was not the same as the UK approach. Prisoners were disenfranchised if they were found guilty of certain specific crimes or if they were sentenced to a particularly long jail term. When a person was jailed for between three and five years, they faced a five-year ban on voting. If jailed for more than five years, then the ban on voting was permanent.[113] The Grand Chamber, by a 16–1 majority, held that this was not a breach of P1–3. The Grand Chamber indicated the *Frodl*

---

[106] *Hirst v United Kingdom* (Grand Chamber), paras 79–80.

[107] *Hirst v United Kingdom* (Grand Chamber), para 84.

[108] *Frodl v Austria* App no 20201/04 (2011) 52 EHRR 5.

[109] *Calmanovici v Romania* App no 42250/02 (1 July 2008).

[110] *Scoppola v Italy (No 3)* App no 126/05 (Chamber, 18 January 2011).

[111] *Greens and MT v United Kingdom* App nos 60041/08 and 60054/08 (23 November 2010).

[112] *Frodl v Austria* App no 20201/04 (8 April 2010), para 34.

[113] *Scoppola v Italy (No 3)* App no 126/05 (2013) 56 EHRR 19 (Grand Chamber), para 28.

judgment had taken too wide a reading of *Hirst*. States could require an individualised judicial assessment, but they could also let the legislature strike the balance between the different interests as long as there was no 'general, automatic and indiscriminate restriction'.[114] The Grand Chamber upheld what it saw as the central point in *Hirst*: that a general, automatic, indiscriminate ban on prisoners voting, regardless of the length of imprisonment or the nature or gravity of the crime, breached P1–3.[115] The Grand Chamber concluded the Italian measure did not breach this central holding: it applied only to certain offences or cases where a long prison sentence was involved; there was a distinction based on the length of sentence; it was possible to apply to recover the right to vote.[116] Judge Björgvinsson dissented, not seeing any relevant distinction between the Italian and UK laws.[117] Indeed, as he pointed out, in some ways the UK law was more lenient: the Italian ban extended beyond the length of the prison sentences and sometimes for life. The dissent argued that the majority were giving a narrow reading to the *Hirst* judgment and it is difficult to disagree with this.[118]

The Court has upheld the *Hirst* judgment, as interpreted in *Scoppola No 3* in several subsequent cases involving different European countries: *Anchugov and Gladkov v Russia*,[119] *Söyler v Turkey*,[120] *Brânduse v Romania*[121] and *Kulinski and Sabev v Bulgaria*.[122] It has also reaffirmed the holding in cases involving the United Kingdom.[123] This has not been without controversy. In *Firth v UK*, two judges dissented, and one – Judge Wojtyczek – criticised the *Hirst* and *Scoppola No 3* reasoning at length. Even more controversial is the

---

[114] *Scoppola v Italy (No 3)* (Grand Chamber), para 102.

[115] *Scoppola v Italy (No 3)* (Grand Chamber), para 96.

[116] *Scoppola v Italy (No 3)* (Grand Chamber), paras 106, 109.

[117] David Harris, Michael O'Boyle, Ed Bates and Carla Buckley, *Law of the European Convention on Human Rights* (Oxford University Press 2018), 921–922.

[118] '[I]t is difficult to see in the *Scoppola v Italy No 3* judgment anything other than a partial overruling of the former judgment [*Hirst*].' Judge Wojtyczek in dissent in *Firth*.

[119] *Anchugov and Gladkov v Russia* App no 11157/04 (4 July 2013).

[120] *Söyler v Turkey* App no 29411/07 (17 September 2013). In passing, the case also indicates that Turkish law disenfranchises privates, corporals and students in military schools. One would imagine that, absent very special circumstances, such bans might be difficult to justify in Strasbourg.

[121] *Brânduse v Romania* App no 39951/08 (27 October 2015).

[122] *Kulinski and Sabev v Bulgaria* App no 63849/09 (21 July 2016).

[123] *Firth v United Kingdom* App nos 47784/09, 47812/09, and others (2016) 63 EHRR 25; *Millbank and others v United Kingdom* App nos 44473/14, 70874/14, and others (30 June 2016). Some applications have been deemed inadmissible for procedural grounds: *Toner v United Kingdom* App no 8195/08 (15 February 2011); *Dunn v United Kingdom* App nos 566/10, 7408/09, 578/10 and others (2013) 56 EHRR SE 5; *McLean and Cole v United Kingdom* App nos 12626/13 and 2522/12 (28 June 2013).

The Right to Vote

fact that the UK has still not amended the legislative ban in question, but has rather adopted a modest set of administrative changes to satisfy the *Hirst* ruling.

Nor is the UK the only state to have resisted the prisoner voting rights case law, as is evident from *Anchugov and Gladkov*. In this case the ban on prisoner voting was stated in the Russian constitution, and Russia asserted a number of novel procedural arguments. The government argued that the Court could not review a provision of the Russian constitution, and that the applicants had not exhausted domestic remedies – they should have tried to begin a procedure to change the constitution. The Court rejected these novel arguments.[124] As with *Hirst*, there is evidence of domestic resistance to implementing this ruling. The Russian Constitutional Court has reaffirmed the supremacy of the Russian Constitution over the possibility to apply international law domestically, and Russia has passed a law allowing the executive to bring a case to the Constitutional Court on the impossibility to apply a European Court of Human Rights judgment compatibly with the Constitution.[125] In the wake of this, the Constitutional Court has ruled that, for the most part, the *Anchugov and Gladkov* judgment is impossible to implement.[126] The Constitutional Court did leave open an avenue for the state to implement the ruling in part by modifying not the constitution, but categories in the criminal code.[127]

The Court has identified the core ruling in *Hirst* and hewn to it despite significant criticism (including judicial criticism in the Court itself as well as from senior UK judges) and recalcitrance on the part of states. It has declined to give advice to states on what they must do to comply with P1–3, despite governments seeking this in cases before it. From *Scoppola No 3* we can see that a five-year ban on voting in the event of someone sentenced to three years and a lifetime ban in the case of a five-year sentence can be compatible with the Convention (albeit there was also a possibility to recover the right to vote in Italy). It is surprising that a lifetime ban could be considered proportionate except for the most serious of offences. *Scoppola No 3* does not indicate a

---

[124] *Anchugov and Gladkov v Russia* App no 11157/04 (4 July 2013). The Court confirmed that Russia's rules breached the Convention in *Isakov v Russia* App no 54446/07 (4 July 2017).

[125] European Commission for Democracy through Law (Venice Commission), *Opinion No. 832/ 2015 Interim Opinion on the Amendments to the Federal Constitutional Law of the Constitutional Court of the Russian Federation* (Council of Europe Pub., Strasbourg 2016).

[126] Judgment No. 12-П/2016 of 19 April 2016 of the Russian Constitutional Court. English translation at <www.venice.coe.int/webforms/documents/default.aspx?pdffile=CDL-REF(2016)033-e> accessed 14 August 2019.

[127] Olga Chernishova, 'Electoral Rights in Russia: Mapping the Situation at the European Court of Human Rights' in Helen Hardman and Brice Dickson (eds) *Electoral Rights in Europe: Advances and Challenges* (Taylor & Francis 2017), 127.

196   *The Right to Vote*

minimum sentence that would justify disenfranchisement. In *Frodl*, the Court found that a rule disenfranchising prisoners who were sentenced to prison for more than a year breached the Convention; while some of the reasoning in *Frodl* has been criticised, the Court still cites it as good law.[128] This suggests a minimum threshold of somewhere between one and three years before prisoner disenfranchisement is permitted, bearing in mind always that there may be other circumstances to consider. This does suggest something of arbitrary line-drawing, though it reflects at least the point that persons sentenced to relatively short periods of time should not normally lose their right to vote. Given the cogent criticism of the *Hirst* and *Scoppola* reasoning some articulation of why persons jailed for short periods should not be disenfranchised would provide more coherence to the case law. The alternatives would be to regard Hirst as a mistake (as the UK has argued) or to strengthen the Court's defence of prisoners' political participation rights.

There are arguments for strengthening the position. Both *Hirst* and *Frodl* contain language suggesting that removal of the right to vote should only be done where there is a relevant link between the offence and the punishment of disenfranchisement; furthermore, they also include language suggesting the need for a more individual judicial determination. While the Court has indicated that the P1–3 rights are subject to limitations, it has also said that restrictions on the 'active' component of the P1–3 rights, that is the right to vote, will not be as easy to justify as restrictions on the right to run for office; in his dissent in *Scoppola No 3*, Judge Björgvinsson draws a more compelling distinction between those aspects of P1–3 that concern the running of elections generally and the specific individual right to vote. He argues that any margin of appreciation must be narrower in the latter case.

Insisting on a narrower margin of appreciation, and consequently a more rigorous review of prisoner voting rules, would also reflect the democratic principle that that which touches all must be decided by all. Prisoners are affected by the laws of society in the most direct and thorough way possible – through deprivation of liberty, restrictions on contact with society and supervision of activities. The restrictions are legitimate in so far as they can understand themselves as authors of the law by which they are imprisoned (or at least as participants in the process by which criminal laws are decided). Restrictions on persons simply because they are prisoners targets a group that is already vulnerable. While the Convention system accepts the legitimacy of imprisonment (indeed envisages it in article 5), no reader of the Convention

---

[128] *Söyler v Turkey*, para 43.

Substantive Democracy

case law can ignore the multiple violations of prisoners' rights across Europe. A human rights instrument should ensure that groups in vulnerable positions such as prisoners are able to participate in the political process so as to vindicate their rights. The Court's case law on prisoner voting seems to have influenced some states to move towards prisoner enfranchisement, further reinforcing the claim that this is required by European democracy.[129]

SUBSTANTIVE DEMOCRACY

Substantive democracy can exist in different varieties – one might claim the centrality of a particular type of society, based on a particular conception of the common good. Another might focus on a more limited conception based on protecting the values essential to a liberal democratic society. The right to vote case law demonstrates both approaches.

A commitment to a substantive democracy of the first type is implicit in the Court's unreflective acceptance of nationality-based restrictions. The exclusion of non-nationals from voting rights implies that there is an identifiable people who presumptively include nationals and presumptively exclude others. The early case law of the Commission and the Court easily accepted age, residence and nationality-based restrictions on the right to vote. As the case law has evolved, the Court has treated much more seriously arguments about residence-based restrictions which apply to nationals than nationality-based restrictions, even though these issues are related. This assumption is applied even though P1–3, unlike the Universal Declaration and ICCPR, does not expressly so limit the right. That the Court easily accepts nationality-based restrictions even in cases like *Makuc* and *Kurič* is disappointing.

The more limited substantive conception – focused on defending liberal democratic values – is also present in the case law, almost from the very beginning. As noted above, the Commission in several early applications noted that states could deprive people of their political rights for treasonous activities such as collaboration during the Second World War. In *Hirst*, the Grand Chamber reiterated that states could restrict the electoral rights of persons who abused a public position or sought to undermine the rule of law and democracy.[130]

---

[129] Kanstantsin Dzehtsiarou, 'Prisoner Voting Saga: Reasons for Challenges' in Helen Hardman and Brice Dickson (eds) *Electoral Rights in Europe: Advances and Challenges* (Taylor & Francis 2017).

[130] *Hirst v United Kingdom* (Grand Chamber), para 71.

PARTICIPATION AND EFFECTIVE INCLUSION

As is evident, the Convention institutions have dealt with a considerable range of formal exclusions from the right to vote, and have generally subjected most exclusions of adult resident nationals to close review. This review of formal exclusions is important but also highlights a general limitation, to date, of the Convention jurisprudence in this area. It is focused on formal inclusion in the electoral process. Formal inclusion is important but not sufficient. If voting rights are important, then it should be possible for rightsholders to exercise them effectively.

Voting rights might be effectively denied in numerous circumstances. Some of these relate to the design of the overall electoral process and raise concerns about types of voting systems or organisation of the franchise, and these are discussed in Chapter 9. Other practices affect effective inclusion at a more individual level.

For instance, voting processes may effectively require that people be able to read and understand material presented to them. This is not because of any formal sight, literacy or mental competence test, but because the voting instructions are available only in written text. This has the potential to exclude certain categories of people – those who are illiterate, or persons with sight impairment or a mental disability. Facially neutral and universal laws might have a disproportionate impact on certain groups[131] – and especially where these groups are vulnerable and disadvantaged minorities, the European Court of Human Rights needs to respond.

Effective inclusion must therefore include mechanisms to permit people in these positions to vote effectively. This might include processes like allowing the voter to bring another person of their choice with them to help read, though this impairs the secrecy of the vote.[132] Alternative ballot papers or ballot designs could be made available, for example with photographs or party emblems, or available in braille, or voting booths could be equipped with audio facilities. Guidance in these matters is also found in more recent human rights instruments. For example, article 29 of the Convention on the Rights of Persons with Disabilities specifies that voting procedures,

---

[131] The lead case on such indirect discrimination involving education rights is *DH v Czech Republic* App no 57325/00 (2008) 47 EHRR 3 (Grand Chamber). The right to education, like the political participation rights, is found in Protocol 1 to the Convention.

[132] Article 29(a)(iii) of the Convention on the Rights of Persons with Disabilities envisages this option; Convention on the Rights of Persons with Disabilities, New York, 13 December 2006, in force 2 May 2008, UNTS vol 2515, p 3.

Participation and Effective Inclusion

facilities and materials should be 'appropriate, accessible and easy to understand and use'.[133]

In this regard a case like *Alajos Kiss* is an important milestone in the development of the case law; while recognising that formal exclusions are subject to strict scrutiny, it can borrow more from article 14 developments to insist on positive obligations to make the right to vote real and effective. The Chamber in *Sitaropoulos and Others v Greece* expressly referred to the existence of positive obligations and thought the proper inquiry in that case was to 'ascertain whether the national authorities took all positive measures necessary to enable the applicants to effectively exercise their right to vote'.[134] While the Grand Chamber reversed the Chamber judgment, this reference to positive obligations could still be appropriate in other cases.

Residence requirements were discussed above; while generally unproblematic, they do have the potential to affect certain categories of people disproportionately. These include people without any formal address. This might include the homeless or people with no other fixed address or minorities with nomadic lifestyles such as Travellers and Roma, or internally displaced persons.

Voting venues may be inaccessible to people with mobility difficulties, wheelchair-bound, etc. It would be important that voting venues adopt such reasonable adjustment as would be necessary to enable persons with mobility difficulties to access them. The Court's judgment in *Molka* suggests a surprising degree of indifference to this issue, albeit that the Court had already held P1–3 inapplicable in that case.

Indeed, the practice of designated voting venues disadvantages certain categories of people who are unable to attend on a designated day. This might include people travelling for work (including work required of them by the state), people in hospitals, mental institutions, prisons, people unable to leave their homes due to injury or illness, and persons with a nomadic lifestyle. Consideration may also be given to the needs of certain observant religious groups if elections fall on designated holy days.

The attitude of the Convention institutions towards minority groups has been one of tolerance rather than positive action – they have accepted the legitimacy of state action to protect minority groups but not so far required state action in this field. If voting practices systematically disadvantage historically disadvantaged and marginalised groups, then there is an argument for a Convention obligation to ensure or at least encourage their participation.

---

[133] Article 29(a)(i).
[134] *Sitaropoulos and Others v Greece* App no 42202/07 (Chamber, 8 July 2010), para 39.

An obvious issue is the inclusion of nomadic communities like the Roma and Travellers and persons with disabilities.

Effective exercise of the right to vote also assumes certain other features, e.g. that the electoral process is well organised and that electoral registers are accurate. It is difficult to see how elections can secure the 'free expression of the opinion of the people' if these basic administrative systems are flawed. As noted above, the Court recognised the importance of an accurate electoral register in the *Georgian Labour Party* case.

DELIBERATIVE DEMOCRACY

Deliberative democracy, as presented by Habermas, requires the co-articulation of democracy and rights; that is to say there is no primacy for democracy or rights in his model. This means that the contours of rights, including democratic rights, must be delineated through the democratic political process, while at the same time giving effect to rights. This suggests that the Court needs to consider whether any restrictions on rights have been the subject of democratic decision-making.

The right to vote jurisprudence does suggest that there is a degree of requirement for a democratic consideration of the limitations on the right to vote. It is noteworthy that in the Belgian example, the Court has referred to the democratic endorsement of the consociational arrangement in Belgium.[135] Again in *Doyle v UK*, the Court drew attention to the fact that the UK Parliament had debated and approved the rules on non-resident nationals voting.[136]

In *Shindler*, the Court expressly referred to the existence of domestic parliamentary scrutiny of restrictions as being relevant to, even if not decisive in, its proportionality analysis.[137] In that case, the Court noted that the residence requirement had been the subject of Select Committee reports and debate in Parliament. The Court, though, was careful to explain – no doubt with an eye on the prisoner disenfranchisement saga – that the fact of Parliamentary scrutiny, 'even repeatedly', did not necessarily mean that a measure complied with the Convention; this was simply a factor to take into account.[138]

---

[135] *Mathieu-Mohin v Belgium*, para 57.
[136] *Doyle v United Kingdom*.
[137] *Shindler v United Kingdom* App no 19840/09 (2014) 58 EHRR 5, para 103.
[138] *Shindler v United Kingdom*, para 117.

Conversely in *Alajos Kiss v Hungary*, the Court noted that, even though the restriction was contained in the Constitution, there was no evidence that the national legislature had given consideration to the restriction in question; in particular, there was no evidence it had ever considered its proportionality.[139] In the Russian prisoner disenfranchisement case *Anchugov and Gladkov*, the government sought to rely on the fact that the ban was contained in the constitution which had been adopted in a referendum after extensive technical and public discussion; this argument the Court rejected, as there was no evidence to suggest the process had involved consideration of the interests and proportionality involved in prisoner disenfranchisement.[140] The Russian argument, if successful, would have created significant problems for rights protection across Europe, and the Court was right to reject it.

And in *Hirst v UK*, both the Chamber and the Grand Chamber attached importance to a perceived lack of deliberation in the legislature about the specifics of the voting ban. Both concurring and dissenting judges in the Grand Chamber were critical of this approach. In a concurring opinion Judges Tulkens and Zagrebelsky warned that here the 'two sources of legitimacy meet, the Court on the one hand and the national parliament on the other. This is a difficult and slippery terrain ...'[141]

At some point it is likely the Court will have to consider the response of the UK to the *Hirst* judgment. When it does, it will need to consider what weight to give to the very long political process in which the issue has been considered at multiple stages in consultations, committee inquiries and the voting chamber, but which resulted in a merely administrative response. While the domestic debates in one sense support the legitimacy of the UK position, it is notable that a joint parliamentary committee had recommended a more generous rule on prisoner enfranchisement.[142]

CONCLUSION

This chapter has charted the Court's case law on the right to vote, noting how the Convention institutions moved to recognise this as a subjective right protected in P1–3 to developing a more inclusive system of voting rights protection. This has seen the Court criticise voting restrictions based on race,

---

[139] *Alajos Kiss v Hungary*, para 41.
[140] *Anchugov and Gladkov v Russia*, para 109.
[141] *Hirst* (Grand Chamber), concurring opinion of Judges Tulkens and Zagrebelsky.
[142] Joint Committee on the Draft Voting Eligibility (Prisoners) Bill *Draft Voting Eligibility (Prisoners) Bill* 2013) HL 103 / HC 924 (18 December 2013).

mental capacity, bankruptcy and prisoner status. As noted, there is controversy over the prisoner voting rights cases, and the Court could give somewhat clearer guidance on what it expects here. This is especially important given the decision of the UK to implement the *Hirst* judgment using a minimal administrative response.

The Court has generally upheld traditional age, residence and nationality restrictions. The age-based restriction seems compatible with democratic theories, though there may be some queries about exact ages in different contexts. The residence-based restrictions also seem compatible with the idea that democracy requires that those people affected by political decisions be entitled to vote in the relevant elections. Recent cases have required the Court to examine this issue from first principles again, though reaffirming its approach to largely defer to state restrictions and regulations in this area. This has extended even to state regulations which at first glance at least appear somewhat arbitrary, even discriminatory. Nevertheless, in light of the evolving national practices in this area, it is one where the Court may have to revisit its reasoning.

More troubling, though, is the acceptance of nationality-based restrictions; indeed, the logic behind the residence cases seems to imply the finding that non-nationals should be entitled to voting rights in at least some cases. However, in no case has the Commission or the Court substantively engaged with this argument, unlike the detailed and convincing consideration in *Shindler*.

While this case law typically considers notions of formal inclusion and exclusion, this chapter has argued that the Convention also requires measures to ensure that the right to vote is effective and not illusory; this will imply positive obligations and accommodation to ensure especially that marginalised and disadvantaged groups can effectively participate. The argument for positive obligations in these cases is much stronger than the argument for positive obligations accepted in the Chamber in *Sitaropoulos*; here we are talking of groups typically excluded from the political process and often from the social and economic spheres. From a human rights perspective these are precisely the groups who need to be included in the political process. The nature of the positive obligations are further likely not to be as extensive and wide-ranging as those required for voting arrangements abroad, especially where the state has a large diaspora spread across the globe.

This is also important to efforts to develop a more deliberative model of democracy based on the Convention. As outlined above, the Court has to some extent encouraged deliberation by taking into account the domestic democratic analysis of voting restrictions and in particular how they address

Conclusion

the human rights issues. Deliberative democracy, though, must not collapse into a mere technocratic expectation of better evidence and reasoning. While undoubtedly that is a part of deliberation, the core normative insight is that all must be able to deliberate on measures. While practically not everyone can participate in a legislative assembly, it is essential that the franchise for this should be as extensive as possible and that this not be limited to formal inclusion.

8

The Right to Run for Election

This chapter considers what the Court oddly calls the 'passive' aspect of the P1–3 rights – the right to run for election. The Court has suggested that it adopts a less strict approach to state regulations in relation to the right to run for election than it does in right to vote cases.[1] In right to vote cases, proportionality looms large, while in right to run for election cases, the Court is concerned with ensuring there is no arbitrariness as regards any restrictions.[2]

The following sections will review how the Court has applied the principles of legitimate aim, legality and proportionality in the right to run for election case law. Later the chapter considers the approach of the Court towards cases involving the inclusion of minorities and the possibility to promote deliberative models of democracy.

LEGITIMATE AIM

The Court has indicated that states may advance any legitimate aim that is coherent with P1–3. States are not limited by the lists which are found in articles 8–11. While this may seem to indicate a difference of approach between P1–3 and the articles 8–11 rights, it is not a very significant one: the legitimate aims in articles 8–11 are extremely broad, encompassing public order (article 8) and the rights and freedoms of others (article 11).

The Court has accepted, in *Podlkolzina v Latvia*, as incontestable the legitimate aim of the state in 'ensuring that its own institutional system functions normally'.[3] The normal functioning of the institutions includes

---

[1] David Harris, Michael O'Boyle, Ed Bates and Carla Buckley, *Law of the European Convention on Human Rights* (Oxford University Press 2018), 912.

[2] *Occhetto v Italy* App no 14507/07 (12 November 2013), para 47.

[3] *Podkolzina v Latvia* App no 46726/99 (9 April 2002), para 34.

204

questions of linguistic competence. To this end, it is legitimate for the state to ensure that candidates can speak effectively the language which is the working language of the national Parliament. In the first post-independence Latvian elections, some candidates from the large Russian-speaking minority (nearly 40% of the population) had been elected who did not speak Latvian, and this caused problems in parliamentary discussions.[4] The Court indicated that the choice of a parliament's working language is 'in principle one which the State alone has the power to make'.[5]

The normal function of the institutions also includes ensuring a degree of transparency from electoral candidates. In *Krasnov and Skuratov v Russia*, the Court accepted that it was legitimate for the state to ensure that voters were properly informed of certain facts about the candidates, including their employment and party membership; consequently, it was also legitimate to expect the candidates to supply information 'accurate to the best of their knowledge'.[6]

Protecting the expression of the will of the people in a general election is a legitimate aim. In *Cernea v Romania*, the Court accepted that the state could require that candidates in a by-election had to be members of parties elected at the previous general election. This was to ensure respect for the expression of the will of the people at the general election and preclude parties or candidates circumventing that decision and using a by-election as a backdoor into the legislature.[7]

Eligibility criteria on the right to stand for election serve to ensure the independence of the members of parliament and the 'electorate's freedom of choice'.[8] The latter refers to the need to protect voters from the fear that a candidate who holds a senior public service position might be in a position to make decisions affecting their interests.[9] The Court has accepted as legitimate a concern that if some political candidates can campaign from a position of being senior public servants, then they may have an unfair advantage over competitors.[10]

---

[4] *Podkolzina v Latvia*, para 27.
[5] *Podkolzina v Latvia*, para 34.
[6] *Krasnov and Skuratov v Russia* App nos 17864/04 and 21396/04 (2007) 47 EHRR 46, para 44.
[7] *Cernea v Romania* App no 43609/10 (27 February 2018).
[8] *Gitonas v Greece* App nos 68/1996/687/877–879 17/1997/801/1004 and 23/1997/807/1010 (1998) 26 EHRR 691, para 39.
[9] *Gitonas v Greece*, para 40.
[10] *Gitonas v Greece*, para 40.

The state may impose restrictions on candidates to discourage frivolous candidates from running, according to the Court in *Sukhovetskyy v Ukraine*.[11] More broadly this guarantees 'the right to effective streamlined representation by enhancing the responsibility of those standing for election and confining elections to serious candidates, whilst avoiding the unreasonable outlay of public funds'.[12] In this case it meant upholding a deposit requirement. In coming to this conclusion, the Court referred to the practice of Member States, but also the opinion of the Venice Commission.

The Court has also accepted that a requirement that a candidate produce a number of signatures from voters supporting the candidacy within strict deadlines serves the purpose of assuring a timely electoral process.[13] This will be the case even when the number of signatures is quite high, e.g. over 100,000, provided at least this is in line with the Venice Commission's recommended maximum of 1 per cent of the electorate and there are procedural safeguards in place.[14]

The Court has accepted a residence requirement for voting as legitimate, and accepts even stricter residency requirements for candidates.[15] Residence requirements serve interconnected legitimate aims of ensuring that the people participating in the political process are genuinely concerned with it and familiar with it, of recognising the difficulties in presenting political issues to people abroad; recognise the influence of residents on politics and the correlation between participating in elections and being bound by the decisions of the elected parliament.[16] (These points underline again the problems with excluding non-national residents from electoral rights.)

The state may act in the interests of preserving its national security and independence and its democratic order. This is manifest from the lustration cases where recently democratic states have taken steps to limit the political rights of those associated with the previous totalitarian regimes.[17]

---

[11] *Sukhovetskyy v Ukraine* App no 13716/02 (2007) 44 EHRR 57, para 61.

[12] *Sukhovetskyy*, para 62.

[13] Decision *Brita da Silva Magno v Portugal* App no 26720/06 (17 June 2008). A state could require a number of signatures by reference to a percentage of the electorate even if this meant different numbers of signatures were required in different parts of the country: *Asensio Serqueda v Spain* App no 23151/94 77B DR 122 (European Commission of Human Rights). A state could also impose such a requirement only on parties not already represented in parliament: *Soberanía de la Razón v Spain* App no 30537/12 (26 May 2015).

[14] *Mihaela Mihai Neagu v Romania* App no 66345/09 (6 March 2014).

[15] *Melnychenko v Ukraine* App no 17707/02 (2004) 42 EHRR 39, para 58.

[16] *Melnychenko*, para 57.

[17] *Zdanoka v Latvia* App no 58278/00 (2006) 45 EHRR 17; *Ādamsons v Latvia* App no 3669/03 (24 June 2008).

The protection of a fundamental feature of the constitutional order may also serve as a legitimate aim before the Court. Thus Turkey may act to protect its legitimate interest in securing the principle of a secular state.[18] The maintenance of a system of decentralisation which is designed to reflect different interests (territorial, linguistic) was the accepted aim in *Mathieu-Mohn* itself.[19]

As is often the case with qualified rights, it is difficult to find a case where the Court has actually rejected as illegitimate an aim put forward by the state. In *Tănase v Moldova*, the Court considered whether loyalty to the state could be a legitimate aim. The Grand Chamber emphasised that loyalty to the government could not be a legitimate aim. Loyalty to the state might be a legitimate aim, though in that case the Grand Chamber expressed some doubt as to whether that was the actual aim behind changes to the electoral law on dual nationality; however, it decided not to rule on that point.[20] In *Petkov and others v Bulgaria*, the Court noted that a state could not choose to ignore a decision of its own courts in electoral matters simply because it disagreed with the decision.[21] One of the other occasions on which the Court has come closest is *Kovach v Ukraine*.[22] A local electoral commission had concluded that there was some irregularities at specific polling stations in its district and had simply nullified all the votes derived from those polling stations. Given that Kovach would have won if the votes from all the stations had been counted, this had the effect of determining the election result. Without ruling specifically on this, the Court said it had 'doubts' as to whether such a practice, done without any regard for the extent of the problem or the impact on the result, could be said to serve any legitimate aim.[23]

LEGALITY OR LAWFULNESS

As noted earlier, the oft-cited quote from *Mathieu-Mohin* does not explicitly include a reference to the principle of legality or lawfulness; nevertheless, and unsurprisingly, it is clear from the case law that any restrictions on these rights must respect the principle of legality – several cases specifically refer to the importance of the rule of law or the pre-eminence of law.[24] Often, however,

---

[18] *Kavakci v Turkey* App no 71907/01 (5 April 2007), para 43; *Sobaci v Turkey* App no 26733/02 (29 November 2007), para 28.

[19] *Mathieu-Mohin and Clerfayt v Belgium* App no 9267/81 (1987) 10 EHRR 1, para 56.

[20] *Tănase v Moldova* App no 7/08 (2011) 53 EHRR 22 (Grand Chamber), paras 166–170.

[21] *Petkov and others v Bulgaria* App nos 178/02, 505/02 and 77568/01 (11 June 2009), para 64.

[22] *Kovach v Ukraine* App no 39424/02 (7 February 2008).

[23] *Kovach v Ukraine*, para 52.

[24] *GK v Belgium* App no 58302/10 (21 May 2019), para 57.

208   *The Right to Run for Election*

the discussion of legality is intermingled with considerations of proportionality.[25]

In an early decision, the Court showed itself willing to accept national legislation on eligibility that was complex; the Court was reluctant to 'embark on its own analysis of the relevant legislation' for fear it would become 'a further level of jurisdiction superimposed' on the national courts.[26] As we will see, the modern Court has not always shared these scruples.

In *Krasnov and Skuratov v Russia*, the Court found that the P1–3 rights of the second applicant had been violated. The national legislation required a candidate to list details about his or her 'present place of work'. The second applicant had noted that he was acting head of the constitutional law department of a university. He had not, however, specifically noted that he held the office of professor. The national commissions and courts ruled that he had failed to indicate his 'principal place of work', though they gave conflicting reasons for this. These reasons included that he did not indicate all of his duties (i.e. that he was a professor as well), that he had not explained all the changes in his employment status and also that he should have indicated his permanent (not 'acting') post. The Court ruled that this situation violated the legality principle: the term 'principal place of work' did not clearly indicate any of these contested meanings, and furthermore the reasoning of the different commissions and courts was 'inconsistent'. This situation did not enable the applicant to foresee the consequences of any action he took.[27]

In the exceptional case of *Melnychenko v Ukraine*, the Court exercised its 'limited' competence to verify that domestic law was complied with.[28] The applicant had served with the security detail of the Ukrainian president. He allegedly made recordings which implicated the president in the murder of a journalist. The applicant was forced to flee Ukraine. He was subsequently recognised as a refugee in the US. Whilst resident in the US as a matter of fact, his internal passport still showed him as residing in Ukraine. He sought to run for election in Ukraine, but the electoral authorities concluded that he was not a resident and so was not entitled to run. The Court concluded that, on a reading of the Ukrainian legislation, the electoral authorities should have

[25] *Podkolzina v Latvia*, para 36; *Krasnov and Skuratov v Russia*, paras 59–60.
[26] *Gitonas*, para 43.
[27] *Krasnov and Skuratov v Russia*, paras 59–60.
[28] *Melnychenko v Ukraine* App no 17707/02 (2004) 42 EHRR 39, para 60. In other cases the Court has declined to look at the interpretation of national legislation, this being a matter for the domestic courts: *Ādamsons v Latvia* para 118. Similarly, it is not for the Court to resolve any conflicts which exist in a domestic legal system between domestic law and directly enforceable international law: *Tănase and Chirtoaca v Moldova* App no 7/08 (18 November 2008), para 106.

Legality or Lawfulness

accepted the indication of residence in the internal passport. The legislation did not clearly distinguish between 'official' and 'habitual' residence, and the electoral authorities had some discretion in the manner. Given that they usually accepted the official residence as indicated in the internal passport, they should have done so in this case, all the more as the applicant had been forced to flee the country.[29]

In *Kovach v Ukraine*, a local electoral commission discounted the votes from several polling stations, thus changing the result of an election. The local commission did so on the basis of legislation which allowed it to disregard the votes in certain specified circumstances or 'in other circumstances' where it was impossible to establish the voters' wishes.[30] The Court found that it was unclear what 'other circumstances' amounted to, and in particular whether that power allowed commissions to ignore other, more circumscribed powers to invalidate results. Along with the somewhat unclear decisions of the electoral authorities, this allowed the Court to find a violation of P1–3.[31] The Court treated this in relation to proportionality, but the overlap with legality principles is evident. This conclusion also allowed the Court to avoid ruling on allegations of bias on the part of local electoral commissioners, some of whom had signed a public statement supporting the election of the applicants' opponents.[32]

Again, in *Petkov and others v Bulgaria*, the Court found a legality type violation in relation to its proportionality consideration. Shortly before the Bulgarian elections, the state changed the electoral law, to allow parties to remove candidates from their electoral lists, if a lustration body (the Dossiers Commission) certified they had collaborated with the former Soviet-era security services. The applicants were thus removed by their political parties. Before the election they contested the legality of these decisions and won judgments ordering their reinstatement on the lists. These judgments came down two days before the election, and, in the case of one applicant, after the election.[33] The Court ruled that the failure of the state to comply with a binding and final ruling – apparently because the state authorities believed the relevant court had acted outside its jurisdiction – was a violation of the fundamental principle of the rule of law.[34]

In *Grosaru v Romania*, the applicant complained that he had not been allocated a seat as a representative of the Italian minority in Romania; the seat

---

[29] *Melnychenko v Ukraine*, paras 60–66.
[30] *Kovach v Ukraine*, para 57.
[31] *Kovach v Ukraine*, paras 58–60.
[32] *Kovach v Ukraine*, paras 6–7.
[33] *Petkov and others v Bulgaria*, para 66.
[34] *Petkov and others v Bulgaria*, para 62.

had been allocated to another candidate who had a larger number of votes in a single constituency, whereas the applicant had a larger number of votes across multiple constituencies.[35] The Court found that the Romanian legislation was unclear on this point, and that the Central Electoral Office interpreting the legislation did not explain sufficiently why it selected the interpretation that went against the applicant.[36]

Despite the overlap between legality and proportionality, there is an important advantage to deciding a case on legality grounds rather than proportionality grounds. This emerges very clearly in the concurring opinion of Judges Garlicki, Zupančič and Gyulumyan in *Adamsons v Latvia*.[37] As we will see, the majority concluded that a prohibition on an ex-member of the Soviet-era Border Guard service from running for election was disproportionate. These three judges concurred that there was a violation of P1–3 but based themselves on the legality principle. The legislation in question imposed a ban on 'agents'[38] of the KGB; according to the concurring opinion, this was too vague a term. A lack of precision in legislation leaves the way open for arbitrary decisions and potentially politically motivated manipulation of the law. The concurring opinion expressly warned against applying the proportionality principle given that it would inevitably take Court judges into the arenas of politics and history.

There are then advantages to relying on more procedural grounds, like legality, rather than proportionality as a proportionality inquiry is more likely to involve looking at the substance of the case. This may mean the Court has to review a state's policy and not just the clarity with which it is expressed. The Court has deployed some elements of proportionality analysis in some cases, though even here we start with more procedural aspects.

PROPORTIONALITY

Despite the view that P1–3 does not involve the same sort of analysis as is typical of the qualified rights, the Court has deployed some elements of proportionality analysis in right to run for elections cases. This sometimes

---

[35] *Grosaru v Romania* App no 78039/01 (2015) 61 EHRR 1.

[36] *Grosaru v Romania*, para 52. A further case concerning unclear legislation and its application is *Seyidzade v Azerbaijan* App no 37700/05 (3 December 2009); the legislation precluded clergymen from running for election where they were engaged in 'professional religious activity' but did not specify how terms like 'clergyman', 'religious activity' or 'professional' were to be defined.

[37] *Ādamsons v Latvia* App no 3669/03 (24 June 2008).

[38] The meaning of the term used in the Latvian legislation was contested in the case. Judge Fura-Sandstrom dissented because she thought the language very clear.

Proportionality

211

concerns matters of procedural fairness which, like legality-type cases, avoid substantive issues of policy choice. On other occasions, though, the Court has looked to see whether the essence of the right has been violated or whether a restriction was disproportionate in not considering individual circumstances.

Procedural Fairness

In 2002, the Court offered some guidance on the requirements of proportionality in relation to P1–3. In *Podkolzina v Latvia*, the Court stressed that the rights in the Convention had to be given a 'practical and effective' interpretation, not a 'theoretical and illusory one'. The right to run for election would be illusory if one could be deprived of it arbitrarily. Therefore, any decision to rule a candidate ineligible must be made by 'a body which can provide a minimum of guarantees of its impartiality'; the discretion open to such a body 'must be circumscribed, with sufficient precision, by the provisions of domestic law'; finally, the procedure must be 'fair and objective' and 'prevent any abuse of power'.[39] As with the earlier quote from *Mathieu-Mohin*, this is now regularly cited in the jurisprudence. It is noteworthy for putting the stress on procedural fairness.

In *Podkolzina* itself, the applicant was a Russian speaker who had been ruled ineligible to run for election because of her insufficient knowledge of Latvian. She possessed a certificate of competence in Latvian. Despite this, the authorities required her to undergo two more processes of verification. One of these involved a thirty-minute interview with a single civil servant who – to the surprise of the Court – asked questions about the applicant's political beliefs.[40] She was also subject to a written examination of which she had been given no advance notice. None of these procedures were clearly set out in legislation, and there was a want of 'procedural fairness and legal certainty'.[41] The Court accordingly found a violation.[42]

The requirement of procedural fairness applies not just to questions of eligibility but also to processes concerning the ending of a representative's mandate. The Court made this explicit in a case from Belgium, *GK*, where the applicant had resigned as senator but then sought to withdraw her resignation. She alleged that she had only signed a letter of resignation under

---

[39] *Podkolzina v Latvia*, para 35.
[40] *Podkolzina v Latvia*, para 36.
[41] *Podkolzina v Latvia*, para 36.
[42] On the need for procedural fairness when denying someone the right to run for election, see also *Abil v Azerbaijan (No 2)* App no 8513/11 (5 December 2019).

pressure from senior colleagues. The Court highlighted that P1–3 required respect for legality principles and procedural fairness in such a case. Procedures for dealing with resignations in the Belgian Senate were unclear.[43] Furthermore, the process did not embody fair procedures. The applicant had alleged that certain colleagues put her under undue pressure to resign, but these senators were allowed to participate in the decision-making on her case, both in the bureau of the Senate and in plenary.[44] There was a further denial of fair procedures in that the bureau of the Senate did not explain why it rejected the applicant's arguments and then the applicant was not allowed to make her case heard in the plenary.[45]

Essential Minimum

One element of a proportionality inquiry is to investigate whether a restriction merely qualifies a right or whether it can be said to abolish the essential minimum core of the right. The Court has identified one minimum requirement of the right to run for election; where a person has been lawfully chosen by the electorate to take a seat in the legislature, only imperative reasons would justify subsequently removing that person from the legislature. This emerges very clearly from a series of Turkish cases where the Constitutional Court ordered a number of sitting parliamentarians to be excluded from exercising their mandate because their party had been declared unconstitutional. The Court has qualified such decisions as 'incompatible with the very substance of the applicant's right to be elected and sit in parliament ... and infringed the sovereign power of the electorate who elected them as members of parliament'.[46] This last phrase links the Court's ruling to the express words of P1–3 which speak of determining the 'opinion of the people'. The Court has repeated this finding in later cases, though perhaps modifying the strength of the prohibition by noting that the Turkish measure was an absolutist one which did not allow for individual assessment of culpability.[47]

The Court has referred to the very substance of the right to stand for election in other cases. In *Lykourezos v Greece*, the applicant had been elected to parliament in 2000. A constitutional amendment was then introduced which prohibited parliamentarians from holding any professional position.

---

[43] *GK v Belgium* App no 58302/10 (21 May 2019), paras 58–59.
[44] *GK v Belgium*, paras 62–63.
[45] *GK v Belgium*, paras 61–63.
[46] *Sadak and others v Turkey* App nos 25144/94; 26149/95 to 26154/95; 27100/95 and 27101/95 (2002) 36 EHRR 23, para 40.
[47] *Kavakci v Turkey* App no 71907/01 (5 April 2007), paras 44–46.

Proportionality

This was a strikingly sweeping disqualification rule, but even more striking was the fact that the Supreme Court ruled that the amendment applied to sitting members of parliament and not merely to anyone elected as a result of new elections. The Court saw this as affecting the very substance of P1–3 which was aimed at

> identifying the will of people through universal suffrage. Equally once the wishes of the people have been freely and democratically expressed, no subsequent amendment to the organisations of the electoral system may call that choice into question, except in the presence of compelling grounds for the democratic order.[48]

In so ruling, the Court did not need to rule on whether the sweeping incompatibility rule (as opposed to its retrospective application) violated any convention rights. In partly concurring opinions, Judge Louciades concluded that the sweeping exclusion violated P1–3, while Judges Spielman and Tulkens found that the disqualification rules violated the implicit right in article 8 to a private *professional* life.

A further case from Greece again concerned a controversial court decision interpreting the electoral law. In *Paschalidis and others v Greece*, the applicants had been elected to the legislature.[49] Their election was challenged in court cases, where the Supreme Court reversed a long-standing interpretation that blank votes were not to be counted for the purposes of determining the quota for the election. The Court ruled that they should be counted. On this basis, the applicants lost their seats. The legislature subsequently changed the electoral law to clarify that blank votes should not be counted. The Court ruled that this unforeseeable Supreme Court decision had altered the expressed will of the electors.[50] Furthermore, the interpretation in this case violated the idea of equality in that it had the effect of creating two types of parliamentarians: those elected according to the new rule and those not.[51] In such a case the very substance of the right had been violated.

The very essence of the P1–3 rights may also be endangered if the state appears to be trying to exclude the political opposition from power; where measures seem to impair the opposition parties from securing electoral success, the Court must examine them very carefully.[52]

---

[48] *Lykourezos v Greece* App no 33554/03 (2008) 46 EHRR 7, para 52.
[49] *Paschalidis Koutmeridis and Zaharakis v Greece* App nos 27863/05 28422/05 and 28028/05 (10 April 2008).
[50] *Paschialidis v Greece*, para 32.
[51] *Paschialidis v Greece*, para 34.
[52] *Tǎnase v Moldova* (Grand Chamber), para 179.

Necessity and Individualisation?

The references in *Podkolzina* to procedural fairness and the stress in the Turkish cases on the removal of a sitting parliamentarian as being a denial of the very substance of the P1–3 right might suggest a limited conception of proportionality in P1–3 cases. It might suggest that the Court does not examine P1–3 cases to determine if a limitation of the right is necessary in any particular case.

This indeed is the suggestion of the Grand Chamber in one of the lustration decisions: *Zdanoka v Latvia*.[53] Here the Grand Chamber considered a 1995 Latvian provision banning certain members of the former Communist Party from running for office in domestic elections. The legislation applied to those members of the Communist Party who actively participated in the Party after 13 January 1991, when there was a coup attempt against the independent government of Latvia. The applicant was a member of the Communist Party at that time and subsequently sought election in local and parliamentary elections in Latvia as well as the European Parliament. She was successfully elected to the European Parliament but was disqualified from the domestic bodies because of her Communist Party past.

The Grand Chamber indicated that P1–3 does not require the same approach as one of the qualified rights in articles 8–11; the approach is less stringent than under those rights.[54] This more relaxed approach to the P1–3 rights applies even more so with regards to the passive right to run for election. The Grand Chamber accepted that this measure was justified in order to protect the democratic system from those involved in an earlier effort to subvert it.[55] The Grand Chamber did not find it surprising that the measure was only adopted in 1995, given that a young democracy would need some time to decide on the rules of its democratic system.[56] It also emphasised that the ruling was context specific and that what was appropriate in a young democracy emerging from totalitarianism would not be acceptable in a well-established democracy.[57] The Grand Chamber was reassured by the fact that the Latvian legislature regularly reviewed the measure and the Latvian Constitutional Court closely scrutinised it and had indicated it should be a temporary measure.[58]

---

[53] *Zdanoka v Latvia* App no 58278/00 (2006) 45 EHRR 17 (Grand Chamber).
[54] *Zdanoka v Latvia* (Grand Chamber), para 115.
[55] *Zdanoka v Latvia* (Grand Chamber), para 122.
[56] *Zdanoka v Latvia* (Grand Chamber), para 131.
[57] *Zdanoka v Latvia* (Grand Chamber), para 133.
[58] *Zdanoka v Latvia* (Grand Chamber), paras 134–135.

Despite the language in *Zdanoka* suggesting a fairly limited role for proportionality inquiries in relation to the right to run for election, there are several cases which suggest a more searching necessity inquiry.

In *Krasnov and Skuratov v Russia*, two candidates were disqualified from running because the information they supplied about their place of business was allegedly inaccurate. In the case of Krasnov, he had claimed to be the head of a district council, whereas in fact he had been dismissed from this position several months before. The Court accepted that the decision to disqualify him was proportionate. The situation was different with Skuratov (the constitutional law department head). The Court referred to legality type principles (as noted above) but also stressed that Skuratov had acted in good faith. The authorities should have made the requirements clear to him, and their failure to do so, according to international observers, may have permitted 'selective' decisions.[59] Furthermore, the Court did not believe anyone would be swayed by knowing that Skuratov was a professor, and he was already a renowned figure because of other posts which he had held. All of these factors, combined with the failure to give proper guidance on the electoral registration requirements, justified a finding that P1–3 was violated.[60]

In *Ādamsons v Latvia*, a Chamber of the Court addressed at some length the question of individualisation in another lustration case.[61] The applicant had been a former member of the Soviet-era Border Guard; following independence, the applicant occupied various positions in the Latvian services, as minister for interior and as a parliamentarian. He was subsequently disqualified from running for election to parliament because the courts ruled that the legislative prohibition on 'agents' of the KGB running for election applied to him. The Chamber majority took some care to distinguish the prohibition in *Ādamsons* from that in *Zdanoka*. The ban in *Zdanoka* had applied to a narrower range of people – those involved in the Communist Party of Latvia at a time when the Communist Party was opposing the move to democracy and independence.[62] The restriction was very different from that in *Ādamsons*, and so a proportionality inquiry required a more individualised consideration.

A more searching approach to proportionality is also seen in *Sukhovestkyy* where the Court upheld a deposit requirement in Ukraine. While the Court found no violation, and did refer to the importance of allowing the

---

[59] *Krasnov and Skuratov v Russia*, para 61.
[60] *Krasnov and Skuratov*, para 64.
[61] *Ādamsons v Latvia* (App no 3669/03) (24 June 2008).
[62] *Adamsons*, para 114.

policy-maker a wide margin of appreciation,[63] it also canvassed many features before concluding that the measure was proportionate: the role of national deliberation, a comparative study of deposit requirements, the fact that the deposit requirement did not preclude a large number of candidates (including some with low incomes) from participating in the elections, and the facilities provided to election candidates.[64]

Again in *Tănase and Chirtoaca v Moldova*, the Court held that the Moldovan authorities could have addressed the question of candidates with dual nationality in a less drastic manner than prohibiting their candidature – Moldova could have introduced a loyalty oath for parliamentarians according to the Chamber[65] or could have relied on criminal sanctions for specific offences according to the Grand Chamber.[66] While the Grand Chamber might have shown more deference to a measure adopted in the immediate aftermath of independence, the argument for such a restriction diminished with time, especially when the state freely undertook obligations under the European Convention on Nationality.[67]

Finally, in *Sarukhanyan v Armenia*, we see again the Court taking the issue of proportionality seriously, not just looking for violations of the essential minimum or of procedural fairness.[68] The applicant was disqualified from running because he had not included a joint tenancy in his declaration of property. The Court found that excluding him from running was disproportionate – the applicant had relied in good faith on an official document which did not indicate he was a joint owner;[69] the state had failed to make the relevant privatisation rules clear;[70] there was no rationale behind concealing such a small property interest;[71] the domestic courts did not consider all these factors adequately;[72] and there was no reason to believe the electorate would be swayed by such a small property interest.[73]

---

[63] *Sukhovetskyy v Ukraine*, para 68.
[64] *Sukhovetskyy*, paras 63–74.
[65] *Tănase and Chirtoaca v Moldova* App no 7/08 (18 November 2008), para 109.
[66] *Tănase v Moldova* App no 7/08 (Grand Chamber, 27 April 2010), para 175.
[67] *Tănase v Moldova* (Grand Chamber), paras 173–176.
[68] *Sarukhanyan v Armenia* App no 38978/03 (27 May 2008).
[69] *Sarukhanyan*, para 44.
[70] *Sarukhanyan*, para 46.
[71] *Sarukhanyan*, para 47.
[72] *Sarukhanyan*, para 48.
[73] *Sarukhanyan*, para 49.

SUBSTANTIVE DEMOCRACY

As we have noted, there are different notions of what might be the core of a substantive conception of democracy. One approach to substantive conceptions would be to see democracy as being tied to a particular type of society or communitarian ideal. When considering issues of language and nationality, the Court leaves open the possibility for states to reinforce the type of society the political system serves. States can decide on the working language of their legislature and insist on linguistic competence for candidates. Nationality-based restrictions on candidacy are acceptable, as is the legitimate interest in protecting loyalty to the state (as opposed to loyalty to the government). While the Court is generally accepting of special measures to support minority representation and consociational systems, it does not usually require them.

Nevertheless, even on these issues the Court is careful to strike a balance. Linguistic competency rules and tests must not be arbitrary (*Podkolzina*). And even if the Court is clear it wants to stay out of language politics, it will find a violation if a state restriction has no pressing need in a particular context such as where a minority language politician is speaking to citizens who do not speak the majority language. And where the Court does accept consociational provisions, it is concerned to avoid practices which exclude racial or ethnic minorities.

The second type of substantive democracy affirms that a liberal democratic state must be based on some values such as those of pluralism, tolerance and broad-mindedness, and these the liberal democratic state can defend. The right to run for election case law demonstrates some adherence to the second type of substantive democracy. The Grand Chamber has acknowledged the legitimacy of a democracy defending itself from subversion.[74] This notion of a democracy capable of defending itself is often called militant democracy, though the Court did not use this term. Thus, the Convention institutions have held that states can ban former members of the Waffen-SS from running for election,[75] and also ban candidates with racist and xenophobic tendencies.[76] A newly established and young democracy like Latvia may find it

---

[74] *Zdanoka v Latvia* (Grand Chamber), para 100, referring to the earlier case of *Vogt v Germany* App no 17851/91 (1996) 21 EHRR 205.

[75] *Van Wambeke v Belgium* App no 16692/90 (European Commission of Human Rights, 12 April 1991).

[76] *Glimmerveen v Netherlands* App nos 8348/78 and 8406/78 (1979) 4 EHRR 260, (European Commission of Human Rights).

218   *The Right to Run for Election*

necessary to ban individuals who had been involved in an anti-democratic coup attempt from participating in elections.[77]

INCLUSION

One of the most important issues in democratic politics is the representation of different groups, minorities or communities who may be excluded or disproportionately underrepresented in representative institutions. From a deliberative democratic point of view, it is important that the different groups in society be able to contribute to political discourse. This is as a marker of equal respect for all, to ensure that all interests are represented, to encourage participants to appeal to justice and to ensure the democratic process has access to all relevant knowledge.[78] If deliberative democracy does not allow all voices to be heard, then it risks becoming 'little more than a pious attachment to informed over ill-informed decisions'.[79]

Practically, these concerns can be expressed in a range of different institutional policies and practices. These include adoption of measures to ensure representation of women, allowing for the inclusion in democratic politics of members of a minority on conditions of equality, and consociational or power-sharing arrangements for the main communities of a state.

In many democratic systems legislators and executives are significantly wealthier and better educated than the average citizen. In terms of inclusivity, participation and deliberation, this also raises problems, and for some this disconnect is one of the explanations in the rise of populism.[80] Strikingly, while there have been cases concerning these status-based distinctions, there have been few addressing problems of economic status or educational attainment and representation.[81]

---

[77] *Zdanoka v Latvia* (Grand Chamber).
[78] Iris Marion Young, *Inclusion and Democracy* (Oxford University Press 2000), 115.
[79] Anne Phillips, *Which Equalities Matter?* (Polity 1999), 117.
[80] Roger Eatwell and Matthew Goodwin, *National Populism: The Revolt against Liberal Democracy* (Penguin UK 2018), 106–116.
[81] One of the few examples is *Sukhovetskyy v Ukraine* App no 13716/02 (2007) 44 EHRR 57. Harris and others note that this case arguably leaves too much discretion to the state; they also raise concerns about the position in *Sitaropoulos and Others v Greece* App no 42202/07 (15 March 2012); David Harris, Michael O'Boyle, Ed Bates and Carla Buckley, *Law of the European Convention on Human Rights* (Oxford University Press 2018), 917, 928.

Representation of Women

The case of *Staatkundig Gereformeerde Partij v Netherland* (*SGP case*) contains a very short Court decision denying admissibility, but the issues it raises belie the short decision. The applicant, Staatkundig Gereformeerde Partij (SGP), was a confessional political party in the Netherlands. As part of their religious convictions, they did not believe women should hold positions of political power, though they did include women among their members. Whether the party had a formal rule barring woman from being nominated for political positions was not entirely clear on the facts; the applicant denied there was any formal impediment.

The Dutch courts had ruled that the party discriminated against women in denying them the possibility to be nominated for political office; the Dutch executive, though, had not taken any steps to enforce these rulings. The SGP nevertheless complained to the Strasbourg Court that these rulings violated their rights under articles 9–11. The Court rejected the complaint as inadmissible given the importance that the Convention and Council of Europe attach to the principle of the equality of the sexes.[82] In passing, the Court did acknowledge that political parties can be organised on the basis of religious beliefs provided they used legal and democratic means to achieve their aims and their aims were compatible with democracy.[83]

What is interesting, though, is the reasoning of the domestic courts. The domestic courts reached their conclusion that political parties must not discriminate on grounds of sex because of the requirements of international treaties and specifically article 7 of the Convention on the Elimination of Discrimination against Women (CEDAW), as well as articles 2 and 25 of the International Covenant on Civil and Political Rights (ICCPR). These treaties are directly effective in Dutch law. If this logic is accepted, it applies also to other states that have ratified CEDAW, though not all countries make international conventions directly enforceable in the same way. From the ECHR point of view, though, it is striking that the Court in *SGP* says that the same conclusion applies to the ECHR and specifically P1–3 and article 14.[84] The implication of this is that political parties cannot discriminate on grounds of sex. This would also presumably apply to other protected characteristics. The corollary is that the state has positive obligations to deal with such

---

[82] *Staatkundig Gereformeerde Partij v Netherlands* App no 58369/10 (10 July 2012), paras 73 and 77.

[83] *Staatkundig Gereformeerde Partij v Netherlands*, para 71.

[84] *Staatkundig Gereformeerde Partij v Netherlands*, para 77.

discrimination, though the Court did not spell that out. The Court did indicate, however, that it (like the domestic courts) could not direct the state as to how exactly to deal with the situation. One of the lower domestic courts had targeted state providing funding for parties, but the Dutch Supreme Court held it could not be prescriptive about that. The *SGP* case is also an extreme one in that the view of the party was explicitly based on sex. It is more likely that in many parties there is no such explicit view, but practices, unconscious bias or structural features disadvantage women (and minorities) from advancement. The article 14 case law is clear that such indirect discrimination is also prohibited by the Convention.[85]

More recently, the Court has considered a challenge to the application of a gender parity law in *Zevnik and others v Slovenia*.[86] Candidate lists drawn up by the applicants had been deemed invalid because they did not meet a requirement of 35 per cent inclusion of each gender – women were under-represented. The applicants did not challenge the principle of the gender parity law but argued that it was unclear and applied in a disproportionate manner.

The Court rejected these arguments and declared the application inadmissible. Citing the *SGP* case, it noted the importance of gender balance in European democracy, a principle that had been asserted by multiple Council of Europe institutions. It dismissed the applicants' argument that the legislation was unclear and also rejected their argument that the Slovenian authorities should have adopted a less severe measure than disqualification of the lists.

Minorities

At one level the need to ensure inclusion of minorities requires basic recognition of liberty and non-discrimination rights, for instance the liberty to speak in one's own language. This was affirmed by the Court in a Turkish case, *Şükran Aydin and Others v Turkey*.[87] The applicants were candidates for election in Turkey at a time the state banned the use of languages other than Turkish during electioneering. The applicants' mother language was Kurdish and they had been addressing audiences which included people who did not understand Turkish. Turkey was the only state the Court could identify in a

---

[85] *DH v Czech Republic* App no 57325/00 (2008) 47 EHRR 3 (Grand Chamber).
[86] *Zevnik and others v Slovenia* App no 54893/18 (5 December 2019).
[87] *Şükran Aydin and Others v Turkey* App nos 23196/07, 49197/06, 50242/08, 60912/08 and 14871/09 (22 January 2013).

survey of twenty-two states that had such a criminal sanction. In this specific type of situation, the Court found that the applicants' article 10 rights had been violated. This affirmed the rights of minority speakers in Turkey, but it is noteworthy that the Court included numerous caveats. The Court was evidently wary of getting involved in reviewing language policy, stressing that this area called for a 'particularly wide' margin of appreciation, and that the Convention imposed no requirements about the right to use a particular language for official communications or the choice of a parliamentary language.[88] In this regard the Court's attitude was also clear from the earlier case of *Podkolzina*.

The possibility for linguistic minorities to participate by running candidates in an election was directly at issue in *Podkolzina*.[89] The Court resolved that case in favour of the applicant but on procedural and legality grounds. However, the Court's position on the substantive question is troublesome from the viewpoint of allowing for minority participation in political institutions. The Court seemed to accept that states had a free choice in deciding on the working language of the national parliament, and that therefore it was legitimate to exclude persons who did not have a satisfactory understanding of that language, provided it was done in a lawful and procedurally fair way. It is understandable that the Court believes parliamentarians need to be able to understand each other. However, it is not clear that this justifies such a deferential approach to scrutinizing how a state implements such a policy. Such a relaxed view of the state's competence to choose a working language seems to ignore the situation of linguistic minorities, and the technical feasibility of providing for translators and simultaneous interpretation.

In *Tănase*, the Court considered rules which excluded persons holding dual nationality from running for election in Moldova. This is not merely a technical question about persons holding dual nationality. Such persons are presumably likely to belong to minority ethnic, linguistic or religious groups. The decision of the Court that the prohibition violated the Convention is welcome from the viewpoint of ensuring different groups can be represented in Parliament.[90] Interestingly, the Court also referred to the large numbers of

---

[88] *Şükran Aydin and Others v Turkey*, paras 50–51.

[89] *Podkolzina v Latvia*, para 35.

[90] However, one of the reasons for the Chamber's (though not the Grand Chamber's) conclusion – that the state could have imposed a loyalty oath – may also raise problems for some minorities. The European Commission of Human Rights had earlier rejected a claim that the oath of loyalty to the UK monarch required of UK parliamentarians violated the Convention: *McGuinness v United Kingdom* Admissibility Decision App no 39511/98 (8 June 1999). The applicant in that later became the deputy First Minister of Northern Ireland.

222   *The Right to Run for Election*

voters who held dual nationality and observed that they had the right to be represented by parliamentarians who reflected their own 'concerns and political views'.[91]

Consociationalism and Power Sharing

The final type of cases under this heading includes consociational or power-sharing arrangements. These tend to be controversial for several reasons: they can be very complicated constitutional institutions and procedures; they are often devised in situations of post-conflict societies or societies with deeply entrenched divisions; and they frequently labour under the accusation that special arrangements for communities are difficult to reconcile with democracy. Ironically, the very first P1–3 judgment and one of the most recent P1–3 judgments concern consociational arrangements.

The *Mathieu-Mohin* case concerned complex consociational systems in Belgium. Belgian legislators were divided into Dutch-speaking and French-speaking groups (representatives from officially bilingual Brussels could choose which group to adhere to).[92] In addition, there were three political Regions – for Dutch speakers, French speakers and Brussels – and four linguistic regions (the above three plus a German-speaking region). Finally, there were three Communities – Dutch speaking, French speaking and German speaking. There was a Flemish Council which concerned itself with community and regional matters, while there was a Council for the French Community and a Walloon Regional Council.

The applicants came from a region within the authority of the Flemish Council, but wherein there was a French-speaking minority, to which they belonged. Persons elected from this region to the legislature might choose to take the parliamentary oath in either French or Flemish, but if they took it in French, they would not be allowed to participate on the Flemish Council.[93] The European Court ruled that this did not violate the rights in P1–3, though it was a split decision, with five of the eighteen judges dissenting. The majority was influenced by the fact that the system was intended to strike a balance between the different interests in Belgium, that it was approved by large majorities after considerable debate and further by the fact that the system

---

[91] *Tănase v Moldova* (Grand Chamber) para 174.
[92] *Mathieu-Mohin and Clerfayt v Belgium* App no 9267/81 (1987) 10 EHRR 1, para 16.
[93] *Mathieu-Mohin and Clerfayt v Belgium*, para 39.

Inclusion 223

was still a 'work in progress'.[94] The dissenters considered that this was language-based discrimination.[95]

Sejdic and Finci v Bosnia and Herzegovina is a judgment where the Grand Chamber has had to grapple with the distinctive consociational arrangements adopted after the Dayton peace agreement. The applicants self-identified as Roma and Jewish and not as one of the three constitutive people: Bosniacs, Croats and Serbs. Under the constitution, only members of the three constituent peoples were eligible to become members of the three-person Presidency or the Chamber of Peoples, the upper house of the legislature. As the Grand Chamber recognised, these provisions were put in place in order to resolve a 'brutal conflict marked by genocide and "ethnic cleansing"'.[96] The Grand Chamber nevertheless found that the provisions were not a proportionate response. According to the Grand Chamber, the political situation in Bosnia and Herzegovina had improved significantly since the 1990s; the state had voluntarily accepted obligations in Council of Europe treaties without reservation, and perhaps most importantly, other mechanisms existed to protect power-sharing without excluding persons based on race or ethnicity.[97] The Grand Chamber's reasoning on these matters was relatively brief, largely because having established this as a matter of racial or ethnic discrimination, it would become very difficult to justify any exclusion from the political process. The dissents indeed complained of the majority's failure to devote more attention to the historical context. While the historical context is undoubtedly important, the existence of alternatives (outlined by the Venice Commission and quoted in the judgment)[98] which would protect the consociational nature of the system but eliminate the discriminatory aspects is an important aspect of the majority's reasoning. The exclusion of individuals because of their race or ethnicity is not just a serious violation in itself but also reflects a major risk of consociational arrangements that they reify group distinctions and disrespect the diversity and fluidity of identities. The proportionality inquiry in allowing the state to protect consociational arrangements provided non-discriminatory alternatives are implemented seems sensible and principled.[99]

---

[94] *Mathieu-Mohin and Clerfayt v Belgium*, para 57.
[95] Joint dissenting opinion of Judges Cremona, Bindschedler-Robert, Bernhardt, Spielman and Valticos.
[96] *Sejdic and Finci v Bosnia and Herzegovina* App nos 27996/06 and 34836/06, 22 BHRC 201 (Grand Chamber), para 45.
[97] *Sejdic and Finci v Bosnia and Herzegovina* (Grand Chamber), paras 47–49.
[98] *Sejdic and Finci v Bosnia and Herzegovina* (Grand Chamber), para 22.
[99] See also *Zornić v Bosnia and Herzegovina* App no 3681/06 (15 July 2014), *Šlaku v Bosnia and Herzegovina* App no 56666/12 (25 May 2016), *Pilav v Bosnia and Herzegovina* App no 41939/07

DELIBERATIVE DEMOCRACY

One aim of this book is to highlight circumstances in which the Court may promote a specifically deliberative model of democracy. The importance of deliberation in political regimes – as opposed to simple interest voting – comes across in some of these decisions.

In *Sukhovetkyy v Ukraine*, the Court considered the Convention compatibility of the deposit system in Ukrainian elections. The deposit was set at sixty times the tax-free monthly income (160 Euros); the applicant's annual income was 140 euros and he was unable to pay the deposit. Further, the deposit was only returned to the successful candidate. Against this the state provided electoral support for candidates.[100] The Court held the deposit requirement was compatible with the Convention. One of the factors which influenced the Court was that the measure had been subject to considerable debate in Ukraine and the parliament had considered the competing interests.[101] The Court contrasted this with other cases where national legislatures had not seriously considered the justification for restriction on the right to vote and where violations had accordingly been found.[102] Similarly in *Mathieu-Mohin*, the Court was influenced in finding no violation by the extensive domestic discussions on the consociational arrangements.

The Grand Chamber also emphasised the importance of dialogue in *Tănase*, albeit in fairly general terms:

> Pluralism and democracy must be based on dialogue and a spirit of compromise, which necessarily entails various concessions on the part of individuals or groups of individuals which are justified in order to maintain and promote the ideals and values of a democratic society. . . . In order to promote such dialogue and exchange of views necessary for an effective democracy, it is important to ensure access to the political arena for opposition parties on terms which allow them to represent their electorate, draw attention to the preoccupations and defend their interests.[103]

(9 June 2016). In *Pilav*, the applicant was a member of one of the constituent peoples, but because he was a Bosniac living in the Republika Srpska, he was excluded from standing in the presidential elections. This was a violation of P12.

[100] *Sukhovetskyy v Ukraine* App no 13716/02 (2007) 44 EHRR 57.

[101] *Sukhovetskyy*, paras 65‑67.

[102] *Matthews v United Kingdom* App no 24833/94 (1999) 28 EHRR 361, *Aziz v Cyprus* 69949/01 (2005) 41 EHRR 11, *Hirst v United Kingdom (No. 2)* App. no. 74025/01, (2005) 42 EHRR 41.

[103] *Tănase v Moldova* (Grand Chamber), para 44.

CONCLUSION

The right to run for election case law evinces judicial caution. Several of the cases demonstrate a desire to reach a decision on narrow ground without reaching larger issues. This approach – associated with Alexander Bickel, Justice Frankfurter and Cass Sunstein in the US – might be called judicial minimalism.[104] It may entail relying on issues of legality and procedural fairness rather than looking more at questions of substance where this might involve treading on policy decisions. Ruling on procedural grounds may also allow the Court to avoid making rulings which directly criticise the impartiality of domestic officials.[105]

In *Melnychenko*, the Court – unusually – examined how the decision to exclude the applicant from running for elections was not compatible with an interpretation of Ukrainian law. This avoided any need to rule on the larger question of residence requirements while still allowing a finding in favour of this particular applicant – and without ramifications for other cases. The dissenting opinion of Judge Loucaides considered that the national authorities had reasonably applied a residence requirement, and stressed that the 'political background and political features were not our concern to the extent that there were not fully relied on or established by the applicant.'

In *Petkov*, for instance, there were major issues about the nature of lustration laws, the role of political parties and the scope for amending electoral law shortly before an election. For the most part the Court ignored these, confining itself to the question of whether the state should have respected a final and authoritative judicial decision (though the Court did have to touch on the timing question).[106] That narrow question was an easy one for the majority. Ironically, two judges dissented because they thought the domestic judicial decision 'an unnecessary disturbance of the free conduct of the elections'.[107]

The minimalist approach is also seen in the emphasis on fair process. There is a positive obligation to ensure that eligibility decisions are made by impartial bodies, whose discretion is circumscribed by domestic law, which follows fair and objective procedures that preclude any abuse of power.[108] There must be an effective remedy under article 13 for any violations of the P1–3 rights. The

---

[104] Cass Sunstein, *One Case at a Time: Judicial Minimalism on the Supreme Court* (Harvard University Press, 1999).
[105] *Kovach v Ukraine*, para 62.
[106] *Petkov and others v Bulgaria* App nos 77568/01 178/02 and 505/02 (11 June 2009), para 18.
[107] *Petkov* dissenting opinion of Judges Maruste and Jaeger.
[108] *Podkolzina*, cited in *Kovach v Ukraine*, para 54.

226 *The Right to Run for Election*

scope of the remedy must not be limited to the provision of compensation, and must, in extreme cases, include the power to annul the election result.[109] Further, the remedy that is available must be one that the alleged victim can initiate.[110]

The Court has shown itself willing to rely on other European institutions in reaching its decisions. This shields the Court from an accusation that it is stepping outside the European norm, and also allows it, at least when treaties are involved, to say that it is only enforcing obligations the state has freely accepted. For example, in *Sukhovestkyy*, the Court was willing to conclude that Ukraine's deposit requirement did not violate the Convention, partly because the Venice Commission had issued an opinion finding that an even higher deposit requirement in Armenia was acceptable.[111] In *Tănase v Moldova*, the Court relied on the fact that Moldova was a party to the European Convention on Nationality and that European institutions such as the Venice Commission, and the European Commission on Racism and Intolerance had criticised the Moldovan rule in finding a violation.[112] Further, Moldova had modified its electoral law about a year before the relevant election, thus ignoring Council of Europe recommendations on the stability of electoral law.[113] In *Petkov*, the Court relied on the work of the Venice Commission on at least two points. First, the Court invoked the Venice Commission principle that the electoral process must provide an 'effective system of electoral appeals' to judicial institutions.[114] Second the Court rejected the state's argument that it did not have the time to implement judicial decisions: one of the reasons for the last-minute judicial appeals was the fact that the electoral law had been reformed less than three months before the election – in violation of the Venice Commission's recommendations on the stability of electoral law.[115] The Court relied on an OSCE report of the elections as well – one critical of the late and vague efforts to clarify the requirements of the electoral law.[116]

There is some limited support for the notion that states have to demonstrate that restrictions on electoral rights are themselves the product of considered democratic deliberation internally. The Court at least has taken this into consideration in some cases like *Mathieu-Mohin* and *Sukhovetkyy*.

---

[109] *Petkov*, paras 79, 80.
[110] *Petkov*, para 82.
[111] *Sukhovetskyy v Ukraine* App no 13716/02, (2007) 44 EHRR 57, para 70.
[112] *Tănase v Moldova* (Grand Chamber), para 177.
[113] *Tănase v Moldova* (Grand Chamber), para 179.
[114] *Petkov*, para 63.
[115] *Petkov*, paras 52, 66.
[116] *Petkov*, para 66.

Conclusion 227

On the issue of minorities, the Court's approach is somewhat mixed. As will become clear in Chapter 9, the Court's approach seems to be permissive of state measures to facilitate minority representation, but is not highly prescriptive and does not generally require them. There is some support to protect the liberty rights of minorities to speak their own language, but no support for the proposition that the Convention requires adjustments or special measures for minority languages. And specifically, in relation to consociational systems, the Court accepts these in principle but importantly requires that they not have the effect of excluding minority racial or ethnic groups from eligibility for legislative or (where P12 applies) presidential office.

The unusual case of *SGP* does indicate the possibility for arguments to tackle the problem of sex discrimination in political parties. Whilst the admissibility decision is brief, it is explicit in signalling that P1–3 combined with article 14 lead to the same conclusions as under article 7 CEDAW and article 2 and 25 ICCPR. Whilst the Court did not draw out the conclusions from this, it could lay the basis for a positive obligation on states to tackle sex discrimination in political parties.

9

Regulation of Elections

The previous two chapters focused on the individual rights to vote and to run for election; this chapter examines the systems and processes. That P1–3 has the effect of protecting the system as well as individual rights is reflected in the case law; for example, the Court has sometimes spoken of a more general right to benefit from legislative elections that conform to the principles in P1–3.[1] It has also specified that as well as individuals, in some cases political parties can be victims entitled to bring applications about P1–3.[2] This chapter examines key issues including the choice of the electoral system, how elections are regulated and the role of electoral commissions, the drawing of constituencies, campaign and party financing.

The early cases in these areas demonstrate a considerable degree of deference shown to the state. This may well reflect a view that there is a difference between cases concerning primarily an individual's rights and cases which concern more structural issues, with the latter requiring a greater margin of appreciation. In cases concerning the technical design of an electoral system, the Court will show considerable restraint.[3] This seems broadly appropriate given the diversity of political systems across Europe and the different and competing purposes they serve. Nevertheless, in some cases the European Court of Human Rights has intervened when the electoral process seemed arbitrary or unfair.

---

[1] *Partija 'Jaunie Demokrati' and Partija 'Musu Zeme' v Latvia* App nos 10547/07 and 34049/07 (29 November 2007).

[2] *Russian Conservative Party of Entrepreneurs v Russia* App no 55066/00 (2007) 46 EHRR 39; *Georgian Labour Party v Georgia* App no 9103/04 (2008) 48 EHRR 14.

[3] *Davydov and Others v Russia* App no 75947/11 (2018) 67 EHRR 25, para 287.

TYPES OF ELECTORAL SYSTEM

There are broadly two types of electoral system: majoritarian and proportional representation. There are, of course, many variants of each and some mixed variants. Majoritarian systems may be based on simple plurality (first-past-the-post) voting or require absolute majorities (either in two rounds or using preferential voting). Proportional systems generally use party lists, though the proportional representation by the single transferable vote (PRSTV) system does not. Party lists may be open or closed (i.e. the list of candidates can be amended by the voters or not). Many countries use mixed systems of election with some candidates elected using a majoritarian system and some using a proportional system. Countries may use different systems at the same time: the United Kingdom employs the simple plurality system for the House of Commons, proportional representation by the single transferable vote in Northern Ireland, party list systems for European Parliament elections and mixed systems for the Scottish Parliament and the National Assembly for Wales.

The European Court of Human Rights recognises this diversity of historical practice. As it frequently notes, electoral systems are designed to achieve a variety of sometimes scarcely compatible purposes. This being the case, there are necessarily trade-offs made in the design of electoral systems. Majoritarian systems frequently have large numbers of 'wasted votes' and do not ensure fair representation in the sense that the elected assembly represents political parties proportionately to their share of the vote. Highly proportional systems ensure a fair representation, but this may lead to fragmentation of political parties in the legislature and hence political instability. Some electoral systems (typically majoritarian) favour a direct link between the representative and the voters. Other systems may encourage the representation of women or minorities.[4] The Venice Commission for Democracy through Law has highlighted these and other diverse aims of electoral systems, concluding there is no such creature as the 'best' electoral system but each must be assessed in its own individual context.[5]

These general considerations were summarised by the Court in its first P1–3 case, *Mathieu-Mohin v Belgium*:

---

[4] European Commission for Democracy through Law (Venice Commission), *Study no. 352 / 2005 Report on Electoral Law and Electoral Administration in Europe* (Council of Europe Pub., Strasbourg 2006), para 178.

[5] European Commission for Democracy through Law (Venice Commission), *Study no. 352 / 2005 Report on Electoral Law and Electoral Administration in Europe* (Council of Europe Pub., Strasbourg 2006), paras 178–179.

54. As regards the method of appointing the 'legislature', Article 3 (P1–3) provides only for 'free' elections 'at reasonable intervals', 'by secret ballot' and 'under conditions which will ensure the free expression of the opinion of the people'. Subject to that, it does not create any 'obligation to introduce a specific system' ... such as proportional representation or majority voting with one or two ballots.

Here too the Court recognises that the Contracting States have a wide margin of appreciation, given that their legislation on the matter varies from place to place and from time to time.

Electoral systems seek to fulfil objectives which are sometimes scarcely compatible with each other: on the one hand, to reflect fairly faithfully the opinions of the people, and on the other, to channel currents of thought so as to promote the emergence of a sufficiently clear and coherent political will. In these circumstances the phrase 'conditions which will ensure the free expression of the opinion of the people in the choice of the legislature' implies essentially – apart from freedom of expression (already protected under Article 10 of the Convention) (art. 10) – the principle of equality of treatment of all citizens in the exercise of their right to vote and their right to stand for election.

It does not follow, however, that all votes must necessarily have equal weight as regards the outcome of the election or that all candidates must have equal chances of victory. Thus no electoral system can eliminate 'wasted votes'.

For the purposes of Article 3 of Protocol No. 1 (P1–3), any electoral system must be assessed in the light of the political evolution of the country concerned; features that would be unacceptable in the context of one system may accordingly be justified in the context of another, at least so long as the chosen system provides for conditions which will ensure the 'free expression of the opinion of the people in the choice of the legislature'.

The Convention institutions had their attention drawn early on to the well-known problems with majoritarian systems of voting, especially in the UK. Majoritarian systems can produce quite arbitrary results depending on the location of voters across constituencies. Typically, they disproportionately favour the largest national parties and regionally based parties while disadvantaging small national parties. They produce results which do not guarantee any proportionality but normally produce stable governments.[6]

---

[6] Traditionally these were among the claimed benefits of a simple plurality system. Of the three House of Commons elections held in the UK during 2010–2017 using this system, only one produced a single-party majority government; this highlights that the benefits are contingent on other factors.

Types of Electoral System

In *X v the United Kingdom*, the applicant pointed to the considerable disproportionality in UK elections especially as regards the 'third' national party in the system, the Liberal Party.[7] For example, in October 1974, the Liberals received more than 5 million votes but only 13 seats. The Conservatives, with approximately 10.5 million votes, obtained 277 seats, and Labour, with approximately 11.5 million votes, obtained 319 seats.

The Commission rejected the complaint as manifestly ill-founded. For it, the free expression of the will of the people implied that voters should be free of pressure to vote for one party or candidate; furthermore, different political parties should be given reasonable opportunities to present candidates. The Commission rejected the notion that P1–3 required that the legislative assembly proportionately reflect the votes case for it. When P1–3 was adopted, European systems used both majoritarian and proportional systems of elections, and these were part of the common European heritage. In addition, the Commission noted that the *travaux préparatoires* also supported this interpretation: the text of P1–3 was adopted in preference to an earlier proposal which might have required proportionality.

The Commission had occasion to apply this reasoning also to the proportional representation by single transferable vote system (PRSTV) in another UK case, *Lindsay*.[8] The applicants objected to the use of the PRSTV system for elections in Northern Ireland to the European Parliament when this system was not used throughout the UK for European Parliament elections. They argued that the PRSTV system would favour the Irish Republican voters and indeed its adoption in Northern Ireland was intended to 'appease or bribe' this community.

The Commission noted that PRSTV was a type of proportional system and so was compatible with P1–3. The Commission noted that in certain circumstances, proportional representation could facilitate the representation of an ethnic or religious minority, if voting split on such lines and one group was in a minority in all constituencies. Proportional representation would make it easier for the people to express its opinion freely in that situation. That the system was different from the rest of the UK was justified as the type of ethnic or religious division and voting was peculiar to Northern Ireland.[9] The Commission also rejected an argument based on article 14 and an argument

---

[7] *X v United Kingdom* App no 7140/75 (1976) 7 DR 96 (European Commission of Human Rights).

[8] *Lindsay v United Kingdom* App no 8364/78 (1979) 15 DR 247 (European Commission of Human Rights).

[9] *Lindsay v United Kingdom* 251.

that the system violated the applicants' dignity and was degrading under article 3.

The Commission subsequently returned to consider the UK's simple plurality system when it heard a complaint from the Liberal Party (along with a number of individuals).[10] The applicants pointed out that the disproportionality had become more marked since 1970 given the decrease in votes for the two major parties. It meant that 400,000 voters were needed to elect a Liberal Party member compared to approximately 40,000–43,000 for the two main parties. Neither of the two major parties had an interest in changing the system, as it disproportionately benefitted them. The applicants characterised the approach as one of indirect political discrimination – they pleaded article 14 read with P1–3.

The Commission acknowledged that the simple majority voting system could lead to different results – it was even possible for a party to secure a minority of votes but a majority of seats, and smaller parties might not be represented at all. However, the Commission stressed it could not get around the wording of the text. Article 14 did protect the voter against discrimination but it did not guarantee 'equal voting influence for all voters'; P1–3 referred to a 'secret' ballot but did not include 'equal' as a qualification.[11] Notwithstanding the important political consequences, the Commission had to recognise that the majoritarian system was one of the two main electoral systems and was used in many democratic countries, and had been upheld as constitutional by different courts such as the German Federal Constitutional Court and the US Supreme Court. It dismissed the complaint as inadmissible.

Interestingly the Commission did leave open one possibility for the future – it noted that a voting system might exclude certain religious or ethnic groups from representation if there was a voting pattern along these lines. Whether this would violate the Convention the Commission left open.[12]

More recently in *Le Lievre v United Kingdom*, the Court rejected as inadmissible a complaint about the highly unusual situation on Sark, part of the Channel Islands. In 2008, the Sark legislature was significantly reformed; formerly it had been a feudal legislature with places reserved for landowners. The historical context as well as the small size of the population – just under 500 voters – made it difficult to devise a satisfactory electoral system. The system chosen treated the island as a single constituency. The voters elected

---

[10] *Liberal Party v United Kingdom* App no 8765/79, (198c) 21 DR 211 (European Commission of Human Rights).
[11] *Liberal Party v United Kingdom* 224.
[12] *Liberal Party v United Kingdom*, para 225.

twenty-eight representatives with these terms staggered so, apart from the first election, there were fourteen vacancies at each election. In each election each voter had fourteen votes and the system was a straightforward majoritarian one – the candidates with the most votes were elected. The applicants complained that this meant there might be no representation for minority viewpoints on the island.

The Court rejected the complaint as inadmissible. It would always be difficult to devise an electoral system for such a small population – traditional proportional or majoritarian systems were ill-suited.[13] The voting system permitted voters to vote for whom they wished, and provided a high degree of representativeness with one representative per about thirty-five to thirty-six voters.[14] The Court noted that the staggering of the elections might increase the possibility for one dominant viewpoint to prevail, but the Convention did not require that all candidates be elected at the same election.[15] Most important, though, was the context: the 2008 reform had sought to introduce genuine democratic elections and erase a system tainted by feudal notions. It was incomparably superior to the previous system and had only been adopted after some difficulties. The reform was only approved after being closely scrutinised to make sure it complied with human rights obligations. For all these reasons the Court found the system to be within the UK's margin of appreciation.[16]

PROPORTIONAL REPRESENTATION SYSTEMS: THRESHOLDS

The Court has also shown a wide margin of appreciation in cases concerning party list systems.

Specific questions related to proportional electoral systems include how any quotas are calculated and in particular whether there is a threshold before a party can claim seats. As noted above, there are different imperatives to consider in electoral design, and as the Court recognises, these are sometimes difficult to reconcile and balance. Several electoral systems directly or indirectly seek to avoid the fragmentation of parties in the legislature and seek to ensure the formation of a stable government. This is what threshold rules do

---

[13] *Le Lievre v United Kingdom* App no 36522/15 (2016) 62 EHRR SE 20, para 47.
[14] *Le Lievre*, paras 48–49.
[15] *Le Lievre*, para 48.
[16] *Le Lievre*, paras 50–51. The applicants also complained that the Seigenur – a historical feudal owner of the island – retained a seat in the legislature, albeit with only a voice and no vote. The Court noted that the UK courts had closely examined this and had found no violation; the Court saw no reason to depart from this: para 56.

in proportional representation list systems, and it is also supposed to be what is achieved by the simple plurality system. Proportional list systems often impose a threshold so that a party with only (say) a 0.5 per cent share of a national vote cannot claim a seat in a 200-seat legislature. These rules are generally intended to avoid excessive fragmentation in the legislature, a problem that can lead to political instability.

The Convention institutions have generally accepted threshold requirements. In *Tete v France*, the Commission considered a complaint from the Green Party in France that France's 5 per cent threshold rule violated P1–3 (alone or in combination with article 14).[17] The Green Party also complained about rules requiring deposits which were non-refundable for parties that did not meet the 5 per cent threshold and that only permitted refunds of propaganda expenses for parties that met the 5 per cent threshold. The Commission recited the *Mathieu-Mohin* principles on the flexibility shown to states in the choice of electoral systems bearing in mind in particular that electoral systems pursued aims that were difficult to reconcile. The Commission held that all the measures were 'designed to foster the emergence of sufficiently representative currents of thought. This is quite a legitimate aim . . .', particularly given that similar rules existed in other European countries.[18] The Commission rejected the complaint as manifestly ill-founded.

Thresholds in proportional list systems may impact regional minority parties that do not have an appeal outside their core region. This issue was discussed by the Commission in *Magnago and Sudtiroler Volkspartei v Italy*.[19] This case concerned the operation of Italy's 1993 electoral law which adopted a mixed majoritarian and proportional representation system: 75 per cent of seats were allocated using a majoritarian system and 25 per cent using the list system with a 4 per cent national threshold. The applicants represented German- and Ladin-speaking minorities in Trentino-Alto Adige. They were able to elect three members for the majoritarian seats but none for the proportional representation sets due to the 4 per cent national threshold. The applicants complained that this discriminated against them on grounds of language and association with a national minority.

The Commission, after highlighting the flexibility shown to states in the choice of electoral systems, observed that the 4 per cent threshold was

---

[17] *Tete v France* App No 11123/84 (1987) 54 DR 52 (European Commission of Human Rights, 9 December 1987).

[18] *Tete v France*, paras 68–69. The Commission reiterated these views in *Fournier v France* (1988) 55 DR 52 (European Commission of Human Rights).

[19] *Magnago and Sudtiroler Volkspartei v Italy* App no 25035/94 (European Commission of Human Rights, 15 April 1996).

Proportional Representation Systems: Thresholds

'intended to promote the emergence of sufficiently representative currents of thought', and that similar provisions existed elsewhere in Europe. Furthermore, even if a system set a 'relatively high threshold', this would not exceed the states' margin of appreciation. The Commission noted the law applied to all parties and there was nothing in the Convention which required 'positive discrimination in favour of minorities'. While the Commission did not allude to it in its reasoning, the party had obtained some seats under the majoritarian element of the mixed system and so was not left without any representation.

The Court agreed that such threshold measures were compatible with the Convention in *Federación Nacionalista Canaria v Spain*.[20] The applicant party had obtained 28 per cent of the votes in one constituency (Lanzarote) in the Autonomous Community of the Canary Islands. Under the electoral law, parties could obtain seats if they obtained 30 per cent of the votes in one constituency or 6 per cent of the votes across the Community. The applicant had achieved neither and argued that this breached P1–3, noting that other Autonomous Communities used slightly lower thresholds.

The Court restated the *Mathieu-Mohin* principles but also borrowed language from the article 10 jurisprudence on the principle of pluralism: the state was the 'ultimate guarantor of the principle of pluralism'. This required it to hold elections that complied with P1–3 to ensure the 'free expression of the opinion of the people'. According to the Court,

> Such expression is inconceivable without the participation of a plurality of political parties representing the different shades of opinion to be found within a country's population. By relaying this range of opinion, not only within political institutions but also – with the help of the media – at all levels of social life, political parties make an irreplaceable contribution to political debate, which is at the very core of the concept of a democratic society.[21]

This statement of principle, borrowed from the article 10 jurisprudence, is interesting for a number of reasons. It hints at the nature of a democratic society which requires pluralism and debate across all spheres so that these can feed into – through the mediation of political parties – the political sphere. It also lays the seeds for potential arguments about when the flexibility otherwise shown in P1–3 case law might not be appropriate. Presumably if state regulations of elections undermined this vision of pluralism, then the Court would find a limit to this flexibility.

---

[20] *Federación Nacionalista Canaria v Spain* App no 56618/00 (7 June 2001).
[21] *Federación Nacionalista Canaria v Spain*. The Court cites *Informatinsverein Lentia v Austria* and other article 10 cases for the principle of pluralism and debate.

236 *Regulation of Elections*

The Court did not find this limit was reached in this case. It noted that the legislation had offered two different routes to party representation including the possibility for a party to be represented if it obtained 30 per cent of the votes in one constituency. Furthermore, the Constitutional Court of Spain had examined the complaint, and that examination demonstrated no evidence of arbitrariness, disproportionality or a thwarting of the free expression of the opinion of the people.

In a number of cases after this, the Court limited itself to recounting the general principles and accepting thresholds on the order of 4 or 5 per cent.[22] The Court, and specifically the Grand Chamber, soon found, however, that it had to examine the issue of thresholds more carefully, both on the issue of principle but also how the thresholds worked in the actual practice of elections.

The case of *Yumak and Sadak v Turkey* was heard at both Chamber and Grand Chamber levels and considered the electoral threshold in Turkey set at 10 per cent nationally. The 10 per cent threshold had been adopted in 1983 after the military regime of 1980–1983. The threshold was adopted because of a history of governmental instability. Between 1961 and 1980, Turkey had had twenty different governments, whereas in the 1983–2006 period it had had six – three coalition governments and three single-party governments.[23] The consequence of this was that significant numbers of voters were left without any representation, as the parties they voted for did not meet the threshold. In three of the elections in the 1980s and 1990s, this figure of the unrepresented was between 14 per cent and 19 per cent.[24]

The 2002 general election saw a dramatic development. The election took place in the context of a series of economic and political crises. Of the eighteen parties which contested the election only two – the AKP and CHP – passed the 10 per cent national threshold. The AKP with 34.26 percent of the votes secured 66 per cent of the seats, while the CHP with 19.4 per cent of the votes secured 33 per cent. Nine independents were elected. This meant that 45 per cent of voters had voted for parties which obtained no seats in Parliament.[25] In the case of the applicants, their party had obtained nearly 46 per cent of the vote in their province, but the province's three seats were shared between the AKP (with less than 15% of the vote in the province) and

---

[22] The Court accepted a 4% threshold on the basis of these earlier cases in *Gorizdra v Moldova* App no 53180/99 (2 July 2002). A 5% threshold was accepted in *Partija 'Jaunie Demokrati' and Partija 'Musu Zeme' v Latvia*.

[23] *Yumak and Sadak v Turkey* App no 10226/03 (Chamber, 30 January 2007), para 55.

[24] *Yumak and Sadak* (Chamber), para 44.

[25] *Yumak and Sadak* (Chamber), paras 11–13.

Proportional Representation Systems: Thresholds

an independent.[26] None of the governing parties in the previous coalition government obtained any seats in the 2002 election.

The 10 per cent threshold would appear to be the highest in Europe. Most states adopted a 5 per cent or lower threshold; some states even had none.[27] The 10 per cent threshold in Turkey had been criticised by the Parliamentary Assembly of the Council of Europe.[28]

The Chamber noted that the election results were the most unrepresentative in modern Turkish history, but the electoral system as such did not block parties representing political alternatives from success.[29] The Chamber noted the 10 per cent threshold appeared to be the highest in Europe and it might be desirable for it to be lowered or for counter-balances to be adopted; but the issue needed to be left to the discretionary judgement of the national authorities. The Chamber noted that the threshold was the subject of public debate.[30] Judges Cabral Barreto and Mularoni dissented, noting that the threshold had been criticised by the Council of Europe, that it allowed for no counterbalancing measures, and that it disadvantaged regional parties, which was an issue in a large country like Turkey.

Following the Chamber judgment and before the Grand Chamber judgment, Turkey had a further election in 2007. In this election there was a strong showing of independents; in addition, several parties used different tactics to circumvent the 10 per cent threshold. One party (DSP) campaigned under the banner of another one (CHP), while the pro-Kurdish DTP candidates campaigned as independents. While only three parties formally reached the 10 per cent threshold (AKP, CHP, MHP), by these ruses the DSP and DTP were also represented in the Parliament.[31] The AKP with 46.58 per cent of the votes secured 62 per cent of the seats and formed a government.

The Grand Chamber comprehensively reviewed the Convention principles identified in previous cases, including the role of the state as the ultimate guarantor of pluralism.[32] It then explained that, since the threshold limited P1–3 rights, it had to examine whether this was for a legitimate aim, and whether there was any arbitrariness or whether there was a reasonable degree of proportionality. In examining those two elements of legitimacy and

---

[26] *Yumak and Sadak* (Chamber), para 11.
[27] *Yumak and Sadak v Turkey* App no 10226/03 (2008) 48 EHRR 4 (Grand Chamber), para 64.
[28] *Yumak and Sadak v Turkey* App no 10226/03 (2008) 48 EHRR 4 (Grand Chamber), paras 58–59.
[29] *Yumak and Sadak* (Chamber), para 74.
[30] *Yumak and Sadak* (Chamber), paras 76–77.
[31] *Yumak and Sadak v Turkey* (Grand Chamber), paras 23–25.
[32] *Yumak and Sadak v Turkey* (Grand Chamber), para 106.

238   *Regulation of Elections*

proportionality it would seek to determine if the measure impaired the very essence of the right.[33]

The Grand Chamber noted that the measure served the legitimate aim of promoting sufficiently representative currents of thought.[34] It also indicated that states could adopt an electoral system based on the notion of a unitary state and that the Convention did not guarantee representation for parties with a regional base only; however, if an electoral system tended to exclude such parties from representation, this might raise issues.[35]

Turning to proportionality, the Grand Chamber noted that the Turkish threshold was the highest in Europe and one of only four above 5 per cent.[36] The Grand Chamber did not consider that this by itself automatically created a problem: there were diverse practices in Europe, and each electoral system had to be assessed in light of its own context. This led the Grand Chamber to examine the 'correctives' which attached to the Turkish system. In this regard the safeguards included the possibility to run candidates formally as independents (described as a 'makeshift' solution)[37] and to form a coalition for campaigning purposes to 'circumvent' the prohibition on joint lists.[38] The Grand Chamber noted that the contested 2002 elections were unusual both in the comprehensive rejection of the governing parties and in the unusually high percentage of voters who were left unrepresented.[39] The Grand Chamber also stressed the vigilance of the Constitutional Court in monitoring the electoral system.[40] With a certain degree of misgiving – pointing to both the criticisms of the Council of Europe and the non-transparent correctives – the Grand Chamber concluded by a 13–4 vote that the measure was proportionate.[41]

The majority judgment showed a certain reticence about the conclusion, and the joint dissent picked up on this and disputed the conclusion. The dissent criticised even the view that there was a legitimate aim given that in practice (except for the 2002 elections), smaller parties could be represented and that the high threshold limited the possibility for minority or regional

---

[33] *Yumak and Sadak v Turkey* (Grand Chamber), para 118.
[34] *Yumak and Sadak v Turkey* (Grand Chamber), paras 125 and 122.
[35] *Yumak and Sadak v Turkey* (Grand Chamber), para 124. In a case against Russia, the Court criticised Russian legislation for effectively eliminating regional parties by requiring establishment of regional branches: *Republican Party of Russia v Russia* App no 12976/07 (2015) 61 EHRR 20.
[36] *Yumak and Sadak v Turkey* (Grand Chamber), para 129.
[37] *Yumak and Sadak v Turkey* (Grand Chamber), para 138.
[38] *Yumak and Sadak v Turkey* (Grand Chamber), para 139.
[39] *Yumak and Sadak v Turkey* (Grand Chamber), paras 141–143.
[40] *Yumak and Sadak v Turkey* (Grand Chamber), para 146.
[41] *Yumak and Sadak v Turkey* (Grand Chamber), para 147.

parties to enter Parliament. The dissent also disagreed on the proportionality point. It disputed the exceptional nature of the 2002 elections given that the threshold applied to elections before and after (this particular critique seems to miss the point that the electoral result was exceptional), and was highly critical of the argument that 'stratagems' were legitimate correctives; indeed, if anything, they undermined the legitimate aim.[42]

The dissent's view that the correctives in question were problematic seems convincing. The correctives introduced a variety of complications into the electoral system, not least that they were of problematic legality, and entailed certain disadvantages in terms of access to broadcasting time and different rules for non-residents voting (see Chapter 7). Compliance with Convention requirements in such a fundamental area should hardly depend on uncertain ruses like these.

In *Yumak and Sadak*, the majority had referenced the importance of the domestic Constitutional Court. In an even more deferential approach, the European Court of Human Rights sometimes limits itself to ensuring that a domestic body has properly considered the arguments in light of the Convention. This was the approach in another case involving thresholds, *Filini v Greece*, where the applicant objected to the different calculations used in relation to votes for parties which did not reach the 3 per cent threshold: different rules were adopted in relation to party lists seats and constituency-based seats. Here the Court simply verified that the applicant had had the benefit of a full examination of the issue in the domestic courts and found the complaint inadmissible.[43]

Electoral thresholds were also considered in a case with a slightly unusual twist from Germany: *Strack and Richter v Germany*. The applicants had voted in the European Parliament elections in Germany. Germany had adopted a 5 per cent threshold for these elections, the maximum permitted under European Union law. The twist is that the German Constitutional Court had decided that the threshold requirement was unconstitutional in respect of the European Parliament, and the applicants were complaining that the Constitutional Court refused to order a new election or to re-allocate the seats. This case highlights the potential far-reaching consequences of violations in relation to the electoral process.

The European Court of Human Rights rejected the applicants' arguments. The Court noted that it had accepted that domestic constitutional courts had

---

[42] *Yumak and Sadak v Turkey* (Grand Chamber) joint dissent of Judges Tulkens, Vajić, Jaeger and Šikuta.

[43] *Filini v Greece* App no 30244/11 (6 May 2014).

discretionary remedial powers and in particular could decide that a measure was unconstitutional but set a time limit for its replacement rather than voiding it forthwith.[44] The Court accepted the Constitutional Court's reasoning that there would be a negative impact on the work of the European Parliament if the Constitutional Court were to either void the election or reallocate the seats.[45] This was in the context that the European Court of Human Rights had shown a wide margin of appreciation on the substantive question as to what sort of threshold could be set.[46]

While the Court has shown considerable leniency in assessing threshold rules, it is worth noting it has shown scepticism towards another means of achieving the same end: restricting the number of political parties. In an article 11 case, *Republican Party of Russia v Russia*, the state had refused to register changes to the registration of the applicant political party and subsequently dissolved the political party. The dissolution was based on the party's failure to meet requirements as to total number of members (50,000) and to have branches with more than 500 members in 45 districts. These restrictions were based on a perceived need to reduce the number of political parties in operation for financial reasons and to avoid threats from separatist parties. They succeeded in reducing the number of political parties from forty-eight to fifteen.[47] The applicant party was dissolved for failing to meet the requirements of membership and branches; this was despite being one of the oldest political parties (established in 1990) and never having been accused of posing a threat of violence or separatism.[48] The Court found that the applicant's article 11 rights had been violated both by the failure to register the amendments and also the dissolution. The minimum membership requirement was not shown to be necessary. The financial argument was unconvincing given that Russia did not provide unlimited funding to all parties but only to parties with more than 3 per cent of the vote share and then in proportion to their share of the vote.[49] Similarly the argument against excessive fragmentation in Parliament was misplaced given Russia also operated a relatively high threshold of 7 per cent and required parties to lodge signatures before they could contest elections.[50] The Court believed that even small minority groups were entitled to organise to see if they could secure parliamentary representation.

---

[44] *Strack and Richter v Germany* App nos 28811/12 and 5C303/12 (5 July 2017), para 29.
[45] *Strack and Richter v Germany*, para 32.
[46] *Strack and Richter v Germany*, para 37.
[47] *Republican Party of Russia v Russia* App no 12976/07 (2015) 61 EHRR 20, para 117.
[48] *Republican Party of Russia v Russia*, para 120.
[49] *Republican Party of Russia v Russia*, para 112.
[50] *Republican Party of Russia v Russia*, para 113.

Furthermore, the membership requirement had the intention and effect of reducing the number of opposition political parties and therefore required considerable justification.[51] The Court also found the effective ban on regional political parties to be a breach of the Convention. Regional political parties should be generally permitted, as they were across nearly all of Europe. The Court did accept that there might be a need in a newly established democracy to limit free association but found that the decision to adopt these reforms only in 2001 suggested they were not necessary; furthermore, the state had other tools at its disposal to counter genuine threats, e.g. party dissolution for violent or anti-democratic parties.[52]

The *Republican Party of Russia* case is striking in that it shows the Court being willing to rule on a sensitive matter in relation to Russia's political system, upholding the rights of the applicant political party but also making very strong criticisms of the Russian system. The case makes a strong stand in defence of regional parties and indicates that the Court is willing to look at the political context. In this instance the state adopted a measure which severely restricted opposition parties and the Court appropriately insisted on very strong justifications for the measures. It is important to note that this is an article 11 case rather than a P1–3 case and suggests the Court will review with more vigour restrictions on the classic liberal rights in articles 10 and 11 than it will issues that more narrowly concern electoral design.

PROPORTIONAL REPRESENTATION SYSTEMS: LIST MEMBERSHIP, CLOSED PARTY LISTS AND BONUS SEATS

One feature of most proportional representation systems is that they rely on party lists, i.e. one votes for a party rather than individual candidates.[53]

This system requires that parties publish their ordered list of candidates. Naturally the most prominent candidates will feature highly on such lists. The Court has recognised that states have a legitimate aim in promoting bonds between the top-listed candidates on a party list and the entire party list. This was recognised as a legitimate aim in *Russian Conservative Party of Entrepreneurs v Russia*. In that case the applicant party was denied registration when its second-listed candidate was deemed to have withdrawn because of a failure to

---

[51] *Republican Party of Russia v Russia*, paras 114–120.
[52] *Republican Party of Russia v Russia*, paras 126–129.
[53] Harris and others note an argument that the Court may too willingly accept the primacy of political parties in such electoral systems and overlook the argument for an individual right to stand for election: David Harris, Michael O'Boyle, Ed Bates and Carla Buckley, *Law of the European Convention on Human Rights* (Oxford University Press 2018), 923.

make full financial disclosure. This triggered a rule which prevented the registering of a party list if one of the top three candidates withdrew. The Court accepted this was a legitimate aim but found the measure nevertheless disproportionate: in that case the entire party and the other candidates of the party were being punished even though they had done nothing wrong.[54] This is one of the few cases concerning the design of an electoral system where the court has found a violation, and even here the problem was not so much with the system as with how it was operationalised in practice to exclude one party.

Party list systems also came under scrutiny in a case from Italy. In *Saccomanno and others v Italy*, more than ninety applicants challenged two features of the party list system adopted in Italy in 2005.[55] The reform introduced closed party lists whereby the lists of candidates were determined by parties and voters had no choice over the individual candidates or their ordering on the party lists. The second reform that was criticised was the system of 'bonus' seats: if the largest party or coalition did not obtain 340 out of 630 seats in the Chamber of Deputies, then it would receive bonus seats up to 340, i.e. 54 per cent of the seats.

The Court noted the importance of the P1–3 rights, which, alongside the right to vote and to run for election, also included a more general right, a right to have the benefit of legislative elections conforming to the P1–3 principles.[56] It reiterated the large margin of appreciation and that electoral systems vary according to the historical and political conditions of each state; they must be assessed in the light of the political evolution of each state.[57]

The government argued that the closed list system served diverse aims: it sought to prevent the machinations of criminal organisations infiltrating centres of political power; to prevent any trade in votes and the risk of candidates getting into debt, and to favour candidates with specific competences.[58] The Court noted that other European countries used the closed list system. The Court's comparative survey indicated that of twenty-two countries using the party list system, thirteen used closed lists, while five opted for open list systems where voters could express a preference for some of the candidates on the list.[59] According to the Court, such a system could be justified given the constitutive role of political parties which were essential for the proper

---

[54] *Russian Conservative Party of Entrepreneurs v Russia*, paras 63 and 65.
[55] *Saccomanno v Italy* App no 11583/08 (13 March 2012).
[56] *Saccomanno*, para 47.
[57] *Saccomanno*, para 52.
[58] *Saccomanno*, para 55.
[59] *Saccomanno*, paras 26 and 62.

functioning of democracy.[60] There was nothing to indicate people were prevented from participating in politics or that the system favoured any particular party. The Court also attached importance to Italy's specific history, possibly a reference to concerns about organised crime.[61]

Turning to the bonus seat provision, the government argued that this was intended to avoid parliamentary fragmentation and to support governmental stability, in the context that Italy experienced a fragmentation of political parties.[62] The Court noted that some European countries used thresholds in order to achieve the same aim, or used analogous measures. The Court's comparative survey on bonus seats indicated that only three others used bonus seats while thirteen used other mechanisms (such as D'Hondt calculations) to advantage larger parties.[63] In light of *Yumak*, and considering the size of the bonuses in question, they did not seem to affect the balance between the principles of governmental stability and fair representation.[64]

The finding in relation to bonus seats is somewhat troubling. The use of bonus seats serves to promote a stable government. This is the same aim served by threshold rules and the normal operation of the simple plurality system, though it achieves the aim in a more direct way. Nevertheless, this is a procedure that is open to abuse. It could systematically favour one party and could even be used to avoid the normal restraints on a constituted power. In a political system it might be normal that one party is consistently the largest, for instance, and it is not unusual for constitutions to require supermajorities in parliament for amendment purposes. It should be emphasised that in the Italian case, the Court did not find that the size of the bonus negatively impacted on the balance between fair representation and governmental stability. Presumably if the bonus was excessive – say, conferring a constitution-amending power on a party or coalition this might be excessive.[65]

One aspect of the party list system is that it raises questions about the mandate of individual representatives – if they are elected under a party list and subsequently leave the party, must they resign from the legislature? The

---

[60] *Saccomanno*, para 63.
[61] *Saccomanno*, paras 60 and 64.
[62] *Saccomanno*, para 68.
[63] *Saccomanno*, para 27.
[64] *Saccomanno*, para 74.
[65] If a party secures enough seats to have the power to change the constitution without opposition support, this leaves the way open to undermine liberal democracy. Halmai tracks some of the changes introduced by Fidesz in Hungary when it secured a parliamentary supermajority: Gábor Halmai, 'An Illiberal Constitutional System in the Middle of Europe' (2014) European Yearbook of Human Rights 497.

244

Venice Commission recognises that party list systems mean that parties select the order of candidate in advance but has criticised policies permitting parties to remove representatives from the legislature after an election has taken place.[66] The European Court of Human Rights has had to deal with this issue in *Paunović and Milivojević v Serbia*. Serbia operated a party list system, and the applicants' party had required its candidates to sign undated letters of resignation. Following differences between the applicants and their party, the applicants signalled that they withdrew their earlier undated letters of resignation; the party nevertheless dated them and sent them in. The European Court of Human Rights focused on the legality question rather than the substantive position. The Court indicated that the legal position in Serbia supported the notion that candidates had an individual mandate and could only resign if they did so individually.[67] Given the failure to comply with what the Court saw as the domestic Serbian legal requirements, this was a breach of P1–3.

This is one of the rare cases where P1–3 arguments about the electoral system itself results in a finding of a violation. It is a cautious judgment; the Court does not go as far as the Venice Commission would and instead relies again on a legality basis to find a violation. Nevertheless, it is important in recognising that representatives, once elected, cannot be restricted by party discipline, at least to the point that they have to resign their seats. This is important from a deliberative democratic point of view in that representatives must be able to change their views once elected as they consider the force of different arguments.

ELECTORAL SYSTEMS AND CONSTITUENCIES

The nature of constituencies can also raise difficult issues in democracies. Equal suffrage would suggest that all constituencies in an election should represent equal numbers of persons, i.e. the ratio of people to seats should be the same. However, in some countries the argument may be made that certain constituencies should have a different ratio of people to seats. This may be to avoid diluting the interests of a particular region or regions in the national parliament. Another issue might be whether any constituency drawing is based on a reliable and recent census or other population count. A separate issue would be the actual drawing of any boundaries. While the ratio of

[66] European Commission for Democracy through Law (Venice Commission), 488/2008 *Report on the Imperative Mandate and Similar Practices* (Council of Europe Pub., Strasbourg 2009).

[67] *Paunović and Milivojević v Serbia* App no 41683/06 (24 May 2016), paras 63–65.

Electoral Systems and Constituencies

persons to seat might be the same in different constituencies, a cunning boundary designer might devise boundaries which enhanced the votes of some groups or diminished those of others – this is the classic political gerrymander.

The Commission considered the Icelandic proportional representation system in a case that also touched on the issue of constituencies, *X v Iceland*. The electoral system consisted of forty-nine representatives elected by proportional representation in eight constituencies, with an additional eleven representatives allocated to parties so as to ensure proportionality. One of the by-products of the system was that the two most populous districts did not return as many representatives as their size would suggest if there were a strict principle of all votes being equal.

The Commission rejected the application as manifestly ill-founded. Protocol 1 prohibited any pressure in the choice of candidates and required that political parties must have reasonable opportunities to present candidates but did not require 'equal voting influence for all voters'. The Icelandic situation reflected migration patterns whereby people moved to the more populous districts; it also, however, reflected a deliberate choice to ensure representation for the more scarcely populated areas even at the expense of the more populous ones. Indeed, if the system ensured full equality of voting influence, then most representatives would come from a small part of the country.[68] The Icelandic system was not 'arbitrary or abusive', and there was no evidence it favoured any particular party or candidate.[69] Indeed, the system included provisions to ensure proportional representation of the parties. It is interesting that the Commission noted these last points – it is not clear that the same can be said of the UK's electoral system as described in the *Liberal Party* case.

The only case in which the Court seems to have considered these sorts of arguments in relation to constituencies is *Bompard v France*.[70] Here the applicant complained about the 2002 elections in France and specifically that they were based on boundaries drawn up in 1986 notwithstanding two censuses in the intervening period in 1990 and 1999. She alleged that population changes meant constituencies no longer reflected the populations. The Court rejected the application as manifestly ill-founded, though not without making some interesting comments.

The Court rehearsed the *Mathieu-Mohin* principles, in particular the rejection of the view that 'all votes must necessarily have equal weight as

---

[68] Interestingly, even though the Commission had referenced the US Supreme Court in the *Liberal Party* case, it made no references to the US Supreme Court's 'one person, one vote' case law in the Icelandic case.

[69] *X v Iceland* App no 8941/80 (European Commission of Human Rights, 8 December 1981).

[70] *Bompard v France* App no 44081/02 (4 June 2006).

regards the outcome of the election or that all candidates must have equal chances of victory.' According to the Court, the French legislative principles were compatible with P1-3 – the principles prioritised demographic balance but also permitted certain other imperatives to be taken into account such as natural boundaries. The Court noted that there was no convincing evidence of actual discrepancies which would cause the election to falsely portray the opinion of the people. The Court accepted the government's arguments for not redrawing the constituencies in light of the 1999 census: the results of this only became confirmed in 2000, and electoral law prohibited changes in the year before an election (while the Court did not mention this, this is in line with the Venice Commission Code of Good Practice); this left only a short space of time to redraw the constituencies, and it was argued this was too complicated a task to rush.

Whilst the Court found this application inadmissible, it is noteworthy that it gives a fair degree of consideration to the specifics of the complaint and the government response. This suggests that it is open to considering other arguments based on population shifts if these can be shown to affect the free expression of the opinion of the people.

One particular challenge will arise if and when the European Union accedes to the Convention and Protocol 1. The seats allocated to each country in the European Parliament are allocated based on degressive proportionality rather than strict proportionality. This mitigates against the risk that the larger states of the Union will dominate the Parliament. In the context of a supra-national organisation like the European Union, such a system may have its own logic. The Convention institutions have not endorsed a principle that there must be a similar ratio of electorate to seats throughout a jurisdiction; at the same time, parties should not be allowed to depart from it without good reason. That the European Union is a supranational (and unique) institution involving cooperating sovereign states but with extensive powers requiring democratic legitimation may be a good reason in this context.

Frequency of Elections

Article 3 of Protocol 1 explicitly requires elections at 'reasonable' intervals, but there is little guidance as to what would be a reasonable period.

The issue was considered by the European Commission of Human Rights in *Timke v Germany*.[71] The applicant complained that the Niedersachsen Diet

---

[71] *Timke v Germany* App no 52731/95 (1995) 20 EHRR CD 133 (European Commission of Human Rights).

had altered the period between elections from four years to five. The Commission rejected the application as manifestly ill-founded – the period of five years fell within the bounds of 'reasonable' intervals. The Commission elaborated that the notion of reasonable interval had to be understood with respect to the underlying purpose of elections. Legislatures must reflect prevailing public opinion and have a period of time to implement a legislative programme – this required some time. On the other hand, the interval must not be so long as to result in a petrified parliament that no longer represented the will of the people. The five-year period was reasonable in this context. This does not give much guidance on the upper and lower limits of reasonableness, though it is clear from the Greek case that simply abolishing parliament or refusing to constitute a new one indefinitely will breach Protocol 1.

CLARITY OF ELECTORAL LEGISLATION

The legislation regarding elections should be reasonably clear, which does not mean that it needs to predict every eventuality. The legislation sometimes needs to be clarified through judicial interpretation. The Court may have given too much leeway to Russia in *Zhermal*, where the legislation for the election of the regional governor was significantly ambiguous. One reading of the legislation for the election was that it required a majoritarian system over two ballots unless someone obtained an absolute majority on the first ballot; the alternative reading was that the legislation provided for a simple plurality majority on the first ballot and only required a second ballot if two candidates had the exact number of votes. The Russian courts ultimately decided in favour of the second interpretation. The Court concluded that the imprecision in the legislation did not actually constitute any sort of pressure on the applicant as an elector, even though it would have been preferable had the imprecision been avoided, and rejected the application as manifestly ill-founded.[72] Given the significant ambiguity about a central part of the electoral system, this does seem an overly deferential approach.

THE TIMING OF AMENDMENTS TO ELECTORAL LAWS

The regulation of elections requires legislation and unsurprisingly states frequently review the content of their electoral legislation. Regular review of important legislation is no doubt desirable, and some states seem to

---

[72] *Zhermal v Russia* App no 60983/00 (28 February 2008).

248 Regulation of Elections

experiment relatively frequently with different electoral systems. The timing and frequency of such amendments, though, may come under scrutiny. Excessive tinkering may end up confusing the electorate or give rise to founded or unfounded suspicions that the government is seeking to fix an election.[73] The risk is not just that the government might be manipulating the electoral process, but that it might be perceived as doing so which risks undermining faith in the legitimacy of the electoral process. For this reason the Venice Commission recommends against frequent changes to the essentials of electoral systems (the choice of electoral system itself, membership of electoral commissions and rules on constituencies) or changes in the twelve months before an election.[74] The Venice Commission notes that one possibility might be a rule providing that any changes to these electoral elements would not affect the next election (at least if it is due within twelve months) but only the ones after that.[75] The European Court of Human Rights has attached some weight to these prescriptions.

In the *Georgian Labour Party v Georgia* case, the Court expressly mentioned the timing issue and affirmed the value of stability in the essentials of the electoral law as recommended by the Venice Commission.[76] In that case, though, there were exceptional circumstances which justified the decision to change the voter registration system radically shortly before an election. The November 2003 election had been annulled in the wake of the Rose Revolution, partly because of concerns, including international concerns, about a wholly inadequate electoral register. New elections were called for March 2004, and the Central Electoral Commission took radical action to compose a new register requiring voters to actively register to vote. The new system was not without flaws but represented a significant effort to improve upon the previous one in a very short space of time. Despite the change in the process a month before the election, the Court concluded this was justified in the unusual circumstances.[77]

The Venice Commission Code of Good Practice guidance on this timing issue was central to the case of *Ekoglasnost v Bulgaria*.[78] The applicant party was a small one, but one which had managed to elect some representatives

---

[73] European Commission for Democracy through Law (Venice Commission), *Code of Good Practice in Electoral Matters (Guidelines and Explanatory Report)* (Council of Europe 2002), para 63.

[74] *Code of Good Practice in Electoral Matters (Guidelines and Explanatory Report)*, para 65.

[75] *Code of Good Practice in Electoral Matters (Guidelines and Explanatory Report)*, para 66.

[76] *Georgian Labour Party v Georgia* App no 9103/04 (2008) 48 EHRR 14, para 88.

[77] *Georgian Labour Party v Georgia*, para 89.

[78] *Ekoglasnost v Bulgaria* App no 30386/05 (6 November 2012).

The Timing of Amendments to Electoral Laws

from time to time; in 2001 elections it had received less than 0.75 per cent of the vote and sent no representatives to Parliament. The applicant party objected to three new conditions imposed in April 2005 on parties wishing to contest elections – with the next elections due in June 2005. The legislature had adopted a new electoral law partly because of concern about excessive numbers of small political parties contesting elections. The applicant objected to the requirement that it had to present its accounts for the previous three years, lodge a deposit equivalent to approximately 10,000 euros and present a petition with 5,000 signatures of people professing an intention to vote for the party.

The European Court of Human Rights indicated that, in themselves, each of these rules was perfectly clear and compatible with P1–3.[79] They were compatible with previous case law and served the legitimate aims of ensuring only viable and sufficiently representative parties participated in elections and of ensuring the transparency of finances.[80] The necessity of these measures and in particular their timing was another matter. Regarding the rule on the accounts, the Court noted that this was a development of an earlier rule; the applicant party had ignored the earlier rule because the only sanction was a denial of state funding to which it would not be entitled anyway. The Court did not regard this as a good reason to be allowed to avoid the new rule given the 'particular importance' attached to the need for transparency in party finances; furthermore, the new rule had been introduced in Parliament in 2003 and the applicant party could have anticipated its adoption.[81]

Regarding the deposit and the signature requirement, the situation was different. These requirements were only introduced into the legislative proposal in February 2005 and were the subject of much debate; given the measures were only approved in April, this effectively gave the applicant party one month to comply with the new conditions.[82] The Court reviewed the Venice Commission principles and its own earlier comments in the *Georgian Labour Party* case and *Tănase*. The Court noted that the list of the essential elements of an electoral system in the Code of Good Practice was not intended to be exhaustive and concluded that conditions for the participation of political parties in elections must also be treated as part of the essentials.[83] While, as the Court noted, some small political parties had been able to

---

[79] *Ekoglasnost v Bulgaria*, paras 62–63.
[80] *Ekoglasnost v Bulgaria*, para 64.
[81] *Ekoglasnost v Bulgaria*, paras 65–66.
[82] *Ekoglasnost v Bulgaria*, para 67.
[83] *Ekoglasnost v Bulgaria*, para 69.

comply with the conditions, and these had been introduced to deal with a serious problem, there was no good reason why the Bulgarian Parliament could not have acted earlier, more than twelve months before the 2005 elections, and so the Court found a violation of P1–3.[84]

This approach makes good use of the Venice Commission's Code of Good Practice in order to flesh out the requirements of the Protocol 1.[85] The approach also has the advantage from the Court's point of view that it focuses on process rather than substance – the state was allowed to introduce different reforms but had to do so using a process that would protect it from suspicions of tampering with the electoral system to favour certain parties. The approach should encourage good governance in electoral reform.

ELECTORAL COMMISSIONS

Increasingly states trust different aspects of the electoral process to independent commissions – these might deal with matters like constituency drawing, the conduct of the vote, issues around financing of parties or political advertising, or electoral disputes.

In the *Georgian Labour Party v Georgia* case, the Court commented at length on the importance of an independent electoral commission.[86] The applicant political party had representatives on the Central Electoral Commission and complained about the dominant role played by members of the CEC appointed by the president or his party, as well as alleging improper conduct. The Georgian CEC had fifteen members; the president appointed five plus the chairperson, while his political party also had a nominee, so a total of seven members were appointed by the president or his party. The Court stressed the importance of a neutral civil service and underlined that it was 'particularly important for an agency in charge of electoral administration to function in a transparent manner and to maintain impartiality and independence from political manipulation'.[87] While acknowledging the diversity of practices across Europe, the Court indicated that this was a high percentage of positions to be nominated in effect by one political party, and especially

---

[84] *Ekoglasnost v Bulgaria*, paras 71–72.
[85] See also on the timing of changes to the laws on political parties in *Republican Party of Russia v Russia* App no 12976/07 (2015) 61 EHRR 20, para 116.
[86] *Georgian Labour Party v Georgia* App no 9103/04 (2008) 48 EHRR 14.
[87] *Georgian Labour Party v Georgia*, para 101.

Electoral Commissions

when they outnumbered other nominees of political parties; the Court was unconvinced that any declaration of impartiality by the office-holders was a sufficient guarantee of neutrality.[88] However the Court concluded that, while this might create the potential for fraud, that was insufficient – the applicant had failed to show any actual fraud or harm to their P1–3 rights. Two judges, Mularoni and Popovič, dissented on this point – they thought there was sufficient evidence of arbitrariness in the actions of the CEC to find a violation in relation to the composition.

The Court's finding of no violation after the strong criticism of the independence of the CEC comes as something of a surprise. It is understandable that the Court might be more interested in substance than form, but formal guarantees of neutrality seem important in this area (indeed, the Court itself makes this clear!). The P1–3 rights are not phrased in the same manner as the article 6 right to a fair trial, but certainly in its article 6 case law the Court would not hesitate to find a violation solely on the basis that a court was not independent. Insisting on actual evidence of harm might indeed simply encourage members of a commission to find some subterfuge. The Court would have done better to insist that electoral commissions regulating important matters must be independent. The Court's finding of no violation on this ground (and for this reason) is all the stranger because it promptly went on to find a violation due to the seemingly arbitrary actions of the CEC. This concerned the actual conduct of the election and the voting process.

While the Court did not find a violation due to the composition of the Electoral Commission in the *Georgian Labour Party case*, it has been prepared to do so in another case. In *Grosaru*, the case concerning the unclear Romanian legislation on the allocation of seats to representatives of national minorities, the Court took issue with the composition of the Central Electoral Office because of the preponderance of political members. Given that the Electoral Office in this case was acting as an avenue of complaint, the Court found that the composition with a large number of political members did not give sufficient guarantees of independence.[89] The case involved not necessarily a preponderance for the governing party but a preponderance of political members as opposed to independent members. In this sense the composition may not have been as problematic as in the *Georgian Labour Party case*, but the fact the commission was hearing a complaint seems to have triggered more concern about its independence.

---

[88] *Georgian Labour Party v Georgia*, paras 105–107.
[89] *Grosaru v Romania*, para 54.

INTEGRITY OF THE ELECTORAL PROCESS

The Court has been faced with several cases having as their focus the actual conduct of an election including the voting and counting processes. In these, the Court has stressed the need to avoid any appearance of arbitrariness. The earliest cases saw the Commission and Court briefly satisfy themselves that there had been no arbitrariness in the domestic review of complaints about the voting process.[90] Since the first decade of this century, the Court has had to engage more deeply with allegations concerning the integrity of the electoral process. In these the Court has stressed that the electoral authorities must 'function in a transparent manner' and 'maintain impartiality and independence from political manipulation'.[91]

One of the first of these cases was the *Georgian Labour Party v Georgia* case in which the Court considered several complaints about the conduct of the 2004 election. Several of these (about the electoral register and the role of the electoral commission) have been considered elsewhere; in relation to those, the Court found no violation. On a third argument, though, the Court did find a violation. This concerned the decision of the Central Electoral Commission to annul the results in two districts and the failure of the authorities to arrange elections in those districts. The government argued that there were problems in the districts, and the importance of summoning a new parliament required such measures. The Court was very critical of the government's position. It noted that the Central Electoral Commission's decision smacked of arbitrariness given there were no hearings or investigations and it was decided hurriedly; furthermore, there was limited reasoning and in particular no explanation as to why irregularities in other districts did not attract this sanction.[92] The effective disenfranchisement of 60,000 Ajaran voters in the two districts was a drastic step, and the Court was critical that the government had not invoked article 15 at the time or provided any evidence of the disturbances allegedly taking place in the districts.[93] On this ground, therefore, the Court found a violation of P1–3.

This emphasis on the need to avoid arbitrariness is also manifest in *Kovach v Ukraine*. Here the applicant complained that the entire vote in four electoral districts had been invalidated because of allegations of fraudulent voting.

---

[90] *IZ v Greece* App no 18997/91 (European Commission of Human Rights, 28 February 1994); *Babenko v Ukraine* App no 43476/98 (4 May 1999).

[91] *Georgian Labour Party v Georgia*, para 101.

[92] *Georgian Labour Party v Georgia*, para 130.

[93] *Georgian Labour Party v Georgia*, paras 131, 133.

The difference in vote between the two leading candidates was very slim, and this decision to invalidate the results in the districts decided the election against the applicant.

The Court noted that the case did not concern eligibility conditions but rather the domestic review of electoral processes; while this was subject to a broad margin of appreciation, the European Court of Human Rights could still review such decisions.[94] The Court expressed its doubts about a policy of invalidating all the votes at a polling station because of alleged fraud if this was done irrespective of the extent of the alleged fraud; it went so far as to say it doubted whether such a policy could have a legitimate aim.[95] However, the Court decided the case on proportionality grounds and specifically found that the decision to annul the vote in four districts (and thus deciding the election) was arbitrary. The national legislation regulating the electoral commission's powers to do this was ambiguous, specifying this step could be taken if certain conditions were met or in 'other circumstances'; in making the decision the commission had not considered the ambiguities of the language, the credibility of the claims of fraud or whether any fraud had made it impossible to ascertain the will of the voters.[96]

Significant numbers of cases involving flawed electoral processes have come from Azerbaijan. In the 2010 case of *Kerimova v Azerbaijan*, the applicant complained that election results in a constituency she was contesting as part of the 2005 legislative elections had been invalidated even though the fraudulent behaviour had apparently been aimed to help her opponents and had not succeeded in registering enough votes to displace her lead. Nevertheless, the results in her constituency were annulled. The Court found considerable evidence of arbitrary behaviour: it was clear the applicant had won the election; any fraudulent behaviour had been intended to help her opponents; the electoral commission decision to invalidate the results was essentially unsubstantiated; the electoral commission failed to consider the possibility of a recount and ignored electoral law provisions which seemed to protect the applicant's position; and the courts failed to engage in any detailed review of the electoral commission's decision.[97] The Court used strong language to criticise the authorities: the electoral commission's decision was 'alarming' and 'troubling', and showed a 'lack of concern for integrity of the electoral process'.[98]

---

[94] *Kovach v Ukraine* App no 39424/02 (7 February 2008), para 55.
[95] *Kovach v Ukraine*, para 52.
[96] *Kovach v Ukraine*, para 60.
[97] *Kerimova v Azerbaijan* App no 20799/06 (30 September 2010), paras 47–53.
[98] *Kerimova v Azerbaijan*, paras 49, 51, 53.

254   *Regulation of Elections*

As part of the electoral process required by P1–3, there must be an effective domestic system to consider complaints and appeals on electoral matters. Without such a system the P1–3 rights would be merely illusory.[99] The European Court of Human Rights cannot constitute itself an election court of course,[100] but another Azerbaijani case, *Namat Aliyev*, indicates that it will verify that any domestic process ensures reasonable steps are taken to investigate irregularities. In that case the applicant alleged extensive and serious electoral wrongdoing in the 2005 legislative elections, and backed up the claims with affidavits, audio tapes and other evidence. The Court found that the Constituency Electoral Commission had not effectively considered the allegations – they had, for instance, relied on written explanations from electoral officials who were the subject of some of the allegations.[101] The Central Electoral Commission had ignored the applicant's complaint, and the domestic courts had relied on purely formalistic reasoning in rejecting his appeals.[102] Yet again the Court was highly critical of the Azerbaijani processes – there was an apparent 'lack of any genuine concern for the protection' of the applicant's rights.[103]

Subsequently, in a number of cases, Azerbaijan acknowledged that there had been violations of P1–3 due to the same sort of problems as in *Aliyev*, and the Court agreed to strike out those claims; it did, however, continue to examine complaints which raised different if related issues.[104] In *Hajili*, for instance, the Court was faced with a *Kerimova*-type situation where the votes in the applicant's constituency (again in the 2005 legislative elections) were invalidated by a decision of the Central Electoral Commission that was unsubstantiated and that ignored certain possible safeguards.

The 2005 legislative elections in Azerbaijan were again the subject of criticism in *Karimov*. In this case the applicant had been a candidate in a constituency with more than thirty polling stations. He lost to a candidate who derived significant and disproportionate electoral support in just three stations – two established on military grounds and one in a prison. The applicant complained of multiple violations, including that the polling stations were established on military grounds in breach of domestic law, that the polling

---

[99] *Namat Aliyev v Azerbaijan* App no 18705/06 (8 April 2010), para 81; *Davydov and Others v Russia* App no 75947/11 (2018) 67 EHRR 25, para 274.

[100] Unless the circumstances of the case make this unavoidable: *Hajili v Azerbaijan* App no 6984/06 (10 January 2012), para 49.

[101] *Namat Aliyev v Azerbaijan*, para 83.

[102] *Namat Aliyev v Azerbaijan*, paras 84–85.

[103] *Namat Aliyev v Azerbaijan*, para 90.

[104] *Hajili v Azerbaijan* App no 6984/06 (10 January 2012).

Integrity of the Electoral Process

station electoral commissions were dominated by military officers and that support in those stations for the winning candidate was coerced.

The European Court of Human Rights noted that special military polling stations created a risk that voting might not be uncoerced; it derived support for this from the Venice Commission's Code of Good Practices as well as OSCE/ODIHR observations on the 2005 elections and its own case law on the Azerbaijani elections.[105] The Court grounded its assessment in the principle of the rule of law – even though the legality principle was not explicitly mentioned in P1–3, it was 'inherent' in every right.[106] In this case, the Court explained that the establishment of military polling stations was in breach of domestic legislation. The domestic legislation only permitted this step if three conditions were met – the unit was located away from populated areas, it would take more than an hour to reach a polling station using public transport and the military unit had more than fifty personnel. In this case only the last condition was fulfilled; there were ordinary polling stations within a short walk of the military units.[107] The Court was critical also that this was evidently part of an overall policy, as seen in the OSCE/ODIHR report; it dismissed as 'contrived' the response of domestic courts rejecting the applicant's complaints.[108] Having reached the conclusion it did on legality grounds, the Court did not address the other criticisms made by the applicant.

These cases from Azerbaijan show there were systematic problems with the Azerbaijani elections of 2005. In them the Court took seriously the position of other European bodies – notably the Venice Commission and the OSCE/ODIHR. Still, however, the Court sometimes does not go as far as it might. In *Karimov*, the reliance on the legality point meant that some of the other extraordinarily serious allegations of the applicant were not fully considered. It is understandable the Court would choose such a strategy, but concerning that, allegations about excessive military involvement in the 2005 election were only partially addressed.

The flaws in the 2005 Azerbaijani elections were apparently not remedied by the time of the 2010 elections. In 2015, in the case of *Gahramanli*, the Court again found a violation of P1–3 because of a failure on the part of electoral commissions and the courts to thoroughly consider allegations of voting irregularity; the Court also criticised the Constitutional Court for certifying the election results even though there were appeals going to the

---

[105] *Karimov v Azerbaijan* App no 12535/06 (25 September 2014), paras 39–40.
[106] *Karimov v Azerbaijan*, para 42.
[107] *Karimov v Azerbaijan*, paras 45–46.
[108] *Karimov v Azerbaijan*, para 49.

256   *Regulation of Elections*

Supreme Court about them. Much of the criticism was reminiscent of that in the earlier Azerbaijani cases. The Court also noted the criticisms made by Council of Europe bodies of the composition of electoral commissions in Azerbaijan. These, in practice, were dominated by nominees of the majority party. The Court indicated it was desirable the authorities should reform this structure, though it did not find a violation simply based on the structure of the commissions.[109]

The Court has also expressed concerns about the integrity of the electoral process in cases from Russia. In the case of *Yabloko Russian United Democratic Party and Others v Russia*, the applicant party had been excluded from participating in the Karelian Legislative Assembly. The Karellian Supreme Court had cancelled the party's registration because it had submitted an invalid version of its charter and it had a system of membership based on two tiers where only a small number of 'registered' members were involved in selecting candidates.[110] The European Court of Human Rights found that the issue about party membership was not clearly provided for in national legislation.[111] It commented on the role of political parties and noted that in principle legislation could provide rules on party organisation. The Court drew attention to the Venice Commission guidance in the area and the principles of party autonomy and principle of internal (party) democracy, principles which can be in tension.[112] The Court also found the reasoning of the Supreme Court about an invalid charter being submitted to be formalistic and disproportionate. The relevant rules were similar to earlier versions of the charter and no member of the party itself had made any complaint.[113]

The Russian elections of December 2011 came under scrutiny in *Davydov and others*.[114] The applicants were voters, candidates, electoral commission members and observers, who highlighted numerous flaws with elections to the St Petersburg Legislative Assembly and Federal Duma. In particular they alleged that there were discrepancies between vote tallies at different levels, that votes for the governing party were increased in this way and through recounts, and that they were denied any effective review of their complaints domestically.

---

[109] *Gahramanli and Others v Azerbaijan* App no 36503/11 (8 October 2015), para 79. See also *Shukurova v Azerbaijan* App no 37614/11 (27 October 2016).

[110] *Yabloko Russian United Democratic Party and Others v Russia* App no 18860/07 (8 November 2016), para 76.

[111] *Yabloko Russian United Democratic Party and Others v Russia*, para 76.

[112] *Yabloko Russian United Democratic Party and Others v Russia*, para 79.

[113] *Yabloko Russian United Democratic Party and Others v Russia*, para 80.

[114] *Davydov and Others v Russia*, App no 75947/11 (2018) 67 EHRR 25.

The European Court of Human Rights stressed that its role in such cases was subsidiary – to ensure there was a procedurally adequate domestic examination of the complaints and that the findings of such a domestic examination were not 'arbitrary or manifestly unreasonable'.[115] The Court agreed that the applicants had raised an arguable claim of serious electoral problems. There had been recounts in almost half of the precincts where the applicants had made complaints; such a high incidence of recounts was itself indicative of a 'serious dysfunction' 'capable of throwing serious doubt on the fairness of the entire process'.[116] Inadequate reasons were provided for the ordering of recounts.[117] Furthermore, opposition party observers were frequently excluded from the recount process, and in many cases precinct electoral commission members were not told that the results in their precincts were being cancelled.[118] The recounts were carried out with remarkable rapidity: in one case, more than 6,000 votes were recounted in 45 minutes.[119] The recounts changed a significant number of votes (of the precincts for which there were figures, more than one-fifth), and these generally favoured the governing party.[120] Unsurprisingly the election had been criticised by external independent observers.[121] On this basis, the Court did not find a violation but did hold the claimants had raised an arguable claim which called for an effective domestic examination.[122]

The applicants had pursued multiple avenues of complaint at domestic level, including appealing to electoral commissions, the prosecutors, the ordinary courts and the Constitutional Court. The electoral commissions did not consider the complaints on their merits but forwarded the complaints to the prosecutor's offices.[123] The prosecutors did not take any effective steps to investigate the complaints.[124] Courts had refused to consider complaints raised by individuals, on jurisdictional grounds.[125] Such cases as were considered were unsuccessful, as the courts focused on trivial procedural issues about the evidence presented by the applicants; when witnesses were called, they offered

---

[115] *Davydov and Others v Russia*, para 288.
[116] *Davydov and Others v Russia*, para 299.
[117] *Davydov and Others v Russia*, para 301.
[118] *Davydov and Others v Russia*, paras 303–304.
[119] *Davydov and Others v Russia*, para 306.
[120] *Davydov and Others v Russia*, para 307.
[121] *Davydov and Others v Russia*, para 309.
[122] *Davydov and Others v Russia*, para 311.
[123] *Davydov and Others v Russia*, para 315.
[124] *Davydov and Others v Russia*, para 318.
[125] *Davydov and Others v Russia*, para 324.

testimony supporting the applicants.[126] This failure to provide an effective investigation violated P1–3.

The Court's thorough examination of this case involving Russia (the case is more than 100 pages long) and its frequently unflinching criticism are welcome. The insistence on a strong procedural guarantee makes strategic sense from the viewpoint of the European Court of Human Rights. It would put the Court in a difficult position if it were to say that the elections themselves were unfair; at the same time, given the serious flaws in the election exposed by the applicants and indeed the domestic review process, it is somewhat disappointing the Court has adopted a self-abnegating stance on the issue of substance. And it is disturbing that the fairness of Russian elections would appear to have deteriorated since the 1999 elections considered in the *Russian Conservative Party of Entrepreneurs* case (discussed in Chapter 4).

CAMPAIGN AND PARTY FINANCE

Money is crucial to the operation of modern democratic politics. Political parties engage in multiple activities from developing membership to funding electoral campaigns to publicising their views and developing links with other organisations at home and abroad. The money to pay for this may come either from the party members' own resources, donations by individuals and other bodies, or state-funded contributions, including facilities like guaranteed free airtime, or some combination thereof. This is all inevitable but also raises important challenges. A key one here is the threat to political equality, if those with deep pockets are allowed unrestricted possibilities to fund political activity. The wealth required for political activity might be such that only the very rich can afford to participate. There is also the risk of corruption on very different scales. There is a risk that the costs of politics and particularly elections might spiral. Given the fundamental importance of funding political activity, but also ensuring these challenges and threats are addressed, states adopt different measures from insisting on transparency, subjecting political parties' finances to scrutiny, regulating donations to political parties, through to funding of political party activities (see also Chapter 4). There is an important point of balance here as well. Having no restrictions or requirements on the role of money in politics risks the inequality that stems from private wealth. At the same time there is also a risk with excessive state control

---

[126] *Davydov and Others v Russia*, paras 328–331.

Campaign and Party Finance

and funding that it subordinates freedom of political parties and politicians to the state.

The European Court of Human Rights has consistently recognised that states have a legitimate aim in requiring political parties and candidates to make disclosures about property, earnings and income. This is permitted to ensure the overall fairness of the electoral system and to enable voters to make informed choices.[127] According to the Court, 'it is essential that parliamentary candidates are shown to be persons of integrity and truthfulness. By obliging them to put themselves forward publicly, in a full and frank manner, the electorate can assess the candidate's personal qualifications and ability to best represent its interests in parliament.'[128] As well as employment and party political membership, states may require candidates to disclose information about their property, as a 'candidate's fortune' is 'a factor not unimportant for forming an opinion about the candidate'.[129]

The Court recognises that the state has a legitimate interest in scrutinising the accounts of political parties. This, however, must be done in a way that respects the Convention rights. These points were emphasised by the Court in *Cumhuriyet Halk Partisi v Turkey*.[130] The finances of the applicant party had been scrutinised by the Turkish Constitutional Court which found them lacking in certain respects. Notably the Constitutional Court criticised some of the accounts as not demonstrating that the activities funded were for the proper purposes of a political party or were inadequately evidenced.[131] The applicant party had some of its state funding reduced and subsequently also paid money to the state in respect of the criticised finances. The sums involved were more than a million euro, and this seriously affected the party's activities and organisation.

The European Court of Human Rights at the outset noted that scrutiny of political parties' finances was appropriate in that it supported 'accountability and transparency' and thus supported 'public confidence in the political process'.[132] In this case, though, the sanctions had a serious impact on the party and interfered with its article 11 rights. This raised the question of justification, which the Court examined in terms of the legality principle. Here the Court recognised the risk that state scrutiny of party finances might

---

[127] *Russian Conservative Party of Entrepreneurs v Russia* App nos 55066/oo and 55638/oo (2007) 46 EHRR 39, para 62.

[128] *Melnychenko v Ukraine* App no 17707/02 (2004) 42 EHRR 39, para 57.

[129] *Sarukhanyan v Armenia* App no 38978/03 (27 May 2008), para 42.

[130] *Cumhuriyet Halk Partisi v Turkey* App no 19920/13 (26 April 2016).

[131] *Cumhuriyet Halk Partisi v Turkey* App no 19920/13, para 12.

[132] *Cumhuriyet Halk Partisi v Turkey* App no 19920/13, para 69.

be used as a 'political tool to exercise control over political parties', and therefore it required the legal measures to demonstrate a high degree of foreseeability.[133] The Court found that there were serious problems about the foreseeability of the effects of the legislation; notably it was not clear what would count as legitimate expenditure and what would be illegitimate; the Constitutional Court itself had been inconsistent in how it treated different expenses; and it was unclear which sanctions would apply to what type of infringements.[134] Having found a breach of the legality principle, the Court did not need to consider the legitimate aim or proportionality requirements.

Where the state adopts rules on state funding for parties and provision of media resources such as time on television and radio, it may pay attention to the support that parties have. The Court made this clear in a case from Greece, *Antonopoulos v Greece*.[135] The applicant represented the 'Party of Human Rights' which received only 0.019 per cent of the votes in the 1999 election. Among various matters, the applicant complained that the party had not received any state financing and had received only five minutes of broadcasting time. Under Greek law, only parties with seats in the European Parliament or which obtained 1.5 per cent of votes in the election received financial support. The Greek measures on broadcasting time allocated time based on support for parties, with the smallest parties only receiving five minutes of broadcasting time.

The Court observed that states were free to organise their electoral systems, taking into account the need to ensure the stability of the political system and the credibility of the parties represented in Parliament. The principle of equality was not offended if states did not offer support to parties with very limited appeal among the electorate. By favouring the more representative parties – which themselves represented diverse ideological currents – the system allowed these currents of thought to be represented and representative. In this event, the Greek system did envisage some broadcasting time even for the smallest parties.

The same principles apply in relation to the provision of public funding for political parties. In *ODP v Turkey*, the Court considered a Turkish rule which required a party to have 7 per cent of the votes in order to receive public funding. This 7 per cent figure was the highest in the Council of Europe, and so the Court had to examine it to see what effect it had on the political system. This was less than the 10 per cent threshold rule required for a party to be

---

[133] *Cumhuriyet Halk Partisi v Turkey* App no 19920/13, para 88.
[134] *Cumhuriyet Halk Partisi v Turkey* App no 19920/13, paras 90, 96, 103–104.
[135] *Antonopoulos v Greece* App no 58333/00 (29 March 2001).

represented in Parliament, and so it meant some parties not represented in Parliament received public funding. For the majority this was significant, as was the fact that the applicant party actually had significantly less than 7 per cent support in elections – less than 1 per cent, in fact.[136]

In another case, the Court considered whether the fact that certain parties had breached campaign finance laws meant that the election results should be voided as not representing the free expression of the opinion of the people. In *Partija 'Jaunie Demokrati' and Partija 'Musu Zeme' v Latvia*, the applicant parties complained that two other parties had been found to have breached campaign finance laws; these other parties had won seats, while the applicants had not. The Supreme Court had agreed there was a violation of campaign finance laws but had decided not to annul the election results, as the violations were not of such a gravity as to affect the free expression of the will of the people.

The European Court of Human Rights saw its role on this point as being to review the decisions of the domestic authorities. The Court noted that only two of the twenty-nine parties contesting the election had been found to have breached the law, and furthermore this had been discussed during the electoral campaign itself. While the breach of the campaign finance law was important, it was not possible to establish a direct causal link between excessive expenditure and voting results. The applicants had benefitted from a domestic judicial procedure which had considered all the issues, and the domestic court had not adopted an arbitrary approach. The Court held the complaint inadmissible as manifestly ill-founded.

ELECTORAL SYSTEMS AND MINORITIES

Almost by definition electoral systems disadvantage 'minorities' – those parties with the fewest votes or seats will lose out unless they can play a part in a coalition. Classic liberal democratic theory suggests this is not a problem if there are safeguards in place to protect the basic rights of everyone from majority rule and if today's electoral minority can see itself as tomorrow's majority. The possibility of alternative governments normally tempers the electoral majority when in power and succours the electoral minority. These assumptions may break down when voting occurs along ethnic, linguistic or religious lines and one group is in a permanent minority status. Electoral

---

[136] *Özgürlük Ve Dayanişma Partisi (ÖDP) v Turkey* App no 7819/03 (10 May 2012), para 45.

systems if applied in a 'neutral' manner are likely to disadvantage certain minorities in that situation.

The Convention institutions, taking into account the Council of Europe's Framework Convention on National Minorities 1995, recognise that it is legitimate for associations to form to defend the interests of minorities.[137] This means the state must not merely respect existing different identities, but also create 'appropriate conditions enabling them to express, preserve and develop this identity'.[138]

The Convention institutions recognised that electoral systems could unfairly disadvantage permanent ethnic, religious or linguistic minorities very early in the P1–3 jurisprudence. In *Lindsay v United Kingdom*, the Commission was faced with a classic situation whereby voting occurred along ethnic or religious lines and one group was in a permanent minority.[139] This was the situation in Northern Ireland. The Commission accepted the legitimacy of adopting a proportional representation voting system in such a situation and even accepted the legitimacy of having a voting system in Northern Ireland that was different from the one operating in the rest of the United Kingdom.[140]

Certain voting practices have a clear potential to disadvantage minorities in the sense here. One such practice is that of electoral thresholds used in party list systems. Other Council of Europe institutions have recognised this and called for consideration of exceptions to thresholds if this would enhance minority representation.[141]

The Convention institutions have generally not required any form of positive action to ensure minority representation. The Commission early indicated that positive action might be permitted but was not required: *Magnago and Sudtiroler Volkspartei v Italy*.[142] This case was decided before important developments in minority rights, notably the adoption of the Framework Convention on National Minorities 1995. The European Court of Human Rights had occasion to revisit this issue in *Partei Die Friesen v*

---

[137] *Gorzelik v Poland* App no 44158/98 (2005) 40 EHRR 4 (Grand Chamber), para 93.

[138] *Gorzelik v Poland*, para 93.

[139] *Lindsay v United Kingdom* App no 8364/78 (1979) 15 DR 247 (European Commission of Human Rights).

[140] While representation is important, it is not sufficient. Irish Nationalists won seats in the Old Northern Irish Parliament between 1921 and 1972 but were in a position of being a permanent minority and frequently adopted an abstentionist policy.

[141] European Commission for Democracy through Law (Venice Commission), *Report on Electoral Rules and Affirmative Action for National Minorities' Participation in Decision-making Process in European Countries* (Strasbourg: Council of Europe Pub., 2005), para 68.

[142] *Magnago and Sudtiroler Volkspartei v Italy* App no 25035/94 (European Commission of Human Rights, 15 April 1996).

Germany.[143] This case concerned the application of a 5 per cent threshold rule in Lower Saxony. The applicant party, claiming to represent the Friesen minority, secured 0.3 per cent of the vote. It alleged that the threshold rule had a chilling effect on potential voters and noted that there were exemptions from thresholds for minorities at the federal level and in some other *Lander.*

The Court recognised the developments in terms of minority rights referring to the work of the Advisory Committee on the Framework Convention and the Venice Commission; however, while these bodies had indicated that exemptions from thresholds should be considered and might be useful in furthering minority participation, this did not amount to a clear legal obligation to exempt minority parties from threshold requirements.[144] The Court rejected the comparison drawn with elections at federal level or in other *Lander*; being in different systems, the situation was not analogous.[145] The Court found there was no violation.

Where a state does have special rules to provide for the participation of national minorities in the political process, then it is also legitimate for the state to make sure that these rules are not circumvented by other groups who do not themselves meet the definition of a national minority. This was the Court's position in *Gorzelik v Poland*. The applicant had sought to register an association to protect the interests of Silesians; the Polish authorities declined to register the association on the grounds that the registration documents contained a paragraph that seemed to have the purpose of labelling the association as a national minority. This would have given the association benefits in the political process to which it was not entitled, as Poland did not recognise the Silesians as a national minority. The Grand Chamber agreed that the state's actions did not breach the Convention, particularly as the state's position was that the issue could be resolved easily by removing the problematic paragraph.[146]

Parties representing national minorities may also have particular issues with rules on party organisation or party funding. Parties representing national minorities are likely to have links with entities outside the territory of the state. State rules, however, may be based on the assumption that a political party's activities are confined to its own territory. This assumption does not necessarily hold in the case of national minorities; it is also questionable in the context

---

[143] *Partei Die Friesen v Germany* App no 65480/10 (28 January 2016).
[144] *Partei Die Friesen v Germany*, para 43.
[145] *Partei Die Friesen v Germany*, para 39.
[146] *Gorzelik v Poland* (Grand Chamber), para 105.

of European political movements. Both of these issues came up for discussion in the case of *Parti nationaliste basque v France*.

In the case, the applicant party was denied official state funding from France because it received funding from the Spanish Basque Party. The French Law on party funding provided that a party could not receive state funding if it received funding from a foreign state or legal entity, and the domestic courts concluded that foreign legal entity included foreign political parties. The European Court of Human Rights treated this as an article 11 case, rather than a P1–3 case, given that the party's electoral rights were not specifically interfered with.[147] The Court reviewed the wider Council of Europe standards and guidance from the different Council of Europe organs. This revealed considerable disparity of practice. The Venice Commission recommended bans on donations by foreign governments and enterprises, but was more open on donations by foreign political parties or parties within the European Union.[148] The Court itself acknowledged that while the necessity of a ban on receiving funding from a foreign government was easy to see, this was not so obvious in the case of a donation from a foreign political party.[149] Nevertheless, it was prepared to accept that the restriction fell within the margin of appreciation, particularly given that the sanction was relatively mild. The party was not precluded from receiving donations, only from receiving French state funding if it received donations from a foreign legal entity; it was free to seek financial support from other sources.[150]

CONCLUSION

Unsurprisingly, the case law on electoral systems and processes shows the Court at its most deferential, certainly significantly more than when it comes to individual rights, be these the electoral rights like the right to vote or run for election or the more broadly political rights of free expression and free association and assembly. Nevertheless, the picture that emerges is one where there are serious problems with the quality of democracy in several European states (most notably Azerbaijan and Russia).

The acceptance of a wide variety of electoral systems suggests that the Court is not open to arguments that certain electoral systems support more

---

[147] *Parti nationaliste basque v France* App no 71251/01 (2007) 47 EHRR 47.
[148] *Parti nationaliste basque v France*, paras 16, 29–32.
[149] *Parti nationaliste basque v France*, para 47.
[150] *Parti nationaliste basque v France*, paras 49–51.

Conclusion

deliberative models of democracy, or at least this would not be a straightforward argument.[151] Practices like simple plurality majoritarian systems, high thresholds in party list system or bonus seat mechanisms all serve to rationalise the different views that may be expressed in a legislature, but the Court accepts they are all legitimate in principle.

On matters of electoral design, there are almost no cases where the Court has found a violation. The Court itself has explained well just why it is reluctant to be exacting in such cases. The design of electoral systems can pursue different aims, and these different aims are often not even compatible, most obviously in terms of balancing the need for fair representation with the creation of coherent currents of thought and stable government. There are different ways of securing similar outcomes, e.g. stable government might be facilitated by simple plurality voting, thresholds in party list systems or bonus seats. Context may be everything – Iceland, for instance, has challenges securing representation outside the capital city due to population changes; hypothetically, the European Parliament and its practice of degressive proportionality would be a very different context from national elections. Assessments are also subject to contingency; witness the difference between the 2002 Turkish general election and the 2007 one, both considered in *Yumak and Sadak*. Or, of course, witness the degree of stability traditionally in UK political system with the Brexit-induced difficulties after the 2017 general election. In this context the choice of an electoral system is one which, in principle, each state may make 'alone'.[152]

This does not mean that questions of electoral systems and process are effectively immune from European scrutiny. When faced with questions of how the process has unfolded, the Court has been much more willing to consider evidence of arbitrariness (*Kerimova*). Here the keyword has often been process. So state authorities are welcome to adopt different rules and even to change them, but if they change them shortly before an election and so disadvantage some parties, this will call for closer scrutiny (*Ekoglasnost*). And if individuals and parties are dissatisfied with the electoral process, they must have access to effective complaints procedures (*Namat Aliyev, Davydov*). The emphasis on process in these cases is understandable. The Court will be more familiar with the notion of due process and so readier to assess the adequacy of process. Furthermore, it avoids the Court more directly criticising

---

[151] James, for instance, defends alternative vote and single transferable vote systems as more likely to encourage voters to see others as deliberative partners: Michael Rabinder James, *Deliberative Democracy and the Plural Polity* (University of Kansas Press 2004), 167–176.

[152] *Paunović and Milivojević v Serbia* App no 41683/06 (24 May 2016), para 60.

the state for the conduct of its elections: saying a state did not provide for an adequate complaints mechanism about arguably irregular practices is less damning than saying there were irregular practices.

This process-oriented approach could be used to strengthen other parts of the jurisprudence on electoral systems. The role of independent electoral commissions has been highlighted. Here the Court could be more robust in upholding standards of independence. The *Georgian Labour Party* case could have done more to enforce this principle of independence by finding the composition of the Central Electoral Commission to be a violation of the Convention. And electoral commissions could offer one solution to cases involving alleged problems with constituency boundary-drawing; when faced with allegations of political gerrymandering, the Court could insist that boundaries be drawn by an independent commission.

The Court could also develop a requirement for a more deliberative consideration and adoption of democratic rules themselves. In *Le Lievre*, for instance, the Court drew attention to the fact that the reforms to the Sark legislature were closely scrutinised both when designing the system and when under review in the domestic courts to ensure that they reflected human rights principles.

Apart from these process considerations, the Court does use some language to indicate that it may be willing to find a problem with an electoral system if it systematically excluded certain types of parties, or systematically favoured some parties. These are no more than hints. The former Commission, for instance, left open the question as to whether an electoral system that excluded certain religious or ethnic groups from representation raised a problem (*Liberal Party*), and the same might be so if a system excluded regional parties (*Yumak and Sadak*, Grand Chamber). In several cases the Convention institutions emphasised that the rules they were considering did not seem to favour any one political party (*X v Iceland, Saccomanno*). If a governing party adopted a system (or a set of rules) that systematically favoured it in an electoral contest, then that would call for very close scrutiny in Strasbourg.[153]

Where a government and ruling party has so designed an electoral system that no transfer of power is imaginable, we are in the realm no longer of the

---

[153] *Tănase v Moldova* App no 7/08 (2011) 53 EHRR 22 (Grand Chamber). Similarly in relation to article 11, see *Republican Party of Russia v Russia* App no 12976/07 (2015) 61 EHRR 20, para 118; *Christian Democratic People's Party v Moldova* App no 28793/02 (2006) 45 EHRR 13, para 71.

Conclusion

liberal democracy envisaged by the ECHR, but rather approaching a 'defective democracy',[154] 'semi-authoritarianism'[155] or 'autocratic legalism'.[156] In such a circumstance the Court should examine electoral measures favouring the government with considerable scrutiny.[157] Just as it recognises that a newly emerging democracy may be permitted to take measures that a well-established democracy would not be permitted to take, a state where political and legal constraints on a government are being eroded must be subject to more intense scrutiny. It would be important to adopt a heightened model of scrutiny given the risks that a governing party might use carefully crafted legal and other stratagems to support itself in power and a numerical majority of voters might accept it or even support it.[158] The context is critical here, as some regimes may cleverly deploy legal changes that are unproblematic elsewhere but in their own context consolidate a specific regime in power.[159]

---

[154] Jan-Werner Müller, *What Is Populism?* (Penguin UK 2017), 58.

[155] Marina Ottaway, *Democracy Challenged: The Rise of Semi-Authoritarianism* (Carnegie Endowment for International Peace 2003), 15.

[156] Kim Lane Scheppele, 'Autocratic Legalism' (2018) 85 University of Chicago Law Review 545.

[157] This may be the case with changes to the electoral system in Hungary and Russia, for instance: Helen Hardman and Brice Dickson, 'Conclusions' in Helen Hardman and Brice Dickson (eds) *Electoral Rights in Europe: Advances and Challenges* (Taylor & Francis 2017), 211.

[158] Marina Ottaway, *Democracy Challenged: The Rise of Semi-Authoritarianism*, 17.

[159] Kim Lane Scheppele, 'The Rule of Law and the Frankenstate: Why Governance Checklists Do Not Work' (2013) 26 (4) Governance 559.

Conclusion: Deliberation, Inclusion and Participation

The survey of the political and electoral rights case law of the European Court of Human Rights reflects a particular approach to the concept of democracy and the Court's vision of how to protect it. Central to the Court's vision is the ideal of a liberal representative democracy with the emphasis placed on protecting the key liberal rights of free expression, assembly and association.

Some of the cases lend support for more substantive visions of democracy. In so far as these seek to restrict the rights of those who would use violence or undermine the principles of pluralism, tolerance and broad-mindedness that are the values of European democracy, the Court is right in principle to accept such restrictions. However, this calls for very careful scrutiny of the restrictions in question to ensure they do not smuggle in excessively substantive conceptions of the social order. Some of the older free expression cases involving public morals are troubling in this regard, as is the 2003 *Refah Paritisi* case.

The Court recognises the importance of the more explicitly electoral rights in P1–3, but also indicates caution – usually – when interpreting these rights. It says regularly that the P1–3 rights are not to be applied in the same way as the qualified rights in articles 8–11. It also says that more caution is required in cases concerning the passive right to run for elections as compared to cases on the active right to vote. And when it comes to questions of electoral design, it becomes more cautious again. It is rare indeed to find a judgment where the Court has found a state in breach of the Convention because of the choices it has made in designing an electoral system.

The support for liberal representative democracy does raise questions about whether the Court's approach falls into the trap of replicating democratic flaws in this model of democracy. Representative democracy might be seen as a very limited form of democracy in which most persons simply choose every few years between different groups of leaders. In this sense, most people do not

Conclusion: Deliberation, Inclusion and Participation 269

experience any real exercise of self-government. Furthermore, this model of representative democracy may be a form of aggregative democracy or preference-counting democracy where individuals simply vote their preferences without having the possibility to deliberate on them and exchange views and reasons about different courses of action. Liberal representative democracy also risks marginalising different groups in some contexts. Ethnic, linguistic and religious minorities may not be able to influence the political system in a representative system that after all favours majority rule. In many political systems women are systematically underrepresented, though some European states have made significant strides in this area. The focus on elections for the legislature excludes consideration of other forms of participation and consultation; this is extremely problematic for members of certain groups who can only participate through participation and consultation, such as children and adolescents.

And then there is the influence of money. Underrepresented groups in the political system may include the poor, unemployed and economically disadvantaged. Private wealth has the possibility to shape public decision-making through political donations and advertising as well as social media campaigns and support for different pressure groups. Structural problems lurk here – economic inequality always has the potential to skew political debate; persons struggling to make do will lack resources and time to influence politics; the need for economic prosperity will usually mean that politicians give particular heed to the interests of business.

These are classical concerns with representative democracy even at the best of times. These are not, however, the best of times. In twenty-first-century Europe, we have political leaders who praise 'illiberal democracy', governments which seek to use referendums to enhance executive power, a British government willing to suspend parliament for weeks during a major political debate, and a Russian government seemingly indifferent even to fundamental principles of international law. The European Union's responses to the financial crisis, sovereign debt crisis and migration crisis cast doubt on its ability to respond in ways that are fair, democratic, even humane. And this is in a wider economic context where the economic and political success of democratic Western European states for a few decades in the mid-to-late twentieth century seem very far away and have been overtaken by decades of neoliberalism, the financial crisis and austerity.[1]

---

[1] Berman notes the importance of those decades of prosperity when liberal democratic states tamed the markets: Sheri Berman, *Democracy and Dictatorship in Europe: From the Ancien Régime to the Present Day* (Oxford University Press 2019), 400–403. Similarly, see Roger

Conclusion: Deliberation, Inclusion and Participation

These democratic challenges of the twenty-first century may well reflect the weaknesses of the type of liberal representative democracy envisioned by the Convention. The traditional model of liberal representative democracy may enable some of these problems or even worse may be conducive to them. There has to be some concern that a human rights regime devised largely in the 1940s to deal with certain threats of the mid-twentieth century is limited in how it can respond to twenty-first-century threats. The Convention was drafted with one eye on the past depredations of totalitarian fascist regimes and one eye on the emerging communist regimes behind the Iron Curtain. In numerous ways the threats to human rights, including political rights, in the twenty-first century are significantly different from those facing the Convention drafters.

In part this reflects important changes such as the development of supra-national institutions, the development of globalisation and the increased realisation that non-state actors are vitally important in relation to the protection and promotion of human rights. It also reflects important technological changes such as the rise of the internet and digital media. There is also a concern articulated by Scheppele, that in some ways twenty-first century would-be autocrats have become more subtle and legally astute in how they seize power, or rather how once they win power, they consolidate their position to make it difficult for electoral and civil society opponents to succeed.[2]

Nevertheless, as we know, the Court interprets the Convention in an evolving manner so as to make it an effective instrument for the protection of rights. The concern about the subtle erosion of the ability of electoral opposition and civil society to oppose a government can be addressed if the Court is willing to consider the wider context in which certain restrictive measures are adopted. This fits in well with the Court's own rhetoric and sometimes its practice. It is a sensitive matter: if the Court says that there are some practices which would be fine in the Netherlands or the UK but not Hungary or Poland due to the context, then there are multiple risks. Nevertheless, the Court has indicated it will sometimes take this into account, where, say, a dominant political party adopts measures which disproportionately affect the opposition (*Tănase v Moldova*). Similarly, the Court has somewhat exceptionally invoked article 18 of the Convention as an independent ground of

---

Eatwell and Matthew Goodwin, *National Populism: The Revolt against Liberal Democracy* (Penguin 2018), chapter 5.

[2] Kim Lane Scheppele, 'Autocratic Legalism' (2018) 85 University of Chicago Law Review 545.

Conclusion: Deliberation, Inclusion and Participation 271

criticism where a state has limited rights for purposes not permitted under the Convention (*Navalnyy v Russia*).

Such jurisprudential responses would address some of the concerns that twenty-first-century autocrats are simply more clever than their twentieth-century predecessors. However, it is also necessary to consider whether the model of liberal representative democracy offered by the Convention and the Court can itself be supplemented. The Convention does offer some, albeit limited, resources to address these concerns about the inadequacy of liberal representative democracy and to develop practices that are more deliberative, inclusive and participatory.

A commitment to the importance of democratic deliberation (and to a degree consultation and participation) is seen in some of the case law. The general principles of the Convention reflect very well a deliberative democratic model whereby democratic bodies have the responsibility to legislate for human rights but have to take the content of these rights seriously. The doctrine of the margin of appreciation and the possibility in respect of most rights for there to be proportionate restrictions indicates that the Convention does not presuppose a natural rights model where the content of rights are simply pre-given. Rather, domestic authorities, and in particular the democratically legitimated domestic authorities, have the possibility to shape the content of rights. At the same time this is not an unlimited discretion but one constrained by a need to implement the rights taking account the limits of legitimacy, lawfulness and proportionality. In this sense the discretion of domestic democratic authorities is limited by the rights that are prescribed by the international legal order to which the state has signed up. While this operates at a level of principle, in some instances the Court reviews this closely in terms of how it plays out institutionally in domestic settings.

So there is some scope in the article 10, article 11 and P1–3 case law to argue for a more deliberative and participatory model of democracy. Indeed there is an argument that article 8 may also offer support for this. Article 8's right to respect for private and family life has been interpreted to include respect for health, working relationships and certain environmental concerns. In at least some of the article 8 case law concerning environmental matters the Court has looked at the process by which the state has regulated article 8 rights to see if there has been consultation and thorough examination.[3]

In several cases the Court has indicated that it will regard state decisions as more likely to comply with the Convention where there has been democratic

---

[3] Rory O'Connell, 'Towards a Stronger Conception of Democracy in the Strasbourg Convention' (2006) European Human Rights Law Review 281–293.

272   *Conclusion: Deliberation, Inclusion and Participation*

domestic consideration of the measure. Sometimes, this has been a modest requirement of democratic consideration.[4] The Court's respect for domestic democratic consideration is likely to be most pronounced when the relevant domestic institutions have carefully considered the human rights issues through political and expert processes, including careful judicial consideration of the rights involved.[5] Where there has been no dedicated consideration of a measure by the domestic institutions, this has counted against the state. This was the case in the original *Hirst* judgment as the Court observed the UK Parliament had simply reinstated traditional restrictions on prisoner voting.[6] A thorough rights-based examination of the issues may mean the Court approves measures that in other contexts it would find violated the Convention. The *Animal Defenders International* judgment shows how the Court looks more favourably on domestic decisions which have been the product of sustained democratic debate and forensic analysis that explicitly considers how to balance the Convention rights.

In requiring states to demonstrate that they have carefully considered the human rights issues, pursued different consultative processes and assessed proportionality, the Court would be nudging states to adopt more rational deliberative processes; in this sense these suggestions are examples of the procedural turn in the Court's case law.[7] This is desirable in itself, but it is also a limited approach.[8] What happens, after all, if the state goes through such a process and arrives at the same conclusion? And without addressing wider issues of participation, inclusion and equality, it is no more than a call for better evidence-based decision-making.

The prisoner voting saga may offer a test case of how the Court should approach a claim that the state has engaged in a thorough consideration of a restriction on a Convention right and concluded that the restriction was justified. The Court has indicated that a blanket ban on prisoners voting is a breach of the Convention, but the UK (and apparently the Committee of

---

[4]   *Hirst v United Kingdom (No. 2)* App no 74025/01 (2006) 42 EHRR 41.

[5]   Not covered in this work, but the efforts of some European states to weaken judicial independence is also problematic.

[6]   *Sukhovetskyy v Ukraine* App no 13716/02 (2007) 44 EHRR 57.

[7]   Robert Spano, 'The Future of the European Court of Human Rights—Subsidiarity, Process-Based Review and the Rule of Law' (2018) 18 Human Rights Law Review 473; Oddný Mjöll Arnardóttir 'Organised Retreat? The Move from "Substantive" to "Procedural" Review in the ECtHR's Case Law on the Margin of Appreciation' (2015) *European Society of International Law (ESIL) 2015 Annual Conference (Oslo)*; Janneke Gerards and Eva Brems, *Procedural Review in European Fundamental Rights Cases* (Cambridge University Press 2017).

[8]   Peter Cumper and Tom Lewis, 'Blanket Bans, Subsidiarity, and the Procedural Turn of the European Court of Human Rights' (2019) 68 International & Comparative Law Quarterly 611.

Conclusion: Deliberation, Inclusion and Participation 273

Ministers) believe this requires only tokenistic administrative changes. This issue will no doubt come back to the Court. Is this a situation like *Animal Defenders International*, where the Grand Chamber (narrowly) agreed that the UK's careful assessment of free expression in the context of political advertising justified a finding of non-violation even though there was considerable precedent suggesting otherwise? There are, however, differences between the *Hirst* situation and the *Animal Defenders International* situation. In the *Hirst* case the Court found that the situation in the UK itself breached the Convention. This is not just a matter of the UK having to consider what the Convention principles mean in relation to decisions involving other states. The Court's view has been repeated in many cases from the UK, and reaffirmed by the Grand Chamber in *Scoppola*. Further, the restriction on prisoner voting goes to the very substance of the right in a way that the political advertising restriction did not. The applicant in *Animal Defenders International* had other means to engage in political advocacy through appearing on broadcasted programmes, advertising in print media, social media and so forth. Convicted prisoners in the UK system are effectively completely disenfranchised, leaving aside the possibility of temporary release on licence. A final distinction is that whereas the restriction in *Animal Defenders International* was adopted in order to support political equality, the prisoner disenfranchisement rule cuts against inclusion in the political process. For these reasons, the domestic consideration of (and support for) the restriction should not lead the Court to find the situation compatible with the Convention.

This highlights the importance of Anne Phillips's critique that deliberative democracy must not just be a plea for better deliberation but must include considerations of equality and inclusion. The Court has largely worked to promote more inclusive voting rights across Europe, addressing problems of exclusion based on race, mental disability and bankruptcy, for instance. The Court has striven to ensure universal suffrage, even if this phrase was not included in P1–3's text. There is more to be done and which can be done within the confines of the Convention. First, the Court will need to consider how to uphold its core ruling in the prisoner disenfranchisement cases, else responses like the UK's to *Hirst* will largely void that decision of meaning. This is not just a UK challenge; Russia has also shown itself reluctant to address prisoner voting rights.

Second, the Court needs to be open to considering argument about practical inclusion in the electoral process. Most of the voting rights cases to date have concerned formal exclusions. Yet people can also be excluded because of any number of indirect means, practices and structures. Persons with nomadic lifestyles, disabilities (physical and mental) and literacy

274 *Conclusion: Deliberation, Inclusion and Participation*

problems must also be offered the opportunity to participate in electoral politics. So Travellers and Roma may not have settled addresses for electoral registration purposes; the fact that they have a nomadic lifestyle may even mean they move from one constituency to another (or perhaps even across national boundaries). Persons with certain physical disabilities may have difficulty accessing polling stations or reading ballot papers. The same may be true also of those with sight impairment or who cannot read. The elderly and the sick and those in institutions may all in practice have difficulty exercising their voting rights. In such situations the Court must be willing to require exemptions to general requirements and to require reasonable adjustments to ensure that people are not excluded in practice from exercising their democratic rights.

Third, there is one important and common formal exclusion which the Court has so far not addressed. This relates to the position of non-nationals. The Court's unreflective willingness to accept nationality-based restrictions on voting rights is especially troubling on any democratic model. The Court itself has canvassed the arguments on residence-based restrictions in a very thorough and convincing manner, but the very arguments which suggest the legitimacy of residence-based restrictions also point to the illegitimacy of blanket bans on non-nationals voting. Within the context especially of the European Union, European states have made important efforts to recognise voting rights for European Union citizen non-nationals in relation to local elections and European Parliament elections. However, generally speaking, this franchise extension does not apply to national political voting processes. Clearly certain categories of non-nationals are significantly affected by the decisions of national political institutions. This applies especially to those who reside for many years in a host state and have made it the centre of their lives. There are situations where it may be appropriate to continue to exclude non-nationals or certain categories of non-nationals from voting in national political elections, but the acceptance of a blanket ban seems more unjustifiable than even in the context of prisoners. As debates about immigration policy and treatment of resident non-nationals are frequently important in national politics, the exclusion of the persons most directly affected by such policy decisions is problematic.

These issues about inclusion mainly relate to the active electoral right, the right to vote. The Court has indicated that it does not apply the same standards of proportionality in cases involving the right to vote as it applies in relations to articles 8–11. In cases involving the right to run for election and electoral process decisions, the Court has been more deferential still. The Court has developed case law that tackles arbitrariness, problems of clarity and absence

Conclusion: Deliberation, Inclusion and Participation   275

of fair procedures. However, its record on inclusion in this area is even more circumspect than in the right to vote cases. The Court's reluctance to be drawn into issues of language policy means that there is some scope for states to adopt policies that disadvantage linguistic minorities. Even here, though, the Court has indicated there are some limits. The Court has broadly indicated that states are free to adopt measures to promote minority representation and measures to support consociational arrangements. Specifically, in relation to consociationalism, the Court has striven to ensure that special measures for the main groups in society do not have the effect of excluding other minority groups on racial or ethnic grounds. This is evident in cases like *Sejdic and Finci*, albeit that the failure of Bosnia Herzegovina to implement the decision highlights problems of the efficacy of the Court system.

As regards the threat that economic inequality and private wealth can deform the public and political spheres and wield undue influence in politics, the Court has shown some awareness of the issue. The Court has highlighted that states can claim a legitimate interest in requiring political candidates to make disclosures about their personal wealth, for instance. In particular, the *Animal Defenders International* case demonstrates Grand Chamber awareness of the importance of ensuring political equality in the public sphere even if this means regulating free expression, indeed what in many ways is core political expression.

Nevertheless, the Convention itself is of limited effectiveness in the economic sphere. This might well be expected in a system designed to uphold liberal representative democracy. There is little that the Convention can say about issues of economic equality: it says very little even about social and economic rights. It protects free expression, free association, electoral rights, most tellingly perhaps property rights and some social rights like the right to education, but not – explicitly at least – the right to work, the right to health, the right to social security and the right to an adequate standard of living. In the Council of Europe, social and economic rights are more the preserve of the European Social Charter system, with rather different mechanisms of monitoring and enforcement than we are used to in the Convention system. To the extent that this means the main European human rights mechanisms do not address social and economic rights (in the main), this has some risks for democratic practice. Individuals leading insecure lives, lacking resources or leisure and concerned about threats to their livelihood and security may not be incentivised to participate in the political system. Or even more worryingly, they may become disillusioned with the liberal representative model of democracy on offer if they perceive that it has failed them.

There is some possibility for the Convention to offer indirect protection to social and economic rights. To the extent that the Convention can be interpreted to offer some protection to these rights, it should be welcome as moving somewhat towards the goal of a more inclusive and participatory democratic model. It has to be acknowledged that this is necessarily indirect and limited and unlikely to address significant questions of economic inequality that affect political equality. The Court can consider these issues of economic and political equality in other ways.

As mentioned above, the Court has made it clear that states are permitted to regulate, even restrict, political rights so as to protect political equality from the threat of economic inequality. The Court's positive obligation doctrine suggests that something more than mere permission is possible. Consider, for instance, the article 10 case law. Here, the Court has generally underlined the role of the state as the ultimate guarantor of pluralism in relation to free expression. This has considerable bite in relation to state broadcasters, where the state is directly involved as in *Manole*. Yet there are also potential implications here for privately owned and run media. Pluralism and access to diverse viewpoints suggest that private wealth should not be allowed to monopolise key fora for public communication. A deliberative model of democracy would require public decisions to be made based on the exchange of reasons between free and equal participants, in a context where participants can consider diverse opinions, sources of evidence and discourses. This exchange of reasons is endangered if the mass media which helps shape public discourse is itself controlled by a small minority who benefit either from their wealth or having privileged access to the political elite (or both). Such a concentration of control might lead to a narrowing of the range of opinions, evidence and discourses available to persons deliberating. This suggests the state may need to ensure a degree of transparency in communication fora or to adopt rules on ownership. The Court should develop its positive obligations doctrine to require states to make clear who owns different media and to ensure there is not too great a concentration of media resource in a small number of hands. This might require the Court to take a stance on just what amounts to too great a concentration, but this is a task that some constitutional courts have been willing to do.

The danger posed by excessive concentration of media in a small number of wealthy owners is not just a matter of private wealth, though; there may be unhealthy links between powerful economic and political actors. Populist or autocratic legalist regimes (and not just them) may seek to limit the scrutiny they receive by taking advantage of powers in relation to private media. Where the state plays any role in allocating private media resources, it should be done on a transparent and impartial basis, with no room for political favouritism.

Conclusion: Deliberation, Inclusion and Participation 277

Again, in the context of article 10, the Court will also need to consider the role of digital media. While digital media offer enormous potential to allow diverse and free expression of opinion, there are multiple challenges. Digital media can be restricted by the state, manipulated by foreign states or by persons with resources taking advantage of the inertia of the law in responding to new technologies. They can also pose a threat to the inclusivity of political processes, as digital media can be abused to attack women or ethnic minorities. These are issues where the Court will need to consider its traditional regard for a balanced approach – overregulation may stifle free expression while underregulation might allow for manipulation of the political process and harm an inclusive political system.

A deliberative, inclusive and participatory approach to article 10 therefore must consider the scope to develop positive obligations in relation to the risk of private wealth dominating means of communication, as well as considering challenges to deliberation and inclusion in the context of some individuals having access to positions of media influence thanks to political links, and the risks posed by digital media. The development of article 8 and article 10 to include a right to information, in at least some circumstances as defined by the Court, also highlights another avenue to protect participation.

The article 10 case law emphasises the importance of civil society, journalists, academic researchers and others with a watchdog role being able to assess state-held information. However, changes in modern governance suggest that the next avenue should logically be to extend this line of cases to instances where the state has subcontracted its responsibilities in some way to private economic or other actors. The modern state frequently expects private organisations to discharge functions that either used to be discharged by the state or which are state functions. This could include the provision of education services, health services, care homes, even prisons and security. Such organisations are involved in activities that affect the rights of individuals and broader public interests. There is the potential for such private organisations to harm individual rights or the broader public interested, especially if they are organised on a for-profit basis or perhaps motivated by a confessional ethos. To support a participatory model of democracy, such organisations must be open to scrutiny. If police forces can be required to release information in the public interest, then, for instance, so should privately run but state-funded prisons or schools or hospitals. As the Convention increasingly puts the states under duties to regulate certain private enterprises through the Court's positive obligations doctrine – say, those involved in environmentally dangerous activities or care provision – then the watchdog function should mean that there should be access at least to the state-held information about such private bodies, if not indeed direct access to information that such private organisations hold.

278   *Conclusion: Deliberation, Inclusion and Participation*

The article 8 and article 10 case law highlights the potential for journalists, non-governmental organisations, academic researchers and others in civil society to use the Convention to promote more openness and transparency necessary for a more deliberative and participatory democratic system, even in relation to private economic actors. The article 11 case law offers some glimmer of hope that the Court is aware of the need for there to be effective mechanisms of participation in the civil society and the economic sphere. In the first part of this century we saw a series of cases from the UK, Turkey and Russia that developed the Court's approach to trade union rights and specifically collective bargaining. Trade unions are an important voice in the public sphere who, through pooling of individual commitment, can agitate on behalf of individuals and groups that may otherwise have only formal access to power. The defence of trade union rights was therefore to be welcomed even if the Court has indicated in *RMT* that there are limits to how far it will take this case law. The defence is all the more important given concerns about the weakening of labour rights and the waning of the welfare state in the last fifty years. This is a concern not just in states like the UK where trade union rights have been eroded over several decades but also in some states where autocratic legalist regimes or others may seek to undermine or co-opt trade unions.

The above suggestions about articles 10, 11 and 8 highlight the limits and potential of the Convention in promoting democratic practices outside the official political sphere. However, the scope of the electoral rights remains a challenge. The language of P1–3 points to the irony that even within the official political sphere the liberal democratic representative vision of the Convention is surprisingly limited. The Court has consistently refused to bring local elections, presidential elections, referendums and other ways of participating in public life within the purview of P1–3. In this sense the Convention is a much narrower instrument than, say, the ICCPR with its article 25. That P1–3 does not refer to broader notions like participation in public affairs or government of one's own country leaves out significant ways of participating in public affairs. The wider notion of participation in public affairs could include local councils, referendums, presidential elections and indeed other areas like consultative and deliberative practices (deliberative polls or citizen juries), appointments to official bodies and other public appointments. This textual limit means it is difficult to see how deliberation, participation and inclusion can be promoted more broadly.[9] This is not just a

---

[9]   See Iris Marion Young, *Inclusion and Democracy* (Oxford University Press 2000), 149 calling for more group representation not just in national legislatures but wider official bodies and non-official bodies wielding significant political or economic power.

Conclusion: Deliberation, Inclusion and Participation

matter of a missed opportunity to support deliberative, participatory and inclusive democracy; these fora outside the limited formal political arena (for the purposes of the Convention anyway) may be the target of parties with anti-democratic tendencies to colonise the state.[10] Unscrupulous political actors could use referendums to enhance executive power, manipulate elections for local councils or presidential elections, appoint cronies to political appointments and control or avoid consultative and participatory mechanisms. And the Court's current interpretation of the Convention would provide little redress.

Whilst the linguistic difference between P1–3 and article 25 ICCPR provides strong support for the Court's approach so far, it also comes up against the principle that the Convention must be given an effective interpretation, one capable of evolving to address contemporary threats to human rights. Some judges have given convincing reasons as to why referendums should at least sometimes be included in the ambit of P1–3. The Court itself has indicated that there may be the possibility to bring some presidential elections within the scope of P1–3, though it has not yet found a suitable case to rule this way. For the protection of an effective political democracy it would seem important to expand P1–3's scope. Even before the adoption of the Convention, the practical relevance of the legislature in domestic politics was often questionable.[11] The period since 1950 has seen the centrality of the legislature often eclipsed by the role of the executive and the development of links with networks outside of the formal political system. For the Convention vision of a political democracy to be meaningful, this trend must either be reversed or the Convention must adapt. Given the improbability of reinventing a dominant legislature, adaption seems to be the order of the day. And this is especially important given the rise of executive governments in some Council of Europe states that increasingly arrogate powers to the executive, undermine the mechanisms of political and legal accountability and not infrequently do this by means of referendums[12] or other legal mechanisms.

---

[10] Müller gives the example of populist parties that seek to control the civil service: Jan-Werner Müller, *What Is Populism?* (Penguin 2017), 44–45.

[11] Chris Thornhill, *The Sociology of Law and the Global Transformation of Democracy* (Cambridge University Press 2018), 148.

[12] This was the purpose of the (unsuccessful) Italian referendum of December 2016 discussed in Helen Hardman and Brice Dickson, 'Conclusions' in Helen Hardman and Brice Dickson (eds) *Electoral Rights in Europe: Advances and Challenges* (Taylor & Francis 2017), 212–215. It was also the purpose of the successful Turkish referendum of 2017. As this book was being finished, Russia's president announced a package of major constitutional change that might go to a referendum and was widely reported as consolidating his power as he left the office.

While it may go beyond the wording of P1–3, it would be defying the purpose of having a guarantee of voting and candidacy rights if these could be ignored simply by switching power to the executive. And it should not be lost sight of that referendums are not immune to Convention scrutiny if they interfere with Convention rights. State action that limits Convention rights through referendums can be scrutinised, and that scrutiny can, as part of any proportionality inquiry, consider whether the process of adopting a limit was lawful, legitimate, necessary – and deliberative, participatory and inclusive.

The other sense in which the Convention is arguably limited as regards the official political sphere is that its model is one of a national liberal representative democracy. The Court has concluded that P1–3 applies to elections for the European Parliament, and this is welcome but it is difficult to see how the Convention can contribute to enhancing EU democracy until the EU actually becomes party to the Convention. Should that happen, the model of deliberative democracy in particular may be one suited to application to the complex supranational institution that is the EU.

To the objection that these suggestions push the Court in a more activist direction, there are three comments.

First, the suggestions here are modest and based very much on the approach already adopted in the Court's jurisprudence. In most cases they involve incremental development (extending the developing freedom of information approach for example), or adapting existing concepts like positive obligations, indirect discrimination and reasonable adjustment to political concerns.

Second, the Court itself recognises that the interpretation of the Convention must be an evolving and effective one, taking into account contemporary threats to human rights. The benefits of liberal representative democracy must be protected, but we must also acknowledge the limitations of this model of democracy and the changing contexts of the twenty-first century. The liberal democratic model has not precluded the rise of illiberal democracy or autocratic legalism; indeed, the limitations of liberal representative democracy may have facilitated such threats. Enhancing the Convention's ability to promote deliberation, inclusion and participation would at least recognise these limitations. If it is not possible to say they would successfully address them all, they would at least be striking at some of the key problems.

Third, these proposals are aimed at ensuring that all people are included on an equal basis in the political process, that they can participate in decisions affecting them and that they can contribute to public deliberation. All these seem eminently legitimate, even urgent, tasks for a human rights court.

Bibliography

Arnardóttir OM, 'Organised Retreat? The Move from "Substantive" to "Procedural" Review in the ECtHR's Case Law on the Margin of Appreciation' (2015) European Society of International Law (ESIL) 2015 Annual Conference (Oslo)

Arnstein S, 'A Ladder of Citizen Participation' (1969) 35 Journal of American Institute of Planners 216

Barnett A and P Carty, *The Athenian Option: Radical Reform for the House of Lords (Sortition and Public Policy)* (Imprint Academic 2008)

Bates E, *The Evolution of the European Convention on Human Rights: From Its Inception to the Creation of a Permanent Court of Human Rights* (Oxford University Press 2010)

Beetham D, *Democracy and Human Rights* (Polity 1999)

Bellamy B, 'The Advent of the Masses and the Making of the Modern Theory of Democracy' in T Ball and R Bellamy (eds) *The Cambridge History of Twentieth Century Political Thought* (Cambridge University Press 2001)

Berman S, *Democracy and Dictatorship in Europe: From the Ancien Régime to the Present Day* (Oxford University Press 2019)

Brems E, 'Indirect Protection of Social Rights by the European Court of Human Rights' in A Barak-Erez A and A Gross (eds) *Exploring Social Rights* (Hart 2007)

'Positive Subsidiarity and Its Implications for the Margin of Appreciation Doctrine' (2019) 37 Netherlands Quarterly of Human Rights 210

Brunkhorst H, *Solidarity: From Civic Friendship to a Global Legal Community* (MIT Press 2005)

Bugarič B, 'A Crisis of Constitutional Democracy in Post-Communist Europe: "Lands in-between" Democracy and Authoritarianism' (2015) 13 (1) International Journal of Constitutional Law 219

Chahbazian C, 'The Contribution of the Parliamentary Assembly of the Council of Europe to Soft Law in Electoral Matters' in H Hardman and B Dickson (eds) *Electoral Rights in Europe: Advances and Challenges* (Taylor & Francis 2017)

Bibliography

Chernishova O, 'Electoral Rights in Russia: Mapping the Situation at the European Court of Human Rights' in H Hardman and B Dickson (eds) *Electoral Rights in Europe: Advances and Challenges* (Taylor & Francis 2017)

Constant B, *Principles of Politics Applicable to All Representative Governments* in B Constant and B Fontana (ed) *Constant: Political Writings* (Cambridge University Press 1988 [1815])

The Liberties of the Ancients Compared with That of the Moderns in B Constant and B Fontana (ed) *Constant: Political Writings* (Cambridge University Press 1988 [1820])

Cumper P and T Lewis, 'Blanket Bans, Subsidiarity, and the Procedural Turn of the European Court of Human Rights' (2019) 68 International & Comparative Law Quarterly 611

Cunningham F, *Theories of Democracy* (Routledge 2002)

Dahl RA, *On Political Equality* (Yale University Press 2006)

De Beco G, *Human Rights Monitoring Mechanisms of the Council of Europe* (Routledge 2011)

Dembour MB, *Who Believes in Human Rights? Reflections on the European Convention* (Cambridge University Press 2006)

Dickson B, 'Special Issue on Positive Obligations and the European Court of Human Rights' (2010) 61 (3) Northern Ireland Legal Quarterly 203

'Electoral Finances, Human Rights and Fairness' in H Hardman and B Dickson (eds) *Electoral Rights in Europe: Advances and Challenges* (Taylor & Francis 2017).

Dryzek JS, *Foundations and Frontiers of Deliberative Governance* (Oxford University Press 2012)

Dworkin R, 'The Moral Reading and the Majoritarian Premise' in R Dworkin (ed) *Freedom's Law* (Harvard University Press 1996)

'The Moral Reading and the Majoritarian Premise' in HH Koh and R Slye (eds) *Deliberative Democracy and Human Rights* (Yale University Press 2000)

Dzehtsiarou K, 'Prisoner Voting Saga: Reasons for Challenges' in H Hardman and B Dickson (eds) *Electoral Rights in Europe: Advances and Challenges* (Taylor & Francis 2017)

Eatwell R and M Goodwin, *National Populism: The Revolt against Liberal Democracy* (Penguin UK 2018)

Ely JH, *Democracy and Distrust* (Harvard University Press 1980)

Ewing KD, 'The Unbalanced Constitution' in T Campbell, K Ewing and A Tomkins (eds) *Sceptical Essays on Human Rights* (Oxford University Press 2001).

Fishkin JS, *Democracy When the People Are Thinking: Revitalizing Our Politics through Public Deliberation* (Oxford University Press 2018)

Fox G and G Nolte, 'Intolerant Democracies' (1995) 36 Harvard International Law Journal 1

Fredman S, 'Scepticism under Scrutiny: Labour Law and Human Rights' in T Campbell, K Ewing and A Tomkins (eds) *Sceptical Essays on Human Rights* (Oxford University Press 2001)

Human Rights Transformed: Positive Rights and Positive Duties (Oxford University Press 2008)

Ganser D, *NATO's Secret Armies: Operation Gladio and Terrorism in Western Europe* (Frank Cass 2005)

Gearty C, 'Democracy and Human Rights in the European Court of Human Rights: A Critical Appraisal' (2000) 51 (3) Northern Ireland Legal Quarterly 381

Gerards J, *General Principles of the European Convention on Human Rights* (Cambridge University Press 2019)

Gerards J and E Brems, *Procedural Review in European Fundamental Rights Cases* (Cambridge University Press 2017)

Ghosh E, 'Deliberative Democracy and the Countermajoritarian Difficulty: Considering Constitutional Juries' (2010) 30 (2) Oxford Journal of Legal Studies 327

Goldsworthy JD, *The Sovereignty of Parliament* (Clarendon 1999)

Gonzalez-Salzberg D and L Hodson, *Research Methods for International Human Rights Law: Beyond the Traditional Paradigm* (Routledge 2020)

Greer S, *The European Convention on Human Rights: Achievements, Problems and Prospects* (Cambridge University Press 2006)

Habermas J, *Between Facts and Norms* (MIT Press 1996)

The Inclusion of the Other: Studies in Political Theory (Polity Press 1998)

The Crisis of the European Union: A Response (Polity 2012)

The Lure of Technocracy (John Wiley & Sons 2015)

Hailbronner M, 'Beyond Legitimacy: Europe's Crisis of Constitutional Democracy' in MA Graber, S Levinson and M Tushnet (eds) *Constitutional Democracy in Crisis* (Oxford University Press 2018)

Halmai G, 'An Illiberal Constitutional System in the Middle of Europe' (2014) European Yearbook of Human Rights 497

Hardman H and B Dickson, 'Conclusions' in H Hardman and B Dickson (eds) *Electoral Rights in Europe: Advances and Challenges* (Taylor & Francis 2017)

Harris DJ, E Bates, M O'Boyle, C Warbrick and C Buckley, *Law of the European Convention on Human Rights* (4th edn, Oxford University Press 2018)

Hathaway O and S Shapiro, *The Internationalists: And Their Plan to Outlaw War* (Penguin UK 2017)

Held D, *Models of Democracy* (Polity 2006)

Hobsbawm W, *Age of Extremes: The Short Twentieth Century, 1914–1991* (Michael Joseph 1994)

James MR, *Deliberative Democracy and the Plural Polity* (University of Kansas Press 2004)

Judt T, *Postwar: A History of Europe since 1945* (Penguin Press 2005)

Lauren PG, *The Evolution of International Human Rights: Visions Seen* (3rd edn, University of Pennsylvania Press 2011)

Lauterpacht H, 'The Universal Declaration of Human Rights' (1948) 25 British Yearbook of International Law 354

Macpherson CB, *The Theory of Possessive Individualism* (Oxford University Press 1962)

The Life and Times of Liberal Democracy (Oxford University Press 1977)

Malkopoulou A, *The History of Compulsory Voting in Europe: Democracy's Duty?* (Routledge 2014).

Marks S, 'From the "Single Confused Page" to the "Decalogue for Six Billion Persons": The Roots of the Universal Declaration in the French Revolution' (1998) 20 Human Rights Quarterly 459

The Riddle of All Constitutions (Oxford University Press 2000)

Marx K, 'On the Jewish Question' in E Easton and K Guddat (eds) *Writings of the Young Marx on Philosophy and Society* (Doubleday Books 1967, [1843])

Mazower M, *Dark Continent: Europe's Twentieth Century* (Allen Lane 1998)

Mersel Y, 'The Dissolution of Political Parties: The Problem of Internal Democracy' (2006) 4 International Journal of Constitutional Law 84

Morison J, 'Models of Democracy: From Representation to Participation' in J Jowell and O Oliver (eds) *The Changing Constitution* (Oxford University Press 2007)

Morsink J, *The Universal Declaration of Human Rights: Origins, Drafting and Intent* (University of Pennsylvania Press 2000)

Mowbray A, *The Development of Positive Obligations under the European Convention on Human Rights by the European Court of Human Rights* (Hart 2004)

Müller JW, *What Is Populism?* (Penguin 2017)

Normand R and S Zaidi, *Human Rights at the UN: The Political History of Universal Justice* (Indiana University Press 2008).

O'Connell R, 'Towards a Stronger Conception of Democracy in the Strasbourg Convention' (2006) European Human Rights Law Review 281

O'Connell R, A Nolan, C Harvey, M Dutschke and E Rooney, *Applying an International Human Rights Framework to State Budget Allocations: Rights and Resources* (Routledge 2014)

O'Sullivan N, *European Political Thought since 1945* (Palgrave 2004)

Offe C, 'The Union Entrapped: Does the EU have the Political Capacity to Overcome its Current Crisis?' in C Offe and K Preuß (eds) *Citizens in Europe: Essays on Democracy, Constitutionalism and European Integration* (ECPR Press 2016)

Offe C and UK Preuß, 'The Union's Course: Between a Supranational Welfare State and Creeping Decay' in C Offe and UK Preuß (eds) *Citizens in Europe: Essays on Democracy, Constitutionalism and European Integration* (ECPR Press 2016)

Ottaway M, *Democracy Challenged: The Rise of Semi-Authoritarianism* (Carnegie Endowment for International Peace 2003)

Paine T, *Rights of Man* (Penguin 1984 [1791])

Palmer E, 'Protecting Socio-Economic Rights through the European Convention on Human Rights: Trends and Developments in the European Court of Human Rights' (2009) 2 (4) Erasmus Law Review 397

Pateman C, *Participation and Democratic Theory* (Cambridge University Press 1970)

Phillips A, *Which Equalities Matter?* (Polity 1999)

Bibliography

Pishchikova K, 'Between Democracy and Authoritarianism: The Hybrid Nature of Post-Soviet Political Transformation' in S Benhabib, D Cameron, A Dolidze, G Halmai, G Hellmann, K Pishchikova and R Youngs (eds) *The Democratic Disconnect* (Transatlantic Academy 2013)

Rodriguez-Ruiz B and R Rubio-Marín 'The Gender of Representation: On Democracy, Equality, and Parity' (2008) 6 (2) International Journal of Constitutional Law 287

'Constitutional Justification of Parity Democracy' (2009) 60 Alabama Law Review 1171

Rubio-Marín R, 'A New European Parity-Democracy Sex Equality Model and Why It Won't Fly in the United States' (2012) 60 (1) American Journal of Comparative Law 99

Rubio-Marín R and R O'Connell, 'The European Convention and the Relative Rights of Resident Aliens' (1999) 5 European Law Journal 4

Sandel M, *Liberalism and the Limits of Justice* (Cambridge University Press 1982)

'The Procedural Republic and the Unencumbered Self' in S Avineri and A De-Shalit (eds) *Communitarianism and Individualism* (Oxford University Press 1992)

Scheppele KL, 'The Rule of Law and the Frankenstate: Why Governance Checklists Do Not Work' (2013) 26 (4) Governance 559

'Autocratic Legalism' (2018) 85 University of Chicago Law Review 545

Schmitt C, *The Crisis of Parliamentary Democracy* (MIT Press 1988, [1923])

Schumpeter J, *Capitalism, Socialism, and Democracy* (5th edn, Allen and Unwin 1976)

Simpson AWB, *Human Rights and the End of Empire: Britain and the Genesis of the European Convention* (Oxford University Press 2001)

Spano R, 'Universality or Diversity of Human Rights? Strasbourg in the Age of Subsidiarity' (2014) 14 Human Rights Law Review 487

'The Future of the European Court of Human Rights – Subsidiarity, Process-Based Review and the Rule of Law' (2018) 18 Human Rights Law Review 473

Sunstein C, *One Case at a Time: Judicial Minimalism on the Supreme Court* (Harvard University Press, 1999)

Teubner G, 'Quod omnes tangit: Transnational Constitutions without Democracy?' (2018) 45 Journal of Law and Society S5

Thornhill C, *The Sociology of Law and the Global Transformation of Democracy* (Cambridge University Press 2018)

Waldron J, *Law and Disagreement* (Oxford University Press 2001)

Walzer M, *Spheres of Justice* (Robertson 1983)

Watt B, *UK Election Law: A Critical Examination* (Cavendish 2005)

Whitty N, T Murphy and S Livingstone, *Civil Liberties Law: The Human Rights Act Era* (Butterworths 2001)

Wolin SS, *Democracy Incorporated: Managed Democracy and The Specter of Inverted Totalitarianism* (Princeton University Press 2008)

Young IM, *Inclusion and Democracy* (Oxford University Press 2000)

286   *Bibliography*

OTHER SOURCES

Council of Europe, *Annual Report for 2012 of the European Court of Human Rights* (Council of Europe 2013)

Annual Report for 2018 of the European Court of Human Rights (Council of Europe 2019)

Brighton Declaration: High Level Conference on the Future of the European Court of Human Rights (2012) available at <www.echr.coe.int/Documents/2012_Brighton_FinalDeclaration_ENG.pdf> accessed 20 August 2019

Copenhagen Declaration (2018) available at < www.echr.coe.int/Documents/Copenhagen_Declaration_ENG.pdf> accessed 16 June 2020

Collected Edition of the Travaux Preparatoires, Volume 5 (Martinus Nijhoff 1979)

Collected Edition of the Travaux Preparatoires, Volume 3 (Martinus Nijhoff 1976)

Collected Edition of the Travaux Preparatoires, Volume 4 (Martinus Nijhoff 1977)

Collected Edition of the Travaux Preparatoires, Volume 1 (Martinus Nijhoff 1975)

Collected Edition of the Travaux Preparatoires, Volume 8 (Martinus Nijhoff 1985)

European Commission for Democracy through Law (Venice Commission) *Report on Electoral Rules and Affirmative Action for National Minorities' Participation in Decision-making Process in European Countries* (Council of Europe Pub 2005)

Code of Good Practice in Electoral Matters (Guidelines and Explanatory Report) (Council of Europe 2002)

488/2008 Report on the Imperative Mandate and Similar Practices (Council of Europe Pub 2009).

Study no. 352 / 2005 Report on Electoral Law and Electoral Administration in Europe (Council of Europe Pub 2006)

Opinion No. 832/2015 Interim Opinion on the Amendments to the Federal Constitutional Law of the Constitutional Court of the Russian Federation (Council of Europe Pub 2016).

CDL-AD(2017)005-e Turkey – Opinion on the amendments to the Constitution adopted by the Grand National Assembly on 21 January 2017 and to be submitted to a National Referendum on 16 April 2017, adopted by the Venice Commission at its 110th Plenary Session (Venice, 10–11 March 2017) (Council of Europe Pub 2017)

371/2006 Referendum Guidelines (Council of Europe Pub 2006)

Franklin Delano Roosevelt 'State of the Union Address' (1944) www.presidency.ucsb.edu/node/210825, accessed 7 August 2019

Index

advisory opinions, 54
African Union, 61
applications, 55–56
artistic expression, 85–86
Athenian democracy, 9, 19
Austria
  individual petition, 51
  political expression, 89
autocratic legalist, 30, 266, 276
Azerbaijan
  electoral process, 253–254

Basque country, 28
Belgium, 41
  consociationalism, 222
bicameral parliament, 146
blasphemy, 96–98, 117
Bosnia and Herzegovina, 2
  consociationalism, 223
Brexit, 2, 20, 30
Bulgaria
  timing of amendment to electoral law, 248

civic republicanism, 14
civil society, 135, 142
Cold War, 40, 64
Colonels' regime, 42, 55
colonies, 41, 45–46, 48–49, 174
commercial expression, 86
Committee of Ministers, 42, 50, 57
common good, 14, 25
communism, 39
communitarianism, 14
competitive elitism, 12
consociationalism, 27, 187, 222
constituencies, 244

Cyprus
  consociationalism, 187

deliberative democracy, 3, 26, 82, 203, 218, 271, 273, 280
  and free association, 135
  and free expression, 108, 119
  and the right to run for election, 224
  and the right to vote, 201
Denmark, 20, 41
  individual petition, 51
deposit requirement, 206, 215, 224
direct democracy, 19–20

electoral commissions, 209, 250
electoral process
  integrity of electoral process, 252
electoral register, 170
electoral systems, 49, 265
  bonus seats, 243
  majoritarian, 230, 232
  majoritarian and proportional representation, 229
  party lists, 241
  proportional representation by single transferable vote, 231
eligibility criteria to run for election, 205
elitism, 10
equality
  economic equality, 136, 141, 269, 275
  political equality, 13, 24
European Commission of Human Rights, 50
  abolition, 53
European Parliament, 63, 157, 246, 280
  and the right to vote, 163
European Social Charter, 17, 58, 137–138

287

Index

European Union, 1, 15, 20, 29, 41, 62, 156–157, 269, 274
  human rights in the European Union, 62
  preliminary reference procedure, 55

fascism, 39
France, 2, 20, 36, 41
  drafting of Council of Europe Statute, 42
  female suffrage, 38
  individual petition, 51
  ratification of Convention, 51
free assembly, 122
free expression
  during elections, 110
  national security, 92
freedom of information, 115–116, 277

Georgia
  electoral register, 170
  timing of amendment to electoral law, 248
Germany, 28, 36
  thresholds, 239
globalisation, 155
Greece, 1, 28, 41, 55
  disqualification of sitting members of parliament, 213
  voting from abroad, 177

hate speech, 100, 102, 118
homophobic expression, 104
Hungary, 1, 30
  freedom of information, 115
  voting from abroad, 181

illiberal democracy, 30, 269
inclusion, 3, 27, 273
International Labour Organisation, 138
interpretation
  autonomous interpretation, 68
  effective interpretation, 66, 76, 280
  evolving interpretation, 67, 280
  historical interpretation, 69
Ireland, 20, 28, 41
  individual petition, 51
  national security and free expression, 92
Italy, 1, 28, 41
  party lists, 242
  prisoners, 193
  regional councils, 154

language, 204, 211, 217, 221
Latvia
  lustration, 215
  restrictions on certain former members of the Communist Party, 214
  restrictions on former KGB agents, 210
legality, 73
legislature, 145, 152
legitimate aim, 72–73
liberal democracy, 3, 6–9, 81
  and free expression, 89
loyalty to the state, 207
lustration, 209, 214–215
Luxembourg, 41
  individual petition, 51

mandate, 211, 243
margin of appreciation, 78–79
  and electoral systems, 168
militant democracy, 14, 40, 99, 128–130, 217
minority representation, 27, 209, 220, 261, 266
Moldova
  dual nationals, 207, 216, 221
municipal bodies, 153

national identity, 15
national security, 79
Netherlands, 20, 41
neutrality, 14
Northern Ireland, 28, 158, 231, 262
Norway, 41
  individual petition, 51

obscenity, 95–96, 117
Organisation for Security and Cooperation in Europe, 62
Organization of American States, 61–62

parity democracy, 26
parliamentarism, 12, 39
Parliamentary Assembly, 43
participatory democracy, 3, 21–23, 134, 136
perfectionism, 14
petition, 52
pilot judgment, 54
Poland, 30
political advertising, 109, 111–115
political expression, 86
political parties
  and freedom of association, 133
  finances of political parties, 259

Index

289

party dissolution, 126
registration, 170, 240
registration of, 127
sex discrimination, 219
state funding, 260, 264
populism, 21, 30, 164
Portugal, 38
positive obligations, 75–77
right to vote, 202
presidential elections, 147–149, 164, 278
prisoner votes, 272
proportionality, 73–75
public morality, 79, 82, 95

qualified rights, 70–71

racist expression, 99–100
referendums, 21, 149–152, 164, 201, 278
representation of women, 219
representative democracy, 3, 6, 9–13, 18, 21, 25,
    31, 61, 115, 129, 136, 143–144, 157, 166,
    268–269, 275
Romania
    minority representation, 209
Russia, 1, 21
    clarity of electoral legislation, 247
    electoral process, 256
    free expression during elections, 110
    party dissolution, 240
    political expression, 91
    prisoners, 195
    registration of political parties, 170, 240

Slovenia
    erased, the, 183
social and economic rights, 77, 141, 276
social media, 31
solidarity, 25
sortition, 20–21
Soviet Union, 33, 37–38, 40
Spain, 29, 38
    party dissolution, 127
stereotyping, 107
subsidiarity, 78
substantive democracy, 3, 6, 15, 17, 99, 107
    and the right to run for election, 217
    and the right to vote, 197
Sweden, 41
    individual petition, 51

Switzerland, 20
symbolic expression, 85

thresholds, 233–240
trade unions, 22, 135–140, 278
    right to strike, 139
transparency, 205, 215, 259
Turkey, 1–2, 30
    2017 referendum, 151
    national security and free expression, 93
    party dissolution, 126, 130–133
    thresholds, 236
    voting from abroad, 180

Ukraine, 2
    non-resident running for office, 208
United Kingdom, 2, 20–21, 28, 38, 41
    drafting of Council of Europe Statute, 42
    drafting of the Convention, 46–47
    individual petition, 51
    majoritarian electoral system, 232
    national security and free expression, 92
    political advertising, 113
    prisoners, 193
    referendums, 150
    voting from abroad, 179
United Nations, 34, 60
United States, 20, 33
Universal Declaration of Human Rights,
    34–35, 46

Venice Commission, 69, 148, 151, 163, 179–181,
    206, 223, 226, 229, 244, 246, 248–249,
    255–256, 263–264
voting from abroad, 176–183
voting restrictions
    age, 172
    bankruptcy, 188
    mental capacity, 186
    national origin, 187
    nationality, 183, 274
    prisoner status, 197
    residence, 172

West Germany
    individual petition, 51
workload of the Court, 53

xenophobic expression, 101

Lightning Source UK Ltd.
Milton Keynes UK
UKHW010814101120
373118UK00004B/13